AF180537

Governing the Rainforest

Governing the Rainforest

Sustainable Development Politics in the Brazilian Amazon

EVE Z. BRATMAN

OXFORD
UNIVERSITY PRESS

OXFORD
UNIVERSITY PRESS

Oxford University Press is a department of the University of Oxford. It furthers the University's objective of excellence in research, scholarship, and education by publishing worldwide. Oxford is a registered trade mark of Oxford University Press in the UK and certain other countries.

Published in the United States of America by Oxford University Press
198 Madison Avenue, New York, NY 10016, United States of America.

© Oxford University Press 2019

All rights reserved. No part of this publication may be reproduced, stored in a retrieval system, or transmitted, in any form or by any means, without the prior permission in writing of Oxford University Press, or as expressly permitted by law, by license, or under terms agreed with the appropriate reproduction rights organization. Inquiries concerning reproduction outside the scope of the above should be sent to the Rights Department, Oxford University Press, at the address above.

You must not circulate this work in any other form
and you must impose this same condition on any acquirer.

CIP data is of file at the Library of Congress
ISBN 978-0-19-094938-9

For Lior

Contents

Figures and Tables

Figures

Tables

Preface

When I first traveled to Brazil in my early twenties, I was seeking inspiration. I visited Curitiba, the capital city in the state of Paraná, located about a six-hour drive south of São Paulo. Curitiba was heralded by many urban sustainability advocates as one of the "ecological capitals" of the world. While many other cities in the Global South, turned into sprawling, smog-ridden industrial centers in the 1970s, Curitiba had taken a different path. The city developed a bus rapid transit system, created a pedestrian mall in the downtown, retrofitted old quarries and turned them into public parks, built libraries, and had adopted a number of other ecologically oriented innovations. To my relatively novice eye, Curitiba lived up to the sustainability hype. To say I was inspired after my visit is an understatement. I was smitten. After this first trip, I presented some lessons learned from Curitiba to my local city council in Oberlin, Ohio, where I was studying as an undergraduate student. After that first trip, I began learning Portuguese, I trained *capoeira*, and helped a Brazilian rock and roll band go on tour in the United States. Two subsequent return trips to Brazil were similarly inspiring. I visited eco-villages, attended the World Social Forum, interviewed human rights defenders, and met *campesino* farmers and city planners alike, all of whom sparked in me a sense that something hopeful and important was taking place in Brazil, along the lines of what I imagined to be strong examples of sustainable development activism and policies. I was eager to find ways to reproduce sustainable development as I saw it taking shape there. I wanted to encourage people to reach the goal of attaining a perfect triangulation between social, economic, and environmental concerns, all while creating thriving communities that were rich in artistic expression, active political engagements, and cultural vibrancy.

Four trips later, I was headed to distant Altamira, in the Amazon. The more I learned about Brazil, the more I realized the depths of inequality, corruption, and contradictions in policymaking there. I am sure that at times I envisioned myself in a starry-eyed vision of Edenic wilderness, filled with potential plant cures for cancer, blue morph butterflies, and, occasionally, some wise indigenous people sharing pieces of their sacred cultures with a privileged few insiders. At the same time, most of the news I encountered about the region was about worrisome rates of deforestation and biodiversity loss. It was concerning. A saying about how the fate of the Amazon was intertwined with the fate of the world gnawed at me and rattled my conscience about the events taking place in the region. I approached working in the Amazon with trepidation. After all, what can a North American tell the world about the Brazilian Amazon that hasn't already been said by Amazonians themselves?

Soon, I turned away from trying to gauge *whether* sustainable development was working in Brazil and *what* could be reproduced elsewhere, in lieu of a more ethnographic set of questions. I wanted to understand, instead, *how* conservation, social movements, and development issues were intersecting in Brazilian politics. At best, as an outsider I could do the important work of ethnographic inquiry. I could endeavor to explain how and why practices emerging from policies described as sustainable development took shape as they did. Why did some groups come to be viewed by the Brazilian government and international nongovernmental organizations as supportive of Amazonian environmental concerns, while others were positioned as culprits in its destruction? How did people at local levels respond as they simultaneously encountered plans to pave Amazonian highways, learned of projects to dam Amazonian rivers, and participated in an economic-ecological zoning effort for their region? How did discourses and practices involving the green economy and sustainable development in the Amazon take shape on an everyday basis, as co-constituents of grand plans which sought to make the world's largest rainforest economically profitable yet at the same time a place that was environmentally protected and that also respected the needs of the diverse groups of people living there?

In the course of my field research I was based in the city of Altamira. In the Xingu prelature, Bishop Erwin Krautler was rumored to wear bulletproof vests to mass because he had been receiving death threats fairly consistently since the early 1980s for being outspoken against deforestation, the Belo Monte hydroelectric project, and the creation of conservation areas in the more remote parts of the prelature. I traveled by boat along the Xingu River, by car (and often in the back of trucks) along the Transamazon highway, and took buses down the BR-163 highway. I visited artisanal gold mining towns, where stories of shootouts and characters nicknamed "Pit Bull," "Rambo," and "White Jaguar" are locally famous. Influential local power brokers are present as the dominant elite in nearly every small Amazonian town, and these individuals, in collaboration with the police, often rule more by intimidation and violent force than by law. I interviewed some of them, including a few illegal land claimers, as much as my own concerns for safety and security would allow. I spoke with dozens of people who were non-indigenous settlers to the region, hearing their stories of the long migration from other parts of Brazil and learning of the hardships they experienced upon first arriving to the region. Rubber tappers showed me how they traditionally tapped trees for latex and toasted and prepared manioc flour to make the ubiquitous staple of *farinha*. They shared with me stories of giant river snakes, their history of conflicts with land claimers, and we spoke about their hopes and dreams for their children. I met some of the most resilient and kind-hearted people imaginable in these remote parts of the world. Consistently, the people I met believed deeply in the potential of the Amazon region to become a better place for all its citizens, and they were often working to make that vision be possible. At times this was in high-profile career paths and risky public activism; at other times, doing so meant simply engaging in land stewardship and farming in a way that fit within a more personal set of aspirations. During my research, I was reminded by the notion expressed by Paulo Freire that humble dialogue, embodied through theoretical work and practical action, was a world-changing process of transformation. I still cling to this idea in the hope that through dialoguing with words, theory, and action, we might better come closer to certain truths and, in that process, to our own humanity. I am immensely privileged to have been so welcomed into Amazonia through the hospitality and generosity of countless Brazilians, and I am filled with appreciation and thanks for the chances they gave me to join in their lives. Countless individuals encouraged, inspired, and supported me along the way. Inescapably, my gratitude will inadequately suffice to acknowledge all those people.

A few remarkable individuals and organizations do stand out as my bastions for security, advice, and assistance. For support with visa issues and providing me with important supplementary opportunities for scholarly engagement, Louis Goodman at American University, Alexandre Barros of UniEuro in Brasilia, and Reinaldo Corrêa Costa of the Instituto Nacional de Pesquisas da Amazônia (INPA) have my deep thanks. My field research was especially supported by an American University dissertation fellowship and by a Fulbright Scholarship. Incredible generosity of time, office space, and spirit was a gift to receive from the office and staff of the Comissão Pastoral da Terra (CPT) in Altamira and Anapu, and the Fundação Viver, Produzir, e Preservar (FVPP). Tarcísio Feitosa opened up his home and family life to me in important ways, especially in the early months of my field research. Gracinda Magalhães and her family also took me in as one of their own and offered insights—both political and personal—during my research at several important junctures. I additionally am grateful to the following people for their assistance through conversations and insights that left their mark in the development of this book manuscript: Ane Alencar, Brenda Baletti, Robin Broad, Binka Le Breton, Jeremy Campbell, Miguel Carter, Janet Chernela, Christiane Dias, Adam Henne, Kathryn Hochstetler, Nabil Kamel, Craig Kauffman, Vânia Lemos, Renzo Mártires, Marlon Menezes, Andrew Miller, Simon Nicholson, Noemi Porro, Sérgio Praça, Matthew Taylor, Linda Rabben, Malini Ranganathan, Marcelo Salazar, Ana Paula Souza dos Santos, Cristina Velasquez, and Hilary Zarin. Fabiano Toni's comments and suggestions especially helped to strengthen this manuscript, as did comments from one anonymous reviewer. You all have my heartfelt thanks. Special thanks also go to my brilliant academic colleagues and friends who offered important comments and support for this work as it developed: Scott Freeman and Annie Claus, thank you. For their decade-plus of assistance and mentoring, Ken Conca, Paul Wapner, Julie Mertus, and Steve Schwartzman all have my deep gratitude. My graduate research assistants from American University's School of International Service also are owed a huge round of appreciation: Amanda Harris, Mukhaye Muchimuti, and Attiya Sayyed. Additional thanks for their comments on several chapters presented here are due to Laura Shelton, Stephanie McNulty, and Alexandria Poole. I am profoundly indebted to Felipe Storch, a remarkable Acreano and graduate of Franklin and Marshall College, who helped to transform this manuscript with his rigorous attention to detail and keen historical research as a Hackman Scholar. Also from Franklin and Marshall College, Stephanie Schick and Coleman Klein helped steward the manuscript through its final revision with their respective skills in editing and map-making, respectively. For early-stage manuscript comments, thank you to Leo Schlosberg, and for final-stage manuscript preparation help, thank you, Derek Meyer, Adam "Fuzzy" Konner, and the team at Oxford University Press, most notably Alexcee Bechtold, and Angela Chnapko. All my family members, by birth and by choice, and especially my partner Joel Rothschild and my sister Dara Hoppe have my profound gratitude. They spurred me on, nourished and cultivated my love of learning, engaged in innumerable conversations, encouraged and joined in my research and travels, and held me up with meals, hugs, patience, generosity, and humor. Annalee Letchinger was a remarkably thorough editor and offered constant encouragement, well beyond the call of motherly obligation. Thank you, mom. None of this work would be possible had it not been for the support of so many people who informed and inspired this work. It is stronger because of all of them. All remaining inaccuracies and weaknesses in the manuscript are entirely my own and my full responsibility.

Abbreviations

APA (*Área Protegida Ambiental*): Environmental Protection Area

BNDE (*Banco de Desenvolvimento Econômico*): Brazilian Economic Development Bank
BNDES (*Banco Nacional de Desenvolvimento Econômico e Social*): National Bank for Economic and Social Development

CCBM (*Consórcio Construtor Belo Monte*): Belo Monte Construction Consortium
CEB (*Comunidades Eclesiásticas de Base*): Grassroots Evangelical Communities
CIMI (*Conselho Indigenista Missionário*): Indigenous Missionary Council
CNPT (*Centro Nacional para Populações Tradicionais*): National Center for Traditional Populations
CNS (*Conselho Nacional de Seringueiros*): National Council of Rubber Tappers
CONTAG (*Confederação Nacional dos Trabalhadores na Agricultura*): National Confederation of Agricultural Workers
CPT (*Comissão Pastoral da Terra*): Pastoral Land Commission
CUT (*Central Única dos Trabalhadores*): Unified Workers' Central
CVRD: (Companhia Vale do Rio Doce): Rio Doce Mining Company (later re-named Vale)

EIA: Environmental Impact Assessment
ESEC (*Estação Ecológica*): Ecological Station

FLONA (*Floresta Nacional*): National Forest
FUNASA (*Fundação Nacional de Saúde*): National Health Foundation
FUNAI (*Fundação Nacional do Índio*): National Indian Foundation
FVPP (*Fundação Viver, Produzir, e Preservar*): Foundation for Life, Production, and Preservation

GMO: Genetically modified organism

IACHR: Inter-American Commission on Human Rights
IBAMA (*Instituto Brasileiro de Meio Ambiente e dos Recursos Naturais Renováveis*): Brazilian Institution for the Environment and Renewable Natural Resources
ICMBio (*Instituto Chico Mendes de Conservação da Biodiversidade*): Chico Mendes Institute for Conservation of Biodiversity)
IIRSA: Initiative for the Integration of the Regional Infrastructure of South America
IMF: International Monetary Fund
INCRA (*Instituto Nacional de Colonização e Reforma Agrária*): National Institute for Colonization and Land Reform
IPAM (*Instituto de Pesquisas Ambientais da Amazônia*): Institute for Amazonian Environmental Research
ISA (*Instituto SocioAmbiental*): SocialEnvironmental Institute

ISI: Import-substitution industrialization
IUCN: International Union on the Conservation of Nature

MAB: (*Movimento dos Atingidos por Barragens*): Movement of People Affected by Dams
MMA (*Ministério do Meio Ambiente*): Ministry of the Environment
MME (*Ministério de Minas e Energia*): Ministry of Mines and Energy
MDTX (*Movimento pela Desinvolvimento da Transamazonica e Xingu*): Movement for the Development of the Tranamazon and Xingu
MPF (*Ministério Público Federal*): Federal Public Ministry
MPST (*Movimento pela Sobrevivência na Transamazônica*): Movement for Survival on the Transamazon
MST (*Movimento dos Trabalhadores Rurais Sem Terra*): Landless Workers' Movement

NGO: Non-governmental organization

OECD: Organization for Economic Cooperation and Development

PAC (*Plano Anual de Crescimento*): Plan for Annual Growth
PAS (*Plano Amazônia Sustentável*): Plan for a Sustainable Amazon
PIN (*Plano de Integração Nacional*): Plan for National Integration
PDS (*Projeto de Desenvolvimento Sustentável*): Project for Sustainable Development
PRODIAT (*Projeto de Desenvolvimento Integrado da Bacia do Araguaia-Tocantins*): Integrated Development Program for the Araguaia-Tocantins Basin
PROTERRA (*Programa de Redistribuição de Terras e de Estímulo à Agro-indústria do Norte e do Nordeste*) Program for Land Redistribution and Stimulation of Agroindustry in the North and Northeast
PT (*Partido dos Trabalhadores)*: Worker's PartyRESEX (*Reserva Extrativista*): Extractive Reserve

SNUC (*Sistema Nacional de Unidades de Conservação*): The National System of Conservation Areas
SUDAM (*Superintendência de Desenvolvimento da Amazônia*): Superintendency for the Development of Amazonia

TI (*Terra Indígena*): Indigenous Land
TIPNIS: Isiboro Sécure National Park and Indigenous Territory

UNCED: United Nations Conference on Environment and Development, also known as the Rio Earth Summit and Eco '92

WWF: World Wildlife Fund for Nature

1
Introduction
The Sustainable Development Conundrum

An elderly, gaunt woman wearing a brightly colored feather headdress sits upon a retaining wall overlooking the Xingu River. Her wan gaze focuses away, looking upon the quietly flowing water. A dense jungle island is the backdrop for the broad blue waters. The woman picks up a can of Coca-Cola and takes a long drink. "Bye bye Brasil," she says, flatly. The late afternoon sun casts a long shadow as the woman remains still, maintaining her contemplative pose. An eerie silence follows, but for a few chirps of crickets.

This is the scene that gives the title to *Bye Bye Brazil*, a 1979 film by Brazilian director Carlos Diegues. The vignette captures a moment within the changing life in the Amazon. Brazil's entry into the global economy and drive to establish new cities in the jungle is wrapped in melancholy. As indigenous people speak English and drink Coca-Cola in a distant city located along a tributary to the Amazon River, the wilderness meets modernity, and ancient cultures meet global capitalism.

The city in which this scene is set is Altamira, Pará. For the band of traveling circus performers who are the main characters of the film, Altamira represents a place where dreams are made. Filled with the mystique of being deep in the jungle, and rich with cosmopolitan opportunity, Altamira embodies the hopes of a modern Brazil. But in Altamira, the protagonists' relationships experience fissures; big bets are lost, romantic relationships go sour, and instead of fortunes made, the place is full of hard knocks. Along their journey, the travelers meet indigenous tribes fleeing their lands because whites have brought disease and death to their villages. As the travelers drive through recently cut roads through the forest, the landscape is one of skeletal tree trunks and roadkill.[1] Viewers are left with the impression of a gradual and lethal process occurring in the rainforest. It is one that is filled with what environmental writer Rob Nixon calls "slow violence" (2011), in which ecosystem decline; vulnerable, disempowered, and displaced people; and erosions of life-sustaining conditions play out in the everyday experiences of the ecosystems and people living in the region.

This story of cultural losses and ecosystem transformation is relatively ubiquitous in contemporary Amazonia. Similar representations are regularly presented in radio broadcasts, magazines, and newspaper stories around the world, though often these realities are less of a news spectacle than the crisis-driven and "hot" conflict focus that often features in the media and in public activism. The portrayal of a dying rainforest is not only resonant because it captures so much of the reality of rapid environmental change and societal transformations. It also involves some of the most fundamental struggles concerning how humans—both in the Amazon and among concerned citizens across the world—relate to nature. One of the most central debates in the environmental field involves interrogating what an authentic "nature" entails. Second, and more pragmatically, debates rage over how best to protect nature. On this count, arguments are fierce over what the right balances and compromises should entail while ensuring a thriving nonhuman Nature (capital N) along with meeting human needs, such as economic growth and poverty alleviation. The framework of sustainable development is the most common policy and discursive tool for addressing these debates. This notion, in its most basic form, posits that balancing social equity, economic growth, and environmental concerns is possible. As such, sustainable development perennially offers a promise of positive potential, wherein conservationist and development aims might amicably unite.

This book is about development and conservation politics in the Brazilian Amazon. Centrally, it explores how the Amazon region's lands and peoples are shaped by sustainable development plans. The sustainable development framework offers a central (though often inexplicit) set of discourses, values, and policies through which Amazonian social dynamics, politics, economic plans, and natural resources are governed. The drive to transform land and natural resources into economically productive assets holds appeal for national economic planners and corporate interests alike. In contrast, environmentalists argue for the need to protect rainforest biodiversity and emphasize the importance of the Amazon as an essential climate-balancing ecosystem, with intrinsic value for protection and stewardship. The complexity and diversity of indigenous cultures pulls mightily within the struggle over the Amazon's present and future as well, given the long historical context of genocidal conquests and the interlinking of human livelihoods with losses of land. For everyday Amazonians, especially for those who settled in the region when it was made more accessible through the governmental colonization and development efforts in the 1970s, moving into the Amazon was simply about making a decent life. Like the travelers in *Bye Bye Brazil*, Amazonia represented to many Brazilians a bountiful setting to make a fresh start away from the highly unequal and poverty-stricken Brazil they knew, where adventure awaited and where a bold national vision for progress might be achieved.

While often oversimplified in narrations as a vast wilderness of ecological bounty, the realities, values, histories, and experiences that are entangled within the developmental and environmental politics of the Amazon are enormously complex. One of the central aims of this book is to portray those complexities with a richness of historical depth and nuanced attention to the social dynamics that are involved as various governance decisions are made about how to live with and manage tropical rainforest ecosystems.

The main argument advanced in this book is that sustainable development politics in the Amazon yields highly uneven results among different members of society and between different geographies. Despite offering a positive vision for change, the framework instead tends to reproduce and reinforce existing inequalities. The research presented in this book shows how land use and infrastructure plans conducted in the name of sustainable development often perpetuate and reinforce economic and political inequalities. While environmental concerns do play a catalyst role in the Amazon, sustainable development plans at work there tend to give social equity concerns short shrift while prioritizing economic growth and only marginally and occasionally leading to any environmental benefits. The granular examination of sustainable development plans presented in this book illustrate some significant mismatches between the ideas people hold about sustainable development's promise and the actual practice of sustainable development. For the people living in the areas that are geographically the closest to where those plans are being implemented on the ground, the experiences of sustainable development are especially fraught with tension.

The analytical focus in this work is on *governing*, that is, the ongoing processes through which people, institutions, political regimes, and NGOs are involved in policymaking and management of outcomes within a specific geographic area. Environmental governance takes shape in the Amazon through strategic planning and public discussions, and more subtly; under the banner of sustainable development discourses, numerous land organizing and rural livelihood projects are conducted in the region. The outcomes of governing the rainforest are uneven, with ironies, contradictions, and inequalities frequently marking both social and environmental dynamics. By focusing on the recent conflicts and development polices in the region, paying attention to how various actors use the sustainable development framework, we can see more clearly what sustainable development offers for different actors and what it does not. Rather than attempt to solve the riddle or show how closely (or remotely) we have hit the sustainable development mark in the Amazon, this book turns the very idea of sustainable development into the object of study, inquiring into how and why it has continued to hold such power and influence and with what impacts. This focus allows for an examination of how different political processes and relationships orient the lived experiences of sustainable development as a manifestation of political practice.

Nearly twenty-five years after *Bye Bye Brazil* was made, in 2005 I too sat along the banks of the Xingu River. The irony was not lost on me that thanks to the privileges of being an American researcher working in the age of globalization, I was a *gringa* tracing the footsteps of the indigenous woman drinking the Coca-Cola. And, somewhat like the traveling circus performers, I too was drawn to Altamira because of my hopefulness. The Brazilian government had recently created one of the world's largest conservation areas upstream of Altamira, in the Xingu River basin. Despite the fact that the new conservation areas were created in the aftermath of a high-profile assassination, it seemed that things were looking up for many of the people living in the region. The *ribeirinhos*, or river-based peasants, were no longer experiencing armed conflicts with illegal land claimers. A new civil–society managed pool of funds was established from a massive crackdown on illegal mahogany logging, and the monies were being directed toward environmental protection, social projects, and indigenous tribes in the region.[2] Still, the Xingu River was slated to receive a mega-dam within a few years' time. The city of Altamira was abuzz with speculation about when the Transamazon highway would finally become paved. Most people said they wanted "development" in Altamira, meaning that they supported the dam and the highway paving because those infrastructures would bring more jobs and urban growth.

How did these visions of development come to represent a transformative reality for the people in the region? What was their relationship to the Brazilian state as they alternately contested, supported, and acquiesced to plans conducted in the name of achieving sustainable development? This work uncovers how sustainable development is articulated by different actors, ranging from the grassroots level to international agencies, and explores the tensions between their approaches. The primary geographical site for this investigation is not the entire Brazilian Amazon, but rather a specific stretch of the Lower Xingu River basin, located in the state of Pará. The region is one of the world's most symbolically laden and high-profile locations for exploring sustainable development as a concept and in physical forms.

A scholarly focus on sustainable development makes sense because it is something that appears both banal and ubiquitous. Anthropological tradition suggests that by finding something to be strange—whether a discourse, concept, or culture—a better understanding about that "thing" can be gained. It is important to study sustainable development precisely because it is so taken for granted. Examining how the discourse can serve to legitimate and privilege certain interests above others, and how it orients particular visions articulated by state and civil society actors while making other discourses and sets of values more marginal, is ripe for critical examination. How are sustainable development plans embraced, resisted, and represented by local communities? How are NGOs and social movements involved in the design, promotion, and implementation of those plans? What is the role of governmental officials and planning authorities as they shape policies aimed at achieving other versions of sustainable development? As plans for sustainable development come into adoption, how are different ideological visions contested?

A political ecology lens is useful for shedding light on how environmental governance in the Brazilian Amazon affects lives and landscapes. Political ecology is an approach that emphasizes geographical and historical materialist analysis of the political interplay between discourses, material struggles, and social relations, with attention to how society and environmental resources are interrelated.[3] The field examines the narratives, institutions, and political-economic structures that underpin how physical environments (land and water resources, for example) are co-produced with society. Its interdisciplinary basis is concerned with understanding how actors contribute to certain environmental practices while also being situated within ecologies themselves, involving relationships that are shaped by political and economic factors as much as cultural and physical connections. This work aligns with the political ecology scholarship that engages in a more critical approach that seeks to portray the complexity of interrelated political, economic, ecological, cultural, and social dynamics as part of a larger environmental epistemology of political analysis (Forsyth 2008, Peet and Watts 1996, Robbins and Monroe Bishop 2008, Robbins 2004, Zimmerer and Bassett 2003, West 2006).[4] A political ecology approach allows for complexity, insofar as its focus on interrelationships and co-constitutions between humans and nature runs against the essentialist and mechanistic tendencies to explain how actors influence governance and underpin social and ecological change.

This book's analysis begins by taking sustainable development at face value. It is used as a strategy, a name given to different policies, and an orienting worldview, through which the insertion of state power, economic priorities, and conservation-oriented values become enacted in lives and on landscapes. For the sake of present discussion, it is important to remember that sustainable development is often thought of as a product—it is in this sense a noun, a thing that can be achieved through a project or built into a place. The notion thus implies a fixed end-point or set of interventions that suggest we can "get there"—to an imagined sweet spot where three major dimensions of economic, ecological, and social equity goals find balance. When understood as a noun, the implication is that sustainable development is an object or outcome that can be built. It stays relatively fixed. Instead, sustainable development is more usefully conceptualized as an ongoing process. Just as ecosystems are dynamic, so too are the social systems that are the object of sustainable development. Change is the constant of our world, and rather than a harmonious balance, sustainable development is generally full of friction. Even reaching agreement among key constituencies on what the specific targets of the three major axes of sustainable development should involve in specific circumstances is difficult, let alone triangulating effectively between often-competing aims in dynamic economic, social, and ecological environments. Furthermore, while ubiquitous, sustainable development is also commonly recognized as inadequate. It is difficult to imagine *not* wanting to have sustainable development; few would venture to argue that we should not strive for such a laudable objective. But simultaneously, societies and governmental leaders do not fully understand what it means to live within sustainable development as a feature of contemporary times.

Approaching Rainforest Politics

Scholars have long acknowledged that there are power differentials and new subject positions created as neoliberalism and environmental governance mobilize different—and often competing or ambiguous—desires to change the world (Gibson-Graham 1996, 2006, Agrawal 2005). As a discourse and a mechanism of environmental governance, diverse visions are captured within the plans that take shape as sustainable development is enacted. These function to open certain spaces of possibilities for new social, political, and environmental relations, and to delineate the bounds of resistance as well. Inescapably, however, the framework of sustainable development falls short of what it attempts, because its role is one of a relatively incomplete and conservative utopia (Hedrén and Linnér 2009). A *u*topia, it is worth remembering, ultimately means *no* place, coming from the Greek word *ou-topos*. Yet even since Thomas More coined the word in 1512, utopia has had a second meaning. Utopia, More wrote, was intended as a pun, because it sounded identical to the Greek word *eu-topos*, or "good place," which also described his perfect but imaginary world (British Library 2017). Places and spaces, then, become centrally implicated in understanding how sustainable development is imagined. These imaginings, moreover, inform how nature itself is produced, becoming co-constituted through levels of ideas, social relations, and actions, and re-productions of our nature imaginaries through scales of culture, politics, and economics (Lefebvre 1991 [1974], West 2006).

Critically engaging how sustainable development orients different plans for Amazonian landscapes and developmental possibilities, and how certain expectations are established concerning what *could* and *should* be done in the region helps inform scholarship on two counts. First, it reveals a nuanced portrayal of how contemporary approaches involving sustainable development are manifested in the present, through building on a deep historical and political-economic analysis of the past. Second, a critical engagement of this sort with the sustainable development concept opens up new possibilities for research about the future of the Amazon and the future of sustainable development itself. Interrogating sustainable development's history and its on-the-ground manifestations offers us the possibility of escaping the problem-solving approach that all too often has offered incremental and inadequate solutions that are ill-matched for the urgent and monumental problems of climate change, biodiversity losses, and gross social and economic inequalities. Instead, it moves toward transformational, structural analysis of our problems, in hopes of finding meaningful routes out of them.[5]

The specific geographic location within the Brazilian Amazon that is discussed in this work are the central and southwestern lands of the state of Pará, in the vicinity of the Transamazon highway and the BR-163 highway. Pará is in the North region of Brazil, and its capital city, Belém, is located near the eastern mouth of the Amazon River delta, about 100 km from the Atlantic Ocean (see Figure 1.1).

In the region, we are witness to sustainable development planning which, upon a surface-level examination, seems to embody significant contradictions: highways that run across the rainforest are paved, the world's third-largest hydroelectric dam is proposed to be built, and at the same time new conservation areas and forestry regulations are established, all within the same geographic space. Operating in concert with one another, these new physical infrastructures are intended to be harmonized with ecological conservation, and together they become the basis of environmental governance interventions in the region.

Governing for Sustainable Development

The approach taken here focuses on how the ongoing process of governing society takes shape. I understand governing as involving a purposeful effort to steer, guide, control, and manage (sectors or facets of) society, both through singular acts and as constellations of political interventions (Kooiman 1993, Kemp, Parto, and Gibson 2005). Governing happens as new environmental norms are shaped, as certain institutional forms become entrenched, and as actors, who often have divergent interests, find places of convergence with ascertainable coherence and legitimacy (Baletti 2014). Focusing on governing helps inform the question of how governance is playing out in practice, at various levels of actors and discourses. Through centering our interrogation around how particular policy interventions transform lives and land into spaces of spatial, cultural, and economic production, we may gain greater insight into how power is exerted, how it shapes social and ecological realities, and how those realities are navigated by different actors (Lefebvre 1991 [1974], Brosius 1999, Bunker 1985, Bunker and Ciccantell 2005).

This book's theoretical focus is informed by the seminal urban geographer Henri Lefebvre, insofar as it attempts to excavate these dynamics within the

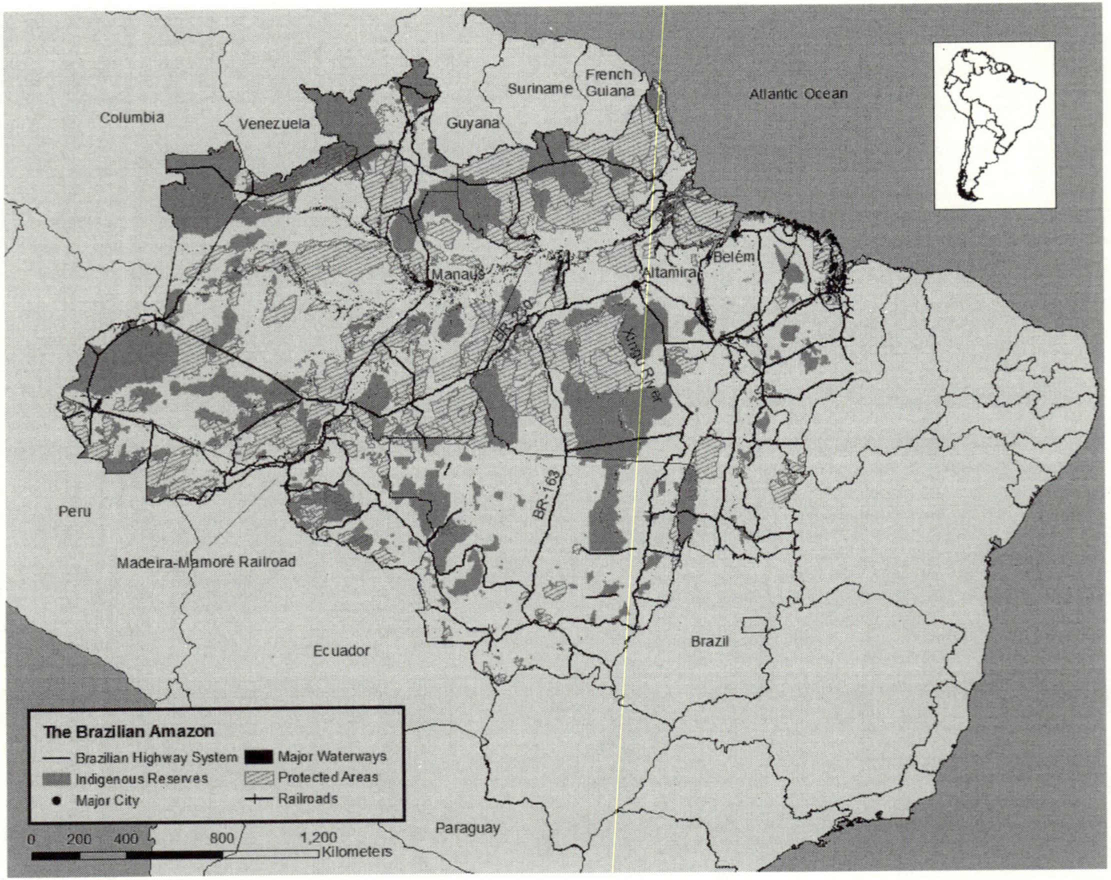

Figure 1.1 The Brazilian Amazon with major infrastructure, environmentally protected areas, and indigenous reserves depicted.

particular spaces in which sustainable development operates. Understood as mental, social, and physical spaces, Lefebvre encourages an understanding of a trialectic between lived space, produced through co-constitutions of objective spatial practices; conceptualizations of space; and lived experiences (1991 [1974]). In Lefebvre's view, "ideologies of space" form a bridge between subjects' perceptions and their lived spaces of activity. In everyday life, ideologies articulate with science, make coherence of spatial practices, and are the forces through which everyday life is practiced in all its contradictions.

> Socio-political contradictions are realized spatially. The contradictions of space thus make the contradictions of social relations operative. In other words, spatial contradictions 'express' conflicts between socio-political interests and forces; it is only in space that such conflicts come effectively into play, and in so doing they become contradictions of space. (Lefebvre 1991 [1974], 365)

Using Lefebvre as a foundation for understanding how space is co-constituted in the modern world, this book endeavors to unpack how sustainable development is imagined, negotiated, and physically enacted. As an element of modern state practice, sustainable development is manifested in specific spatial cultures through social, physical, economic, and cultural expressions.

A good part of the theoretical foundation for answering the question of how sustainable development is manifested in lives and landscapes also derives from the concept of the production of nature. As Neil Smith (1996) argues, the urge for capital accumulation shapes nature both discursively and materially. Understanding nature as a co-constituted element of social relations (which are simultaneously constituted by economic and political forces), or a socio-nature, establishes capitalism within contingent and contested historical-geographical processes that position society and nature as inseparable.[6] New natures are produced across space and time in these ongoing processes, and because of this, the idea of a pristine nature, untouched by humans, is increasingly problematic. Lefebvre's call to capture socio-nature requires tracing through a complex maze of power relations and natural processes. The production of socio-nature is understood through moments of relation between representational visions, symbolic-level expressions, and material practices. These elements may each embody characteristics that tend to internalize dialectical relations, but none of these are reducible to or determined by the other (Lefebvre 1991 [1974]). For Lefebvre, process and fluctuation "becomes interiorized in moments (lived, perceived, conceived) of the production process, but always in a fleeting, dynamic, and transgressive manner" (Swyngedouw 2015, 21). In this epistemological perspective, there is no fixity; flows of social relations, language, discursive constructions, material and cultural practices, biochemical and physical processes, and ideological processes are interacting in processes of creative destruction. The focus on understanding process over fixed ends helps in conceptualizing sustainable development as an ongoing set of actions and imaginaries, and it is as relevant to the nature of cities as it is to the remote regions of the Amazon.[7]

The political ecology of capitalism is deeply intertwined with the idea of sustainable development, which through assemblages of socio-nature becomes manifested and co-constituted by the economic, political, and social forces interacting on multiple levels. But how can those levels be understood within such complex metabolisms and shifting relationship dynamics? Environmental governance scholarship offers a path forward, recognizing that both "the politics of scale and the politics of networks" (Bulkeley and Betsill 2003, 3) need sensitive treatment. The close observation skills of anthropological methods inform subtle turns of phrase and social relations, and political science yields insight into how governance implicates a whole range of actors, including states, international institutions, private corporations, epistemic communities, domestic NGOs, local governments, and transnational civil society groups. Interrogating the interdependence and fluid frontiers between the public, private, and associated spheres of action, intervention, and control is central to being able to understand how sustainable development is manifested (Kooiman 1993, Barros-Platiau 2010).

The treatment of govern*ing* in this book, importantly, is distinct from traditional governance scholarship, which is a robust and distinctive field of its own. A brief discussion on governance versus governing, and the merits of each, is certainly warranted. Governance is concerned with the political and economic variables and mechanisms that lead to specific policies, outcomes, and political practices. The scope of governance extends beyond governments to focus on regulations, influential actors, and different organizational forms. Environmental governance is a domain concerned with how interventions change environment-related incentives, knowledge, institutions, decision making, and behaviors. This type of analysis can be applied to a variety of topics, such as climate change, ozone depletion, water pollution, species preservation, forest loss, or any number of other environmental issues (see, for example, Bulkeley 2005, Delmas and Young 2009, Hempel 1995). Governance for sustainable development is generally considered a sub-field of environmental governance, which often emphasizes participatory processes, coordinating policies, sharing information, establishing common criteria for success, and a host of other criteria that help establish effective institutions and incentives for desired outcomes to be achieved (Kemp, Parto, and Gibson 2005). The bulk of international relations research on environmental governance in practice tends to model the actors and networks that ultimately wield political influence, and it debates the extent to which such networks are multilevel, primarily domestic, or primarily transnational in nature (Delmas and Young 2009, Bernstein 2002, Backstrand 2006, Ivanova 2003, Cronkleton 2008). These studies examine key events and political relationships, among other pathways, formal and informal, in order to explain how environmental reforms take shape. Yet even as convergence takes shape around norms, interests, institutions, and environmental values, contradictions also arise, as the often-stated goals of governmental bureaucracies may diverge from the actual sociocultural conditions taking place in any given project's elaboration. Studying the messiness of such contradictions has generally fallen to anthropological treatments, much more than political science (see, e.g., Campbell 2012, Mathews 2011, Wolford 2005).

The importance of achieving good governance looms large as a paradigm in development practice, involving extensive lists of institutional changes and capacity-building initiatives that are frequently considered preconditions for economic and political development. Designing effective governance institutions and organizational structures that provide rule-ordered behavior and that get the process right for managing rules and sanctioning contrary behaviors is a key concern, especially in terms of environmental management in a developing-world context (Ostrom 1980, Ostrom 1999, Uphoff 1986). Developing effective institutions, especially in the relationship between the state and civil society organizations, is an important part of achieving effective governance (Grindle 2011, Evans 2002, Jordan, Wurzel, and Zito 2005). Shifts away from such extensive criteria and toward the notion of basic minimums of good governance, or "good enough governance," are a newer and relevant corrective in international development scholarship and practice (Grindle 2011). The scholarship on governance is certainly important and useful, but it tends to position specific governmental structures, policies, and interventions as fixed interventions of bureaucracy and institutional design. The problem of understanding how ongoing and co-constituted forms of social and environmental interaction take place is ultimately not well served, however, because the dynamism and tensions that arise as processes of governance play out through governing are ignored.

In Brazil, institutions are notoriously entangled within layers of jurisdictional authority, unfinished and sometimes contradictory processes, and institutional redundancy; the uncertainty that results from these gaps and redundancies creates formidable obstacles to building effective organizations and management regimes (Abers and Keck 2013). Policymaking is often driven by domestic actors, and those who are most successful in shaping policy outcomes are distinguished not by the overall strength of the institutions in which they operate, but by their individual experiences and abilities to experiment and rescale their efforts depending on different institutional limitations (Abers and Keck 2013).

Substantive roles, especially in the often contradictory and nonlinear world of Brazilian environmental politics, are also played by multilevel governance and international norms (Hochstettler and Keck 2007).

The approaches that are concerned with explaining who holds most influence over certain political outcomes goes a long way toward explaining the rationale of the state's institutions or certain political outcomes. However, they do relatively little to answer questions concerning how international norms, economic arrangements, and politics converge with local-level realities. Such complexities are expounded upon well in the anthropological literature on conservation and development (West 2006, Tsing 2005, Agrawal 2005), and this is where governing gains a strong analytical foothold. Through focusing on how attempts at influencing norms and political outcomes are made, too, the contradictions and entanglements of the Brazilian political sphere can be discussed with significantly greater depth than typical governance scholarship allows. Hence, my focus concerns governing, which involves seeing governance at multiple scales coming together to shape on-the-ground experiences in the Amazon, and interrogating the meanings that are made as the rainforest is shaped by and contested through the framework of sustainable development. This book navigates through these issues by engaging sustainable development as a reality-orienting discourse that is shared across these disparate groups of actors and becomes manifested in practice through a variety of policies, projects, and interventions.

The general goal of bringing environmental governance to the Amazon is the orientation through which a host of sustainable development projects and plans are established. That is, environmental governance is discussed as a normative good, involving clear rules for land use, property titling, forestry regulations, streamlined permitting, and the like. Moreover, governance more broadly is used to describe the need to confront assassinations, the often-shocking rates of rural violence, and deep social inequality. Citizen groups at local and transnational levels voice the need for a more robust criminal justice system and more rule of law, while bemoaning the absence of governance. In its various forms, environmental governance becomes manifested in material practice in addition to representation and semiotics; it situates the ambiguous policy idea of participation, which also serves as a "mobilizing metaphor" (Porter 1995) in development projects. This book offers an exploration of the co-constituted relationships that are formed as sustainable development discourses and policies gain legitimacy, involve compromises, and entail competing notions of what success should look like. The "terrain of struggle" (Li 1999, 316) of sustainable development in Amazonia is both geographical and relational. Through exploring this terrain, we are able to examine how environmental governance is worked out in uneven, dynamic ways.

Articulations and Identity

Through a focus on articulations of sustainable development, we will be able to gain a more granular understanding of the social and political realities of Amazonia, with appreciation for the complexity of those dynamics. In using the notion of articulation, I build upon the work of Antonio Gramsci (1971), Stuart Hall (1996), and Tania Murray Li (2007), who all suggest that articulations describe a process in which a position, an identity, or a set of interests is rendered and then conjoined with other convergent identities and interests within historical contexts. In other words, articulations involve the temporal overlap of individual elements; the concept helps explain how people present their positions and then come together around shared senses of place, culture, or values. Articulations may function to unite people with a sense of shared interests, common purpose, and social unification. These, in Gramscian interpretations of social power, can be configured within broader hegemonic contests to amass political power. Articulations, in both Antonio Gramsci and Stuart Hall's work, may be symbolic (that is, through words, narratives, and symbols) and also institutional, manifesting in political actions, campaigns, and institutional developments (Smucker 2017). The unity between two positions that form an articulation may be only fleeting, based on how different elements combine within a set of conditions and relationships. Stuart Hall explains:

> You have to ask under what circumstances can a connection be forged or made? So the so-called 'unity' of a discourse is really the articulation of different, distinct elements which can be rearticulated in different ways because they have no necessary 'belongingness'. The 'unity' which matters is a linkage between that articulated discourse and the social forces with which it can, under certain historical conditions, but need not necessarily, be connected. Thus, a theory of articulation is both a way of understanding how ideological elements come, under certain conditions, to cohere together within a discourse, and a way of asking how they do or do not become articulated, at specific conjunctures, to certain political subjects . . . [It] asks how an ideology discovers its subject rather than how the subject thinks the necessary and inevitable thoughts which belong to it; it enables us to think how an ideology empowers people, enabling them to begin to make some sense or intelligibility of their historical situation, without reducing those forms of intelligibility to their socio-economic or class location or social position. (1996:141–2)

Articulations are only more or less conscious; they can be thought of more as a derivative of spontaneous conjectures than fully rational, calculated actions or statements that aim to portray a fixed identity (Li 2007, Rose 1999). Rather, articulations shift and are responsive within historical contexts and are contingent on processes of agency, political openings, and having a fluidity in their formations of self that are historically rooted and iterative. The representations of struggles that often are imposed by outsiders frequently deny agency to the subaltern voices, instead ascribing to them distortions or idealized versions of their lives and livelihoods. By tracing the processes of articulation, subaltern perspectives can gain more agency over their self-representation, and more complexity can be gained as the realities of power relations and identities are explored (Li 2000, 2007).

The work on articulation and the complexity and hybridity of identities is increasingly adopted by anthropologists, but relatively little scholarship focuses on the political questions of how articulations shape policies and inform institutional structures as well as the local activism that responds to those structures. As Maarten Hajer's work on environmental discourses shows, successful discourse coalitions can consolidate beliefs about physical realities, leading to institutionalization and further reinforcement of discourses and beliefs (Hajer 1995). Illustratively, Hajer's analysis of acid rain and other forms of non-incidental environmental pollution suggest an increasing articulation of sustainable development as a means of further institutionalizing the policy itself (Hajer 1993, 43). Social movement scholar Jonathan Matthew Smucker contends that the "we" that is articulated when activists speak of "we in the environmental community" functions sometimes unconsciously to the detriment of building broader and more inclusive political mobilization efforts (Smucker 2017). One of the dimensions of analysis in this work entails exploring how different manifestations of environmentalism become used in policy frameworks or as ideological justification by well-meaning outsiders. In some cases, as with the *ribeirinhos* of the Terra do Meio region discussed in Chapter 5, locals may be forced to "twist and subvert" roles and presentations of their identity in to serve their own advantage (Lohman 1993, 203). The "middle ground" (Conklin and Graham 1995) that is often the only space left when certain identities are conscribed remains a space where pragmatic gains may be made in the face of predominant representations but where actions are confined to a particular identity "slot" (Li 2000) without adequate attention to how those categories and conscriptions became delineated in the first place.

All too often, overly simplistic narrations conscribe the Amazon and its population into homogenous and passive recipients of ideas, rather than acknowledging their agency. Much of the scholarship and narration of the history of the region tends to ignore or downplay the development concerns and aspirations of some Amazonian populations (Fisher 1996). The complexity of Amazonians' own political spaces are often subsumed by romanticized narratives about the non-human forest and its preservation (Hecht and Cockburn 1990), or to concentrate only on indigenous populations and rubber tappers, as if they are the only residents of the region worth discussing. Instead, an articulation-based analysis helps reveal how knowledge systems and identities are personal, flexible, and accommodating of variability (Harris 2006, Bratman 2011). More recent treatments offer some helpful new directions; anthropologist Jeffrey Hoelle tackles development issues directly by studying cattle culture in the Amazon (2015), as does Jeremy Campbell, whose excellent scholarship on property and land regimes focuses on the ranchers and loggers in the South of Pará (2015). These contributions add much-needed anthropological correctives to the English-language writing on the Amazon, presenting views that expand beyond the tendency to focus on Amazonian populations as indigenous groups or rubber tappers; and by focusing on the multiple ways in which development is articulated in the region, our understanding of the motivations, political constraints, and relationships of larger-scale landholders in Amazonian societies is considerably enhanced. Drawing upon such scholarship, it is important to recognize the hybrid, mutually constituted, and dynamic relationships that the many people of the region experience. From there, exploration may continue with a more dynamic and nuanced assessment of how power relations between specific actors inform the prevalence of certain formulations of values and identities within the geographical space of the Brazilian Amazon.

The Sustainable Development Conundrum

Sustainable development is broadly understood as a discourse and a policymaking framework that assumes a balance can be achieved between short-term needs and long-term economic growth, ecological health, and social equity. Social, economic, and environmental win–win–win situations can sometimes be found, but they are all too rare and fleeting. Ultimately, "doing" sustainable development in a manner that is satisfactory may be akin to the geometrical puzzle of squaring the circle: an impossibility (Robinson 2004).

Scholars have dismissed the utility of the idea of sustainable development since nearly the inception of the term, but especially since it persists so often in actual use, it is important to the scholarly endeavor to engage it. Environmental philosopher Timothy Luke pointedly asserts that sustainable development has become "one of the world's most unquestioned environmental philosophies" (Luke 1997, 75). There are legion uses of the term *sustainable development*; so many, in fact, that some scholars have identified over eighty different current definitions of the term (Williams and Millington 2004). This definitional fuzziness of sustainable development should not be mistaken for impotence. Quite the contrary; fluidity of characteristics of both *sustainability* and *development* proliferate within the concept of sustainable development and imbue it with staying power. Moreover, the multiplicity of expectations and discrepancies that emerge over what success itself looks like is part of what explains the frequent use of the term, giving it almost self-perpetuating qualities.

The central scholarly criticisms of sustainable development argue that the concept is too vague and too based in business-as-usual. Some contend that sustainable development shortchanges environmental issues, others assert that it shortchanges social justice and cultural concerns, and still others maintain the position that sustainable development is so broad a concept that it is ultimately impotent (Hedrén and Linnér 2009, Cruickshank, Schneeberger, and Smith 2012, Sachs 1993, Clusener-Godt and Sachs 1995, Adams 2001). Yet through its regular invocation as a political solution, the discourse of sustainable development often goes unquestioned, gaining still more salience. It is commonly held to be a central value, orienting how landscapes are imagined, how people participate, and how traditionally conflicting goals, such as conservation versus development, might instead become harmonized.[8]

Despite many well-recognized inadequacies, sustainable development nevertheless remains the predominant discourse that governmental and civil society actors have adopted for coping with the multidimensional challenges in the Amazon and in many other parts of the world. Sustainable development and its ancillary concepts are everywhere in Amazonian land use and environmental politics. There are agrarian reform models called Projects for Sustainable Development; Ecological-Economic Zoning initiatives orient land and resource use; the "Sustainable BR-163" plan involves paving an Amazonian highway to facilitate soybean exportation; local Agenda 21 council meetings take place in many municipalities; Extractive Reserves are established throughout the Amazon basin in order to meld conservation goals with local livelihoods. In response to assassinations and conflict, invoking sustainable development promises more citizen participation in planning and orients proposals for stronger police and justice systems. Sustainable development appears in land uses policies, in labor practices, in enforcement activities aimed at quelling illegal logging and land speculation, and as justification for constructing new hydroelectric dams. Through sustainable development economic planning, new markets for ecosystem goods and services are promoted, with an aim for turning conservation areas—and those people living within them—into economically thriving communities and places.

As a policy frame, sustainable development is powerful: the very theoretical emptiness of the term allows any number of actions to be justified in its name. Simultaneously, the rhetoric of sustainable development still carries a legitimacy that confers certain desirability upon those who use and successfully deploy the idea to orient policies, land uses, project proposals, and any number of other initiatives (Adams 2001). It begs the question: what is ultimately meant by "development," and who is the target of such development? Is sustainability meant as an adjective to modify development, understood implicitly as economic growth? How long of a time horizon is involved with sustainability? What is aimed to be sustained? And so on.

While the discourse of sustainability is widely used, there is a persistent gap between articulated best practices and the realities of implementing sustainability (Mosse 2005b, Büscher and Dressler 2007). Put simply, the idea here is that sustainable development is considerably easier said than done. When sustainable development becomes operationalized, and discussions about bringing it into practice take place, "opinions and actors fragment again or appeared never to have been coherent in the first place" (Büscher and Dressler 2007, 593). With such constant fragmentation, figuring out what regulatory limits should be established, how to achieve intended outcomes in both the short and longer term, and what resources to mobilize to most effectively achieve the desired changes presents a significant governance challenge.

Ironically, the imprecision of the term has not stopped sustainable development from becoming ubiquitous. The UN's development agenda for 2030 is oriented around the Sustainable Development Goals, and economist Jeffrey Sachs observes that the concept defines our era (2015). Natural resource management schemes, infrastructure proposals, territorial organization initiatives, and new regulatory regimes tend to form the major currencies of sustainable development. These take shape under the general paradigm of instilling environmental governance into places that are understood to need interventions of planning and policy, most often from actions led by the state.

Sustainable development is here to stay. The term *sustainable development* arose in UN policies in the late 1980s, and despite the many critiques launched against the concept, it is currently used in settings ranging from corporate boardrooms to elementary school classrooms and community gardens. Given that sustainable development arose to such popularity as a framework of environmental governance in such a relatively short period of time, a brief historical discussion to illustrate why and how this came to be the case is offered below.

A Brief History of Sustainable Development in Global Environmental Politics

Most studies concerning the origins of the term *sustainable development* trace its origin to a 1980 document prepared by the International Union on the Conservation of Nature (IUCN), entitled the *World Conservation Strategy* (WCS) (Redclift 1989, Adams 2001). The concept sought to put words to the idea that a reduction or avoidance of the environmental harms caused by economic growth could be achieved. The WCS was an outgrowth of the June 1972 United Nations Conference on the Human Environment held in Stockholm.

The Stockholm Conference was led by countries of the Global North, which were mainly concerned about pollution from industrialization, and was only "partly and belatedly" concerned with issues faced by the developing nations of the Global South (Adams 2001). Nations from the Global South were dismissive of the conference from the very start, and most developing nations did not send high-level officials to attend. Notably, however, Indian president Indira Gandhi did attend, and she made a statement that amounted to a seismic shift in the foundations of global environmental politics. "Poverty is the worst form of pollution," she declared, linking together the previously separate issues of development and environmentalism. The statement was considered an inconvenient blurring of two separate issues by many at the time, but nevertheless it established a connection between issues that shaped the discourse, institutions, and governance surrounding global environmental affairs thereafter (Wapner 2011). This intervention slightly shifted the previously environmentally dominated discourse into one where development issues gradually entered the global environmental realm. Overall, the WCS's treatment of sustainable development derived primarily from the political priorities of wealthier nations. As a result, it bungled the question of economic development—instead, privileging the conservation of living resources as one of the central problems of economic development—and presented lifestyle shifts as a framework for addressing poverty (Adams 2001, Lélé 1991).[9]

The *sustainable development* term gained more traction in the international arena beginning in 1983, when the United Nations established a World Commission on Environment and Development (WCED), chaired by Norway's former Prime Minister, Gro Harlem Brundtland.[10] The Brundtland Commission's final report, a 1987 document entitled *Our Common Future*, articulated sustainable development in a number of ways, while including a seminal formulation of the concept that remains predominant as a definition: "development which meets the needs of current generations without compromising the ability of future generations to meet their own needs" (Brundtland 1987, 41). Sustainable development, according to the WCED definition, was undergirded by two significant norms. First it sought to treat basic needs, with an emphasis on development actions that served the needs of the poor. Second, and differing significantly from the WCS, environmental limits were based on social and economic objectives. In other words, by premising development objectives upon economic growth, physical measures of environmental health and ecosystem balance were relatively devalued (Adams 2001). Environmental limits followed from achieving human development goals, it argued. The environmental impacts that accompany economic growth (e.g., greater consumption, energy and raw materials use, and pollution) were not characterized as contradictory to the sustainable development framework:

> In the short run, for most developing countries except the largest, a new era of economic growth hinges on effective and coordinated management among major industrial countries designed to eliminate expansion, to reduce real interest rates, and to halt the slide of protectionism. In the longer term, major changes are also required to make consumption and production patterns sustainable in a context of higher global growth. (Brundtland 1987, 67)

This 1987 formulation of sustainable development provided the grounding for most subsequent international discussions and policies on the topic of environmental conservation and development issues.

The Organization for Economic Cooperation and Development (OECD), International Monetary Fund (IMF), and the World Bank had been moving in the direction of win–win prospects for merging economic growth with environmental protection since the mid-1980s.[11] As international social structures converged around the importance of alleviating developing countries' debts in the late 1980s and early 1990s, the primacy of market-based mechanisms for trade and state sovereignty over environmental resources became a near-universal consensus in global environmental politics (Bernstein 2000).

The WCED's enunciation of sustainable development paved the way for the 1992 Rio Conference on Environment and Development (UNCED, also referred to as the Earth Summit or Rio '92). The Earth Summit is relevant to global environmental governance on several counts; not only was it one of the largest civil society gatherings to have happened, it also laid the groundwork for sustainable development as the orienting paradigm for global environmental politics (Wapner 1996, 2011). Moreover, as host nation for the summit as well as the subsequent Rio +20 Summit which took place in June 2012, Brazil rose to a position of perceived leadership among nations on environmental issues (Ferreira et al. 2014, Loyola 2014). The nation's explicit championing of development concerns within negotiations put questions of poverty and economic growth at center stage amid the global environmental discussions at these meetings.

One relevant outcome of the Earth Summit was that it placed environmental issues *wholly within* the context of development. Principle Four of the Rio Declaration states: "In order to achieve sustainable development, environmental protection shall constitute an integral part of the development process and cannot be considered in isolation from it." This centrality of development, which at the time was a discussion primarily about economic growth, was led by the countries of the Global South. No longer, they argued, should northern countries blame pollution and environmental problems on the poor. Rather, development was framed as a right, and nations had "common but differentiated responsibilities" for supporting development while upholding the integrity of the global environment. Plans for sustainable development would be captured through Agenda 21. This document, at 600 pages long and with insufficient funding allocated for implementation after the conference, became a catch-all for plans in the name of sustainable development.[12] Despite these caveats about the relevance and implementation of the Rio '92 proposals, the framework established at the meeting laid the groundwork for sustainable development's dominance as a paradigm in global environmental governance. The Earth Summit was an important moment of worldwide agreement that economic growth was the starting point of concern within the sustainable development framework, and environmental protection stemmed from the necessity to perpetuate global economic expansion.

The Global South emphatically prioritized the sovereignty of nation-states over environmental resources at the Rio '92 Earth Summit, and central to their concern was the necessity to achieve poverty alleviation and greater economic growth through industrialization strategies. The already-wealthy nations emphasized environmental protection responsibilities, but the developing world perceived this as a luxury they had little use for, much less money to afford. The Group of 7 nations (G7), representing the concerns of the Global North, urged the developing world to preserve and protect their natural resources for the good of the whole planet and offered technology transfers and financing. Sparse results were ultimately manifested on a global level. In 2002, ten years after the Rio Earth Summit, another global conference was held in Johannesburg, South Africa, and global leaders signed on to a Declaration on Sustainable Development as well as an implementation plan. Again, however, much of the implementation never actually came into fruition (Wapner 2003). At the conference, national sovereignty was reiterated as the basis for addressing natural resource management issues, although democratic decision making, innovative partnerships between governmental and nongovernmental actors, and stakeholder participation were emphatically incorporated into the conference as important parts of global governance (Backstrand 2006). At both conferences, sustainable development seemed a pragmatic means of reaching global agreement. The central sticking point of achieving a globally acceptable compromise was the divide over the importance given to environmental protection and the need for economic development. Generally, the developing world gave priority to development needs, while the already-developed world urged conservation. The idea of sustainable development appeared to negotiators as a framework through which to achieve both goals without significant compromise.

Around this concept of sustainable development, international conferences created new agencies and established international environmental and development policies. Sustainable development became the orienting framework through which any number of other global issues—including forest loss, biodiversity, desertification, access to clean drinking water, access to improved sanitation, ozone-depleting substance pollution, and climate change are all addressed. At local levels, governments and citizens alike have organized strategies and initiatives for tackling environmental concerns hand in hand with economic growth. Practices such as local-level participation in environmental decision making, achieved through valuing democratic processes of stakeholder engagement, have also become central strategic components of sustainable development (Backstrand 2006).

By the early 2000s, the concept of sustainable development had received a scholarly battering. It was too vague, too lofty, too incremental, and ultimately, too intellectually empty for most scholars to champion. Yet it persisted to a significant extent in UN statements, NGO projects, and national planning. Related concepts, such as the green economy, had initially emerged around the same time as the sustainable development concept took hold.[13] Barely discussed since then, however, the green economy reemerged in UN arenas around 2008, revived by the global economic recession and financial instability (UNDP n.d.). Exemplified by the UN Environment Program's Green Economy Initiative (GEI) and subsequently featured as a major theme of the 2012 Rio+20 UN Conference on Sustainable Development, the central assumptions of the sustainable development framework remained intact.[14] The green economy discourse, along with adherent discussions that promote "green jobs," "green development," and "green growth," encourage the idea that economic growth and low-carbon ("green") futures for the world are something of a silver bullet, much like sustainable development (Cook and Smith 2012). Social justice issues, meanwhile, are perpetually under-privileged within both the frameworks of the green economy and sustainable development. In the realm of international development, ensuring environmental sustainability was one of the eight Millennium Development Goals for 2000–2015.[15] The Millennium Development Goals were superseded by the Sustainable Development Goals (SDGs) in 2016. The SDGs placed substantially more emphasis on environment and developmental linkages in the more recent iteration. Notably, the SDGs include addressing climate change, urban sustainability, life on land, and life below water each as separate goals. The reformulated goals—of which there are 17, along with 169 targets—orient the world's collective targets and priorities for addressing poverty and inequality, participation, urban development, education, along with climate change, environmental and biodiversity protection, and achieving a more peaceful world.[16] The wide-ranging goals firmly establish that the discourse and framework of sustainable development will be the predominant modality for addressing global challenges until 2030, if not well beyond.

Theoretical Underpinnings of Sustainable Development

Two central sociopolitical theories related to the sustainable development concept help to explain why the concept has attained so much political and ideational importance. They are ecological modernization and liberalism. First, the theory of ecological modernization has strongly influenced the sustainable development concept as it evolved in the late 1990s. Ecological modernization posits that technological innovation and scientific knowledge should be embraced as a means of *ecologizing the economy*, and by implication argues for *economizing ecology*, namely through adopting market efficiency logics. These include appropriate economic accounting for environmental resources and pollution as a means of fostering compatibility with environmental concerns. A combination of technological innovation and environmental policies work toward modern, market-oriented economic systems under ecological modernization (Beck, Giddens, and Lash 1994). Ecological modernization also positions the state as an instigating actor that should seek to encourage private enterprises to get involved in efforts to be more environmentally concerned (Sezgin 2013, York, Rosa, and Deitz 2010, Latour 1998). Social movement actors, meanwhile, are positioned more as participants in sustainable development initiatives than as watchdogs over such processes of change, which are led by the state and private enterprises (Olsson, Hourcade, and Köhler 2014, Mol 2010). As Bruno Latour's work contends, an entrenchment within modernity problematically tends to reproduce the perception of a dualism between man and nature, without adequately encompassing the hybridity of nature–society relationships. Through the managerial approach and the confidence in our own ability to know the world that is implicit in the modernist paradigm, we lose sight of the side effects that ultimately entangle us even further into the pursuit of modernity (Latour 2003).

Sustainable development became subsequently infused with ecological modernization in significant ways,[17] particularly in terms of its ability to position ecological, social, and economic concerns as in harmony rather than opposition to each other.

As much as sustainable development is related to the concept of ecological modernization, it is important also to note the second foundational theoretical underpinning of sustainable development, which is anchored in the liberal political tradition.[18] It is widely recognized that the norms established within the notion of sustainable development are predicated on liberalism, understood as a championing of free trade principles, environmental cost accounting, and individualization of responsibility (Hobson 2013, Bernstein 2002, Zelli, Gupta, and van Asselt 2013). Sustainable development is the "breakthrough idea" that further institutionalized the liberal approach in environmental governance in the 1980s, which then became further embedded in Agenda 21 and subsequent global environmental agreements (Bernstein 2002). Liberal norms of economic efficiency and environmental improvements, achieved through privatization, deregulation, and market-based governance mechanisms, tend to orient the logics of global environmental governance. They have not been eclipsed by neoliberalism, although they have sometimes coexisted (Bernstein 2002, Zelli, Gupta, and van Asselt 2013, Bernstein 2000). These norms have held considerable sway over environmental governance, influencing everything from the principle that polluters should pay for their environmental damages to biodiversity agreements and climate change negotiations (Bernstein 2002, Zelli, Gupta, and van Asselt 2013).

Increasingly, too, the marks of neoliberal political and economic relations have influenced the ways in which environmental politics take shape and in which nature itself is configured through politics.[19] Under the juggernaut of free market logic and the values of classical liberalism, nature itself, and land in particular, became seen as things which could be commoditized, privately controlled, and individually held (McCarthy and Prudham 2004). Under global neoliberalism, states have become centered upon protection of individual property rights and the facilitation of free movement of capital, while environmental regulations have suffered concomitantly with labor protections and social entitlement programs. The discourse of sustainable development has become wrapped into the language of neoliberalism's central institutions (Goldman 2005). Rather than rejecting environmentalism, sustainable development has become a platform through which environmental concerns can be assimilated, even if achieved at the cost of corporate greenwashing and rather weak sustainability values (Bakker 2010, McCarthy and Prudham 2004). Recent critiques even more sharply contend that at times, the language of sustainable development continues to further entrench colonialist mentalities, since it often euphemistically urges poor countries to develop along a different path than the already-wealthy nations, while ignoring the inequitable distributions of power, responsibility, and participation in decision making within the global system (Ghosh 2016). Understanding the assumptions embedded in the concept, whether explicit or implicit, goes a long way toward explaining how it maintains its predominance. The Amazon is an especially interesting location to witness sustainable development in action as a discourse and a policy framework, since it has such a variety of important social and environmental characteristics in addition to being located largely within Brazil, which led many of the developing nations in the UN summits pertaining to the topic of sustainable development.

An Open-Air Laboratory for Sustainable Development

The Amazon is a tremendously important region in terms of its contributions to global ecological integrity. Amazonian deforestation (and the lack thereof) has significant implications for global climate change, and its freshwater resources are similarly implicated in global desertification and rainfall dynamics (Fearnside 2012b, Nepstad et al. 2008, Nepstad et al. 2014). Among the Amazon's hundreds of indigenous tribes, nearly a quarter of indigenous peoples remain isolated or completely uncontacted, and scant knowledge exists about their ways of life (Walker and Hamilton 2014).[20] Capturing the potential of the Amazon's flora and fauna for scientific and medical purposes is also an area where there is considerable room for new discovery; Brazil is the most biodiverse country on Earth, and the Amazon region has a virtual pharmacopia of potential to address human needs (Davidov 2013).

The international stage for debating sustainable development has often been set in Brazil, and for good reason. Brazil's status as a leader in global environmental politics is almost *sui generis*, given its wealth of natural resources. The nation contains 12 percent of the world's freshwater, and somewhere between 15 and 20 percent of the world's biodiversity. The Amazon region has the largest tropical rainforest in the world, over sixty percent of which is located in Brazil. The region is estimated to contain about 10 percent of the world's known species and 20 percent of the world's known bird species. Its human diversity is impressive, too: there are 21 million people living in the Brazilian Amazon, and around 400 different indigenous tribes there. Only 6.6 million Amazonians live in rural areas, however; the other 70 percent of the population is urban (Padoch et al. 2008). The rainforest plays a critical role in balancing the global climate, meaning that the loss of the forest could have severe implications for carbon emissions and other greenhouse gases.

The international political and scientific focus on the future of the Amazon has been framed in global environmental negotiations since the late 1980s around a predominant perception of problematic deforestation occurring in the region. Brazil, as host to more than half of Amazonian rainforests, has endured most of this concern (Cleary 1991, Monteiro, Seixas, and Vieira 2014). Around 20 percent of the total Brazilian rainforest has been lost in the past fifty years. Measurement of deforestation first began in the 1980s when satellite imagery technology allowed for such data to be obtained. At the same time as Brazil's deforestation rates began alarming people all over the world, the nation's economic growth was its major priority. Strong correlations between rainforest loss and economic development appeared in other nations as well (López and Gregmar 2005). Researchers and politicians alike began questioning whether rainforest loss was the price of economic achievement. There is good reason to believe, however, that achieving economic growth in Brazil and reducing deforestation may both be achievable, in contradiction to the sometimes-held assumption that environmental protection and economic growth are at odds. The significant decline in deforestation during Brazil's economic growth period of 2004–2012, while agricultural production rates surged, is a significant counterpoint to this assumption (Butler 2014).[21]

The all-too-human strife in the Amazon is often obscured by predominant characterizations of Amazonian environmental problems, captured in images involving felled trees and statistics about vast tracts of land becoming deforested. The harsh daily realities faced by most people in the region, however, have less to do directly with rainforest loss than the public imaginary would portray. Think, instead, of the experience of struggle that happens when small-scale farmers get malaria, or how children may not have a consistently paid teacher staffing their schools. The Amazon's highways are unpaved roads, and cars and buses get stuck in the mud along them with a frustrating frequency during the rainy season. Smaller cities often turn a blind eye to the sewage that is produced by their ever-growing numbers of residents, dumping the waste straight into the rivers. Not far downstream, those same rivers are the primary livelihoods for small-scale fishermen and indigenous tribes. Persistent budgetary shortfalls and bureaucratic hiccups often stymie projects to improve local sanitation, drinking water, hospitals, or road improvements. Those problems are compounded by pervasive corruption dynamics that position such projects to be exceedingly costly and dependent on kickbacks. These realities are not uncommon in many parts of the world, especially in low- and middle-income countries. They certainly are not unique to Brazil, although they are universally disturbing. It is important to bear these realities in mind when considering how sustainable development politics in the Amazon are lived out, given that the prioritization of forest protection is frequently discussed without regard to these mundane but pressing social and development needs but instead alternately privileges the protection of trees or the creation of jobs as the predominant mode of gauging developmental success.

The statistics and the less-known stories of Amazonian social frictions and impunity are noteworthy. Between 2003 and 2013, nearly 2,500 rural workers received death threats in Brazil, and in just the first eight months of 2016, 39 people died violently in conflicts over land.[22] These conflicts entail struggles over property rights that become arbitrated through threats and hired gunmen rather than in courts. The human rights group Global Witness reported that Brazil was the worst place in the world to be an environmental defender in 2015, with 50 killings taking place, most of them in remote parts of the Amazon and over hydroelectric dams, mining, logging, and land conflicts (2016). Figure 1.2 portrays assassinations, violence indices, and rural land conflicts with historic and more

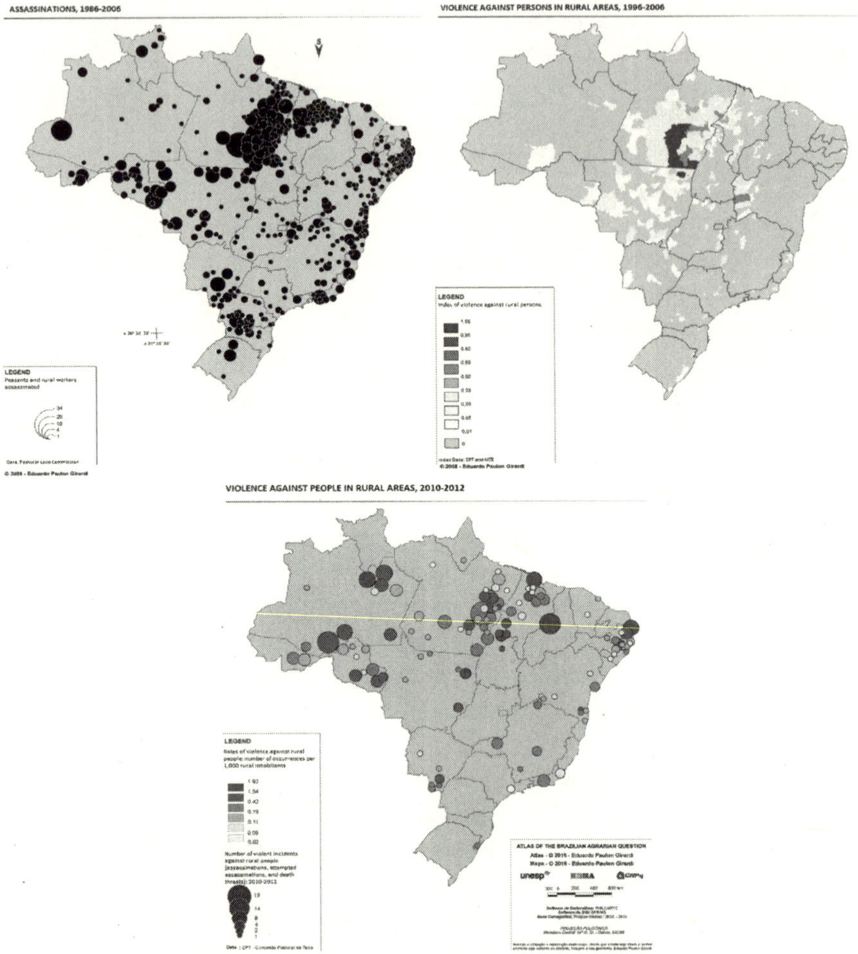

Figure 1.2 The state of Pará is a hotspot for land conflicts, which frequently lead to assassinations. The concentration of rural violence in the South of Pará, which is the focus area for the case studies presented in this research, are among the highest rates in all of Brazil. Map credits: Eduardo Paulon Girardi

current data, and portrays the prevalence of such aggressions in the Amazon and in the state of Pará relative to the rest of Brazil.

In 2012, 3,000 people reported being subject to forced labor conditions—a manifestation of modern-day slavery—in the Amazon.[23] Governmental efforts increased to improve labor conditions in various supply chains between 2014–2016, with over 4,000 people being freed from "slave-like" conditions and 349 companies experiencing penalties (Human Rights Watch 2017). In the Amazon, people involved with the cattle ranching industry, which is mostly dominated by wealthy individual landholders that operate outside of governmental supervision, are largely the culprits for such acts. Cattle ranching is linked both to illegal land claiming and deforestation, and to labor abuses (Greenpeace 2003). The logging sector, agribusiness, and ranching interests often hold substantial political control, and together tend to constitute local political alliances. It is also not uncommon to hear the expression that *o dono é quem desmata*—the owner is whoever deforests (Torres, Doblas, and Alarcon 2017). The dynamics are explained succinctly by those living in the region, who, envisioning a more transparent, impartial, and responsive federal government, complain that "the state is absent." The predominant view is that rule-of-law measures can best be accomplished through a greater presence of the state itself. And, paradoxically, the government's track record from the 1960s until the mid-1980s was to unapologetically bolster deforestation and encourage Amazonian resource exploitation in the name of economic growth, with little attention to social and environmental costs (Hall 2008). Typically, this notion of governance conceptualizes the state as accountable and democratic. It posits that the presence of regulations and environmental enforcement personnel, as well as clearer processes for legalizing land uses and business practices, will ultimately lead to better social and environmental outcomes.

Given the commonality of such views, it is important to acknowledge that the Amazon is often narrated as the new "wild West" or as a frontier. This current of scholarship was especially popular into the mid-1990s.[24] Incursions of people and capital into Amazonian lands was concomitant with a relative lack of brakes on the state and private enterprise (Sawyer 1990). Conversely, frontier closure and consolidation involves regulating and restricting settlement on new land, often through territorial and environmental governance, including through actions such as the creation of parks and indigenous reserves, demarcations of land holdings, regulations on logging, and strategic planning for where and how new infrastructures and agricultural activities take shape (Sawyer 1984).[25] Given competing property claims and competition for the control of natural resources in the Amazon, violence and conflict over lands and resources become manifested in visceral ways—on bodies marked by violence, in denuded landscapes, and always-on-guard social relations (Aldrich et al. 2012, Walker et al. 2011, Campbell 2015, Hoelle 2015). Frequently, maps portray an arc of deforestation which butts up against indigenous reserves and conservation areas in the rainforest, evoking clear delineations of property boundaries and territorial control.

It is worth briefly noting that the frontier notion embedded in these framings also implies a significant amount of taming and control that take place as civilization encounters the "wild."[26] The frontier notion is not inaccurate, but it does tend to portray Amazonians[27] as having little autonomy over their own historical process. Instead, residents are positioned as relatively powerless subjects of outsiders' agendas or as purely beholden to the state's enforcement regimes. Within a global environmentalist imaginary, the Amazon is seen sometimes as a 'second Edenic paradise,' filled with pristine and mysterious natural wonders, meant to be left alone by most humans (Slater 2002). Along with this vision, Amazonian residents are collectively framed as ideal conservationists and are often portrayed as "noble savages living happily in perfect harmony with nature" (Sachs 1995, 103). Alternatively, Amazonia has historically been characterized as a sort of "green hell" by some observers, which implies that the lands must be tamed and brought under human control, or at least better understood, in order to become bounteous. The Amazon's vast expanse, according to this worldview, presents a threat to human survival unless land there can be tamed and exploited, usually by projecting state power and amassing wealth (Slater 2015, 2002, Cronon 1995).[28] In the 1970s, this view suggested that human settlement in the region was necessary in order to further national development goals and capitalist expansion, while scientific study and sound management would help the region lose its "wild" quality, leading to the triumph of human ingenuity. Other portrayals center humans in Amazonia quite differently; when framed as the "lungs of the world," this conceptualization of the Amazon emphasizes its vital importance for the climate-regulating functions which the trees provide. Similarly, the narrative of the rainforest as a 'pharmacopeia' wherein a bounty of miracle cures are held within a de-nationalized space present an imaginary of the Amazon as a part of the global commons (Davidov 2013).

On a basic level, such Amazonian portrayals are congruent with environmentalist narratives of pristine nature, in which a relatively untouched wilderness experiences the deleterious effects of human settlement and encroachment. Overly simplistic media accounts frequently subvert the complexity and hybridity of Amazonian realities, ultimately excluding certain important constituencies. For example, common portrayals of larger landholders often involves characterizing those who have land and wealth as actors who are centrally motivated by capital accumulation and land acquisition, who hold little regard for laborers or the environment.[29] A dichotomy of overly simplistic interpretations of Amazonian actors also results in a popular discourse wherein "environmental" interests, understood as representative of indigenous populations and rubber tappers, are pitted against the "pro-development" actors represented by bourgeois classes comprised of cattle ranchers and business owners, many of whom are also in local political control.

This problem of oversimplification is not only present in media accounts but also in scholarship. For example, take the relevant but distinct case on the question of what role indigenous knowledge plays in Amazonia today. Noted

Amazonian scholars historically maintained a rather static and one-way view that knowledge was passed from indigenous populations to Europeans in the Amazonian peasantry. Historian Charles Wagley writes that "It might be said that all Indian residues in contemporary Amazon culture relate directly or indirectly to the environment" (1967, 227). Ecologist Emilio Moran's similar description is that "In almost all aspects which deal with man's relation to the environment, the indigenous ways are still practiced today through the cultural adaptations of the *caboclo amazonense*"[30] (1974, 139). These representations present knowledge systems as if they are linearly accumulating and impersonal, coming from a culture or tradition writ large. The unfortunate consequences of reliance on these abstract categories and unnecessarily simplistic portrayals are multiple. Such dichotomous and one-way thinking tends to reduce the diversity of Amazonian actors and their interests. Moreover, it ignores how developmental and environmental values are understood, become predominant, and gain staying power. If we are to understand how sustainable development plays out in the Amazonian context, it is essential to start from a point of recognition of the diversity of Amazonian populations, and to acknowledge the myriad differences in how environmentalism, development, and territorial control are inflected upon the region as a site of global and national importance.

The Amazon in Relation to Global Environmental Politics

Brazil's importance in global environmental politics was attenuated by its will for political leadership, expressed through the role it played as host to the 1992 Rio Earth Summit and the subsequent Rio+20 Summit in 2012. Brazil gained credibility for showing goodwill toward addressing global environmental issues as it increasingly participated in global environmental negotiations from 1992 onward. Since that time, Brazil has actively engaged in global environmental negotiations, whether over issues such as genetically modified organisms, global biodiversity, or climate change.

While earlier stances had mainly involved a "veto-state" position in relation to environmental issues articulated by countries in the Global North, the intransient strategy pivoted toward one of emerging negotiator. Brazil made more active contributions to agreements on biodiversity, climate change, and trade-related environmental issues as the nation's diplomats came to recognize how participation in global environment and development negotiations could ultimately protect and promote national interests and national sovereignty (Barros-Platiau 2010). Brazil's positions, too, have frequently derived from strong pressures exerted by national and international civil society groups. Rather than major institutional or ideational shifts in international affairs, Brazilian environmental decisions have often hinged on the activism of multi-scalar networks. These networks have had some impressive campaign successes, often using the government's sensitivity and responsiveness to international media attention as their main strength (Keck and Sikkink 1998, Brown and Purcell 2005, Bulkeley 2005). A robust set of domestic laws and legal accountability processes, moreover, helps to enforce domestic environmental laws (Hochstetler and Keck 2008), although funding shortfalls at times plague environmental enforcement agencies in Brazil.[31]

Within South America, Brazil is the predominant regional power. Two-thirds of the Amazon basin is located within Brazilian territory, although Brazil does not stand out as a particularly progressive leader on environmental issues in relation to some other Amazonian countries. Ecuador and Bolivia, for example, both incorporated the idea of the rights of nature into their legal frameworks. The concept of rights of nature is based on indigenous views of nature as a sacred and undivided community of living beings. The idea offers a wholly different paradigm for understanding human–nature relations from that of sustainable development. Instead of a production and consumption based economic model, the rights of nature paradigm is based on living well—*sumak kawsay*, or *buen vivir*—and posits that public policies should be guided by living in harmony with natural limits (Kauffman and Martin 2017). Even as the leadership of the "new Left" governments was strengthened throughout the region in the early 2000s, Brazilian policies tended to diverge from the stronger legal frameworks for environmental protection and indigenous rights that were articulated in Bolivia and Ecuador. Brazil's emphasis instead tended to follow a more reformist approach, rooted in the sustainable development framework and finding economic incentives to achieve conservation aims. Brazil looked toward more neoliberal conservation approaches, at times following the lead of Guyana, which was an early adopter of Reduced Emissions from Avoided Deforestation and Degradation (REDD+) financing schemes for forest protection.[32] It made strides for forest protection largely through creating new conservation areas, especially between 2003–2008, and focused on developing funding for Amazonian conservation from international sources, such as through the Amazon Fund, which steered over $1 billion in foreign investments into outcomes-based environmental initiatives in the region.[33]

Traditionally, Brazilian leaders cared little about global handwringing over Amazonian forest losses. National sovereignty and the imperative to exert a strong state presence over the distant territory of the Amazon were priorities instead.[34] Protecting the region from invasion was a strongly articulated goal of Brazil's military regime, which lasted from 1964 to 1985. The Brazilian emphasis on territorial control in the Amazon also centered upon a vision for expanding the economic productivity of the region, which led to irreversible consequences in the form of deforestation and social conflicts as natural resources were exploited (Castro 2012).

While global leaders were discussing the importance of global environmental protection at the Stockholm Conference of 1972, Brazilian leaders touted national sovereignty and the importance of deforesting the Amazon as a national development priority (Hecht and Cockburn 1990).[35] The centrality of the idea of territorial protection and control in the Amazon also coupled with the economic growth logics and carried forward into Brazil's re-democratization, which began in 1985 and lasted through a multiyear period of gradual political opening and the adoption of a new constitution in 1988.

Tensions between environmental protection and economic development strategies marked the Brazilian approach to sustainable development in the late 1980s and early 1990s. The government accorded scientists a stronger role in shaping strategies for Amazonian conservation, and established greater land rights and legal protections to the indigenous and traditional populations in the country (Alonso, Costa, and Maciel 2005, Hochstettler and Keck 2007). Even as these efforts persisted, however, the desire to build infrastructure in the region remained a significant priority of national development strategies. A similarly relevant contradiction was present regarding international pressure and national policies; in public discourse, Brazilian politicians outwardly rejected other nations' influence over their sovereign affairs, but the country in practice was quite sensitive to outside pressure.[36]

At the Rio Earth Summit in 1992, such contradictory positions became obvious. Brazil stymied efforts to establish a global convention on combating deforestation, ultimately diluting resolutions about deforestation and relegating them to become nonbinding Forest Principles. The question of deforestation was also linked to climate change and desertification issues in other agreements. Brazilian insistence that global environmental agreements should incorporate a right to development and financing for technology transfers also marked the nation's positions in environmental negotiations (Castro 2004). A Pilot Program for the Protection of the Brazilian Tropical Rainforests, or PP-G7, brought considerable funding to bear upon Amazonian conservation research and policies. In keeping with the notion that sustainable development projects should be participatory and locally based rather than top-down in orientation, projects proliferated that aimed to engage communities in natural resource management initiatives and to establish common property management systems in the Amazon (Le Tourneau et al. 2013). The basic approach toward sustainable development planning was one where funding and local-level interventions were welcomed, but binding commitments and constraints on national planning efforts were resisted. For most national infrastructure and economic planners, capitalizing on the region's potential role in economic growth through extracting natural resources appeared a significantly higher priority than conserving its natural resources or using them renewably. Brazil's market-oriented and modernization-conscious emphasis on conservation and development strategies have long marked its approach toward Amazonian lands.

It is possible that eventually Amazonian landscapes will become valued globally within schema that leverage markets for conservation and management of working forest ecosystems in the region. But, for the most part, today's global market system continues to privilege single crops and products from the region (soy beans, timber, beef) much more than viewing agro-ecosystems and intact forest landscapes when sustainable development is articulated (Clement 2006). Essentially, writes Gustavo Fonesca of the Global Environment Facility, the current paradigm of sustainable development "has not (yet) succeeded in changing the essentially exploitative nature of resource-based development in the Amazon. In most cases, it manages only to mitigate the most egregious negative impacts" (Fonesca, preface in Killeen 2007, 4). Fonesca argues that a new development paradigm shift may be necessary in order to gain more substantial changes. Meanwhile, understanding how—and why—we continue to perpetuate the existing paradigm of sustainable development, particularly within a region so marked by its presence, begs further investigation.

The aim of this work is to explore how the disjunctures between sustainable development in policy and in practice function as a lived reality. Often, the representations of more powerful countries construct the realities of Brazil, and inform the lived experiences of people on the ground in the Amazon. Such reality-shaping ultimately molds encounters between the developed and underdeveloped, the First and Third Worlds, empire and colonies (Doty 1996). Further, domestic state practice and civil society re-appropriations and resistances play important roles in the political dynamics of territorial control and change. In what anthropologist Anna Tsing terms "frictions," or the contingencies and awkward engagements that take place as global universals are interconnected and translated into people's lives (Tsing 2005), more powerful economic and political actors shape local realities that are often contradictory to plans that are articulated on paper and to the goals that are held by natural resource managers, community organizers, and infrastructure planners alike. This work follows from the long tradition of scholarship that explains how visions established from "above" by governments, international NGOs and development banks, and even by domestic groups, are then resisted and locally reinterpreted by grassroots actors (Ferguson 1994, Escobar 1995, Scott 1998). This is also a part of the seemingly inescapable process through which conservation and development ideals are unevenly put into practice (Li 2007, Tsing 2005, West 2006, Scott 1990, 1985, Mosse 2005a, Ferguson 1994).

A Brief Overview

The next two chapters of this book offer a historical tracing of Amazonian environmental governance and development, oriented centrally around the idea that sustainable development is articulated through land use practices and policies that have strong underpinnings in modernity. The subsequent chapters use case studies to engage a more granular portrayal of sustainable development politics in practice. These chapters examine several levels of actors with a focus on sustainable development interventions including road paving, creating new conservation areas, and mega-dam construction projects. The case studies offer a more nuanced perspective on the social and political dynamics of sustainable development plans, and tell the stories of who wins, who loses, and why.

Chapter 2 traces the ideational struggles over the Brazilian Amazon from the early explorations of the region by non-indigenous explorers into the 1980s. The chapter specifically highlights the important theoretical undercurrents of how seeing the tropics and the push for modernity in Amazonia became manifested through grandiose development projects and deeply symbolic exertions of state power. The chapter situates the Amazon region as a space fraught with the tension between ecological concerns and state economic planning priorities that often take uneven, incomplete, and erratic forms. These make lasting marks on the landscapes and societal structures in that region, and ultimately provide the ideational foundation for later sustainable development articulations. The historical discussion continues in Chapter 3, which focuses centrally on the host of plans and policies for sustainable development conducted in Brazil beginning in the late 1980s, when the concept of sustainable development was introduced into the mainstream of global environmental politics. Chapter 3 also elaborates on the contemporary major players of Amazonian sustainable development politics, focusing on the roles and historical formations of the Catholic Church, social movement groups, socio-environmental activism in relation to various projects, and the socio-environmental struggles of the late 1980s and into contemporary times. Illustrative cases of Brazilian infrastructure and developmental priorities for the Amazon are discussed to illustrate the primacy of national integration and consolidation of state power—in other words, economic priorities with a strong modernization orientation—well above environmental protection and social equity considerations.

Chapters 4, 5, and 6 take a more granular approach that investigates how sustainable development plans are enacted in projects and policies for regional development. The focus in these chapters concerns the socio-natures of roads, conservation areas, and a river. The three areas are geographically proximate—all within the state of Pará. The focus in these case study chapters is to illustrate various articulations of sustainable development, with emphasis on how the concept of sustainable development functions to regulate and constrain actors' identities and to shape land uses. The chapters develop the central argument of this book, which is that with few exceptions, sustainable development ultimately serves to reproduce and reinforce existing inequalities and yields highly uneven social and environmental results. The socio-natures of Amazonian realities show how injections of capital and state influence disproportionately consolidate the power of capital and the state, even as they are contested by members of civil society. The experiences of sustainable development explored in these chapters reveal how techno-managerial coordination and capacity plays out on vulnerable landscapes and frequently marginalized populations, with consequences that are full of friction and imbalanced privilege. They also reveal how historically constituted relationships and understandings of self in relation to others inform development projects, often reproducing long-standing inequalities.

Chapter 4 focuses on the legacy of modernization-oriented planning processes, which are reinforced through transposition into the language and logics of sustainable development planning concerning how lands bordering the Transamazon and BR-163 highways will be protected, even as those roads are paved. Chapter 5 elaborates a counterpoint to this perspective; it explores the creation of conservation areas in the region known as the Terra do Meio, a process that involved the collaborations of state actors with local and international civil society groups and ultimately transformed a region of substantial isolation and lawlessness into one of the world's largest and most important biodiversity corridors. The chapter highlights how the sustainable development forms taking shape suggest the ways in which territories of conservation are circumscribed by strategic alliances and political moments and entail different, often contradictory, ideas of place and identity that are articulated by different actors. In Chapter 6, competing visions behind sustainable development articulations are analyzed based on the case study of the Belo Monte hydroelectric project, which is located along the same Xingu River where the conservation areas discussed in Chapter 5 were created a few years earlier. The chapter reveals how the framework of sustainable development promotes the logics of state planning for the promotion of macro-economic and growth-oriented goals, while concealing the social and environmental consequences of the infrastructure under the auspices of democratic engagement.

The conclusion of the book, Chapter 7, zooms back out to explore the sustainable development framework as it informs state–society relations and uneven manifestations in lived experiences of place. The conclusion also examines prospects for the transformative potential of sustainable development as a utopic vision, and offers reflections on the possibilities for sustainable development discourse to become more deeply emancipatory through adopting a new metaphor, involving embroilment—as a means of better grasping the fundamental realities of the concept as it is practiced.

Bruno Latour reminds us that a policy idea or political design is not an automatic success or a foregone conclusion from its inception. Rather, policy and political success arise from society's abilities to build support, perpetuate the idea, and impose "growing coherence on those who argue about them or oppose them" (Latour 1996, 646, Mosse 2005b). Authoritative interpretations have to be made and nurtured socially in order to become politically reproduced. In the consolidation of environmental norms and in development projects, communities must come together to translate, interpret, and participate in certain established orders so that these endeavors can be sustained, particularly as they are predicated upon certain socially constructed representations of reality.

This book begins by exploring the historical undercurrents of the entanglements that are present as ideas, discourses, and political and economic power collide. Then, the case studies presented here are intended to portray the complexity of Amazonian realties, which do not neatly conform into a fixed analytical framework or predictive model. In offering this structure, I draw upon ethnographic "thickness" of description to render meaningful the relationships between policies and political superstructures.

Early on in my research, I was cognizant of what I hoped to find: I longed to see a sweet spot of sustainable development being actuated in the Amazon, where I could find inspiration. The findings presented here are not parsimonious, nor are they particularly inspirational; indeed, much of the overarching story is one of disappointment and disillusionment rather than hope. Having Altamira as the "home base" for my field research, I often returned to the physical location of that scene with the indigenous woman drinking a Coca-Cola in *Bye Bye Brazil*, and thought about the contradictions it evoked in me on an emotional level: loss, disappointment, and helplessness that the ineffable global forces of change were so fiercely being enacted on such a beautiful place. Yet the world-changing work of emancipatory transformation, as Paulo Freire (1970) has observed, comes through humble dialogue, embodied through theoretical work and practical action. In that spirit, I hope this book offers grist for discussion, new insights, and critical thinking about how sustainable development can and should become enacted in practice.

2

Capital in the Jungle

On these banks of the Xingu, in the full Amazon jungle, the President of the Republic initiates the construction of the Transamazon [highway], in a historical jolt to conquer this mammoth green world.

—Commemorative bronze plaque on the stump of a brazil-nut tree in Altamira, unveiled by President General Emílio Garrastazu Médici, 1970

In the mid-seventeenth century, the explorer José Palacios wrote that the Amazon was the "perfect paradise" (1869, 120). The area being explored by Palacios and others between 1749 and the late 1800s followed the Madeira River along a 250-mile stretch of unnavigable upstream waters that forced portages along the way. Despite the hardships, travelogues and official reports from these early expeditions involved exuberantly poetic descriptions of the vegetation, resources, and animal life of the region.[1] The early explorers measured river depths, widths, currents, topography, and botany of the region. "It seems as if Nature strove to hide her richest treasures in those unfortunately pent-up regions," Palacios wrote (1869). There was just one catch. Paradise had a serious accessibility problem.

The nascent rubber cultivation taking place in the region during early Amazonian colonization was highly profitable. But the rubber could not get out to market because of transportation challenges. Travels were so back-breaking and slow-going that only three round trips on the river could be made per year (Jackson 2008). In the 1880s and 1890s, landlocked Bolivia competed with Brazil in striving to gain a firmer foothold in the rubber industry. The nations disputed the territory of what is the present-day Brazilian state of Acre as the rubber-rich area was still being surveyed, claimed, and land prices rose in the region (Hecht and Cockburn 1990).[2] Eventually, as the territorial conflicts in Acre subsided, Brazil began collaborating with the Bolivians; it was pragmatic for both governments to harness the wealth coming out of the frontier territory.[3] Their cooperation yielded a dogged effort to construct a railway through the remote region. The effort became perhaps the earliest and most formidable boondoggle in the history of Amazonian infrastructure.

Investors and governmental officials alike were wooed by the argument that the railway would foster communication, wealth, and political power for this remote but bounteous part of the world. Ultimately backed by the Brazilian government, an ambitious American investor and engineer named George Earl Church managed to raise 1.7 million British pounds sterling for an enticing railway project. It was intended to become a land route between the Madeira and Mamoré rivers and give the Bolivian rubber access to the Atlantic (Jackson 2008).[4] Church began planning the railway in 1861 and, about a decade later, sent his first British crews to begin field work. British engineers set out for the region in 1872, but their boats sank along the treacherous cataracts of the rivers, and they were attacked by Capurine Indians. Sick with fevers, crew members wandered beleaguered through the forest, with many dying from tropical diseases and the poor conditions of toiling in the heat. By 1873, the London-based company's stock had plummeted, and the workers who remained in the forest abandoned the project, leaving their equipment behind to rust when they heard that the company had gone bankrupt. "The region is a welter of putrefaction where men die like flies" wrote a British assessor of the project (Hecht and Cockburn 1990, 78). Undeterred, Church went back to Philadelphia and continued promoting the railroad to foreign investors for sixteen years, recruiting personnel and pursuing investors for the project. Church was called the "indomitable" man by the Brazilian emperor Dom Pedro II for his perseverance (Neeleman and Neelman 2013). Accounts say that some 80,000 men applied to become the contracted engineers and laborers that would travel to and work in the Amazon. By January of 1878, Church's project re-launched and again monumentally flopped, this time because of the atrocious labor conditions along the railway.[5] Another twenty-five years passed before the project would be revitalized.

The project of building the Madeira–Mamoré railroad was given new life after the turn of the twentieth century, following the 1903 Petrópolis Treaty in which Brazil and Bolivia committed to finishing the railway. This time, the project would be financed largely by another American magnate, infrastructure developer and briefly politician, Percival Farquhar (Hecht 2013). Farquhar was a tycoon, to say the least, in Latin American infrastructure investments.[6] In 1906, he bought concessions in the Eastern Amazon aimed at building the Port of Pará in Belém. This would facilitate mass transportation of rubber to the Atlantic (Gauld 1964). Only a year later, he bought the Madeira–Mamoré concession for $750,000 from a Brazilian engineer—a sum that is only underplayed by the total of $70 million in European investment that he had capitalized toward his projects between 1905 and 1912. He convinced European bankers to finance the endeavor, even though he had neither personally journeyed west of Belém nor had he gotten any detached expert analysis concerning the economic prospects of the endeavor (Hecht and Cockburn 1990). Regardless, the Amazon railroad project resumed, and this time at a breakneck pace.

The project became commonly known as the Devil's Railway.[7] Once re-ignited, work was so demanding and intensive that within one year, 220 kilometers of the railway were completed. By 1911, there were 307 kilometers of tracks. The process of laying the rail ties and clearing the land through the jungle was grueling. Workers faced precarious conditions and often succumbed to illnesses. At least six thousand workers died, with some estimates suggesting the total death toll was as high as 10,000. The final 57-kilometer stretch of tracks between Porto Velho (now the capital of Rondônia state) to Guajará-Mirim, on the western border of Brazil, was completed in 1912 (Picoli 2006).

However, 1912 was also the year when rubber prices crashed. Just when the Madeira–Mamoré railway was finally ready, the commodity the infrastructure was intended to support became terribly devalued (Sherwood 2010). The railroad was profitable to construct, but nearly as soon as it was completed the railroad lost its main purpose. Left to rust amid the forest, the railroad was forgotten for years.[8] A single railcar remains in Porto Velho, serving as a minor historical attraction for tourists.[9]

The Madeira–Mamoré railroad project is one of the earliest and most poignant examples of an Amazonian Sisyphean effort. Driven by the high hopes that the future of the Amazon could yield an Eldorado-like profitability if only its resources could be harnessed, the promise and work efforts came to a screeching halt. While the railroad is a notable historical example, the history of Brazilian development initiatives is rife with similar cases.[10]

The story of the Madeira–Mamoré railway is illustrative of two central conceptual frameworks for understanding the Amazon as an economic space and as a unique physical place. First, the economic historical narrative about the Amazon typically characterizes the region as involving "boom and bust" cycles. The Madeira–Mamoré project illustrates the economic boom and bust cycle of rubber, and the associated implications of the cycle on infrastructure plans. In each "boom" round, the Amazon became a site for capitalistic expansion. The railroad also illustrates the staying power present in the view that tropical nature should be brought under human control so that benefit from the region's commodities can be received. The project's failure illustrates both the difficulty of achieving major infrastructure development in the region as well as the attitude that conquest over nature will lead to a more robust economy and strengthen political ties. Taken together, both of these themes reveal something important about the drive for modernity which underpins the notion of sustainable development.

This chapter sets the historical stage for understanding how sustainable development politics became so important in the Amazon region. Two themes are central to this history, both of which underpin the tensions experienced as Amazonian sustainable development politics play out in contemporary society and land use politics. The first issue is how the Amazon is conceptualized as a place of tropical nature, which, according to this view, is a space that is meant to be scientifically understood and to be physically tamed to capture its resources. Second is the theme of modernizing Amazonia. Through introducing the notion of modernization, we will be able to see how various interventions to organize and manage natural resources for the productivity of the state and private enterprise figured heavily into regional politics, shaping patterns of settlement, land use, and social relations. This chapter offers readers an overview of the history of Amazonian colonization from the time of the early explorers into the end of the "directed colonization" schemes of Brazil's dictatorship years, which lasted until 1984. I begin with discussion of the naturalists' approach to the tropics, and the early colonial settlements in the region. This historical stage was driven by wealth accumulation during the rubber boom. The discussion then proceeds with a focus on the state-led modernization schemes of the late 1930s through to the early 1960s, which left a lasting mark on Brazilian energy, land use, and economic planning. Last, the discussion turns to the era of bureaucratic-authoritarian rule, in which major infrastructural developments and settlement meant lasting and significant changes to Amazonian lives and landscapes.

The discussion which follows is oriented around three central eras of Amazonian development, in which socio-natural relations are each illustrated as involving inequality and unevenness as Amazonian development takes place. These three major time periods consist first of the colonial experience, then the rubber boom of the late nineteenth and early twentieth centuries, and, finally, a massive wave of new settlement which began during the 1970s under Brazil's military dictatorship. Sustainable development does not enter as a globally popular term until the late 1980s, and it will be the major focus of Chapter Three. The early precursors to sustainable development discussed in this chapter, meanwhile, are foregrounded in the ways in which contemporary Amazonian settlement hinged upon a need to rationalize and control space and people through making order out of a wild nature, encouraging land occupation, and embracing the influence of capital. Through examining these forces, we can gain insight into how the later sustainable development policies and projects were shaped by long-held beliefs and conscribed social and environmental conditions in the region.

Colonialism in the Amazon

Early colonizers and missionaries that set upon Brazil and the Amazon region began perpetuating the idea that Brazil was opulent, abundant, and filled with generous Indians. Writings from the time were filled with ideas about the indigenous populations as noble savages, though the early explorers were euphoric in their descriptions of the forest's richness.[11]

> Each man is able to provide for himself, without expecting any legacy in order to be rich, other than the growth that nature bestows on all creatures . . . They have no private property and do not try to acquire it as other men do. They thus live free from greed and inordinate desire for riches . . . All Indians live without owning property or tilled fields, which would be a source of worry . . . for all are equal in every respect, and so in harmony with their environment that they all live justly and in conformity with the laws of nature." (Balick 2006, 8)

Amerigo Vespucci's 1503 account of his discoveries described the nature off Brazil's coast as a "terrestrial paradise." At the same time, Vespucci described a gory scene of indigenous cannibalism, in which the explorers were induced into a fatal trap:

> When she reached our Christian, she stole up from behind and raising this club, gave him such a blow that it knocked him dead on the ground. And immediately the other women grabbed him by the feet and dragged him toward the mountain, and the men leaped toward the shore to shoot at us with their bows and arrows . . . Yet we fired four charges of mortars at them, and while none of the shots hit anyone, the very sound of them was enough to send them fleeing toward the mountain, where the women were already hacking the Christian up into pieces, and, in a great fire they had built, were roasting him before our eyes, showing us many pieces and then eating them; and the men, indicating by their gestures that they had killed and eaten the other two Christians. (Vespucci 4 September, 1504, 87–89)

Despite the potential of danger in establishing contacts and relations with the natives, the accounts of the time suggest that especially in the Amazon, the Portuguese empire was enticed by promises of gold, silver, quality sugarcane, and a potentially hardworking and submissive workforce in the native Amerindian populations of the Amazon (Boxer 1962, Langfur 2014).[12]

Missionaries continued working in the Amazon, though they had little success in getting the indigenous peoples to give up their own belief systems even as they took interest in Christianity. Slave labor was important to the Portuguese colonists as a means of exploiting the region's resources. The notable exception were the Jesuits, who objected to the way that the colonists practiced slavery and saw enslavement of indigenous peoples as a violence against their would-be-converts.[13]

Missionaries and colonists were drawn in to explore the rainforest, but the economy of the region remained simple. It was largely based on the exchange of natural products produced in the region until 1749, when coinage first was minted in Lisbon and then sent for circulation into the colony. The initial enthusiasm about the forest's abundance turned into more negative descriptions of the hazards and hardship of rainforest life as they struggled to gain both converts and wealth out of the rainforest. This continued into the middle of the nineteenth century, with a predominant view from the major European powers that Brazil was something of a tropical backwater that was not really worth fighting over. Their gaze turned to the African continent for colonization instead (Hecht 2013).

The indigenous population of the Amazon was nearly wiped out by the encroachments of the newly arriving Portuguese colonization efforts beginning in the sixteenth century, and then by the rubber tappers who arrived in droves in the mid-nineteenth century.[14] Epidemics plagued the once-healthy indigenous communities, which quickly became decimated by smallpox, measles, cholera, and influenza (Hemming 2006). Diseases often spread even before the tribes[15] had actual physical contact with peoples of European or African origins (Whitehead 1993).[16] While miscegenation between indigenous groups and other Brazilians living in the Amazon was commonplace, relations between the Amazonian indigenous tribes and the newer settlers in the region were far from harmonious. Confrontations with the newer settlers were openly hostile; skirmishes involved gunfights, kidnappings, and lethal attacks. With few protections from the government, more often than not indigenous lands were encroached upon by new settlers, and many tribes moved deeper and deeper into the rainforest as they experienced threats to their very existence. In 1500, there were at least 3.5 million indigenous people in Brazil. A historical low took place around 1981 when indigenous groups in the Amazon numbered only around 50,000 (Nugent 1981).[17] The near-total losses of the indigenous populations in the Amazon, which took place largely during the sixteenth through eighteenth centuries, were both demographic and cultural. Today's indigenous population is around 350,000, around 0.6 percent of Brazil's total population.[18]

African slaves in the Amazon were less numerous in number than elsewhere in Brazil, although they were a notable part of the workforce. Some people, most notably prestigious scientist and head of the US Naval Observatory Matthew Fontaine Maury, subscribed to the idea of the Southern Manifest Destiny. According to this perspective, the Amazon was a good destination to send slaves, especially because doing so took some pressure off of the American South as they faced the prospect of the Civil War.[19] When slavery was abolished in Brazil in 1888, "slaves just left, and as with the Indians, no one knows where they went" (Harris 2006, 226). Some African-descendant slaves escaped and formed communities called *quilombos,* where they lived as maroons for subsequent generations. The surviving indigenous peoples that did not become acculturated into missions moved into deeper isolation in the forest, presumably aiming to avoid the early deaths and hardships of forced labor. The subsequent perceived voids in population provided a justification for Europeans and Brazilian officials to focus on new "intensive uses" of the estuary (Moran 1993).

Imaginations of Amazonia as a vast wilderness is likely a derivative concept from the American frontier characterization, which were most seminally described in Frederick Turner's 1894 writing about the frontier as free lands that are the "meeting point between savagery and civilization" (Turner 1894). Much like the same frontier vision that shaped the exploration into the North American West, the Amazon is viewed as a vast territory which will gradually become part of a landscape that is influenced, studied, and made productive according to humans' needs.

In the last two decades of the nineteenth century, about 500,000 workers moved to the Amazon[20]—both as migrants and as immigrants drawn (and dislocated) by the international division of labor. Laborers were brought into the region to work in shipbuilding, in rubber tapping, and also on the construction of the railways (Franco 1995). This division took place concomitantly with conditions internally in Brazil that favored domestic migrations (Cardoso and Müller 2008 [1977]). Still, colonization in the Amazon took place rather sporadically throughout the nineteenth and twentieth centuries. It was propelled by the drive to extract natural resources for use as globally traded commodities. Early Amazonian commodity booms include gold, pepper, animal pelts, and mahogany, to name a few.[21] Rubber is probably the most emblematic of the Amazonian commodities to have radically altered economic and social life in the region.

Robin Anderson, a historian of colonial Amazonian human ecology, bemoans these early Amazonian colonization schemes as being devastatingly flighty:

> In comparison to the calm continuity of the Directorate policy, colonization between 1850 and 1911 was a hodgepodge of schemes, programs, plans, projects, and designs. Particularly during the period 1885–1910, new ideas were metamorphosed at an astonishing rate into the "latest and greatest" solution to the problem of settling empty lands. On the positive side, it must be acknowledged that colonization was a popular issue, and the best minds in the province were focusing their attention on it in a heady mixture of trial-by-error philosophy and bulging treasury. . . . Pará proved to be a dynamic laboratory for experimentation in settlement of the humid tropics. (Anderson 1999, 84–85)

The negative dimensions of such initiatives, noted by Anderson, include the irreparable damage done to the upland environment as colonies were carved out of virgin forest. Constant turnover in planning often resulted from frequent changes in administration. While foreign investments and contributions to the Brazilian economy were achieved, the plans awakened a long-lasting appeal of the central role of the state and capital in turning the natural resources of the region into an economic engine for the modernization of Brazil. Such visions would be encoded irreparably into the landscape and the socioeconomic inequalities of the region thereafter.

Exploring the Tropical Frontier

Explorers from Brazil and many other countries ventured to the Amazon as naturalists and frontier adventurers. For Brazilian diplomatic leaders such as the Baron of Rio Branco, however, the resources of the Amazon held an extraordinary potential for nation building, scientific explorations, and putting new technologies into practice (Hecht 2013). The uncharted and newly explored lands and rivers of the Western Amazon promised considerable wealth acquisition because of the rubber trees there.

To the early European and North American naturalists and explorers, the Amazon represented a space of scientific bounty. The naturalists who explored the Amazon most notably included Alexander von Humboldt, but also Alfred Russel Wallace, Richard Spruce, Karl Freidrich Philip von Marius, Henry Walter Bates, and Louis Agassiz, in addition to many artists. These men were influential in establishing a conceptualization of the tropics as a world of particular constellations of plant and animal life that is vast and mysterious, and that is both an aesthetic space and a scientific one (Stepan 2006). American President Theodore Roosevelt's trip exploring the Amazon was emblematic of the adventurous frontier spirit that global imaginaries brought to bear upon the region. From October 1913 through May of 1914, President Roosevelt traveled with a team led by Brazilian Marshal[22] Cândido Mariano da Silva Rondón. The trip was "not intended as a hunting trip but as a scientific expedition" (Roosevelt 1914), but notes from the trip most notably characterized the dangerous rapids and encounters with animals which the adventurers triumphed over during their travels (see Figure 2.1). Rondón's later expeditions, did entail efforts to document encounters with indigenous groups, with attention to photographic and ethnographic filmmaking.

The naturalists' vision of tropicality tended to view the Amazon as the sublime source of nature's bounty, a super-fertile landscape containing a wealth of untapped resources, along with some indolent indigenous people. The more modern perception of the tropics also viewed it as a wild, untamed jungle. Instead of an idyllic Edenic narrative, the tropics were seen as a source of

Figure 2.1 Marshal Cândido Rondon with a group of Paresi indigenous peoples in Mato Grosso, around 1908. The Paresi had a long history of being exploited in their labor for rubber tappers. Rondon later founded the Indian Protection Service and oversaw installation of a telegraph line that ran West from Cuiabá. He encouraged the Paresi to move nearer to the line, establish schools, and to work on maintaining the telegraph infrastructure.

pathological disease, and observers represented it with degenerative rather than productive imagery (Slater 2002, Stepan 2006). Even archeologists have experienced substantial disputes over questions of who has lived in the Amazon and what their civilizations were like. Until the late 1990s, the predominant view, most vocally articulated by the Smithsonian Institution's Betty Meggers, was that the Amazon's soils were of such poor quality that early civilizations were unable to sustain agricultural activities there. Without viable agriculture, they ultimately could not build larger and more complex societies in the region. Meggers argued that the Amazon region was a "counterfeit paradise" (Meggers 1971). The research was not lost on environmentalists, who took heed that a similarly destructive fate would befall both the forests and those who tried to develop it for human purposes (Mann 2006).

The conventional wisdom was upturned two decades later by none other than American President Theodore Roosevelt's granddaughter, Anna C. Roosevelt, who was an archeology curator at the Field Museum of Natural History in Chicago. She re-excavated the lands on Marajó Island, where Meggers had conducted the earlier research, but reached an opposite conclusion; Roosevelt found evidence of a massive civilization, which had planted the rainforest as an extended garden of fruit and nut-bearing trees (Roosevelt 1991, Mann 2006). Supported by a growing body of research on Amazonian dark earth soils and archeology, the newer scientific consensus is that humans were actually able to cultivate lands in the Amazon for centuries, and that the pre-Colombian polities living in the eastern Amazon rainforest involved dispersed but complex civilizations, who cultivated the rainforest as a built landscape that was designed, planted, and managed over thousands of years (Heckenberger et al. 2008).

While archeologists debated the extent of human influence over Amazonian lands, from the early 1980s onwards geographers and sociologists generally envisioned and theorized Amazonia as a dynamic frontier.[23] The characterization of the Amazonian frontier, a topic much debated in the Brazilian literature, is usefully distilled by David Cleary as a space where "the absorption of peripheral regions by an expanding capitalism" takes place (Cleary 1993, 331). This characterization, rooted in a political-economic definition of the frontier, also frequently includes nuanced examinations of how humans integrate with the land and the scale and density of their occupations, which can be determined by including technology, physical infrastructures, soil quality, economic incentives for settlement, and other factors (Almeida 1992). State and institutional influence may also contribute to the expansion or consolidation of the frontier.

> Frontier areas involve a spatial de-concentration of certain economic activities, and also, often, are places that are not well integrated into the State. Frontier populations, whether by political lack of representation, or insufficient strength and organization, often lack recognition and integration with the State. Frontiers, in their dynamism, are often marked by the diversity of outside economic actors, who come into a sparsely populated region, making it have distinctly dynamic shifts in population, culture, and economic activity; the pre-existing populations that are present in the region of an expanding frontier are usually unable to oppose or resist the outside actors and economic shifts that are occurring. (Sawyer 1990, 184)

Frontier expansion can involve a relative lack of brakes on the action of the State and of private enterprise as their economic activities are implemented (Sawyer 1990). Conversely, frontier closure and consolidation involves regulating and restricting settlement on new land, often through territorial and environmental governance, including through actions such as the creation of parks and indigenous reserves, demarcations of land holdings, regulations on logging, and strategic planning for where and how new infrastructures and agricultural activities take shape (Sawyer 1984).

The next section details the second stage of frontier expansion, emphasizing how wealth and landholdings became concentrated in the Amazon during the rubber boom. While it did represent an expansion of global markets, investment, and capitalism in the region, the rubber economy was also highly personalized. It was also an economic boom premised upon a renewable natural resource, which led to unique forms of land management and territorial control.

The Rubber Boom

This section will focus on the rubber boom in order to illustrate the unique form of merchant capitalist exchange that predominated in the Amazon in the late nineteenth and first part of the twentieth centuries. It will explain complex social histories and the inequalities that were produced as rubber was exchanged. Rubber was a central commodity that shows how the political, social, and economic life of the region has been (re)produced and altered over time (Nugent 2006, 1993). The "boom" economy of Amazonian rubber production marks the region's economic integration with the forces of global trade and capitalism, albeit in a way marked by the interpersonal ties and debt structures of the *aviamento* system, and then the subsequent capitalism of an industrial-scale production attempt. Amazonia was an active center of global trade and cultural life, as well as a site through which national and international aspirations for development are encoded.

One of the central themes of modern Amazonian development is a history of commodity production reliant on trade within a globally integrated economy. Hallmarks of such trade are boom and subsequent bust cycles involving those commodities, with rubber being the most notable among them.[24] The volatility of these boom–bust cycles, in many instances, leaves the region's human populations and natural resources vulnerable to the whims of the global economy.

Agrarian peasantries became established in the region in the nineteenth century, as merchant capitalism predominated the economic life of the region. The flow of capital in the Amazon skyrocketed during the rubber boom of the mid-nineteenth century and continued into the twentieth and twenty-first centuries in ways that deeply marked the policies in the Amazon, and the social relationships and landscapes in subsequent fads and development efforts beyond that time. Rather short-lived colonization schemes led by the state have long marked the Amazon region's human settlements.

At different times, Amazonian peasants were also dependent on the production of cattle, cocoa, peppers, and extraction of firewood; all these goods gave people opportunities to use local resources in exchange with a merchant elite (Nugent 1981, 1993, 2002, Harris 2006). But the earliest major Amazonian commodity, significantly overshadowing these aforementioned goods, was rubber. Due to its well-established rubber trees, robust labor force, and relatively unique tropical climate, Brazil was then the only country in the world able to abundantly produce latex, and it did so through production systems embedded within the native Amazonian forests. Beginning around 1840, rubber was Brazil's major link to foreign industrial capital.

The history of rubber dates back several centuries earlier. Latex is a renewable resource, which is harvested by tapping rubber trees (*hevea Brasilienensis*), found mainly in the rainforest area between Bolivia, Peru, and Brazil[25] (Weinstein 1983, Almeida 1993, Keck 1995). The Amerindians of South America began using rubber around 1600 BC, forming smoked latex into a ball for a game called *tlachtlic*. In the West, rubber was introduced by French scientists in the mid-eighteenth century.[26] The first significant commercial uses of rubber were in suspenders, around 1803, and life vests and raincoats in the 1830s. After the vulcanization process was discovered by Charles Goodyear in 1844, rubber was able to withstand significant temperature changes. Subsequently, it became used in bicycle tires, automobile tires, shoes, hoses, piston rings, and a host of other industrial uses (Tully 2011). Rubber became essential to the production and innovation of the Industrial Revolution, and latex was a crucial natural resource for it all. The height of the Amazonian rubber boom took place from the 1840s until around 1911. At its height, rubber comprised 40 percent of Brazilian export revenues, second only to coffee in terms of its national economic contribution (Dean 1987). The Amazonian rubber was sold for export in the cities of Manaus and Belém, though transportation logistics were a major challenge.

Rubber was exchanged through a system of highly personalized chains of vertically dependent economic relationships, known as the *aviamento* system. *Aviamento* involves the commercialization of one—and sometimes several—products,[27] and it is distinctive because of the close personal ties embedded within this system of commodity exchange. Instead of the otherwise impersonal capitalist exchange that marks much of economic life, especially on modern frontiers, *aviamento* often involved long-term debts and loyalties to those at different levels of exchange.

The chain of dependency in *aviamento* extended from the commercial agents (the buyer of rubber and the seller of goods for the consumption and production) to the river-based traders,[28] to the worker in the forest (Cardoso and Müller 2008 [1977]).[29] The *seringueiros* became indebted to the *seringalista*, or rubber barons,[30] in a clientelist relationship of loyalty and barter, as well as formal debt.

Interpersonal ties were established through the *seringalista* offering maintenance of housing, provisions of some basic goods, and generally paternalistic relationships with the rubber tappers (Garfield 2013). The *seringalistas* often lived more opulently than their workers. They enabled the laborers to live on such isolated lands, while hindering the workers' economic prosperity through debt structures (Léna and Oliveira 1991). Rubber tappers' travels to arrive at the distant estates were frequently funded by the *seringalistas*, making debt-based relationships encoded into the rubber tappers' livelihoods from the very start. The isolation of the rural *seringueiros*, as well as their lack of education, meant they had little other knowledge of less-damaging economic possibilities (Mahar 1978).[31] Outside of Brazil, indigenous people were commonly captured and brought to work in the estates, especially in the Peruvian Amazon (Davis 1996).[32] Shared notions of labor reciprocity, barter, and long-term commitment to bosses marked the economic relations in the rubber estates (Weinstein 1983). The state also controlled a significant amount of the surplus capital from the rubber industry, making the entire industry significantly linked to market forces (Barham and Coomes 1994).

The *seringalista*s, too, were linked as dependents to commercial intermediaries. Usually, the *aviadores*, or commercial agents, were based in Manaus or Belém, to sell equipment and tools and also purchase the rubber from the *seringalistas*. The rubber was then sold to major import–export houses. These houses principally serviced the British commercial demand for rubber as new uses for it arose in manufacturing. Often, the *regatões*, or river-based traders, facilitated transport of the rubber and other goods that were exchanged along the rivers of the region as well (Perney 1996, Allegretti 1995).[33] Commercial intermediaries would often receive monetary parcel payments from the *seringalistas*. By accepting parcel payments, the intermediaries thus shouldered some of the debt of the rubber production process. The commercial intermediaries, in turn, incurred financial penalties from the major foreign export–import houses based in Manaus or Belém. These multiple dependencies became integrated into the *aviamento* system as mechanized economic relationships that are still manifested in present-day Amazonia (Cardoso and Müller 2008 [1977], Cleary 1993).

In most parts of the Amazon where *aviamento* occurred, trade relations and division of labor were markedly personalized and unequal. The *aviamento* economies were (and sometimes continue into the present) based on extractive activities including rubber, fish, and Brazil nuts; profitability was premised upon the highly unequal relations of labor and exchange (Hecht 2007, Bunker 1985, Taussig 1980, 1987, Schmink and Wood 1992, Hecht and Cockburn 1990). These relationships were initially formed out of the Cabanagem Rebellion, a separatist revolt that took place in what was then the state of Grão-Pará in 1835. The conflict yielded a more powerful role for traders and middlemen (*aviadores*) to control labor, and leaving the rubber tappers semi-autonomous. The rubber tappers relied on the *aviadores* for supplies, but their labor was controlled through threats of violence and debt-peonage to the *aviadores* (Hecht and Cockburn 1990). The small-scale producer had little choice about what to buy or the price at which to sell.

The rubber tappers and other Amazonian peasants were far from homogenous as a group,[34] and the *aviamento* economy was not a pre-capitalist model of production but rather a merchant capitalist one, in which peasants became separated from the national economy through the debt structures and isolation rather than becoming linked to it through their labor (Nugent 2002). Within the rubber economy, exchange was highly unequal, and while it represented an expansive arena for national economic growth, the relationships that the rubber industry fostered tended to entrench inequalities and clientelism (Bunker 1985).

The expanding zone of capitalism presented by the rubber boom was bolstered by the power of state incentives and massive land concessions, especially through the end of World War I.[35] As these expansions occurred, territorial expansion based upon private landholdings also took place, with river-based explorations leading to massive land claims for the locations of the *seringais*. The *seringueiros*, or rubber tappers, sometimes experienced attacks from indigenous peoples, as they were clearly working on something of the front lines of territorial conquest as economic activity expanded into these areas.

The Brazilian monopoly on rubber production eventually collapsed because of scientific innovation, bolstered by seed smuggling. Rubber seeds, snuck out of Brazil by British entrepreneur Henry Wickam in 1876, led to the cultivation of trees in then British-controlled colonies in Ceylon, Malaysia, and Indonesia.[36] The British succeeded in adapting rubber trees for use in commercial plantations in Asia around 1912, just as rubber prices were falling. Production increased around the world, with a competitive global market for rubber replacing the Amazon's monopoly on the product, which had become highly dependent on high market prices (Barham and Coomes 1994). Brazilian rubber, which had dominated 100 percent of the world's supply between 1840 and 1911, only supplied around 7 percent of the world's rubber by 1922, with the rest coming from Asia (Weinstein 1983). In these new climates, the rubber trees were less vulnerable to pests and diseases, and commercial production thrived in South Asian monoculture plantations. Rubber production in Brazil declined, whereas it was rapidly increasing in South East Asia (Garfield 2013).[37] The price shocks were first felt by trading houses in Manaus and Belém, who closed their doors. As they stopped being able to provide goods to the *seringalistas*, the rubber estates in the Amazon fell into states of disrepair. Many of the rubber tappers and their descendants continued living on the land of those estates, however, relying on hunting, fishing, and small-scale agriculture to survive. As Figure 2.2 shows, these rubber-producing areas were found throughout the Amazon basin.

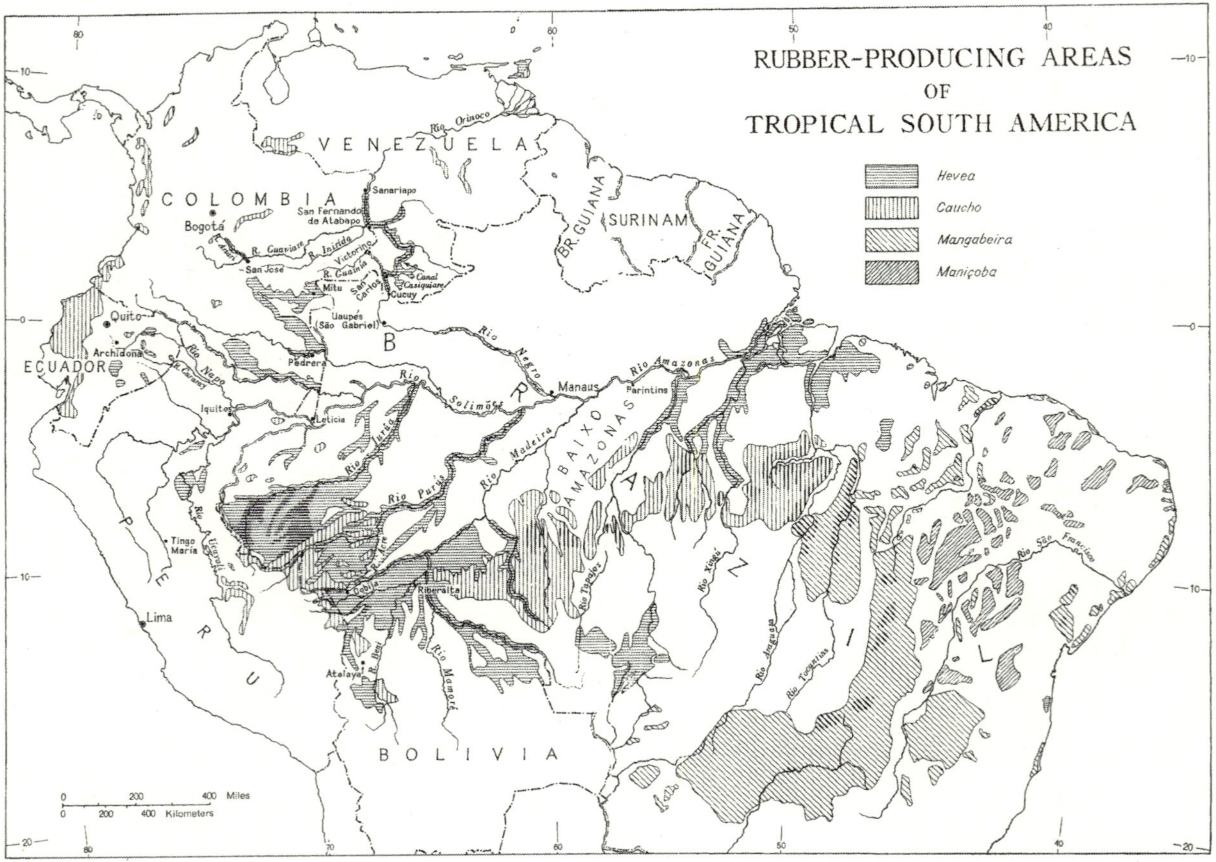

Figure 2.2 Rubber cultivation areas in the Amazon Basin.

It is worth noting that a smaller, more short-lived rubber boom also took place in the Amazon as rubber was traded during World War II, from 1942–1945.[38] During this time, some 25,000 people moved into the Amazon, among them scientists and talented businesspeople. Destitute farmers were also encouraged to contribute to Brazil's war efforts, motivated by both patriotism and a severe drought in the northeast of the country, which made moving to the rainforest seem appealing.[39] Edward Higbee writes: "No greater effort has been made with such stunning disappointment than that to augment the harvest of wild rubber during the early 1940's. Millions of dollars were poured into this discouraging endeavor" (Higbee 1951, 410). The only Allied-controlled rubber-producing region aside from Brazil was Ceylon, and Brazilian campaigns promoted the idea that moving to the Amazon was an important contribution to the war effort (see Figure 2.3). Demand for rubber precipitously increased around the world as everything from airplane and car tires to basketballs and rubber gloves became used for the war effort.[40]

Figure 2.3 Art such as this "More Rubber for Victory" poster served to encourage people to move to the Amazon region as rubber soldiers during World War II, when the economy for Brazilian rubber took on a smaller but renewed economic value.

Fordlândia: A Grand Investment with Little Yield

Like the Madeira–Mamoré railway, rubber continued to entice investment and interest from foreign capital long after the commodity had "busted." The Amazonian lands continued to hold appeal as a site in which to manifest utopic future visions for social and ecological harmonization. Illustrative of these efforts is the case of Fordlândia, which was the company town established by American industrialist Henry Ford. Conceived out of a belief that the Amazon could be a sort of blank slate for creating a vision for an American company town that was slipping away in the United States, near Santarém along the Tapajós River, Ford's vision maintained that productivity would flourish thanks to modern technology and assembly-line production.

The plans for Fordlândia involved turning the jungle into a land productive enough to grow rubber trees in a more intense cultivation than that of the traditional rubber estates.[41] In 1928, Ford's prefabricated company town was built in the state of Pará. At about 2.5 million acres, Fordlândia was around the size of the state of Connecticut. On that land, Ford hoped to turn the complexity of the rainforest into something resembling the efficiency of his automobile assembly lines coupled with idyllic small-town life. Part of Ford's strategy involved applying American values and sensibilities to the project; he built churches, swimming pools, a modern hospital, a power plant, sawmill, and numerous Cape Cod–style cottages. Brazilian workers were encouraged to tend vegetable gardens and grow flowers. Brazilian cultural norms were ignored, as workers were encouraged to eat whole wheat bread, to forgo their traditional white rice in lieu of brown rice, and to eat oatmeal for breakfast (Grandin 2009). Managers enforced no-alcohol strictures, as well as prohibitions on prostitution and gambling. Square dances and poetry readings were planned as the weekend recreational activities.[42] Despite many workers falling ill, medical care remained free, and the workers were well paid. More than 3 million rubber trees were planted, and while lumber was shipped to the United States, actual rubber production was virtually nonexistent.

Predictably, innumerable things went awry with the Fordlândia scheme. The lack of cultural sensitivity applied to its governing rules, which affected everything from worker conduct guidelines to hygienic inspections of houses that involved issuing fines for violations. The design of the town and housing was incongruous with Amazonian traditions and weather conditions, and the foreign foods were fed to increasingly unhappy—and unproductive—Brazilian employees.[43] The hardships of the Amazonian climate were also not lost upon Fordlândia's American managers and their families, most of whom were from the state of Michigan. In addition, the newly planted rubber trees[44] on the lands were planted with little consideration for soil quality, appropriate spacing, or tropical forestry knowledge. With factory managers instead of horticultural specialists supervising the plantation operations, the trees failed to become established. The perfect company town planned by Ford resulted in an immense waste; for only $250,000, Ford sold his interests in Amazonian rubber back to the Brazilian government, while some $200 million had been lost on the project over the seventeen years of its existence (Strochlic 2015). The Fordlândia company town was officially closed in 1945, although today it does operate as a frozen-in-time tourist destination.[45]

As an object of modernity, Fordlândia today represents another historical universe. But it is not detachable from the later rebounds of industrial projects, confidence in rational planning, and technological innovations that occurred within the same spaces in subsequent eras. The logic of the assembly line has not translated into virtuous circuits of higher wages, decent benefits, and expanding markets, as Ford had envisioned (Grandin 2009). The endeavor illustrates the futility that can result from such bold and grandiose designs in the Amazonian landscape, in addition to revealing some of the hazards of arrogant planning and cultural impositions upon foreigners.

As earlier noted, the rubber tappers and other smaller populations of *caboclos* who settled during the commodities booms stayed on in Amazonia. They sustained themselves through a mix of subsistence agriculture and an exchange economy based around hunting, fishing, and extraction of renewable resources. Continuing a version of the *aviamento* system, river-based traders supplied the *caboclos* with necessities such as soap, coffee, and cooking oil in exchange for their products: Brazil nuts, *açaí* fruits, and fish. As during the rubber boom, the system of trade relations remained unbalanced in favor of the traders. Life for the *caboclos* was highly atomistic, largely dispersed, and dominated by patron–client relationships (Nugent 2002, 1993, Bunker 1985, Bunker and Ciccantell 2005).

Rubber tapping is now widely referred to as a sustainable "extractivist" activity because rubber is a renewable resource that has a low-environmental impact, a livelihood that can generate modest but viable incomes for Amazonian residents. In Chapters 3 and 4, the *seringueiros*' contemporary role as local forest stewards will be discussed in more detail. As land conflicts with ranchers and illegal loggers emerged in the rainforest in the 1980s, continuing into the present, the *seringueiros* played a central role in mobilization for forest protection. Though they were briefly nationally recognized as rubber soldiers, the *seringueiros* were generally ignored by the government and only became legally recognized as a "traditional population" in the late 1980s. Gaining this recognition fostered greater public awareness of their roles as caretakers of the rainforest and contributed to a more nuanced understanding about how long-standing but nonnative populations living in the region played important roles in forest conservation.[46]

Once the rubber economy was virtually extinguished, the Amazon languished as a region that was relatively stagnant in terms of its national economic contributions. The transformations that took place ecologically also significantly slowed. The brief discussion that follows conveys the political and economic history of the years between the end of World War II and the 1970s, in which significant emphasis on modernization and economic developmentalism offered the ideological pillars for subsequent colonization interventions. Even as the Amazon fell out of the limelight of Brazilian development politics during this time, state-led interventions began to transform the Amazon into a region that was increasingly perceived as ripe for industrial investments and agricultural settlement.

(Re) Expansion in the Amazon

Beginning with the second wave of the rubber boom during World War II, a national economic focus emphasized a broader nationalistic vision aimed at bolstering industrial production in Brazil. Modernization-oriented development approaches, which especially gained currency in the 1950s, continued to influence Brazilian rural development strategies. The emphasis on capital-intensive agricultural investment is especially a product of this era. Under this strategy, the Brazilian leadership began looking to the Amazon as a fertile region for more human settlement. Small-scale farmers were viewed as poor decision makers over their environmental resources (Pokorny 2013). To remedy the problems of rural unproductiveness, economists emphasized technological advancement, scientifically oriented agricultural methods, and capital-intensive infrastructure investments as interventions for bolstering growth. Most often, the national government was assumed to be the best and most effective actor to implement these strategies (Eicher and Staatz 1990, Barbanti 2013, Lewis 1954).

Early modernization attempts actually began in the Amazon under the administration of President Getúlio Vargas (first 1930–1937, then during the Estado Novo era, 1937–1945, and again in 1951–1954).[47] Following from the nationalist and anti-foreign overtones of populist leadership, their prescription involved increasing the military presence in the region as well as transforming it into an area for eventual agricultural colonization (Schmink and Wood 1992). Gradually, the symbolic and geographical status of the Amazon began to shift away from being considered an isolated backwater and into being a place of national and global economic significance for development.

Beginning in 1938, the westward exploration in Brazil attempted to push the dense northeastern and southern populations into the center and west of the country. Getúlio Vargas said that Brazil's future was in its own backyard, in the lands that had been forgotten for centuries. "In our fertile and vast valleys . . . veins of earth . . . through which the instruments of our defense and our industrial progress should be forged" (IBGE [Conselho Nacional de Geografia] 1942). As this quote reveals, the military rationale for these efforts weighed as heavily as the economic case. The Amazon figured prominently into this vision for conquest. The government supported an initiative called the March to the West,[48] which involved anthropological expeditions into the Amazon region, subsidies for labor migrations, and updated river transportation infrastructures. Again, descriptions of the rainforest as a bounteous paradise were deployed by the government to appeal to the public imagination and to induce new migrants and entrepreneurs into Brazil's remotest areas. For many adventurous spirits, the appeal of settling in a bountiful, untapped, and somewhat mysterious region was likewise impossible to resist.

Migration to the Amazon and initiatives to establish better public health and sanitation there were also encouraged under the Estado Novo. But for the most part, it was the industrially and agriculturally strong southeast and southern parts of the country that remained the predominant geographic focus of Brazil's economic program. Despite a strong pro-American rhetoric of economic liberalism, nationalist solutions were spurred by the reluctance of foreign firms to commit to providing capital in sectors such as petroleum, steel, and energy. A significant dimension of this strategy was import-substitution-industrialization (ISI), which encouraged state subsidies for industrial production and encouraged direct foreign investments in the country. Most notably, Getúlio Vargas also created the giant Brazilian state-owned oil company, through heavy domestic investments. This, coupled with the perceived national security threat of foreign domination in petroleum development, led to a concomitant push for greater federal control (Evans 1979). The ISI strategy in Brazil, as with other Latin American countries where it was attempted, was aimed at reducing dependence on the export-oriented sector. Instead, however, it led to inflation and to numerous foreign companies establishing bases in Brazil without concomitant domestic economic returns.

Attempts to make the Amazon region more economically productive and a significant contributor to the national economy tended to sputter under Getúlio Vargas, but they did leave a legacy of offering governmental impetus to reconsider the Amazon's role as a vibrant economic contributor. In 1953, a plan for the economic recovery of the Amazon (Superintendência do Plano de Valorização Econômica da Amazônia, or SPVEA) was launched. The SPVEA was a weak bureaucratic organization and shifted direction constantly. In 1957, a Free Zone of Manaus established incentives for free trade and industrial production to take place in the long-time urban hub of the Amazon; in its early years, however, the Free Zone of Manaus floundered.[49] Eventually, the SPVEA was replaced with more enduring institutions oriented toward economic growth. These included the Superintendency for the Development of the Amazon (SUDAM), a new Amazon Plan, and a Fund for Amazonian development.[50] These newer programs and institutional arrangements were fraught with corruption and bureaucratic ineptitude. Nevertheless, they were indicative of a more long-lasting commitment of material resources and organizational direction from the national government. Eventually, as Table 2.1 suggests, such moves steered Amazonian land use investments and economic contributions significantly, with a lasting effect on the region's natural and social landscapes.

Table 2.1 Estimated Regional Income for the Brazilian Amazon (1800–2010) [a]

Year	Regional Income (R$ in thousands, 2010) [b, c]	Year	Regional Income (R$ in thousands, 2010) [b, c]
1800	76,883	1910	5,970,944
1810	39,976	1920	1,217,460
1820	60,413	1930	......[e]
1830	64,919	1940[d]	2,530,483
1840	96,764	1950	3,384,697
1850	251,226	1960	7,682,262
1860	493,305	1970	14,443,926
1870	855,699	1980	48,040,734
1880	1,630,610	1990	83,204,481
1890	2,449,421	2000	121,786,358
1900	3,498,358	2010	201,510,748

[a] The Brazilian Amazon refers to the states of the legal Amazon. The two main data sources were Santos 1980 (see Quadro I-1) for 1800–1960 and the Institute of Applied Economic Research, or IPEA, for 1970–2010 (http://www.ipeadata.gov.br/ "regional" and "income / income per capita/geographic area: states/)").

[b] Indexed to 2010 real values (constant values) in Brazilian reais (R$) utilizing the general price index calculation designed by Central Bank of Brazil, which takes into consideration the changes in currency that occurred in the 19th and 20th centuries (see "citizen calculation" under http://www3.bcb.gov.br/).

[c] The Brazilian Institute of Geography and Statistics provides further insight into how to aggregate the calculations (see "Anuários Estatísticos," in IBGE 2016).

[d] Refers to 1939 (see Santos 1980).

[e] Data not available.

Brazil experienced "extraordinary" economic development between 1930 and 1980, largely as the politics of the country coalesced around freeing the country from dependency and emphasizing national economic development as a central aim of planning and political alignments (Bresser-Pereira 2009, 223). From around 1945–1975, Keyensian economic strategies amassed stronger welfare states around the world, and in Latin America, development economics predominated as a strategy for achieving economic growth and fostering greater autonomy from the economic and political hegemony of the Northern industrialized nations.[51] By the 1950s Brazil was transitioning into capitalism, using industrialization and import-substitution as a means to break the predomination of state and private landholders controlling surplus wealth. The Brazilian National Economic Development Bank (BNDE) was established in 1952 and helped channel foreign financing (public and private loans, including from the United States, the Export–Import Bank, the Inter-American Development Bank, and the European banks) into development projects that sought to influence the "economic expansion of the country" (Sikkink 1991, 202). Electric energy, railroad transport, and basic industries were the major sectors of the BNDE's investment. Under the developmentalist economic ideology of the late 1950s, the state played an increasingly strong role in driving the economy (Evans 1979, 91–93). Between 1956–1961, Brazilian industrial production grew at the spectacular rate of 80 percent. Historian Bradford Burns notes the incredible growth of particular sectors during this time: "steel by 100 percent; mechanical industries by 125 percent; electrical and communications industries, 380 percent; transportation equipment, 600 percent. President Juscelino Kubitschek, who has been most historically associated with establishing Brazil's capital in Brasilia, launched a "Target Plan" from 1956–1961 that sought to make fifty years of growth happen in only five years. This ambitious strategy involved some triumphant initial successes, which subsequently led to economic crisis and the demise of Brazilian democratic institutions.

Modernizing Amazonia

Many of the economic ideas that took hold during the late 1960s and 1970s continued to hold sway for several subsequent decades. Among these ideas, the Amazon was seen as playing a key role in igniting Brazilian growth. By 1960, industry accounted for over 20 percent of the gross national product (Burns 1993, 402). Subsequently, however, the growth was not able to be sustained; sharp economic declines in the early 1960s marked both Brazil and Argentinian experiments in developmentalism. The BNDE shifted its lending emphasis as inflation increased and some of the basic industries it had supported—including agriculture and cattle ranching—found other sources for financing.[52] Under the ISI systems, exultant growth rates were experienced, and the urban working class was strengthened, but foreign exchange shortages, poor productivity in export sectors, and erratic prices for exports took their toll on the economy (O'Donnell 1973).

During this same time period the military became increasingly powerful, with some military leaders taking more prominent positions as governmental authorities. The industrialization-oriented economic views held by the military leaders began to increasingly converge with the developmental economic strategy of the government.[53] National security, anticommunism, and pro-industrial settlement became intertwined concerns for the Brazilian administration (Sikkink 1991). Much like other bureaucratic-authoritarian governments in Latin America at the time, the Brazilian army, as guarantor of the authoritarian order, took on a technical, supportive relationship between the state and social groups, doing away with political parties. Coopted through participation within the state's bureaucracy, individuals and private interests collaborated to work within the militarily driven system (Cardoso 1979).[54] Individuals with substantial capital (an "organic elite"), multinational banking and industrial interests, and the military leadership were financially interconnected. Their positions remained secure, even as a confident new cadre of civilian economic leaders and military personnel rose to power in a 1964 coup d'état. The coup gave rise to Brazil's new era of bureaucratic authoritarianism, which lasted for the next two decades.

The new ruling military leaders and economic elites formed a government that emphasized state security and technocratic approaches to economic, social, and land use planning (Dreifuss 1981). The military's capabilities for political leadership were encouraged (often directly through training and financial support by the United States), as a growing emphasis was placed on isolating and "excluding" the popular sector politically, and a security rationale permeated the regime. The strength and political influence of a salaried middle class, meanwhile, gained an increased role as experts and penetrated into state institutions. Brazilian bureaucratic authoritarianism was characterized by a new cadre of governmental technocrats that tended to support a stronger law-and-order approach (O'Donnell 1973, Collier 1979, Cardoso 1979).[55]

In the Amazon, the different economic cycles of extractivism that had formerly predominated in the region, such as rubber extraction and Brazil nut collection, were "totally ruptured" by the colonization plans of 1970. In its place, a new aspirational order triumphed, where "the objective is to create a middle class of rural workers; the utopia to construct an equal society on the periphery of a Brazil that, though full of economic miracles, unconsciously fosters an increasingly unequal society" (Hamelin 1991, 165). In so doing, a new social contract was established. Instead of the strong clientelist relationships of the *seringalistas,* the state and its institutions became the new entity responsible for providing resources and support for Amazonia's new peasantry. It was a seminal era for establishing new social arrangements in the region.

Brazil's experience under the military leadership was not unlike the emergence of other authoritarian regimes elsewhere in Latin America during the same era, where authoritarianism arose as a response to the difficulties of deepening industrialization as ISI models floundered (O'Donnell 1978).[56] But a few important contradictions between the discourse espoused by Brazil's leadership of the time and its actual practice are of significant note. First, although Brazil's military regime was launched in the name of preserving private enterprise and bringing the country "back" from the brink of communism, instead it gave rise to an expanded role of state-led business involvement (Cardoso 1979, O'Donnell 1973). In addition, the Brazilian state's central motivation involved capital accumulation, and it espoused liberal free enterprise in order to achieve that goal. In practice, however, the military allied with national and multinational business interests, and strategically linked repression and the weakening of democratic processes in order to satisfy statist economic interests (Evans 1979). Last, Brazil's leaders were persuaded by a popular notion that the Amazonian territory was being pursued by foreign interests who sought to "internationalize" Brazilian resources and control the lands there, and often promulgated this idea themselves (Hall 1989, Momsen 1968, de Oliveira 2002).

Consequently, their economic plans entailed expansion and assertion of control over resources on a broader scale. But nationally driven investments also involved considerable collaborations with multinational corporations, and the government encouraged joint state enterprises along with multinational investments. As a result, the line denoting where Brazilian economic investments started and other international investments stopped was more fuzzy than hard and fast (Cardoso 1979).

Periodically, especially in the 1930s and again during the military regime that led Brazil from 1964 until the mid-1980s, a euphoric nationalism marked Brazil's economic ambitions (Shohat and Stam 2013, Garfield 2013).[57] These ambitions and the idea of nationhood were especially formative in terms of the Amazonian development planning. Susanna Hecht richly describes the military leaders' perspectives on the region:

> Its river capitals with their crumbling opera houses and decaying palaces were pathetic reminders of an earlier glory, and embarrassing proofs of the meager developmentalist capacities of Amazonian inhabitants. . . . According to the new military masters of Brazil, Amazonia, with its shabby river towns and vast forests, needed a modernist, technical, and technocratic vision, one that would

> transform the inchoate wilderness with its smattering of pointless Indians and its revanchist extractive economy into a theater of statecraft. (Hecht 2011a, 204)

Centrally, the government's concern involved making the region orderly, productive, and integral to national security interests.

Under the bureaucratic-authoritarian regime that followed the coup of 1964, the course of reforms suggested that political and juridical reforms would be necessary, on top of the clear need for economic restructuring. The approach was based in making reforms to the developmentalist economic approach that had caused high inflation rates and state overspending. Celso Furtado, a formidable Brazilian economist, captures this expansive agenda:

> The basic task of the present time is to give more elasticity to [economic] structures. We have to walk with audacity to modify the constitutional relations that permit the realization of agrarian reform and modify the base of administrative machinery from the state level, the fiscal system and the banking structure . . . And, above all else, we have to have a plan for economic and social development of the status of our possibilities and with consonance with the will of our people. (Furtado 1962, 31–32)

Furtado's reference to the agrarian sector suggests a concern with making the country's agricultural system grow through modernization. In so doing, the stimulus of market demand for the application of capital and the incorporation of new technology would help agricultural development (Furtado 1962, Neto 1997).[58] The reforms were not substantially questioned in terms of their necessity within Brazil, as there was widespread agreement that the economy needed to find a way to break out of the "double articulation" bind.[59] It was clear that the earlier model of import substitution had not succeeded, largely as a result of the state's inability to acquire capital goods and appropriately time public sector intervention in the Brazilian economy to pull itself out of economic crisis (Neto 1997).

Ultimately, the Amazon offered a tantalizing geography for escaping the double articulation bind. In the planners' view, the abundance of forest, mineral, and freshwater resources in the Amazon offered a way to bolster Brazilian economic success through making the Amazonian lands "productive" (Castro 2012, Becker 1999, 2005). The sparsity of Amazonian populations relative to its geographic area also made the Amazon an attractive location for land reform investments that could serve security purposes through the attempts to settle more newcomers on the remote lands (Ianni 1975). In addition, the rural northeast experienced a severe drought in 1970, pushing farmers there further into poverty. That region was politically mobilized in support of land reform efforts, so the threat of mass mobilization loomed large, threatening civil unrest. The government responded with a measure that functioned as a pressure release valve. Instead of directly addressing the conditions in the northeast, the Amazonian settlement schemes promised those farmers a literal way out. These contributing factors, which were environmental, economic, social, and geopolitical, provided the impetus for substantial interventions that subsequently took place in the region. Amazonian landscapes and social dynamics were irreversibly altered as a result.

Operation Amazonia

By the mid-1960s, once the military was in power, a doctrine of national security and development proposed that security goals and economic reforms would be addressed together. The doctrine "explicitly considers the contribution of multinational corporations to be by and large positive in the economic development of a nation, in spite of the fact that it may generate considerable internal opposition" (Alves 1985, 23). In 1965, Operation Amazonia was created as an early initiative of the new authoritarian regime under Castelo Branco. Manaus, Belém, and other major cities were established as hubs for trade, private investment, and road connectivity, so that rural goods could access global markets (Browder and Godfrey 1993). In addition to Operation Amazonia's incentives for cattle ranching and urban development, new infrastructure was planned and projected to spur the Amazon region's contributions to national growth. A central goal articulated by the military leaders within Operation Amazonia was to "integrate the region" with the rest of the nation so that it would not become "forfeited" to other nations. These plans aimed to light up the forest, make its farthest reaches accessible, and bring power to mining operations that would capture its mineral wealth. These nationally driven investments also served international geopolitical purposes for Brazil (detailed later in this chapter), as they entailed expansion and assertion of control over resources on a broader scale (Castro 2012, Becker 1999, 2005).

The government's large projects entailed the construction of major dams, which included the Tucurí, Balbinas, and Samuel dams in Amazonia. With these mega-projects, cheap energy from Amazonia would drive the engines of industrial growth in the south of the country (Carvalho 2002, Magalhães 2002). Important, too, were the mining projects, which drew more people to the region and propelled the growth of many Amazonian cities. Mining for iron ore in Carajás, located in the south of Pará, as well as for bauxite, manganese, copper, and gold in many other parts of Amazonia, led to major population migrations and environmental impacts, especially beginning in the late 1960s (Castro 2002, Hall 1989).[60]

These interventions came with significant costs to Brazil's indigenous populations, which had already suffered long legacies of bloodshed throughout the colonization period. A new agency was set up to protect the Indians in 1969, known as FUNAI, or the National Foundation of the Indian. Though initially it promised them restitution and protection, in practice FUNAI began by functioning in the opposite manner. By the following year, the head of FUNAI was found to be issuing operation certificates to large-scale livestock operators. Simultaneously, the federal government was laying plans to construct the Transamazon highway straight through some indigenous territories (Smith 1981, Hecht and Cockburn 1990), putting them at significant risk.

Operation Amazonia's attempts to significantly expand colonization into the region did, however, boost the region's reemergence as a critical site for promoting national economic growth.[61] Operation Amazonia promised tax incentives for entrepreneurs willing to reinvest their profits in the vast expanse of land in the Amazon, and businessmen responded by establishing huge cattle ranches there. At the time, it appeared to scholars that the Amazonian frontier would become increasingly opened through the creation of new markets, migration, and the increasing concentration of land and capital, as capitalism essentially replaced subsistence livelihoods in the political economy of the region (Foweraker 1981, de Souza Martins 1975). Plans for frontier expansion were ". . . elaborated as an authoritarian military government was breaking down the geographical and economic isolation of Amazonia, using all the policy tools at its disposal to foster what was loudly proclaimed as modernising [*sic*] capitalist development" (Cleary 1993, 335).[62] Ironically, in the name of promoting developmental independence, national security, and economic strength, the plans amassed Brazilian debt to multinational bank lenders, and augmented violent social conflict and environmental destruction in the region. Governmental subsidies and tax rebates for cattle ranching and industrial production backfired; instead of becoming a domestic source of economic strength and autonomy, there was greater internationalization in the Amazon because of foreign debt, and disappointing levels of economic growth (Espach 2002). While the military promoted an alliance among the state, domestic capital, and foreign capital to spur investments, including in Amazonia, it simultaneously promoted a nationalist discourse that spurned foreign intervention and that encouraged the occupation of the Amazon region.

Planners sought to build urban centers and infrastructure in the Amazon as a means of connecting the region to national and international networks of economic production and capital accumulation (Corrêa 1987, Browder and Godfrey 1993). Under the first Project for National Integration (PIN), which began on June 6, 1970, the Amazon became slated to receive new "poles of development."[63] These aimed to create stable, self-sufficient populations along newly cut roads to stimulate immigration and give incentives for private capital investments. The new people and infrastructure would allow the potential for natural resource wealth to be extracted from the region, serving the good of the nation as a whole. There were interlinked yet distinct goals articulated in PIN, both economic and geopolitical (Mahar 1978). These aims continued to be currents of subsequent plans as well. Polamazônia, another Amazonian development scheme promoted beginning in 1974, focused on fostering integral uses of different economic potentials of the region, including identification of investment priority areas intended for livestock, agriculture, forest, and mining potentials. The main three areas of focus were grouped into agricultural, wood, and agro-industrial poles. Upon the establishment and stellar growth of mining operations in Carajás, in Pará state, a new Carajás pole became a unit of its own in 1980, and around the same time the Araguaia-Tocantins pole became the more comprehensive Integrated Development Programme for the Araguaia-Tocantins Basin (PRODIAT) (Almeida 1992).

From 1970–1973, the federal government ramped up the Amazonian settlement efforts, aiming to settle the new colonists on the margins of roads that often were freshly cut through the forest. Urban development poles were part of the "directed colonization" strategy, in which the government sought to organize and orient adventurous and hardworking newcomers through settling them on lands for small-scale farming, cattle ranching, and larger commercial production. Ironically, the "directed colonization," as it was called by the government's land reform agency, the National Institute for Colonization and Agrarian Reform (INCRA), was lacking clear direction:

> The families leave from all the states and arrive in Amazonia with a rhythm considerably more intense than our actual capacity to settle them . . . but INCRA will establish a structure that attends to this fluctuation, because we are receiving an exceptional settler, who, having voluntarily dislocated themselves, has already participated in a self-selection. (INCRA 1973, Almeida 1991)

Despite a general aim to install the migrants onto plots of land that conformed with their intended uses, as the quote above illustrates, the Amazonian settlement spiraled out of control, beyond INCRA's management capacity. In effect, the institutional void frequently left it to the newcomers themselves to settle on and claim land, without receiving their anticipated—and requisite—support for building homes, schools, hospitals, and the like. Similarly, there was little guidance and support for turning the poor Amazonian soils into the productive agricultural lands that were hoped for, with the results most frequently being that slash-and-burn agriculture decimated virgin forests while leaving the settlers in continued states of insecure land tenure and poverty. The next section focuses on these colonization efforts more specifically. It portrays the interrelationship of governance with economic developmental strategies and the resultant environmental and social dynamics that emerged.

Colonization Schemes in the Amazon

The idea of territorial integration, wherein the Amazon would be settled and connected with the rest of the country, was present since the inception of the Brazilian Republic in 1889. It was no coincidence that the 1970s wave of *colonization* was called just that, unabashedly. Industrial expansion ruled the day under developmentalism, but the Amazon, especially at first, was a region that generally remained marginal to those efforts for the first few decades of Brazil's experiences of the approach. Overall, and especially relative to the rest of Brazil, the Amazon had very little increase in settlement between 1920 and 1970 (Alston, Libecap, and Mueller 1999). While the Amazon was perceived as demographically "empty," the south and northeast regions of the country, by contrast, were rapidly increasing in terms of population and demand for land titles. By the 1960s, the Amazon was perceived by many bureaucrats and economic planners as the "last frontier in Brazil" (Ianni 1979). Brazil's military leaders and civilian technocrats began to focus upon the Amazon's isolated peoples, virgin lands, and bounteous natural resources as offering the potential for wealth accumulation and a secure source of raw materials (Tavares 2013). They viewed the possibility of settling the nation's poor farmers in the region as a possible release valve to alleviate the mounting pressure (including the prospects of civil unrest) in other parts of the country that was spurred by a demand for land reform (Ianni 1979).

Land reform was considered for decades as a strategy for reducing the economic and social problems from the *latifundio* system, in which large and often unproductive concentrations of land were held by only a few politically powerful individuals. The inequalities of landholdings were attenuated in the south and southeast, with increasingly difficult conditions for the poorer and landless sectors of Brazilian society. Despite a few earlier attempts at land reforms,[64] the popular sector had little power to rectify long-standing inequalities and relatively consolidated social structures aside from its electoral weight and its capacity for social and political protest through strikes, disruptions, and demonstrations (O'Donnell 1973). In 1967, General Médici, then the top leader in Brazil, discussed the northeast as a "problem region" (Ianni 1979). Officials hoped that the Amazon colonization schemes would function as a counter–agrarian reform measure, alleviating pressure from social movement groups like the Landless Workers Movement, who demanded land reform for the northeast and other parts of the country (Almeida 1991). Most of the earlier land reform efforts had taken place under various federal agencies for agrarian policies.[65] Amazonian colonization efforts under INCRA in the 1970s offered the tandem benefits of alleviating the pressure for land reform in other parts of the country while simultaneously securing the remotest territories of the nation through installation of a more active presence of colonists. As Table 2.2 indicates, the populations of new settlers along the Transamazon highway did increase significantly in the first decade of such colonization efforts. The 1970–1980 period had a 200 percent growth rate, with continued population increases in the region in subsequent years.

Instead of a more comprehensive agrarian reform, however, the government offered emergency assistance and employment programs to 500,000 people, mostly from the northeast, to engage in "work fronts" of road-building projects in the Amazon (Fearnside 1984, Alston, Libecap, and Mueller 1999, Furley 1994). This strategy was also thought to resolve the tripartite problem of the Amazon's problematic "empty demography," which would be offset through new settlements and road constructions, as well as fuel economic growth and provide a greater extent of settlement to help bolster national security. Immigration would be stimulated, and greater incentives for private capital, developing infrastructure, and exploring the potential for natural resources would help make the region more integrated into the national and global economy (Ianni 1979). As with the earlier explorers' views, these plans echoed the mentality that the Amazon was open for the taking. Accordingly, if only people could be effectively steered and nature's bounty harvested through efficient, rational management and planning, success would follow.

Directed by Brazil's new cadre of technically oriented bureaucrats and under the supervision of its military government, encouraging a new wave of migrants to settle in the region invoked an idealized version of the American West's development, as leaders promised to "repeat the pioneering feat of the conquering of the Western USA during the first decades of the last century" (Hall 1989). Similarly, José Francisco de Moura Cavalcanti, then president of INCRA, noted: "We give a greater emphasis to colonization, especially on the Transamazon, because we do not comprehend how in the same country there can be the concerning problems of demographic surplus in certain parts, and a demographic void in others" (Cardoso and Müller 2008 [1977], 95). The directed colonization efforts in the region were enormously costly, at around $7.5 billion. Despite the huge costs, only around 6 percent was actually spent on settlements; the rest was spent on roads and building support institutions.

Colonization did ultimately foster conditions for the development of capitalism in the region, but the settlers' needs were largely left unmet. The areas that were especially lacking included access to credit, schooling, education, health care, communication, and agricultural extension services (Almeida

Table 2.2 Population in Municipalities near the Transamazon Highway in Pará, 1970–2010*

Municipality	1970	1980	1991	2000	2010	2016***
São João do Araguaia	15,322	35,774	19,824	12,247	13,155	13,569
São Domingos do Araguaia**				20,005	23,130	24,659
Jacundá	2,219	14,860	43,012	40,546	51,360	56,781
Marabá	24,474	59,881	123,668	168,020	233,669	266,932
Itupiranga	5,346	15,651	37,011	49,655	51,220	51,806
Novo Repartimento**				41,817	62,050	72,347
Tucuruí	9,921	61,123	81,623	73,798	97,128	108,885
Pacajá**			30,777	28,888	39,979	45,596
Anapu**				9,407	20,543	26,271
Altamira	15,345	46,496	72,408	77,439	99,075	109,938
Porto de Moz	7,523	11,805	15,407	23,545	33,956	39,246
Brasil Novo**				17,193	15,690	14,834
Uruará			25,339	45,201	44,789	44,370
Prainha	12,304	45,354	26,782	27,301	29,349	29,132
Medicilândia**				21,379	27,328	30,315
Placas**				13,394	23,934	29,336
Rurópolis**			19,468	24,660	40,082	47,971
Aveiro	8,819	12,749	10,876	15,518	15,849	15,950
Itaituba	12,690	38,573	116,402	94,750	97,493	98,485
TOTAL	113,963	342,266	622,597	804,763	1,019,779	1,126,423
Population Growth Rate[1]	—	200%	82%	29%	27%	10%

* This list excludes municipalities with populations under 10,000 people as of the 2010 census count. Several important municipalities that are near but not directly bordering the BR-230 are included on the list, namely, Jacundá, Tucuruí, and Porto de Moz. Prainha, located near the Amazon River, is included in the list because Medicilândia was a part of that municipality until it was emancipated in 1989.

** Municipality more recently established, data not available in earlier census counts.

*** Estimated population for the municipalities, Brazilian Institute of Geography and Statistics, IBGE 2016.

[1] Population growth rates were based on ten-year period differences (1970–2010) and the six-year population growth estimate (2010–2016).

Source: IBGE, Censo Demográfico 1970/2010. Until 1991, data was extracted from Estatísticas do Século XX, Rio de Janeiro: IBGE, 2007 in the Anuário Estatístico do Brasil, 1994, vol 54, 1994. For 2000, 2010, and 2016, data was extracted from IBGE's database online, which combines data from other institutions.

1992). Some federal programs such as the PIN and PROTERRA (Program for the Redistribution of Land) established financial instruments that strove to positively impact the regional development process, even if they were directed at areas of need where there was little or no direct economic gain to be made (Franco 1995).[66]

Locating and dislocating the workforce was a necessary part of capitalism's growth in Amazonia, although it involved substantial paradox. Cattle ranching was the main economic activity encouraged through state-sponsored financing such as SUDAM, but it only primarily involves labor in the initial stages of cleaning and preparing pastures. Most of the ranch hands derived from the government's workforce goal of absorbing northeasterners into the Amazon region. This was especially the case in the state of Pará, where, of 130,000 migrants to the state, around 75 percent came from the states of Maranhão, Goiás, and states in the Northeast region (Cardoso and Müller 2008 [1977]). Without land titles, and frequently finding themselves without work on the ranches, there was little incentive for the new workers to stay in those initial positions. With little capital, over 65 percent of the migrants moved on within ten years, usually claiming land in unplanned settlement patterns (Moran 1981).[67] In 1970, 18.7 percent of the total population of the Amazon resided in a municipality different from the one in which they were born (Cardoso and Müller 2008 [1977], 48). Settlers moved between sites searching both for agriculturally fertile land and greater degrees of security to the title of the land itself, though they generally tended to stay within the Amazon region rather than returning back to their home states.[68] This migratory and spontaneous form of settlement ultimately expanded capital fronts further into the frontier, even in low-profit small-scale agricultural activities (Léna and Oliveira 1991). In addition to frontier expansion, the result was also greater economic inequality. Under SUDAM financing, extra-regional companies used extraordinary fiscal incentives for cattle ranching in the Amazon to develop their properties with large subsidies. Instead of leading to Amazonian wealth, the profits from such investments ended up in other regions or abroad (Mahar 1978).[69]

Recognizing their inability to adequately settle the newcomers to the Amazon, INCRA's new president, Lourenço Vieira da Silva, announced in 1974 that official colonization would be "readapted." The announcement was concomitant with a report from SUDAM that showed how the spontaneous migratory fluxes that had taken place in the region in the early 1970s had exceeded INCRA's guiding capacity.[70] Cognizant of its failure, the evidence suggested that the colonization schemes had transplanted the agrarian problems and conflicts of the northeast into the Amazon region instead of removing those problems. Historian Charles Wagley describes the Brazilian government as "playing both ends against the middle" by supporting corporate investment projects while at the same time—at least for a brief part of that time—encouraging small holders to settle in the Amazon (Wagley 1974, Lisansky 1990). Consensus was widespread by the early 1990s around the idea that Amazonia could not resolve the social problems of other regions by welcoming both the excluded and the covetous (Allegretti 1995, Léna and Oliveira 1991). Inequality was pervasive in Brazil, and ultimately was worsened by the colonization schemes of the 1970s.

The reform efforts aimed at improving colonization in the Amazon from 1974–1978 were generally to no avail. It was frequently the case that official colonization in fact involved a formal bureaucratic process of recognizing what were already the established facts of spontaneous colonization (Smith 1982). "The construction of roads in the Legal Amazon and for Amazonia created a new "El Dorado" for the marginalized populations, that went there by any means, establishing themselves on the lands they found, without care for if that were public or private, and they would not leave from them, even with a judicial mandate" (Arruda 1977, 27). Many times, public power—federal, state, territorial, and municipal—reacted to these informal migrations in ways that favored the *latifundiário* and businesspeople, often at the detriment of indigenous peoples and smallholders (Ianni 1979). By 1978, around 10 percent of SUDAM's projects had gone to four large landholding projects, all of which ended up in firms held by foreign companies.[71]

Colonization did not play out strictly according to the logics of strategic economic investments and appeasing the diverse interests of different Brazilian classes. Regional prejudices, often dovetailing with racially associated biases, also characterized Amazonian colonization. The lighter-skinned, mostly European-descended Southern Brazilian population was especially encouraged to move north to the Amazon and settle there because of their perceived "entrepreneurial spirit." More often than not, government policies steered toward offering these populations greater incentives to engage in cattle ranching. The northeastern, generally darker-skinned populations were instead encouraged toward farming and received fewer subsidies. "A manager from BASA—the Bank of the Amazon, S.A., in 1968, said that he maintained enthusiasm also for the 'know-how' and dynamism—which comes naturally for Paulistas [people from São Paulo state]—and which at times is more important than mere economic cooperation" (Cardoso and Müller 2008 [1977], 124). The impacts upon indigenous populations because of the colonization efforts in the Amazon were devastating due to the cycle of penetration of their lands that occurred; hostility with new colonists, robbing, contact, lies, and expulsion all marked their experiences of colonization. Meanwhile, the economically oriented newcomers from the northeast and Mato Grosso expressed discontent regarding the region's large indigenous reserves. A common complaint, especially from businesspeople, was that the reserves were wastefully large, containing "much land for a few Indians" (Cardoso and Müller 2008 [1977], 124).

Policies of settler colonization thus trended toward creating new inequalities and augmenting preexisting ones. Furthermore, new dependencies were created, with the Amazonian migrants often reliant on the state for the provision of infrastructure, land titles, and a host of other basic services. The idea of bringing new territory and people under the control of the state held considerable appeal to the planners and business interests behind the schemes despite the disempowering, unequal, and environmentally problematic nature of the entire enterprise.

Geopolitical Concerns and Territorial Control

The last major rationale undergirding Amazonian development trajectories during this era was Brazilian geopolitical security. Consolidating settlement along the Amazonian borders was thought to protect Brazilian territory from possible threats of international encroachment (Ianni 1979). This view was paradoxical; foreign encroachment was a major security concern, yet Brazilian economic policy encouraged investments by multinational private enterprises, many of which had actively shaped Brazilian policies toward the Amazon. Steel and timber corporations from the United States had notably shaped Brazilian governmental policies, including through supporting the Brazilian *coup d'etat* that brought the military leaders to power in the first place (Alves 1985, Almeida 2015, Almeida 1991).

The conflicts Amazonian territories experienced more than fifty years earlier were invoked by the dictatorship to explain the need to settle the western reaches of Brazil's Amazonian territory. The idea of Rondón's early explorations into the Amazon (from 1913–1914) were invoked in the Rondón Project (*Projeto Rondón*), which encouraged youth to participate in the process of Amazonian development.[72] Other rationales played on fears of foreign ownership; a popular science fiction novel, Ignácio Loyola de Brandão's *Não Verás País Nenhum* (translated as *And Still the Earth*), depicted Brazil's future as one in which the country was sold to foreign nations and where environmental destruction left the nation ravaged (Brandão 1981). Works such as this critiqued Brazilian leadership and captured the failures of state planning on massive scales. Government propaganda alleged that foreigners would "steal the green from our flag," in reference to the Amazonian forests (Hecht and Cockburn 1990).

The suspicion of outsiders was not completely baseless—at different times, foreign powers had sought to claim stakes in the Amazon, often couched in beneficent terms. The Hudson Institute, an American conservative think tank, promoted the idea of building a massive dam across the Amazon river to spur

Brazilian migration and provide energy for both the United States and South America; the "Mediterranean Sea" in the Amazon that would be created in the Amazon basin could be a benefit to both nations, they argued (Tavares 2013). The military-led government also butted heads with the Americans over nuclear technology (Cardoso 1979). Capitalizing on a concern that foreign intervention might compromise Brazilian sovereignty convinced many within Brazil that the nation faced significant external threats and adversaries. It also resulted in a disempowered local population, who trusted the distant federal government to provide for and protect them. Amazonian journalist Lucio Flávio Pinto writes that for Amazonian residents, the predominance of state-led control and the notion of a constantly expanding frontier "condemns its inhabitants to not have a vision of their own historical process" and, as such, has disempowered native Amazonians to take control of setting their own agenda for the region's history and its future (Pinto 2002, 111). The fears of outside influence functioned to consolidate nationalist sentiment and simultaneously promoted political apathy on the part of the Brazilian public toward the military regime, especially in the early years of their government.

In addition to concerns that outsiders would exploit and invade Brazilian lands, the military presence in the Amazon also aimed to quell domestic unrest. From around 1967–1974, a group of Maoist insurgents settled in Araguaia, along a river by the same name near the borders of Pará, Tocantins, and Goiás states. The insurgents were part of the Communist Party of Brazil (PCdoB), which had split several years earlier from the PCB, or Brazilian Communist Party, over the issue of whether or not armed resistance should be embraced by the parties. The revolutionaries, inspired by the Cuban and Chinese revolutions, settled in the Araguaia region with the aim of radicalizing local peasants. The guerrilla revolutionaries were squelched, however, between 1972 and 1974, as the military took action against them. More than fifty people associated with the Araguaia guerilla forces were assassinated after being taken as political prisoners in the final military actions of 1973–1974. At least eighty-nine people are known to have died in the fighting as part of the Araguaia rebellion (Almeida 2015). Other low-level conflicts occurred at the Serra Pelada gold mine in Pará, when *garimpeiro* miners conflicted with the state-owned Companhia Vale do Rio Doce (CVRD) between 1980–1983, leading to multiple deaths of peasant miners and significant confrontations between the government and the Catholic Church (Branford and Glock 1992).

Without a doubt, concerns about foreign interference on Brazilian soils and concerns for unequal exchange with foreign powers have marked Amazonian history for more than 500 years (Sartre and Taravella 2009). Suspicion and concern regarding outside imposition in the Amazon was spurred during the military regime, however, as the geopolitical discourse of the generals and political leaders of that era emphasized territorial control as a means of responding to threats, both internal and external. In so doing, they drew upon anticommunist ideologies, especially during the Cold War years (Hepple 1992). The sensitivity toward outsider intervention in the Amazon also manifested itself with a fierce commitment to sovereign determination over how best to use Brazil's environmental resources. While the world convened around environmental issues in Stockholm in 1972, at the Conference on the Human Environment, Brazil's Minister of Planning argued that the nation could "import pollution." "Why not? We have a lot left to pollute" he stated to the *New York Times* (Novitski 1972, 11). Officials expressed resentments toward the northern countries that promoted environmental protection without giving adequate recognition of the violence and injustice that the developing nations experienced due to poverty (Castro 2015 [1992]).

For developmentalists, deforestation in the Amazon was perceived as a sign of national progress. As one Congressman stated in 1977, "The green area of Amazonia should be totally devastated . . . because the forest represents the paralyzation [*sic*] of the country's development" (Giaimo 1988, 537). This vein of thinking continued, even fraught with contradictions,[73] as environmentalism began being popularized and embraced into national policies, and Brazil gradually transitioned out of military control. These views of Amazonian development continue to mark the landscape of the region. To this day, a Brazil nut tree stump nearly two meters wide in diameter sits aside the Transamazon highway, eight kilometers from the city of Altamira (See Figure 2.4). Newspaper accounts from the day that this enormous tree was cut down refer to an "emotional" President Garrastazu Médici. The President enthusiastically applauded while the tree was razed. The commemorative sign placed on the tree stump enthusiastically lauds the progress that the felling represents (1970).

Even as Brazil's military dictatorship relinquished control in the gradual democratic opening that took place between 1984–1988, remnants of the security-and-development ideational marriage continued in Amazonia.[74] The Calha Norte (Northern Trench) Project, launched in 1985, was one of José Sarney's first major initiatives as a new president under Brazil's still nominal democracy. Calha Norte was primarily motivated by a desire to appease military interests and emphasized promotion of regional development. Calha Norte was administered by the Ministry of Defense, and was a highly secretive and authoritarian program that dedicated substantial funding to infrastructure investments (Espach 2002). The program provided financial incentives for cattle ranching and roads, rather than enforcement policies combating illegal logging or land speculation. Low beef prices locally corresponded with increasing the size of cattle herds, which led to the expansion of new roads. Deforestation rates were dramatically affected (Arima, Barreto, and Brito 2005, Morton et al. 2006). Calha Norte continues into

Figure 2.4 The symbolic marker of the construction of the Transamazon highway. The plaque on the tree stump reads: "In these banks of the Xingu, in full Amazonian jungle, the President of the Republic starts the construction of Transamazon Highway, in a historical felling for the historic conquest of this huge green world" (1970).

the present; the project's website declares that its principal objective is to promote "maintenance of Amazonian sovereignty, contributing to the promotion of its sustainable and orderly development" (Calha Norte 2016). Of note, in this current formulation, is the word *sustainable* to modify the phrase "orderly development." The security concept that was so prominent in the past is suggested by the term *sovereignty*. The substance of the work still hinges upon *orderly development*, which, at core, captures the modernist underpinnings of the notion of development that had been a strong historical undercurrent in Amazonian history since the 1930s.

Finally, while the state-led approaches to Amazonian land and agriculture adopted in the 1970s were generally callous toward the environment, a noteworthy historical antecedent to environmental protection that was achieved under the auspices of international security is worth a brief mention. An early, albeit weak, attempt to manage the Amazon's shared ecological resources took place in 1978 with the signing of the Amazon Cooperation Treaty. It was signed by all eight nations of the Amazon basin (Bolivia, Brazil, Colombia, Ecuador, Guyana, Peru, Suriname and Venezuela), and went into effect in 1980. Article I of the treaty articulates the principle of ecological stewardship, protection, and natural resource management as a collective responsibility of the parties. Free navigation of the Amazon River was made possible through the agreement, as was the establishment of national sovereignty in managing natural resources in the region (ACTO 2004). Still, in practice the treaty had little by way of teeth, coordination, or implementation. Even the permanent organization tasked with implementation and guidance of the agreement, the Amazon Treaty Cooperation Organization (ACTO), was not established until 2002.[75]

The Legacy of Amazonian Settlement

It is not inaccurate to sum up the directed colonization efforts as a "failure." However apt in a historical and academic context, this pithy statement might lead a reader to mistakenly believe that the government and the people of the region gave up on the promise of Amazonian development. Instead, it is important to remember, the region's residents and the Brazilian government are far from unanimous about what Amazonian development *could* and *should* look like.

This tracing of Amazonian history has focused on two important themes which continue to echo strongly in the present. First, the prevalence of the tropical imaginary helps explain the colonial impetus to explore and settle the region since the first wave of Portuguese settlements in Brazil. Driven by the tensions between the naturalists' view of the Amazon as pristine nature and by the political-economic impetus to harvest and extract its goods for maximum profit, it is not too difficult to understand why the Amazon has so often been ground zero for the conflicts embedded in the paradigm of sustainable development. The physical challenges presented by Amazonian landscapes (physical distance, climate, and so forth) are linked to an abundance of natural resources (freshwater, precious metals, timber, etc.) in the region, and early explorers in the Amazon saw it as a place of pristine and wild nature that could be scientifically understood and accounted for, usually with a clear purpose in mind and often involving taming the wilderness of the jungle. The contradiction between valuing these natural resources as pristine, while also taming and controlling them, also helps to illustrate the contradiction present in Amazonian conservation and indigenous protection politics of the present. History's lessons in the Amazon clearly show the scars and troubles experienced by indigenous groups and other less powerful non-European minorities, whose populations and land ties were decimated by such interventions.

The second important theme in this historical discussion is the notion of modernity, present since the beginning of the colonial experience and echoed repeatedly in the twentieth century. Modernity entailed viewing the Amazon as a "backward" place with "primitive" peoples, who need to be brought into a different world—a world in need of infrastructure, technology, scientific analysis, and settlement (Posey and Balick 2006). First through missionary work, then through colonial settlement, the Amazon became a frontier as people and wealth moved in, often with impetus from the state but with little other support and direction. The history of Amazonian colonization is one of an expanding capitalist frontier marked by violence, private control of territories, and concentrations of capital (Foweraker 1981). During the rubber boom this was more based on a personalized *aviamento* economy than the later frontier expansions of the 1970s. Even after the rubber boom had turned into a bust, the Fordlândia project is illustrative of the emphasis on ordering nature and harnessing Amazonian lands for the sake of foreign markets, though there, too, the best intentions went awry. The 1970s colonization efforts were driven by three major factors: economic developmentalism, a motivation to alleviate social unrest, and a concern for Brazil's geopolitical security. But instead of colonization yielding considerable benefits to the national economy and a more peaceful society and world order, the efforts to more densely populate the region generally resulted in greater inequalities and a tendency toward increased militarization. Capital accumulated on the frontier in uneven ways, with a tendency toward privileging southerners who had more land access and business interests that were already capitalized (Almeida 1992). The Brazilian state, with its vision for integration of the Amazonian territory into the nation's development, became positioned to take on the role of a hegemonic provider and planner for the region. The frequency and severity of its shortcomings in taking on this role, however, led to worsening social conditions and chaotic settlement dynamics on the frontier, without most of the hoped-for economic growth outcomes stemming from the region's new roads, dams, and mines.

Many of the original colonists who were encouraged to settle in the region in the 1970s are staying in the region, and remain active in demanding a greater governmental presence and better conditions. Others maintain the belief that economic progress is, in fact, best achieved through the ranching and mining sectors, while still other residents in the region argue for alternative development rooted in small-scale farmers, renewable natural resource use, indigenous protections, and social support measures from the state. The government, for its part, did begin reevaluating its role, and increasingly paid attention to environmental issues. As this occurred, however, development goals and environmental issues increasingly collided in contradictory discourses, policies, and agendas. These will be detailed in subsequent chapters of this book.

It was not until the late 1980s, when Brazil had a new democratic constitution, that Amazonians began forming stronger national and international environmental and human rights ties with anthropologists and activists. In due course, too, they began articulating a more vocal political resistance to the infrastructure planning and land use policies that marked the early years of the dictatorship. Such advocacy efforts capitalized on the long-standing importance given to Brazil's international reputation, which was particularly prized by government officials (Castro 2012, Fearnside 1984). At international conferences, the Brazilian government began making efforts to convince the world that its regional and even global leadership role could be environmental as well as economic. These plans, for the first time, were aimed at bringing a set of environmentally responsible policies to the region that balanced social needs with environmental concerns and economic development considerations. It is to those politics, which bear the explicit hallmarks of sustainable development governance, that we now turn.

3

Sustainable Development Meets the Amazon

People have been saying that we have to be sustainable; this became a sort of mantra. There was a Senator from Rondônia who presented a project that was titled "project of sustainable development that expands the clear cutting in the Amazon." [. . .] I pondered: This [project] is not right, but just putting the word "sustainable" in [the title] is how the problem got resolved.

—Marina Silva, University of Chicago, April 9, 2016

In the lead-up to the 2014 World Cup and the 2016 Summer Olympics, Brazil was far from the lighthearted, samba-dancing, ever-sunny place that planners had hoped to show the world. Instead of celebrations, waves of protests marked the advent of the World Cup. In Rio, people took to the streets in 2013, signaling their frustration with higher bus fares; the protests sparked similar protests around the nation concerning corruption and a government that seemed to care more about making positive impressions on foreign visitors than its own citizens. News coverage speculated about whether Brazil was "ready" to host the impending flood of foreign visitors for both events. Jokes were made about how soccer fans would see wet paint signs on the walls of new stadiums, many of which were behind deadline.

In the Amazonian city of Manaus, three construction workers died while working round-the-clock to construct a soccer stadium, called the Amazon Arena, in time for the start of the World Cup games (CNN 2014). Several soccer stadiums were criticized for being white elephant projects. Most notable among them was the 41,000-plus seat Manaus stadium. It took three years to build at $300 million in cost and involved draining a river tributary to prepare the proposed site. Once completed, the stadium hosted exactly four World Cup matches. In the opening Italy versus England World Cup match, stars such as Mario Balotelli and Wayne Rooney graced the pitch, exciting fans. But subsequently the lack of a first- or even a second-division soccer team in the region made the stadium rather useless after the World Cup, and maintenance costs were high (Garcia-Navarro 2015).[1] Once the games were over, people in Manaus speculated that the stadium might become a prison processing center, and noted that it would only occasionally host Evangelical Christian rock concerts (Panja 2013). A bus rapid transit project was begun, originally slated to take World Cup fans from the city center out to the stadium and to serve around 80 km of the city. Subsequently the project stalled so considerably that its anticipated opening was slated for 2020, well after the World Cup (Rocha 2015a).

For World Cup tourists and non-tourists alike, Brazil's troubles were thinly masked. Brazilian leaders hoped to present the nation as a rising power and a newly strong global economic leader. Yet in practice, Brazil's low capacity to effectively manage its ambitious projects was widely apparent. Only two years later the country faced a triple crisis in the lead-up to Brazil's hosting of the Olympics: the mosquito borne Zika virus reached epidemic levels and scared off foreign travelers, especially given warnings from the World Health Organization that pregnant women should not travel there. Compounding the already bad situation, the economic slump in the country was one of the worst in recent memory.[2] Finally, a corruption scandal known as Operation Car Wash embroiled many of the nation's major construction firms and top politicians. Making matters worse, a corruption scandal of epic proportions led to the ousting of Brazil's President, Dilma Rousseff, who then charged that her removal from office was in fact an orchestrated *coup d'etat*. Corruption indictments against numerous other high-level officials caused newly appointed cabinet ministers to step down from office and forced the resignation of the President of the Chamber of Deputies, Eduardo Cunha. In 2010 public confidence in the Brazilian economy was as high as 62 percent, but in 2015 only 13 percent of the population deemed the economy to be in good shape (Zainulbhai 2015).

By the time the Olympics began, the pollution in the Guanabara Bay caused some sailing teams to withdraw from participating altogether. Poor construction and project delays also became a source of public embarrassment, as construction for the Olympic Village in Rio was so behind schedule that the Australian teams opted to check into a hotel instead over concerns that the gas, plumbing, and electrical work were incomplete. Strong waves associated with ocean undertow currents caused the collapse of a sailing ramp, a flagship new bicycle path, and damage to the media building that was being constructed on Copacabana beach less than a week before the games were scheduled to open. The official response to such problems was focused on ensuring that the biggest symbols of success such as the stadiums glistened, even if only for a short while.

The grandiosity of Manaus' Amazon Arena soccer stadium might well be compared to the extravagant opera house in Manaus that had opened over a century earlier, in 1896. The Renaissance-style building was replete with mosaics from France and an elegant tapestry from China. A Portuguese architect was contracted to design the theater, which was built by wealthy rubber barons to show the opulence and cultural prominence of the city. Manaus was the epicenter of wealth generated from Brazil's virtual monopoly on rubber. The opera house took a dozen years to build; some say that the entire endeavor was aimed at luring the famous Italian tenor Enrico Caruso to perform in the remote Amazon city (Morton 2014). But after rubber prices plummeted, the theater fell into disrepair. It sat empty for around ninety years.

It is notable that the world-famous tenor Luciano Pavarotti traveled to the Amazon in the 1990s, compelled to sing there by the idea of following in Caruso's footsteps.[3] Pavarotti traveled by boat and found the theater closed upon arrival (Magiera 2008). A memoir of his career recounts the trip: "[W]e located a piano but found the theatre out of use. Nevertheless, we went in and he sang two arias from *Tosca, E lucevan le stelle* and *Recondita armonia* to an audience of about five" (Kington 2008). Eventually, in 2001, the theater was renovated and restored. Today it is a tourist destination and occasionally hosts concerts. For most national and international visitors, it stands as a reminder of the glory and global importance the city once claimed. On a daily basis, however, the area surrounding the theater is relatively devoid of life. Large groups of cruise ship tourists disembark their boats to visit the theater, but there are few shade-offering trees in the plaza surrounding the building, so street life is lacking in the vicinity. Tickets to shows are expensive, and the area is not considered especially safe for a casual afternoon stroll.

In both the cases of the Amazon Theater and the Amazon Arena, the mismatch between aspirations of grandeur and short-lived usefulness was glaring. Instead of creating infrastructures that symbolized success, the buildings and the process of constructing them became excessive wastes. They were symbolic more of an Amazonia involving dashed hopes and fleeting cameos on the global stage than of durable eminence. For any country, undertaking major projects aimed at showing national achievement would be a source of investment and point of pride during times of economic strength. It was overconfidence in sustained wealth conditions, emphasis on external validation as a mark of success, and the remarkably short periods of usefulness that distinctively marked such endeavors in the Amazon.

This chapter unpacks the contemporary history of development in the Amazon region with a focus on how the discourse and framework of sustainable development began to take hold in policy and practice, along with the disjunctures and contradictions that appear along the way. It builds upon the historical discussion of the previous chapter that established the foundations for capitalist expansion into the Amazon and developmental visions for the future of the region, and focuses on the time period of the late 1980s until the mid-2000s. This chapter's historical treatment centers on the question of how the state and society articulated sustainable development through policies and activism in the Amazon region. More specifically, it examines how geopolitical security interests and the concept of environmental sustainability informed what ultimately are manifested as changes in Amazonian landscapes, the built environment, and mega-projects, as well as complex social dynamics in the region.

Development goals factor into the economic ambitions driven by state planners, whether as a driver of increased commodity production and exportation or as a producer of energy to fuel the nation's rising consumption as it industrializes. For some, especially state planners and military leaders, the Amazon is symbolically wrapped up with a nationalist drive for territorial control. A vision about Brazil's worldwide position as a powerful political actor and a presence commanding respect underpins many of the plans that are made concerning the region, aiming to make it "orderly" (in the common parlance of the Brazilian armed forces and Ministry of Defense) or "legible" (to borrow anthropologist James C. Scott's term for how state planners envision engaging such remote areas) (Scott 1998). For others, the globalist vision regarding the Amazon takes a different tack; the Amazon holds the world's largest freshwater reserves, the forest is a critical carbon sink. Many people see preservation of the rainforest through creation of more parks and wilderness areas as imperative to addressing the global challenge of climate change and biodiversity protection. And then there are those perspectives on the Amazon that lie somewhere in the middle, aiming to provide Brazil with commodity-based economic growth through production of soy and beef that derives from the Amazon but on lands that would involve no new deforestation. Others seek to make viable livelihoods out of the forest ecosystems through protecting land rights and creating more robust economies for Brazil nut gatherers, rubber tappers, fishermen, and the like. All of these involve contested visions for the region, which are positioned in some degree of friction with each other—not to mention the myriad other aspirations and realities that are the stuff of the local experience of living in the Amazon for the millions of residents that call the region home.

The gaps between those visions are present where the terms of how people should live have not been fully established by universal norms or policies (Tsing 2005). Understanding the tensions and gaps that are present between those visions "calls attention to the bad transportability of demarcations of human livelihood versus nature conservation, productive farms versus forest reserves, and settled culture versus the wild" (Tsing 2005, 175). The theoretical framework outlined above helps orient our exploration concerning how certain ideas change based on relationships, context, and necessity. Our historical discussion continues with a focus on the ways in which sustainable development became articulated as a political project in the Amazon.

Conservation or Development? The First Sustainable Development Debates

The notion that there was an "internationalist conspiracy" aiming to steal and control Amazonian resources was first articulated in 1948, in response to a UNESCO proposal to establish an international research center in the Amazon (Sartre and Taravella 2009). Not helping to dispel such paranoia, true quotes from Al Gore, François Mitterand, Margaret Thatcher, and Mikhael Gorbachev encouraged these beliefs, both during the years of military rule and shortly thereafter:

- "Contrary to what Brazilians think, the Amazon is not their property, it belongs to all of us." (Al Gore, senator and later vice-president of the United States, 1989)
- "Some countries must relinquish their sovereignty in favor of global interests." (François Mitterrand, president of France, 1989)
- "Brazil must delegate part of its rights over the Amazon to qualified international agencies." (Mikhail Gorbachev, president of the former Soviet Union, 1992)
- "If the underdeveloped countries do not manage to pay their foreign debt, then they will sell their wealth, their territories and their richness." (Margaret Thatcher, former British prime minister, 1983)

The above examples illustrate clear links between Brazil's natural resources and foreign interests in transnational environmental concerns. For Brazilians, such statements were generally received with resentment or outright objections, as they stoked anxieties about foreign takeovers of sovereign territory and resources in the name of conservation. News stories about the exploitation of Amazonian forest and freshwater resources by non-Brazilians tend to infiltrate popular consciousness and fuel fears about the "internationalization" of Amazonia, even into the present day.[4] Such fears were stoked and popularized during the military era and continue to be prominent in the present.

Aside from such concerns, Brazil did also take some steps toward environmental protection in the 1980s, although a general emphasis was maintained on subsuming environmental issues under more highly prioritized economic goals. An early advent of Brazilian environmental attention was the National Environmental Policy Act (NEPA), first approved in 1981. The legislation sought to "make social economic development compatible with the preservation of the quality of the environment and the ecological balance (. . .) aiming at its rational use and permanent availability."[5] Here, the foundations of a sustainable development discourse are rather blatantly expressed; "social" modifies the phrase "economic development," and compatibility with environmental quality and ecological balance establish the idea of harmonization between the various conceptual foundations of the sustainable development framework. The notion of rational use, further, and the idea that development is becoming compatible with the environment (rather than the other way around) emphasizes that the legislation is essentially not conservationist but rather about reigning in and steering development along a more environmentally friendly trajectory over the longer term. The NEPA became enshrined in Brazil's democratic constitution of 1988, along with a host of local, state, and federal agencies, which were tasked with doing environmental impact assessments as part of the legal requirements for licensing new projects. The public participation component of Brazilian environmental laws is also substantial; once the assessments are completed, the relevant environmental agencies must organize and conduct public hearings about the proposed projects.

1988 was an important year for Brazilian politics and for environmental protection. Brazil underwent a gradual opening-up process of transition toward democracy; José Sarney was the vice-presidential candidate in a ballot led by Tancredo Neves, and they were indirectly elected by the Brazilian Congress in 1985. Tancredo Neves died a few weeks after that, and Sarney took his seat as president of the country in March 1985. By 1988, Brazil's new constitution was approved, and democracy was fully restored. Under President José Sarney, the Brazilian government began acknowledging environmental concerns and drafted a conservation plan called Nossa Natureza—Our Nature. The plan, which was formally approved in 1989, had a nationalist tone: President Sarney said, "Amazonia is ours, even to destroy" (Allen 2006, 66). Still, the plan addressed concerns about pollution from gold mining activities and promoted the creation of new national parks and protected forest areas. Little immediately changed on environmental grounds during the transition from the dictatorship into Brazil's democratic era, but the new constitution of 1988 had a whole chapter devoted to environmental issues. This laid the foundation for new regulations and, eventually, the creation of a national environmental agency. Nossa Natureza is an especially illustrative example of the frictions involved in how Brazil navigated responding to international pressure to address deforestation while maintaining national autonomy and emphasis on economic development.

Nossa Natureza

Amid heated international debate concerning the possibilities of debt-for-nature swaps, Brazil staunchly refused to consider any degree of compromised national sovereignty or territorial concessions in exchange for foreign aid or debt relief. Nossa Natureza attempted to appease international public opinion and simultaneously keep discussion on the Amazon confined to the Brazilian domestic realm (Barbosa 2000). It recognized the traditional populations living in the Amazon, which included *ribeirinhos* (riverine peasants), *seringueiros* (rubber tappers), as well as nut harvesters, coconut-breakers, and other river-based peasant populations and descendants of slaves who had lived lightly off the lands in the rainforest for at least a generation prior to the 1970s colonization efforts. Nossa Natureza also instituted tough penalties for illegal burning of the rainforest, regulated the use of mercury in mining operations, and even suspended some road building projects. IBAMA, the national environmental agency (formally known as Brazilian Institute of the Environment and Renewable Natural Resources) was created through the program.

Spurred by a combination of international pressure, Brazilian social movements, and also by his own initiative, President Sarney showed that some policy, even if imperfect, was still a positive step forward. Nossa Natureza at least offered acknowledgment that the environment was, in fact, an issue that needed a backbone institutionally and legally (Barbosa 2000). Moreover, it granted state recognition to the hitherto invisible populations of forest peoples in Amazonia[6] and incentivized research on the consequences of environmental degradation and protection efforts relevant to those populations. It also sparked the creation of communal, non-privatized landholding, which was aimed as a strategy to address the uncertain land titling and identity status of *garimpeiros* (artisanal gold miners), riverine peasants, and rubber tappers. It recognized the reality that the gold mining areas emitted toxic pollution from mercury, although the regulations often had few teeth in terms of enforcement. New national forests were created in Amapa and Amazonas, national parks were established in Acre and Mato Grosso, and some lip service was paid to the idea that land reform outside of the Amazon should take place to address the flow of migrants into the region (Hecht and Cockburn 1990). In all of those ways, Nossa Natureza was a policy that helped social and environmental protection in significant ways.

While such initiatives would give the appearance that Nossa Natureza offered formidable emphasis on Amazonian environmental protection, a healthy dose of skepticism is also merited about the depth of those commitments. The policy suspended the incentives of the SUDAM (Superintendency for the Development of the Amazon) program for cattle ranching and land clearing, and limited the logging of whole trees for export. Many of these initiatives were already underway and winding down, however. It omitted any treatment of the migrant populations that were already present in the Amazon and said nothing about some of the most blatant ongoing forms of environmental destruction that were taking place in the region. These included massive dams like the Balbina hydroelectric project, the proposed Xingu river dams, and extensive roadbuilding throughout the region. Aside from Nossa Natureza, overall, Brazil remained staunch in its commitment to development, allowing little in the way of environmental considerations to impede national economic growth. Scholars Susanna Hecht and Alexander Cockburn observe:

> . . . what Nossa Natureza made quite clear was that the real Amazonian policy would be covert, or at least undiscussed in public, in much the same manner as the deals made nearly a quarter of a century earlier [when Operation Amazonia was announced by General Castelo Branco in 1966]. (Hecht and Cockburn 1990, 140)

Under Sarney, the land values near roads remained high, the investments in infrastructure were still seen as a means of boosting economic growth and deterring the region from its persistent isolation, and the larger struggles over land remained a constant. For environmentalists, who were growing in numbers and prominence as a movement in Brazil and around the world during this time, Sarney's forays into Amazonian development appeared to provoke a vicious cycle. As ranching, mining, and mega-dams expanded, ecological degradation took place, and conflicts over land frequently became violent.

Chico Mendes and the People of the Forest

Just before Nossa Natureza was scheduled to launch, events in the remote Amazonian state of Acre shook the world. A rubber tapper who lived there named Chico Mendes was assassinated. In the far western Amazon, rural violence and land conflicts were not uncommon, so when his assassination made front page news around the world, Brazilians were shocked.[7] Mendes was a leader of the *seringueiros* and, together with local rural workers' union leaders, their aim was to protect the forest upon which they and their families had practiced sustainable extractivist activities for several generations.[8] Their conflicts frequently involved face-to-face confrontations with chainsaw-carrying workers who were deforesting lands at the behest of powerful local ranchers. Mendes and the rubber tappers organized *empates*, or nonviolent standoffs, to protect their trees from being cut and their land from being claimed by nearby ranchers. The *empates*, practiced since the mid-1970s as ranching was increasing, became a widely recognized protest action. Chico Mendes reflected on the challenges they faced in taking a largely oppositional stance in response to the problem of deforestation and land claiming:

> A moment arrived when we began to get worried, because we had got a fight on our hands, the struggle to resist deforestation, but at the same time we didn't really have an alternative project of our own to put forward for the development of the forest. We didn't have strong enough arguments to justify why we wanted to defend the forest. (Mendes 1989, 37)

As the struggle being waged in Acre gained momentum, the rubber tappers organized into a national movement and became increasingly prominent. The rapid deforestation rates in the Amazon were gaining attention both in Brazil and internationally. The rubber tappers sought to gain government officials' attention by holding the First National Rubber Tappers' Congress of May 1985, in Brasilia: "Why Brasília? Because it was the decision-making centre of the country. Also because most of the authorities thought the Amazon region was just one big empty jungle. We wanted to show them the Amazon was in fact inhabited—there were people living and working in the forest" (Mendes 1989, 39–39). Mendes gained traction with public officials, and the rubber tappers' movement caught the attention of several anthropologists who were working in the region. Chico Mendes was charismatic and articulate, and provided an accessible human voice to outsiders that the rainforest was not just a jungle wilderness devoid of humans. He helped give a public face to the fact the people of the forest—including those who were not indigenous peoples—had long histories of being economic contributors to the nation as well as protectors of the forest.

The prominence of the people of the forest was further bolstered when Mendes began internationally traveling during the 1985–1988 interval as a national leader of the rubber tappers. Through meetings with US Senate Foreign Operations Sub-Committee[9] and officials at the Inter-American Development Bank and the World Bank, the story of the rubber tappers became more politically important and resonant back in Brazil. The death threats against Mendes over a specific local land conflict in Xapuri had been mounting for some time. Mendes' struggle was poignantly articulated to international officials, especially because while under this pressure he raised awareness about the struggle the rubber tappers as a whole faced as the rainforest was being lost to ranchers and new highway projects.

For many, Chico Mendes represented a charismatic personal story about the importance of Amazonian conservation. His presence conveyed to people around the world that threats to the rainforest from ranchers and development projects had a real human impact, in addition to the flora and fauna that were being lost. Ultimately the rubber tappers did come up with a proposal, one that responded to the idea that aside from wanting deforestation to halt, the rubber tappers had an alternative development trajectory they could offer for the region. This was the idea of the extractive reserves (*reserva extrativista*, or RESEX), which were intended to be communally held and managed areas where the rubber tappers and other traditional populations engaged in low-impact, renewable resource–based activities could live off of the forest with minimal impact. Such activities include fishing, rubber tapping, Brazil nut gathering, and even small-scale farming. In a sort of exchange for being the eyes and ears on the ground of forest protection, the resident populations are given a degree of extra support from environmental agency personnel, who ideally help them protect and steward the land with their enforcement capacities.

The RESEXs offered a policy framework for achieving environmental aims in harmony with ecological protection goals. Creating protected areas where long-standing residents could live with a minimal environmental footprint was a win–win: it simultaneously offered the government an on-the-ground presence (in the form of the traditional populations living in the RESEXs) as a form of protection against illegal encroachments by would-be loggers and ranchers, while giving the traditional populations a collective property title that secured their ability to stay living on those lands. The otherwise unregulated land uses in the region were thus put toward conservation, with the people of the forest at the center of the strategy (Allegretti 1990, Allegretti 1995).

When Chico Mendes was gunned to death on December 22, 1988 by a hit man (who was hired through a contractor of one of the local ranchers, named Darly Alves), it was a story of a death foretold. The story resonated with a much wider audience than that in Acre, especially since Mendes had strong international allies and attended meetings that influentially resonated in Brazilian politics (Keck and Sikkink 1998). When Mendes was assassinated, his death reverberated in the international media much more than any of the 1,500 or so prior deaths that had previously occurred in Amazonian conflicts over land and forest protection (Moore 2008). Mendes' assassination was an Amazonian "shot heard around the world" for the problems of Amazonian forest loss, and he became a social movement martyr as an environmental defender (Revkin 1990).

Mendes' defense of the forest—and his death for that cause—had several important implications for Amazonian sustainable development politics. First, it showed environmentalists around the world that social and environmental issues could be addressed in tandem. It functioned to raise awareness of a socio-environmental or "social greens" framework for addressing issues at the intersection of conservation and development (Keck 1995). Second, it weakened some of the nationalist claims that foreign interests were greedily stealing the Amazon as many on the Brazilian left, who would have acceded to this nationalistically driven reasoning, instead began looking inward at the nation's struggles (Hochstettler and Keck 2007, Hurrell 1992). The international response to Mendes' assassination stunned Brazilian officials and put their Amazonian endeavors under increased scrutiny. A few months after the assassination, World

Bank and Inter-American Development Bank financing for highway projects in the Amazon was withdrawn, largely over pressure they were experiencing from environmentalists in the United States and Western Europe (Hecht and Cockburn 1990). Accountability measures to assess the environmental impacts of multinational bank lending and development policies increasingly became part of the banks' standard operational protocols (Rich 1995, Clark, Fox, and Treakle 2003). The assassination made clear that Brazil's new environmental law, Nossa Natureza, would be internationally questioned, and that there could be tough consequences for the nation's development agenda if proper protections were not in place for forest peoples or the land upon which they depended.

Not least, by the mid-1980s the rubber tappers and indigenous peoples were "considered legitimate participants in the debate" in global environmental politics (Dore 1996). Less included in that debate were the small-scale farmers of the Amazon who had been encouraged to colonize the region throughout the 1960s and 1970s. The newer settlers largely were blamed for Amazonian deforestation by the Brazilian government, although they were victims in the sense that they were unable to receive support or encouragement to do much else (Bratman 2011). Incentivized to come to the region, the training, agroforestry assistance, social supports, financial credits, and health conditions that were promised in Amazonian colonization schemes failed to meet their expectations. Given little resources or training to do anything else, the absence of support established conditions for ongoing slash-and-burn practices that depleted soils and spurred unplanned colonization (Schmink and Wood 1992).

In the aftermath of Mendes' death, a gathering took place that united a wide range of forest peoples including indigenous tribal groups, *seringueiros*, and an array of others. The tone of the meeting demanded change: "Things can't be as they were, and to dream that they would be would drive us to ruin" said Osmarino Amâncio Rodrigues to the assembled crowd (Hecht and Cockburn 1990). Among the shifts that were taking place, clear organizing structures began to emerge among rainforest peoples and conservation activists. The composition and formation of those broad domestic social movement alliances, and the international civil society linkages that also influenced the political dynamics of the time, involved considerable conflicts, failures, and successes, all of which inform subsequent debates over how sustainable development should take place in the Amazon. These merit a more detailed discussion, to which we now turn.

Amazonian Social Movements

Well before the sustainable development discourse and the high-profile assassination of Chico Mendes, social movement activism, especially in the form of labor rights and agrarian reform, had been brewing in the Amazon since the early 1970s. A demand, articulated as early as 1973, that a "wide and massive agrarian reform" be executed in the Amazon catalyzed much of the organizing (Almeida 1991). Under the military government, however, trade unions were highly controlled and stifled; but as democratization and civilian rule resumed in the early 1980s, the union movement gained more freedom and considerable momentum (Mendes 1989).[10] Paradoxically, despite the repression of the military era, the rural poor undertook significant mobilizations during this time (Maybury-Lewis 1994). An important explanation for this is institutional, because Brazilian corporatism specified that each county could only have one rural workers' union that was officially recognized by the government. Doing agrarian reform of some sort was "part of the official discourse on transforming Brazil" because the military generals had hoped to avoid a revolution similar to Cuba's by attempting to organize agrarian redistribution (Font 2003, 91). But since the agrarian reform process was so disorganized, violence and land conflicts tended to ignite and mobilize the poor. The organizational and moral support of the Catholic Church was also behind those efforts, strengthening them considerably while shielding them somewhat from the repressive violence that could be leveraged by the military regime.

Church and Union Mobilizations

While there was growing momentum surrounding the extractivist-based and indigenous groups that comprised the peoples of the forest, the newer migrants to the region were getting educated about inequality and social justice issues. Often, such groups did overlap, as both met in Catholic Church settings, where they were spurred to organize into workers' unions and cooperatives. Chico Mendes, for example, was a secretary of the rural trade union in 1975, and in 1977 organized the Xapuri Rural Workers' Union. He did so along with help from Marina Silva, who was once an aspiring nun and later became a national politician and head of the Environmental Secretariat.[11] Such mobilizations were largely thanks to the grassroots ecclesiastical communities (CEBs), which were organized by the Catholic Church as early as 1966. The CEBs were one of the rare forms of social organizing that was allowed during the dictatorship era, largely because of the sway held by the Catholic Church despite the censorship and repression perpetuated by the military leaders of the times. Guided by liberation theology, the CEBs were intended to instill a more profound sense of communion within church life. Leonardo Boff, a liberation theologist, explains some of the religious philosophy behind the CEBs:

> The adjective 'ecclesiastic' is more important than the noun 'community' because it is the principal constitutive of community and gives structure to community. The religious inspiration is Christian and binds together Christians as a group, and confers upon it all of its objectives; both those that are social and liberation-oriented, these are evangelizing characteristics. The consciousness and the explicitness of Christianity constitutes, thus, a characteristic of the CEBs and an element of the discernment in relation to other types of community. (Dornelas 2006)

The Transamazon colonists—especially those involved with the rural workers' unions—were strongly linked to religious life in the Catholic Church. A rural community leader along the Transamazon Highway near the Uruará parish described the ways in which the Church got involved in politics: "Church, union, political party . . . if, at the Catholic mass, you speak of the PT [the Worker's Party], the union, it is a prayer because it's considered a healthy thing. . . . Those that do not participate in the union and in the local commercial cooperatives do not have the right to receive any sacraments, nor to baptize their children" (Araújo 1991, 128). It was not infrequent for Church leaders to ask laypeople about their political participation and engagement in meetings. The Xingu Prelature, in the state of Pará, helped in the formation of the Workers' Party (Partido dos Trabalhadores, or PT) in the region, and organized its rural workers. It is significant too that in this part of the Transamazon, the demand from social movement activists for "working the land" was secondary to their demand for better infrastructure for the region. The paving of the Transamazon, the construction of secondary roads, hospitals, and schools, were always the central demands of the social movements in the region (Araújo 1991, Toni 2006).

Land reform–oriented organizations like the Pastoral Land Commission (*Comissão Pastoral da Terra*, or CPT) and the Landless Workers' Movement (*Movimento Sem Terra*, or MST) emanated from the Catholic Church and the CEBs in the early 1970s as well. The CPT arose out of several heated land conflicts, many of which involved progressive priests supporting peasants in their struggles against the large landowners. In the state of Mato Grosso, a rural prelacy called São Felix do Araguaia was one site of a formative struggle. A 1971 letter from the region notes the importance of the Church in standing up for the poor: "São Felix will be either the Church of the people, or it will not exist! It cannot become the church of calves and cows, which is inevitable if it does not support the resistance of the *posseiros* [small landholders] and Indians against the greed of capital held by modern *latifúndios*" (Poletto 1985, 30). The CPT was created with the intention of being a pastoral branch of the church, focused on the linkages between land and oppression of the poor. The existence of

CIMI—the Indigenous Missionary Council—set a precedent for the Church's involvement in social justice issues, and, at the same time, the CPT was intimately linked to the class-based struggles that were being led by the syndicalist organizations. This closeness and affinity between the Church, the unions, and political parties was explicitly documented and encouraged by the mid-1980s as the social movements collectively gained strength: "Beyond support from above, institutionally, it is fitting for the CPT to stimulate the critical participation of the *camponeses* [peasantry] and rural workers in the syndicate at CUT [the Unified Workers' Central], in the syndical opposition in PT or in other parties, and in forms of organization" (Poletto 1985, 56). The CPT's role in this regard helped to address the challenge of the traditionally perceived distance between the urban working classes and the rural peasantry, despite their common class struggles. The CEBs provided the training ground for activists who later became leaders in the social movement groups and in the PT party as well. In meetings of the CEBs, local organizing used the strength of the Catholic Church to articulate critiques of the military regime.[12] Brazil's Landless People's Movement, or MST, was a major force behind the Church-led and civil society push for agrarian reform as well.[13]

The Church's 1960s and 1970s progressive focus on mounting opposition to the military regime shifted by the early 1980s into building political engagements and a robust cadre of social movement leaders within Brazilian civil society. It is also important to note the presence of the links between union organizing and the church. CONTAG, the National Confederation of Agricultural Workers, was similarly conceived out of the CEBs and the work of the CPT. It also spurred a labor movement of considerable magnitude and variety and played a unique role in influencing Brazilian political parties.

CONTAG emphasized a distinction between agrarian reform and colonization, criticizing the transfers and compulsory removals of colonists and urging immediate action to settle the families in the places where they were already living and cultivating the land (Almeida 1991). Using a top-down model, they organized state and local union groups across the Amazon as early as 1979. Their efforts aimed to build an organizing strategy, so that the unions would influence the nation's eventual opening into a democratic transition.[14] In the Amazon, several strong unions were prevalent. One important union was the Rural Workers Syndicate (*Sindicato de Trabalhadores Rurais* or STR), which organized laborers alongside CONTAG, encompassing many of the new migrants in the region who were working as agriculturists. The unions sometimes politically conflicted with each other,[15] but alliances and overlapping memberships were also common.

Social movement activism in the Amazon became more prominent toward the end of the 1980s and in the early 1990s as Brazil fully transitioned into democracy. A significant derivative of the many meetings and civil society organizations was a robust focus on land rights, class issues, and inequality. In Brazil and other parts of Latin America, conversations emerged on a more widespread basis about how to address environmental and development issues together. The framework was called *socioambientalismo*, or socio-environmentalism. The rising movement of socio-environmentalists saw nature and the lifestyle of regionally based social groups as indissoluble, and it emphasized the political and economic basis for environmental problems (Alonso, Costa, and Maciel 2005, Hecht 2011a).

Socio-Environmentalism

Stemming from leftist discourses and ideology, socio-environmentalism emphasizes the negative effects of capitalist development on the middle and lower classes, and at the same time champions the poor as protagonists in finding environmental solutions (Keck 1995, Hochstettler and Keck 2007). Brazilian socio-environmentalism is strongly linked to concerns about class-based oppression, and integrated a broad swath of the population into its ideological tent, including rubber tappers, river-based peasants, coconut-breakers, and the agrarian reform movement (Esterci 2003). Even as those groups were embraced by socio-environmentalism, the forest peoples themselves did not directly know about or embrace environmentalism and ecology; their narratives happened to run in parallel. Only as the socio-environmental movement evolved did the idea that forest peoples were an embodiment of socio-environmental values become recognized by all parties that were participating within the movement (Rodrigues 2007).

Socio-environmentalism grew at a time when the environmental justice movement in the United States was also gaining a strong foothold, and political ecology was on the rise in Europe. As a Brazilian variant, socio-environmentalism was positioned against both a strong environmental conservation stance as well as more neoliberal perspectives on the economic values of nature. While natural resources and society are often framed as being at odds with each other in the debate surrounding sustainable development, Brazilian socio-environmentalism frames society instead as not only compatible with environmental protection but even as conducive to achieving it. Socio-environmentalism critiques capitalism and capital-intensive farming, as well as the idea that nature should be set aside for biodiversity protection purposes (Hecht 2011b).

By the 1990s, socio-environmentalism was the predominant form of organizing and activism in the Amazon.[16] It embraced inequality and social harm issues head-on, finding natural affinities with the land reform and labor movements as well as the PT party. Poverty and environmental degradation "were part of the same causal story" in socio-environmentalism (Hochstettler and Keck 2007, 109). While sometimes the links were unclear about exactly what steps should be taken using a socio-environmental framework, the democratic transition, the Chico Mendes story, and the Rio Earth Summit all helped to bolster the idea that socio-environmentalism—as both a movement and a set of ideas—offered an important means of conjoining ecological and social justice questions (Hochstettler and Keck 2007).

Other more "mainstream" environmentalist orientations gained ground in Brazil during the 1980s and early 1990s as well, and engaged in political protests.[17] "All the activists were pondering how to make the best use of newly opened channels of political access, whether the opportunities originated in domestic democratization, keystone events like the Rio Conference on Environment and Development, or newly available funding from businesses and the state" (Hochstettler and Keck 2007, 102). The Atlantic forest conservationists formed the SOS Atlantic Forest Foundation (SOS), which became a powerhouse by the mid-1990s in influencing conservation and deforestation discussions for that region. A separate group that was a byproduct of a cross-partisan coalition (the Interstate Ecological Coordination for the Constituent Assembly, or CIEC), put together their own list of endorsements for political candidates in 1986, which was known as the "ecologist platform" (Hochstetler and Keck 2007). A NGO coalition group called Gaia was formed by José Lutzenberger in 1987, aimed at offering a Brazilian organizational basis for tackling global environmental issues. The various NGOs coalesced around anti-nuclear activism and local anti-pollution struggles. Also in 1987, they formed the Brazilian Green Party. Lutzenberger, who had been more of a locally oriented anti-pollution environmental activist in the southern state of Rio Grande do Sul in the 1970s, won the Right Livelihood Award[18] in 1988 in recognition for his work (Rohter 2002). He became a Minister of the Environment in 1990 under President Fernando Collor de Melo (1990–1992) and convinced him to recognize and protect 36,000 square miles of land for the Yanomami Indians in the far northern Amazon. Creating the Yanomami reserve involved expelling considerable numbers of *garimpeiros* from the area, who were decimating the Yanomami tribe and destroying their rainforest habitat (Rabben 1998).[19]

Another important step for the socio-environmental movement, illustrative of the strength of these transnational networks, was the 1988 a meeting of indigenous peoples in Altamira, Pará in protest of the Belo Monte dam. This event, called the First Encounter of the Xingu, captured the spotlight of international media and was the largest gathering of indigenous peoples of the Amazon at the time (Bratman 2015, de Sousa Júnior, Reid, and Leitão 2006, Fearnside 2012a, Hall and Branford 2012, Jaichand and Sampaio 2013, Sevá Filho 2005). As the international environmental movement gained strength worldwide, campaigns were launched against international funding for the Brazilian highway infrastructure projects, on the basis that they were both socially and environmentally irresponsible.[20]

It is also important to recognize the role of transnational advocacy networks in shaping Amazonian political dynamics. Whole books have been written on the topic of activist groups in transnational alliances relation to environmental (and socio-environmental) activism in Brazil and other countries.[21] Of special note were the effectively powerful ties between internationally based scholars and grassroots actors. Darrell Posey, an ethnobotanist, and Janet Chernela, an anthropologist, played central roles in bringing indigenous leaders and Chico Mendes to Washington, DC to meet with officials at the World Bank in 1988 to voice their concerns about financing for Amazonian dams (Rabben 1998). Others, such as the Environmental Defense Fund's Stephen Schwartzman and his mentor, the anthropologist Terrence Turner, also played central roles in understanding the indigenous tribes, brokering meetings for their leaders, and working on lobbying together to bring them into contact with Brazilian officials, US Congressional representatives, and the Inter-American Development bank (Keck and Sikkink 1998).

The role of nationally connected organizations and key individuals in the scientific and applied anthropology communities also played important supporting roles in strengthening these networks.[22] While socio-environmentalist activists in Brazil worked most often at grassroots levels, national-level activism also supported their work, often through partnerships with groups such as the Social Environmental Institute (ISA) as well as the Catholic Church's Pastoral Land Commission, the National Council of Rubber Tappers, and the Landless Worker's Movement. Often, their work was in conjunction with international allies including the World Wildlife Fund for Nature (WWF), Environmental Defense Fund, International Rivers, the Centre for International Forestry Research and, occasionally, organizations with a slightly more conservationist bent such as Greenpeace, Friends of the Earth, Conservation International, and The Nature Conservancy. Multiple Amazonian scientific institutions, such as the Institute for Amazonian Environmental Research (IPAM) and the National Institute for Amazonian Research (INPA), in addition to state-led agricultural extension services, supported local initiatives through research and technical support. A robust epistemic community of researchers had grown since the mid-1970s and effectively raised attention to deforestation and biodiversity concerns taking place in Amazonian geographies.

Facing international pressure that was the result both of the legacy of Chico Mendes' assassination in December 1988 and the lead-up to the Rio Earth Summit in 1992, the Brazilian government began to establish national parks in the early 1990s, which emphasized forest conservation and ecological research.[23] Dovetailing the new emphasis on ecological conservation, indigenous reserves were also created, and these served not only to help protect many of the Amazon's most threatened tribes from the intrusions of illegal land claiming and logging but also to support the goals of forest protection. Table 3.1 details the establishment of the history and magnitude of these protected areas in the Amazon, noting the federal and the state-level conservation efforts. As new reserves, parks, and extractive reserves were created, land speculation was dramatically reduced, and the rates of deforestation began to notably decline in those areas. These plans, for the first time, were explicitly aimed at bringing a set of

Table 3.1 Protected Areas in the Brazilian Amazon (1961–2016)

Presidential Period[a]	Government Type	Total Size Created (ha)[b]	% of Total Conservation Areas
1961–1968	Federal	2,206,221	1.6%
	State	0	–
1969–1974	Federal	5,002,687	3.6%
	State	0	–
1975–1979	Federal	3,349,801	2.4%
	State	0	–
1980–1985	Federal	5,887,116	4.2%
	State	2,634	0.0019%
1985–1990	Federal	6,066,643	4.4%
	State	11,670,318	8.4%
1990–1992	Federal	940,358	0.7%
	State	1,882,425	1.4%
1992–1994	Federal	17,626	0.01%
	State	1,393	0.001%
1995–2002	Federal	12,558,412	9.0%
	State	8,116,027	5.8%
2003–2010	Federal	33,542,885	24.1%
	State	34,851,413	25.0%
2011–2016	Federal	15,820,015	11.4%
	State	424,795	0.3%
Total		139,301,491	100%

[a] Protected Areas were combined in year groups based on who was the president at the time.

[b] Data from the Protected Areas Monitoring Program and Geoprocessing Laboratory of Instituto Socioambiental (ISA). The organization monitors the Federal Official Gazette and the Official Gazettes of the states of Legal Amazonia daily to report any creation of new protected areas. ISA also consults other NGOs, such as the Chico Mendes Institute for Biodiversity Conservation, and administrative bodies to keep track of changes to current conservation areas.

environmentally oriented policies into the region that simultaneously strove to balance social needs.

Through constructing plans for the region's future that included efforts at environmental protection, significant demarcations of indigenous territories, and creation of protected areas for environmental conservation, the Brazilian government began making efforts to convince the world that it could be an environmental leader at the same time as it grew as an economic power. Likely, too, those steps positioned Brazil better as a host for the 1992 Rio Earth Summit, where undoubtedly the nation's track record surrounding deforestation would be scrutinized.

The Rio Earth Summit of 1992

Global environmental political agreements were in need of revitalization by 1992. The Stockholm Conference on the Human Environment (1972) resulted in many unmet hopes for environmental protection, and between the geopolitical shifts, new scientific knowledge about environmental problems, and civil society mobilizations in the twenty years since the Stockholm conference, 178 representatives from different nations recognized the need to rekindle their commitments. Maurice Strong, the Secretary-General for the Rio conference, praised the central role that Brazil would play in giving the "Only One Earth" summit momentum:

> There could be no better place to hold this historic Earth Summit. This great country of Brazil, which takes pride in being a part of the developing world, is a universe in itself, rich in the resources with which nature has endowed it and in the diversity, the vitality, the creativity and the charm of its people. It is, at the same time, one of the world's leading industrial countries and one of its most urbanized, while containing some of its greatest frontier areas. The EcoBrasil exhibition in São Paulo and EcoTech '92 here in Rio have demonstrated, too, the impressive quality and range of Brazil's scientific and technological capabilities. The economic, social and environmental challenges which Brazil is tackling with characteristic vigor and dynamism mirror the whole panoply of issues this Conference is addressing. And the initiatives Brazil has taken under your leadership, Mr. President, in dealing with some of your own critical environment and development problems have set an enlightened example to the international community. (Strong 1992)

The lofty praise set a congenial tone for the start of the conference, but Brazil's way of coping with environment and development problems was by no means wholehearted.

Despite its hope to become an environmental leader, Brazil's embrace of environmental concerns at the Earth Summit was only tenuous. Brazil led nations of the Global South in championing rights for development over conservation interests. As the nation transitioned out of military dictatorship and into a young democracy in the late 1980s and early 1990s, leaders were only reluctantly spurred by international outcry to try to set a new course for the region. José Lutzenberger, who went from the NGO world into becoming Brazil's Minister of Environment, stepped down only a few months before the conference was to begin. At the summit, the nation maintained its stance on the importance of national sovereignty over forest resources, ultimately resisting international efforts to make a treaty to combat deforestation. Largely, environmental issues remained more rhetorically important to the government during this time than substantively encoded as a set of values and enforced policies (da Costa Ferreira and Tavolaro 2008).[24] Each time it faced the international limelight, a somewhat contradictory stance marked Brazil's position. It made gestures toward conciliation with international environmental concerns, even if only rhetorically, but then defiantly asserted its national sovereignty through resoundingly nationalist campaigns (da Costa Ferreira and Tavolaro 2008, Hochstettler and Keck 2007).[25]

By the early 1990s the environmental problems of the Amazon took center stage in global environmental governance debates, particularly those surrounding biodiversity and deforestation. The social and economic efficacy of earlier policies began to be questioned by Brazilian officials, who were confronted with both evidence of the environmental damages such policies had caused as well as substantial international pressure to improve its environmental protection if it was to credibly maintain a leadership position in global environmental debates (Schweickardt 2003). Newly democratized Brazil had any number of political and economic barriers to overcome, but the environmental conditions in Amazonia remained a focus of international attention. The SOS Atlantic Rainforest director, João Paulo Capobianco, left SOS shortly after the Rio Earth Summit and became the founding director of ISA, the Instituto SocioAmbiental, which became the premiere research and advocacy organization working within a socio-environmental approach (Hochstettler and Keck 2007).[26] A growing body of social movement and civil society groups increasingly shaped government priorities concerning environmental issues.

On the heels of contentious arguments at the 1992 Earth Summit over forestry issues, deforestation rates in the Brazilian Amazon continued to rise. Between 1991 and 1994, some estimates cited a 34 percent increase in annual Amazonian deforestation (Serrill 1997). Although significant progress was made in creating new conservation areas and indigenous reserves, deforestation rates climbed continuously higher. [27] Pressure mounted through domestic networks of socio-environmental activists as well as in the international media for the nation to act to counter the shockingly high rates of deforestation occurring in Amazonia. But the general trajectory of environmental losses continued, as is illustrated in Figure 3.1. By 1996, Amazonian deforestation was at record levels, and the rates shot even higher in 1998, when fires burned out of control in Roraima and reduced about 15 percent of the state's forests to ashes (Espach 2002, Muchagata et al. 2003).

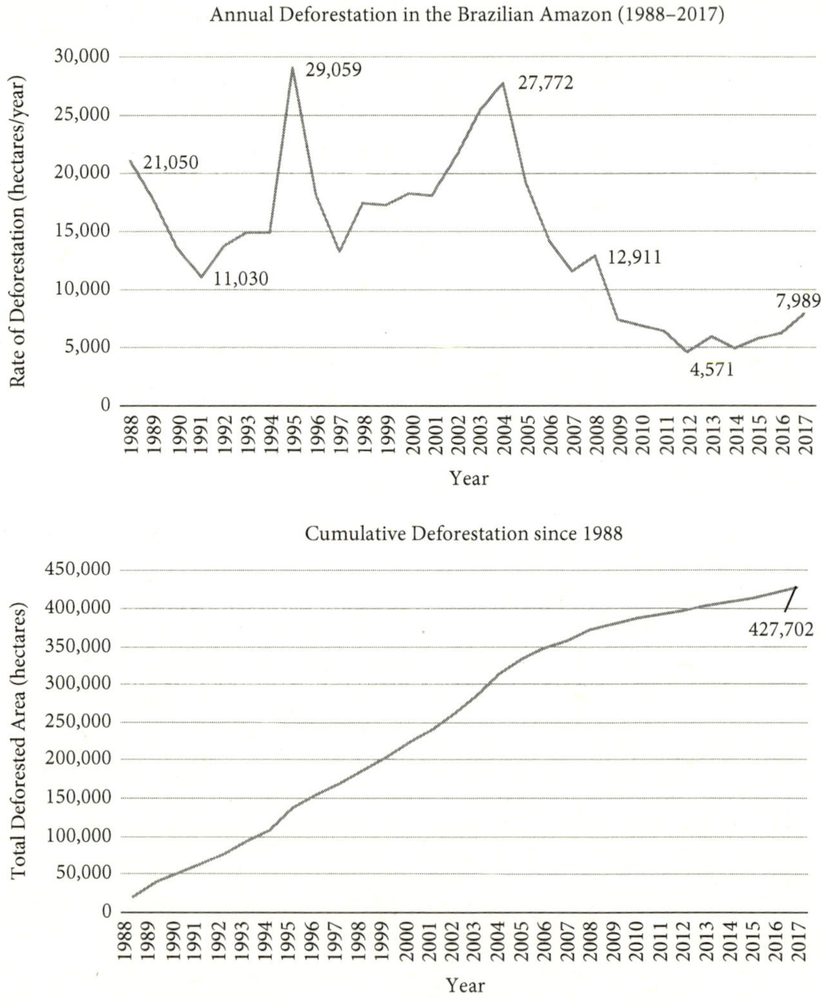

Figure 3.1 Rates of deforestation in the Amazon plummeted from 2004–2007, although subsequently began to rise. The total area of forest losses has continuously increased over time.

The multinational banks, which had a long history of supporting Brazilian federal programs to incentivize cattle ranching, infrastructure, and industrial developments in the Amazon, began to change their approach around this same time. Through the World Bank, Brazil received around $1.56 billion in funding oriented toward environmental research and conservation from the G7 nations in 1991. The Pilot Program to Conserve the Brazilian Rain Forest (commonly known as the PPG-7) sought to provide long-term support for community-based agroforestry activities and to bolster Amazonian production of forest products for commercialization (Espach 2002, Becker and Lèna 2002, de Lima and Buszynski 2011). Sometimes these projects were more valuable to NGO intermediaries than the local peasants whom they were purported to empower and benefit. But the pilot projects did notably encourage a high-level discourse of sustainability, participatory management, and agroforestry activities in relation to the Amazon (Barbanti 2013). Increasingly, a neoliberal orientation began marking Amazonian conservation, with landscapes positioned as having an agro-industrial and modern utility. Export-oriented monoculture production is exemplary of the highest transformed manifestation of such landscapes. As soy was planted in the state of Mato Grosso, especially, the contrast between Amazonian protection and Amazonian "productive" land uses became more marked (Hecht 2011b). Long critical of debt-for-nature swaps, Brazil accepted its first one in 1991 and began embracing the possibilities that international cooperation—including from long-resisted NGO actors—could offer for Amazonian conservation.

The era of sustainable development took hold in the early 1990s, as practices that aimed to avoid juxtaposing environmental strictures and economic development gained momentum. Illustrative of this is the Fernando Henrique Cardoso administration's (1994–2002) progress with the Planafloro program in Rondônia. Despite many long years of negotiations with skeptical NGOs, Planafloro was an ambitious plan for statewide agro-ecological and economic zoning, largely funded by multilateral banks. It was an extremely ambitious plan, intended to limit frontier expansion by intensifying agriculture and infrastructure in already-settled areas, and to do more to protect environmentally vulnerable areas and indigenous reserves (Keck 1998). Rondônia was "environmentalists' object case of colonization run amok," and Planafloro was crafted with considerable disjunction in its aims (Keck 1998, 185). The contradictions persisted well into the plan's implementation. Planafloro was a notable example of sustainable development because it explicitly attempted to address ecological issues and economic growth in tandem. It did so through protection of existing conservation units, creation of extractive reserves, regulation of timber logging, and discouragement of settlement in unsuitable areas, while at the same time it sought to invigorate social infrastructure for local populations and to build new infrastructures for them while expanding farm production and logistical efficiencies. Civil society's activism, both locally in Rondônia and transnationally, also represented a notable level of engagement and concerted efforts to influence such plans (Keck 1998, Rodrigues 2004).

The national Forest Code, which had been first established in 1965, was also strengthened during the mid-1990s. While provisions of legally protected forest reserves and prohibitions on clearing vegetation from environmentally sensitive areas were already in place, the new revisions required that Amazonian landowners maintain 80 percent of their lands as intact forest (Espach 2002, McElhinny 2011). Subsequently, the Forest Code would become a revisited bone of contention as, beginning in 2011, legislative changes weakened the 80 percent protection standard and waived some of the penalties for prior deforestation. The Planafloro program and the Forest Code epitomize early attempts to translate sustainable development theory into practice.

The discourses that entrenched nationalism and national sovereignty that marked the dictatorship's ideological views toward the Amazon continued to be articulated even in this era, however. Illustrative of this is the following snippet of a speech made to the Senate on June 7, 1999, by Senator Luiz Otávio (at the time, a PPB party member from Paraná), criticizing the international NGOs in Amazonia:

> The organizations [NGOs] are captained by our media headlines. Greenpeace, by the way, will set up a base there in the Amazon; they will have their own boat there to travel our territories, our riches, also to interfere with the ecological balance and our resources, of our riches. I give you my alert: *por aí, não*! [not that way!] One cannot think only of the Amazon as the world's lungs, as minerals or as a large biodiversity reserve, forgetting the millions of Brazilians who live in the region and need to support their families . . . They [NGOs] will not intimidate me! As they go there to supervise us, we will also go there, to supervise them!" (Campos 1999)

A former Commander of the 2nd infantry of the jungle for the Brazilian army in Pará, Luiz Otávio supported investigations of international organizations. Despite such resistances, accepting the possibility that environmental issues could be addressed hand-in-hand with economic and social concerns was perceived as a more credible approach by most Brazilian leaders. The role of NGOs in partnership with the Brazilian state became more prominent during this time as well, despite the persistent undercurrent of nationalist sentiment that objected to their presence.

While distinctions between the socio-environmentalists, conservationists, and neoliberal approaches appear sharp in ideological terms, in practice, especially in the present, conservation and development practice in Amazonia is far more muddled. Despite the wide variety of approaches to conservation, the spectrum of voices does tend to find common ground in terms of crafting and advocating for environmental policies (Hecht, Morrison, and Padoch 2014). An early example of this was the creation of Extractive Reserves, and the socio-environmental movement itself is representative of the intersectionality that oriented the activism of many actors in Amazonian civil society.

Renewed Developmentalism in the Amazon

With this context of policy and activism established, it is important to understand how sustainable development in the Amazon was extended through contemporary political-economic models. This section examines how the political economy of renewed developmentalism influenced—and was influenced by—articulations of sustainable development in the Amazon. Beginning in the mid-1990s, Brazil increasingly embraced market-opening policies, which left Amazonian ecosystems more vulnerable to global market prices and technological advances. Especially since the PT party in Brazil rose to power in 2003 under President Luiz Inácio da Silva (Lula), a leftist political rhetoric combined with strategies for intensifying agricultural production and exploiting natural resources (Baletti 2014, Morais and Saad-Filho 2012). Lula's administration adopted a hybrid model for economic development, both embracing neoliberal prescriptions and, in parallel, taking on a new developmental approach.[28] Sometimes called "neodevelopmental," the renewed developmental approach involved constructive interactions between a strong state and the private sector, with the former providing macroeconomic stability, supporting distributive outcomes directly, and nurturing large domestic firms ("national champions") (Morais and Saad-Filho 2012, 790). The emphasis in the renewed developmental approach focuses on encouraging global market competitiveness, and values states' roles as regulators of private enterprise and as providers of infrastructure. The framework of sustainable development also consolidated in the 2000s, as new procedures for possessing and utilizing Amazonian territories were explored (Campbell 2015, 36). Bresser-Pereira argues that new developmentalism involves "a concern with the protection of the environment or with sustainable development that did not exist under old developmentalism" (Bresser-Pereira 2009, 250).

The central aim of renewed developmentalism was to expand states' productive capacity and increase accumulation of capital. At the same time, the renewed developmental approach gives substantial importance to addressing social inequalities as part of the path toward growth (Morais and Saad-Filho 2012,

Siscú, de Paulo, and Michel 2007, Amado and Mollo 2015, Cornwall and Eade 2010, Bresser-Pereira 2011). The renewed developmental approach differed from the earlier developmentalism of the Economic Commission on Latin America and the Caribbean through its recognition of the failures both of import-substitution and of the extensive state intervention in markets. In fact, much of the new approach to developmentalism aimed to correct and mitigate the effects of the earlier developmentalist policies. The renewed developmentalist turn also significantly differed institutionally from Brazilian developmentalism of the 1970s and 1980s, in which a bureaucratic-authoritarian approach led to highly technocratic planning oriented almost entirely upon economic growth (Sikkink 1991, Hochstetler and Montero 2013, Amado and Mollo 2015).

Up until 2004, soybean prices, cattle ranching, and deforestation all spiked, suggesting a new wave of development emphasis concomitantly occurring in the region (Nepstad et al. 2014, Hecht 2014). The satellite images made clear that not only was deforestation increasing from 2002–2004, but also that the greatest rates of deforestation were happening along the same roads where industrial-scale soybean agriculture was being expanded.[29]

As Figure 3.1 shows, in the 2002 rate was similarly high, at 9,845 square miles, a size comparable to the state of New Jersey. The rates were only between 5,000–7,000 square miles per year from 1996–2001, however, so the increase was especially alarming to observers. The steep declines of later years can largely be attributed to strong institutional enforcement, and the uptick in deforestation since 2014 tends to also correlate with other political and economic turmoil in the country (Monteiro, Seixas, and Vieira 2014, Fonseca et al. 2015, Pfaff et al. 2015, Butler 2017). Seeking to continue these trends while still offering high growth rates, renewed developmentalism aimed to couple attention to environmental governance and social policies with a doubling-down on infrastructure plans. Ironically, for Brazil, Ecuador, Bolivia, and Peru, the commodities boom and natural resource extraction in large part offered the funding pool from which financing social policies and conservation activities could be achieved (Strassburg et al. 2014, Gudynas 2016, North and Grinspun 2016).

Paradoxically, a more traditional growth and development model was championed throughout Latin America's "new left" governments at the same time as alternatives to the modern paradigm of economic development were being articulated. In Ecuadorian and Bolivian constitutions, the idea of *buen vivir*, that is, living well within community, was championed, as was the idea of extending the human rights framework to nature through the idea of the rights of nature (Gudynas 2011, Kauffman and Martin 2017). Yet, under sustainable development, especially as far as Brazilian development politics were concerned, the environment–development conflict was accentuated rather than alleviated. One example is the Initiative for the Integration of the Regional Infrastructure of South America (IIRSA), where the discourse behind planning is distinctively couched within the sustainable development paradigm:

> . . . IIRSA's comprehensive approach to projects places a priority on environmental protection and is responsive to a growing awareness of its importance by the people of the region . . . The IIRSA approach of applying the concept of hubs helps address environmental issues in a structured way and offers planners and other stakeholders a vision of development opportunities, alternatives and needs to ensure effective and balanced regional integration. (IDB October 2006, 17, quoted in [van Dijck 2008, 101])

The emphasis on road building[30] and integration fundamentally focused on economic opportunities in each hub of IIRSA infrastructure development projects. The proposed highway through Bolivian Isiboro Sécure National Park and Indigenous Territory (TIPNIS) is a prominent example of this tension. The TIPNIS highway would connect the Amazon to the Andes, motivated largely by the possibility of transporting Brazilian soybean shipments out from Pacific ports to China. Oil exploration rights near the TIPNIS park are also held by Brazilian oil giant Petrobras (Friedman-Rudovsky 2012). The result of TIPNIS was an exacerbated geographical pattern of uneven development and a system of investments that prioritized benefits to multinational firms well above environmental protection and social equity considerations (Castro 2012, Kanai 2016). This brief example illustrates the significance of Brazil's economic strategy in a regional context. Moreover, it highlights the influence of large state firms such as Petrobras and the Chinese government over the development of Amazonian spaces.

In the Brazilian case, the social policies that were also derivatives of renewed developmentalist strategies did have considerable success in reducing extreme poverty and growing the middle class. The push to achieve land reform in the Amazon, and simultaneously to mitigate the concerning rates of deforestation that were occurring in the region, resulted in one especially significant new land use plan known as the Project for Sustainable Development (PDS). The PDS is a type of land reform settlement that involves strict environmental protection protocols while allowing newer (nontraditional) Amazonian residents to engage in farming and settlement. The PDS model is discussed in more depth in Chapter 4. The PDSs were initially created in the western Amazonian state of Acre, and then were scaled up as a planned agrarian settlement model beginning around 2003 (Campbell 2015).

Agrarian reforms, coupled with a strong economy and substantially redistributionist social policies, did go a long way toward reducing inequality and poverty in Brazil. The poverty rate declined by more than 55 percent between

2003–2012, going from around 35.8 percent of the population to around 15.9 percent during that time period (Weisbrot, Johnston, and Lefebvre 2014). Brazil was not alone in its renewed developmental orientation. Across Latin America, leaders such as Evo Morales in Bolivia, Rafael Correa in Ecuador, Kristina Kirchner in Argentina, and José Mujica in Uruguay all embraced resource-intensive production of commodities as a strategy for achieving higher economic growth rates in tandem with conditional cash transfer programs and other distribution-oriented policies aimed at reducing inequality (Escobar 2010).

The renewed developmental approach was ignited with a host of infrastructure-oriented national plans. Under the *Avança Brasil* (Forward Brazil) program initiated under President Fernando Henrique Cardoso in 2000, $43 billion would be allocated for the construction of roads and dams, many of which were in the Amazon. *Avança Brasil* funded the paving of 7,500 km of Amazonian roads, a significant sum considering the region's predominantly unpaved character. Table 3.2 illustrates the extent of road paving throughout the country. It is notable that despite the major funding allocations, there have been only incremental improvements to paved road conditions on both federal and state levels since the early 1990s.

Table 3.2 Road Paving in the Brazilian Federal and State Road Network (1970–2007)

	Federal				State			
Year	Paved	Unpaved	Total	% Paved	Paved	Unpaved	Total	% Paved
1970	24146	27394	51540	47%	24431	105040	129471	19%
1975	40190	28774	68964	58%	20641	86320	106961	19%
1980	39685	19480	59165	67%	41612	105756	147368	28%
1985	46455	14410	60865	76%	63084	100903	163987	38%
1990	50310	13417	63727	79%	78284	110769	189053	41%
1993	51612	13783	65395	79%	81765	110773	192538	42%
2003	57143	14049	71192	80%	84352	111410	195762	43%
2005	58149	14651	72800	80%	98377	109963	208340	47%
2007	61304	13636	74940	82%	106548	113451	219999	48%

Source: Ministério dos Transportes, http://dados.gov.br/dataset/rodovias-federais. Data from after 2007 is not available.

Avança Brasil also supported the rapid expansion of industrial soybean production, and Brazil quickly become a global leader second only to Argentina in terms of soybean exports by 2003 (Baletti 2014, Hetherington and Campbell 2014, Flaskerud 2003).[31] Joining with neighboring countries in South America to build infrastructure projects, Brazil also launched the Initiative for the Integration of the Regional Infrastructure of South America (IIRSA) in the year 2000. In twelve South American countries, the IIRSA plan included 510 infrastructure projects and totaled more than $130 billion in investments, some of which came through public–private partnerships, and others of which were from the Brazilian National Development Bank (BNDES) and regional development banks such as the Inter-American Development Bank. One major IIRSA project was the $1.3 billion Interoceanic highway,[32] which connects São Paulo to the Pacific coast in Peru by traversing through both the Amazon and the Andes (Reel 2014). IIRSA entailed commitments of over $69 billion in roadbuilding, hydroelectric dams, and other major infrastructure projects throughout South America, including in the Amazon region.[33] The strategy contemplates a total of 348 projects for the continent, many of which impact Amazonian ecosystems (Killeen 2007).

An important component of the renewed developmental approach was the pluriannual Plans for Accelerated Growth (PAC), initiated under president Lula and continued by his successor, President Dilma Rouseff. PAC I (2007–2010), at BRL$503.9 billion or around US $153.8 billion, and its tripled-budget successor PAC II (2010–2014), which was a BRL$1.59 trillion plan (around US $485 billion), proposed major investments by the Brazilian government in projects to achieve economic growth through major civil construction projects for highways, energy infrastructure, and support of industrial zones.

Much like the impetus for the Transamazon and the BR-163 highways that were first cut under Operation Amazonia, Brazil's goals from IIRSA and the PAC plans were primarily based on the rationale that territorial integration and global connectivity would lead to a more efficient connection to the global economy.[34] Furthermore, national consolidation could be achieved, allowing greater opportunity for improving cross-country logistics and shorter travel times. An additional contribution was the growth these investments could foster in Brazil's budding tourism industry (van Dijck 2008, Kanai 2016). Throughout South America, the projects exacerbated already uneven territorial development patterns, privileging urban nodes and existing networks for further investment while tending to leave those who live in peripheral areas and who experience more limited economic opportunities and access to governmental programs in continued marginal positions (Kanai 2016).

In the first decade of the twenty-first century, Brazilian annual growth rates hovered at around 5 percent, and the nation joined the echelons of the world's top agricultural commodities producers. Simultaneously, many observers feared what these changes would mean for the Amazon and for the global environment, as the growth strategy was predicated on development models which typically involved substantial losses for the rainforest and the smallholder populations living on its land (Araujo et al. 2008, Nepstad et al. 2014, Aldrich et al. 2012, Martino 2007).[35]

While the renewed developmental policies introduced some social reforms and new monetary strategies into a more leftist orientation of economic strategies, the emphasis on integrated economic engagements, private investments, and market competition was seminal (Escobar 2010, Castro 2012, Baletti 2012, Ban 2012, Hochstetler and Montero 2013). Coupled with Brazil's economic growth from 2003–2011, investments and cooperation with China grew substantially, and Brazil took cues from Chinese state capitalist models for development. The strengthened Brazilian National Bank for Social and Economic Development (BNDES) had a lending portfolio consistently larger than the World Bank's during this time, at around $190 billion USD.[36] The BNDES lent monies to finance export activities and to foreign governments, mostly in Africa. Notably, over 60 percent of the BNDES portfolio was invested in large Brazilian firms including Petrobras, the meatpacking giant JBS, and the world's leading iron ore exporter, Vale (Leahy 2015). State control extended to businesses and stocks as well. In 2011, some estimates suggested that 20 percent of industries in Brazil had the government among their top five shareholders (Ban 2012, 314). As Brazil was "rising," the *Economist* magazine ("Brazil Takes Off" 2009) observed that hubris would be one of the biggest threats to Brazil's economy. Sacrificing a stable, slow, and steady model in lieu of too rapid a reach into major investments without diversification was a recognized risk. But this is indeed what happened; prices dropped for the major commodities of oil, sugar, and coffee, while Brazil's tax and pension systems were severely bloated. The result was that considerable public expenditures extended well beyond the pace of GDP growth. The massive public expenditures from statist policies led to significant public debt and a budget deficit, putting Brazil into economic stagnation from 2012–2015 and, after that, a serious economic decline.

During the economic growth period of 2001–2010, a sense of hopeful nationalism prevailed. Brazil catapulted into becoming the world's sixth largest economy, and President Luiz Inácio "Lula" da Silva's (2003–2010) popular leadership pulled millions out of poverty. Brazil won its bid to host the 2014 World Cup, and Rio de Janeiro won the honor of hosting the 2016 Summer Olympics. Politically, the nation positioned itself to gain a permanent seat on the UN Security Council, clearly aiming for global leadership that was not only economic (Neves 2012, Grant 2014). By 2011, however, the corruption scandal that embroiled the state-controlled company Petrobras, which is Brazil's biggest investor, froze spending, and consumer confidence fell dramatically. Cascading effects with high unemployment rates and downgrades to Brazil's credit rating ensued. The government had little money in its coffers to try to boost more investments.[37]

Public expenditures were so heavily leveraged toward large corporations, in fact, that critics suspected BNDES of crony capitalism, and these allegations were affirmed during the extensive corruption investigations known as *Lava Jato*, or Operation Car Wash. During the investigation, corporate heads of JBS, Petrobras, and a host of other major firms were all found to have been connected to bribes and kickbacks with high-level politicians, including former President Lula da Silva. By 2016, between the economic crisis, President Dilma Rousseff's impeachment, and constant political turmoil from the corruption scandals as well as the outbreak of the Zika virus in the country, Brazil faced a "triple crisis," and the era of renewed developmentalism effectively came to an end.

A significant legacy of renewed developmentalism in Brazil is that of a reshaping of the physical landscape and infrastructures in much of South America. The state-financed encouragement of soybean production, investment in bauxite and other mining operations, and the financial backing of loans for hydroelectric dams intended to increase Brazil's energy infrastructure to fuel continued economic growth, meant permanent shifts in the ecologies of the Amazon (and other regions), leaving notable reminders of extraction-oriented industries, hydrological shifts, and agro-industrial production on the watersheds, flora, and fauna of the region. At the same time, the renewed developmentalism involved a significant emphasis on strengthening governmental institutions for environmental enforcement and regulation. Along with the clear push for global economic integration through commodity production, environmental governance was a strategy offering prospects for reducing deforestation, quelling the "expansion" of the frontier, and substantially reducing or even eliminating rural land conflicts (Baletti 2012, 2014, Fearnside 2007a). Through formalizing relationships between civil society, researchers, the government, and private enterprise, political will to ensure forest conservation at the same time as massive infrastructure investments were taking place was thought by some close observers to be feasible (Nepstad et al. 2002, Campos and Nepstad 2006b, , Nepstad et al. 2014). Such moves involved threading a very fine needle between environmental protection and economic growth, however.[38] In fact, a striking drop in deforestation rates did occur in 2004, with rates precipitously declining by 70 percent over the next decade (Hecht 2011b, Nepstad et al. 2014, Rudel 2013). These declines in Amazonian deforestation can be credited to several factors. These include intensive management of the supply chains for soy and beef, widespread implementation of property registration systems, participatory forms of planning, a substantial increase in territories designated as new protected areas and extractive reserves, substantially improved enforcement regimes that penalized deforestation, and agreement upon new policies for forestry. (Nepstad et al. 2014, Hecht 2011b).

In the longer run, however, maintaining these policies and programs became a dubious prospect. In 2012 and 2013, the Brazilian government revised the Forest Code. In 2014 the size of several conservation areas in the Amazon was reduced, and this happened again between 2016–2017 as over a million hectares (25 million acres) of protected areas were proposed to be removed from protection. Coupled with changing land registration proposals and extensions, the uncertain legal and policy context for environmental protection led to upticks in deforestation. Serious concern was voiced by government ministers (speaking anonymously in the press) that Brazil was "backsliding" on land use and indigenous protections (Arsenault 2017). A stagnant national economy and severe cutbacks of the environmental agency budget (by over 40 percent in 2017) suggested that Amazonian conservation would be sacrificed to the perceived economic imperatives for increasing agricultural production and shrinking state spending (Nepstad et al. 2014, Patterson 2017).[39] One of President Jair Bolsonaro's first steps upon taking office in 2019 was to shift the authority to declare and demarcate indigenous territories from the Fundação Nacional do Índio, (the National Indian Foundation, FUNAI) to the Ministry of Agriculture. Such moves, along with his stated promises to gut the protections on conservation areas and criticism of the number of indigenous territories in the Amazon, gives the trajectory of mining and agribusiness a major boost while simultaneously causing grave concern for environmental and human rights interests.

Finding Common Ground within Sustainable Development

Instead of the traditional opposition between the developmentalist position, which sought to maximize growth and environmental conservation, the embrace of land organizing and environmental governance in the Amazon could be understood as following from a common set of problems (Baletti 2012, Brainard and Martinez-Diaz 2009).[40] Specifically, these logics contended that efficient production could be achieved in tandem with regulation of property rights and adequate mitigation of deforestation risks, thus enabling conditions for an Amazonian development strategy that involved substantial economic productivity, greater social equality, and also reduction and mitigation of environmental damage.

The new model of Amazonian conservation and development that is captured through the environmental governance model, however, remains almost inevitably contentious. As Brazilian socio-environmental activists began embracing renewed developmentalist strategies, increasingly they became implicated in processes oriented toward sustainable development and its policy outgrowths, namely, the "green economy" or what some social movement activists in the Amazon call "green capitalism." Environmental nongovernmental organizations play a substantial role as liaisons within this approach, enabling "participatory" approaches and channeling funding for territorial ordering and environmental planning which takes place at local levels. Environmental activists from across the spectrum of conservationists, socio-environmentalists, and those with more neoliberal orientations maintained a tenuous place of mutual understanding, and could come together to find common ground over land management decisions (Hecht 2011b, 2007). Local activists, as well as the everyday shopworkers, farmers, smallholders, and hired hands (who may be on the front lines but do not generally think of themselves as activists) often experience a subtle form of political control through their participation in environmental governance initiatives as stakeholders in the renewed developmentalist plans, becoming complicit in the green economy (Baletti 2014, Barbanti 2013). The alternative, also uncomfortable for many, is to become coopted by it as they collaborate with the powerful interests of state power, multilateral financial institutions, and global capital. Rather than reducing inequality and domination, this form of governance instead has a concerning tendency to reproduce inequality and the hegemonic power of the state, environmental NGOs (especially large ones), and multinational corporations, and destabilizes the resistance and political action that otherwise would stem from actors organized at local levels.

Articulations of sustainable development that derive from environmental governance are frequently refracted through other cultural and economic boundaries that comprise the diverse social fabric of Amazonian cities and towns. Sociologist Roberto Da Matta has observed that in Brazilian social life, institutional pressure is exerted from bureaucratic norms and laws, but a second key axis of pressure stems from "webs of personal relations to which all are subjected and by the social resources which these networks mobilize and distribute" (Da Matta 1987, 318). Local media outlets and politicians are often tied to families of wealthy businessmen, many of whom represent cattle ranching or logging interests. Those same groups often influence the civil police, typifying the dynamics of small-town Brazil where "everyone knows everyone." Nepotism, personal relationships, and trust are powerful influences in local political dynamics (Prado 1995). The more powerful interests of the economic elite and those "outside" of the politically left-leaning social movement activist groups press on social life in (usually) unspoken but ever-present ways. Not only are material interests and competing values often at stake, but also a fragile sense of trust and safety. Amazonian land conflicts are so frequently marked with death threats and assassinations that suspicions of betrayals and long-standing antagonisms run deep.

As the next chapter will detail, despite the continuous efforts beginning around the year 2000 to put concerted attention into public participation and projects involving road paving, which almost uniformly was perceived by residents, wealthy and poor alike, as something that would bring "progress" and "development," the region continued to wait for such developments to arrive. Sometimes the promise of these infrastructures was met with eagerness and other times with resignation. The road paving and ecological-economic zoning plans for the BR-163 highway area were very much a part of the modern project of sustainable development in the state of Pará. In the BR-163 highway region especially, the results involved shared experiences of grassroots actors being downtrodden by the decades of promises and subsequent failures to follow through on the modernist plans. In Ferguson's description, abjection from development entails a sense of betrayed promises and of being cast outward and downward from the fuller circle of humanity (1999). Despite decades of promises that desired infrastructures and land organizing initiatives would take place, and active public participation toward that goal, land use reversals and infrastructure implementation voids persisted for decades. The people who were left behind from sustainable development plans were often those living in the very spaces those plans were meant to most benefit.

Throughout its contemporary history, the Amazon has been in a process of being reimagined through the lens of sustainable development, which is the focal point of environmental governance. In this imaginary of sustainable development, Brazil has aimed to show the world that its global leadership will be one of strong economic growth as well as some degree of environmental protection in the Amazon, enforced through techno-managerialism. This imaginary is a derivative feature of modernity itself, even as, at times such as under the military dictatorship and in Jair Bolsonaro's presidency, nearly all semblance of environmental protection and most discourses of sustainable development fall by the wayside. Finding a path wherein agribusiness is responsible to commitments to zero deforestation, where hydropower does not damage waterways, and where mining operations do not inflict lasting damage upon the earth is an almost utopian view of what is possible for rural development in the Amazon. As environmental governance strategies take shape, multiple narratives implicating calls for sustainable development are evolving on an everyday basis. Prior to accepting any starry-eyed or doomsday scenario of regional transformation, one should closely examine how the realities of the various plans being made and policies being implemented are experienced on the level of those closest to such plans. The chapters which follow aim to do just this, examining the frictions, contradictions, and power relations that emerge as sustainable development plans and discourses take place in practice.

4

The Roads through the Forest

Modernizing Amazonia

In the Transamazon, the government made a colonization effort, but left them without the possibility for survival. The malaria was more constant, the rains were much harder, and they were outside of their place of origin, and the other factor was the direction that they had, it was incentives just for deforestation, clearing.

—Anapu resident, 2006

The end of the forest is the end of our lives.

—Sister Dorothy Stang

Just after dawn on the morning of February 12, 2005, Sister Dorothy Stang awoke and headed out of the farmer's thatched-roof wooden house where she had spent the night. Sister Dorothy was a 73-year-old Catholic nun, but she was a strong walker and early riser, full of ideas and energy. The struggle for land was heating up in a community where she worked called the Esperança (Hope) Project for Sustainable Development (*PDS-Esperança*). Sister Dorothy was there doing community organizing in solidarity with the landless and recently settled farmers who had moved there in hopes of making a life out of small-scale farming and sustainable community-based forestry. "Hope" was indeed an appropriate name for the project, given the struggle people faced merely to live on that land. In recent weeks several homes had been torched, and families were being evicted at gunpoint by the hired gunmen of the ranchers that also laid claim to the lands in the PDS.

Sister Dorothy was no stranger to violent land conflicts in Brazil. She had worked for over 25 years in some of Brazil's poorest communities since joining the Sisters of Notre Dame de Namur. She moved to Brazil in the mid-1980s, at first living in the state of Maranhão, and then moved to the Transamazon highway region (Transamazon) in 1983. Born and raised in Ohio, Sister Dorothy became a naturalized Brazilian citizen and worked with the colonists who began settling along the Transamazon highway in those early years of the region's colonization. At the outset, Sister Dorothy's work was a far cry from conflict-prone rabble-rousing. She helped start many schools, organized women's empowerment and entrepreneurship groups, and wrote grants for greater financial support to reach the region's impoverished newcomers and support the projects and businesses that they hoped to launch. She wrote grants for and helped install small-scale hydroelectric dams to give energy to places that were still off the grid, and helped the small town of Anapu become independent as a recognized municipality in 1996.[1] The Transamazon, in the state of Pará, became her adopted home. Sister Dorothy was widely loved by the communities in which she worked: she helped many young people in the region stay in school and find scholarships for their studies, and many of those students spoke about Sister Dorothy as if she were a second mother. They started knowing her through the Catholic Church youth groups, and she helped guide, mentor, and educate a cadre of Anapu's rising leaders. She facilitated the Transamazon highway settlers' processes of organizing associations that helped get agricultural production out to markets and helped to establish a small factory for processing fruit pulp used in yogurts and juices. Sister Dorothy was known for her perseverance; if she was told that a bureaucrat was not in the office, she had a reputation for smiling and then just camping out in the office to wait for their return. Sometimes it took days or weeks to get her business taken care of, but Sister Dorothy was not intimidated or easily deterred when challenging intransigent authorities or navigating the notoriously cumbersome paperwork of government administrative offices.

Sister Dorothy's involvements in land reform efforts grew slowly over the course of fifteen years of working in the Transamazon. In 2000, the federal government made some funding available for Amazonian Demonstration Projects, which helped to fund the fruit pulp factory and agricultural extension work for improving agroforestry and fruit cultivation in the region. It was challenging, long-term work, as one person close to those efforts recounted:

> The idea was to recuperate degraded areas and work with management and production of fruits, through *açaí*, and cultivating *cupuaçu*, soursop, pineapple, and bananas. . . . But it takes a really long time for this soil to be good again, for the plants to start producing in areas that are recuperated. (Interview with author 2006)

The fruit pulp factory proposal was the beginning of Sister Dorothy's growing vision for creating more viable approach to rural landholding and livelihoods in the region. "The end of the forest is the end of our lives," she said. Protecting the forest through planting economically beneficial crops, restoring the land, and helping poor farmers stay put on the land while quelling the ranching in the region became Sister Dorothy's life purpose. Concerned both about deforestation and about the tenuous production of farmers in the region, Sister Dorothy wrote up a proposal to create the Projects for Sustainable Development in 2001, explaining the rationale:

1. Approximately 95 percent of the citizens are Northeasterners who migrated (since 1972) in search of better days. As of the present, the vast majority have not found means of sustaining themselves aside from simple survival.
2. The colonization projects and settlements from INCRA have not demonstrated success, stemming from the fact that there was never technical assistance with these projects, which would have helped the agriculturalists to adapt their techniques and practices of cultivation from the Northeast to the Amazonian environment.
3. The reason that brought INCRA [Brazil's land reform agency] to create this new modality of agrarian reform, the PDS, is because in its own evaluations there is a clarity about the problems stated above. These serious and large problems end up with many well-intentioned agriculturalists selling their land parcels, and seeking betterment in nearby cities. When they do not find employment, many return to the countryside to work as farmhands. When they return to rural labor, they end up completing a [vicious] cycle, invading other parcels, because they cannot survive in the city or as farmhands.

The proposal Sister Dorothy crafted refers to many potential—and lofty—benefits that the PDS could offer: preserving forests and forest ecosystems; helping family farmers make self-sustaining use of natural resources; combining agricultural and agroforestry systems with healthy ecological equilibrium and the healthy quality of life and forest resources on land holdings; education and technical assistance for families to be able to have more permanence on their lands and thereby avoid the indiscriminate sale of land parcels. Steering incentives for alternative technologies that are appropriate, with development that is socially just and ecologically adapted for the area, were part of the main rationale for the PDSs. So, too, according to Sister Dorothy's proposal, was a conservationist goal wherein the forest could be defended from "indiscriminate invasions from loggers and ranchers that were destroying the forest as their single source of income." There were two PDS projects for Anapu that were ultimately approved by INCRA: one on the northern side of the Transamazon highway, called PDS Virola-Jatobá, and the other to the south of the road was Esperança. In both areas, though most controversially within Esperança, many of the land parcels within them remained in dispute, despite INCRA's approval. The notoriously long and complicated process of Brazilian land regularization and agrarian reform unfolded with typical slowness in the PDSs. While it may seem confusing to some readers that Brazil's land reform agency approved of the projects and yet did not fully arbitrate and demarcate the land parcels within them, the phenomenon is commonplace and is attributable to the complexity and bureaucratic magnitude of Brazilian land and property laws. Not only do agrarian reform settlements take at least several years, on average, to become official, but INCRA itself is reputed as a notoriously corrupt agency. INCRA often butts heads with environmental protection activists. In the Amazon, for example, INCRA has a history of intentionally encouraging settlers to make contracts with logging companies and settling families on protected forest land rather than already-cleared areas (Valente 2008). The result in Anapu was one of frequent and violent conflicts between Sister Dorothy's landless farmers who primarily sought out agricultural land, and larger landholders, who had logging and cattle ranching aspirations and controlled their claims to each lot by the force of hired gunmen.

One rancher especially, called Tato, was causing problems for the PDS settlers in the Esperança project. Claiming that some of the lots where the PDS was to be implemented were in fact his property, he and some other ranchers had already filed allegations that Sister Dorothy was organizing a militia together with the farmers. Ranchers like Tato were powerful and had strong ties to local businesses and politics. Local officials along with the ranchers aimed to isolate and intimidate Sister Dorothy from having any influence and had officially passed a resolution declaring her *persona non grata* in Anapu. The mayor of Anapu once publicly said: "We have to get rid of that woman if we are going to have peace" (Dear 2007). Sister Dorothy received overt death threats, and, over time, the ranchers amassed a $20,000 USD bounty for her assassination.

Sister Dorothy faced a serious threat, but it was also one that was not particularly unusual in the world of Pará's agrarian struggles, given the region's infamy for its high rates of violent land conflicts. Around the time that Sister Dorothy ran into trouble, 34 percent of the reported death threats in all of Brazil stemmed from land conflicts in Pará (Campbell 2006). Land tensions were so acute that the state concentrated 40 percent of all assassinations in Brazil's rural areas between 2003 and 2005, and around one hundred forty people received death threats ("Pará Concentra" 2005, Rohter 2005). Figure 4.1 illustrates incidents of rural land conflicts in Pará from a historical perspective.

Given these realities, many activists saw the writing on the wall as far as Sister Dorothy's fate was concerned. They were dismayed but helpless to alter the course of events, much though they tried to protect her.[2] When Sister Dorothy encountered two men waiting for her along the road of PDS Esperança on the morning of February 12, 2005, most accounts suggest that she already knew this would be her last conversation.

The scene of the assassination is one frequently told in detail by those living in the region at the time. Instead of facing an ignominious death, as so many of

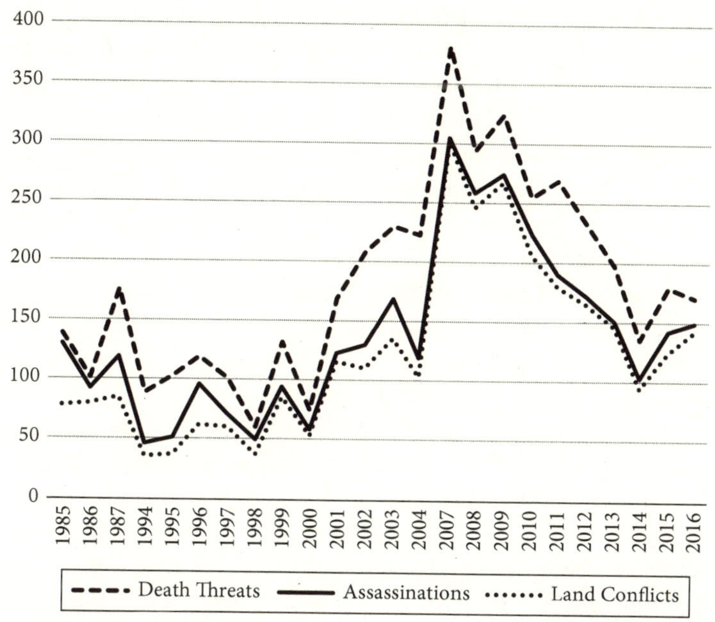

Figure 4.1 Violence in the state of Pará reached precipitously high rates by 2007 and spiked significantly between 2004–2007 (although data is not available for each of those years). Although a tight statistical correlation is not present, it is notable that deforestation during that same interval fell significantly. Chapters 4, 5, and 6 detail the most significant land use and infrastructure changes that were taking place in Pará during this time, which include the creation of conservation areas in the Terra do Meio, the establishment of Projects for Sustainable Development land reform settlements, and the BR-163 Sustainable Forest District.

the assassinations over land conflicts entail, Sister Dorothy's assassination became something of a local legend, and she is considered a modern-day martyr. Accounts from bystanders attested that Sister Dorothy tried to persuade the hit men that their boss, whose land they were planting pasture grass on, was illegally using land that was in fact part of the PDS. The men weren't there to talk, however. Conversation failing, one of the hired gunmen, Rayfran, pointed his .38 caliber gun at her. She pulled out her Bible to read: "Blessed are the pure in heart, for they shall see God. Blessed are the meek, for they shall inherit the earth. Blessed are they who hunger and thirst after righteousness . . . " Four shots were fired. Her blood mixed with the orange-colored clay soils as the February rains poured down in the forest (le Breton 2007, Murphy 2007, Rohter 2005). The physical blood shed over land is a powerful symbol and reminder commonly narrated by people living in the PDSs as a testament to Sister Dorothy's work for a cause worth fighting for. The idea that up until the very last moments of her life Sister Dorothy maintained humility and steadfast faith is also often remarked upon by those living in the PDSs, offered as an example through which to find inspiration and courage.

The assassination was front page news around the world; the Associated Press (2005) assessed that "The killing made her the most celebrated person to die defending the rain forest since Chico Mendes, the rubber tapper and guardian of the Amazon who was slain in 1988." The association of Sister Dorothy's life and struggle with Chico Mendes' was not lost on anyone. Most scholars acknowledge that Chico Mendes did not die in vain (Hall 1996, Allegretti 1995), but it is understandable that local activists wondered how much progress had truly been made. Sister Dorothy's death reverberated in the region with handwringing by other regional activists that she was "too isolated" and "all alone" in Anapu. Local activists expressed anger, regret, a sense of isolation, and tried to keep their fears at bay that nothing significant would change despite all the hardships they were experiencing. "We're all incensed, but at the same time we're also very afraid," Ana Paula Santos Souza, another local activist, told reporters (Rohter 2005).

In the immediate aftermath of Sister Dorothy's death, the government stationed 2,000 troops in Anapu in hopes of establishing a calming presence in the region. Yet the violence in the PDSs flared back up again once they left.[3] The international outcry and posthumous fame for Sister Dorothy was resounding, but when I visited Anapu less than a year after her death, another nun working there told me, "we need to find some other sort of presence" in the PDSs. Father José Amaro, who in many senses was Sister Dorothy's successor to the PDS work, was also based in Anapu and facing serious death threats.[4] Two people died in another land-related conflict in April 2006. Even less could be said for the land regularization processes and the illegal deforestation happening in the PDSs.

Sister Dorothy's story evokes a number of questions about how sustainable development plans take shape in practice: How did the settlers view the possibilities for a better economic and environmental future on the lands of the Projects for Sustainable Development? How did the Brazilian federal government conjoin domestic environmental governance, security, and development aims while planning to pave the Amazonian roads along which they lived?

This chapter focuses on the unevenness of influence and the tensions that were present as sustainable development planning, in the form of both highway paving and agrarian reform, and other land organizing plans for protecting the rainforest, occurred. The discussion centers upon both the Transamazon highway where Sister Dorothy worked and upon the BR-163 highway, which runs perpendicular to the Transamazon through the state of Pará. Through this case study of land use planning, this chapter reveals the contingencies and portrays the developmental and ecological modernization-oriented politics of the Brazilian state as a process of environmental governance that is fraught with contradictions and divergent ideals. The conflicts that emerge through this process ultimately lead to an entrenchment of social and land use patterns that tend to exacerbate violence, forest loss, and inequality rather than ameliorate such concerns.

The north–south axis route, BR-163 (Cuiabá–Santarém highway) connects Cuiabá, a city in the agricultural heartland of Mato Grosso, to Santarém, a port town where the Tapajós and Amazon Rivers merge. The BR-230, more commonly referred to as the Transamazon highway, goes east–west from Brazil's João Pessoa on the Atlantic coast for some 4,000 km to the small jungle town of Lábrea in the state of Amazonas. Sister Dorothy's work in Anapu took place along the Transamazon highway, just east of Altamira and the Belo Monte dam site. Anapu is an independent municipality with a 2016 population of 26,271.[5] The Transamazon highway did become paved near Anapu, with the paving work starting in 2011. Both of these roads were made of pressed dirt in their Pará sections for most of the research that informs this chapter. Asphalt only stretches for a few kilometers outside of each city along their routes.

Roads as Amazonian Development Infrastructures

There are two important conceptual foundations for understanding the ideals that are negotiated within the sustainable development framework in this particular story: modernization and the developmental state. The central axis of Brazilian modernization-oriented strategies during the 1964–1985 military dictatorship years were policies encouraging an industrially focused and export-oriented model of production, spurring massive civil construction project investments in roads, mining, hydroelectric dams, and industries (Fiechter 1975). While little was done during this time to prevent or even to mitigate environmental and social costs of such projects in Brazil, it is noteworthy that globally, the ecological modernization framework came about alongside the sustainable development concept, taking hold by the late 1980s. Positing that no radical sociopolitical restructuring was necessary, minimal environmental costs were seen by state planners as something that would reinforce economic growth. Foundational principles of ecological modernization are the reliance upon technological innovation and macro-economic restructuring, through which both economic growth and environmental quality might be simultaneously achieved (Sezgin 2013).

In practice, a number of factors may affect the likelihood of achieving a successful ecological modernization strategy. Other conducive or even required conditions for ecological modernization include industrialization, regulatory oversight by the state over the market, the presence of innovative companies, strong educational systems, substantial environmental awareness, high purchasing power, open democratic systems, participatory schemes of policymaking, and environmental institutions (Milanez and Bührs 2008). Despite the fact that risk management in the form of the precautionary principle, integrated regulation, and market-based incentives are underpinnings of ecological modernization, the approach "avoids addressing basic contradictions in capitalism" (Christoff 1996, 486). The risk management approach does, however, respond to environmentalist concerns about neoliberalism's deregulatory tendencies (Pepper 1998).

The second theoretical foundation for understanding state rationale in the case of these road paving projects is the role of the developmental state (Hochstetler and Montero 2013). The strength of the Brazilian National Development Bank (BNDES), especially from 2001–2010, bolstered industrial growth, infrastructure, and energy sector projects considerably, with a central emphasis on export-oriented economic strategies (Ban 2012).[6] State-led investments, with an emphasis on transportation infrastructure improvements and connectivity between Amazonian territory and the rest of South America, remain a crucial factor for explaining the fragilities of Brazilian policies as well as their assertive strengths (Kanai and da Silva Oliveira 2014, Morais and Saad-Filho 2012).

Establishing a road network was a centerpiece of the federal government's ambitious project of the 1970s to make the Amazon an economically productive region that was integrated with the rest of the country. Cutting roads through the Amazon was prioritized in 1970 within a national development strategy known as the Project for National Integration (PIN). By creating a network of road infrastructure and settlements in the vast rainforest, it was hoped that new flows of goods, services, and people into the Amazon would benefit the region as never before, and all of Brazil would prosper. The north and south of the country would become connected through the Cuiabá–Santarém highway (BR-163), linking production centers with distribution ports and providing a basis for the lands themselves to be controlled and traversed. The Transamazon highway (BR-230) would similarly connect the eastern coast of Brazil with the farthest western reaches of the Amazon. Other primary road arteries, such as the Belém–Brasília highway, the Cuiabá–Porto Velho, and the *Perimetral Norte* highway (BR-210) also would receive funding in the early 1970s. During this time, these highways were cut but never fully paved. They remained dusty in the Amazonian summer months and muddy throughout the rainy season.

Roads in the Amazon are a rather overdetermined subject as "technologies of destruction" (Campbell 2012a), because so often they are thought to be singularly associated with land speculation and deforestation. Yet roads also are a material form that captures the political and ideational values of economic development, modernization, and social improvements in physical form. As central sites of state-building processes and cultural transformation, the physical realities of roads are not the only features which determine their role in these processes; they are also bound up in people's uses, imaginaries, and figurative relationships, through which they make the material and the ideational-level existence of the road (Campbell 2012a, Hetherington and Campbell 2014, Scott 1998).

Most accounts of Amazonian development suggest that road paving is inimical to achieving conservation goals. The highway projects begun in the Amazon during the 1970s epitomized many of the problems of Brazil's military rule (Chernela 2005, Fearnside 2002, Schmink and Wood 1992). History's lessons indicated that with the advent of these projects, the small-scale farmers and standing forests of the region would both be harmed (Goodland and Irwin 1975, Godar et al. 2012, Godar, Tizado, and Pokorny 2012). Some worried that those failures and disappointments would only be repeated as Brazil's economy was rising in the early 2000s. Millions of dollars were being spent to promote agribusiness through constructing a port for soybean exportation and construction of massive logistical infrastructures, including highway paving projects on both the Transamazon and BR-163 highways.

Operation Amazonia and the developmentalist strategies of the 1970s and 1980s were retrofitted into the sustainable development strategies of the new millennium through a process of political articulation. More people of the region sought out engagements with the state, and government bureaucrats appeared to have more nuanced familiarity with the realities and expectations of local residents. As highways were planned for paving in the twenty-first century, they seemed to offer new attention to people's needs and to more adequately respond to conservationists' concerns. Locally, many residents instead embraced these plans in ways that were intimate and instrumental. At the same time as people publicly showed a willingness to engage and interact with the state, their engagements often blurred between the illegal and the legal (Campbell 2012b).

In the early 2000s, tandem seriousness in achieving national environmental and economic goals oriented the new vision for roads as socially responsible and compatible with conservation-oriented land use planning. Understanding the practices and concerns of citizens was a federal governmental priority, manifested in practices of participatory consultation throughout the region. On the other hand, through their participation, people became reconfigured as both willing allies and hands-tied-behind-their-backs adversaries of sustainable development governance.

Amazonian Roads and Territorial Control

Induced in the 1970s by governmental campaigns to "open up" and "develop" the region, poor families came from all over Brazil to Amazonia.[7] Under the plans, settlers along the roads would gain land, the government's installation of military bases in the region would help national security, and the eventual road paving intended for the region would establish strong local economies. In conjunction, mining operations would be encouraged, and development of major dams along some of the Amazonian rivers aimed to significantly bolster the nation's industrial growth and energy production (Moran 1981).

Critics of the strategy, both in Brazil and internationally, saw the settlers as nothing short of foreign invaders who threatened the safety and integrity of indigenous peoples, who were unable to productively use the land, and who irresponsibly exploited its natural resources (Barbanti 2013, Almeida 1992, Lisansky 1990). Satellite pictures show the forest loss along the Transamazon following a fishbone pattern, with deforestation extending from the highway spine through perpendicular access roads. The same pattern is true with the BR-163 and most Amazonian highway colonization: loggers have access to the forest through the main roads, as do farmers who penetrate the road edges, claiming and clearing land for crops. Over time, the once-forested territories become degraded while landholdings consolidate in the hands of cattle ranchers for use as pasture.[8]

Since they were first cut in 1972 and 1973, respectively, the proposals to pave both the Transamazon (BR-230) and the BR-163 highways were often floated and were politically appealing, but just as quickly those plans were abandoned due to inadequate planning, lack of financial resources, unsuitable working conditions, or some combination of the three. The pressed-dirt roads of the BR-163 and Transamazon highways involved slow and precarious traveling conditions (See Figure 4.2). Trucks were frequently stuck in muddy potholes along the roads when the Amazonian rains were heavy, and the dusty conditions for travelers in the dry season caused respiratory illnesses.

The plans for paving the Amazonian highways would not materialize for nearly forty years. Despite the stacked odds, many poor farmers were smitten by enticing slogans that convinced them that Amazonia offered "land without people for people without land"[9] and a place to make new dreams become possible as pioneers.

> . . . the military regime understood that it would have to attract [the poor] there by promises of land grants, schools, health clinics, and housing. The government hoped to lure people to the Amazon with the promise of land, not only, and perhaps not mainly, to clear new agricultural land, but also to use these people as labour for road and hydroelectric dam building, timber extraction, mining enterprises, partly and precisely because agricultural settlements would in many cases fail. (Perfecto, Vandermeer, and Wright 2009, 111)

Figure 4.2 Transportation challenges along the unpaved BR-163 highway include steep inclines, muddy roads, and precarious bridges. Photo: Eve Bratman (2007)

Even after the government-sponsored colonization effort ended, people continued settling along the new roads, seeking greater opportunity and hoping that conditions would be bountiful for agriculture on lush Amazonian lands. One colonist who had come to the region in the 1970s explained:

> I was always in agriculture, then I was in civil construction but I went back to agriculture working back here in the Transamazon; I didn't want to live always

> working for others. I wanted to live for myself. I didn't have experience with conditions to do work, I think too it was about dignity . . . I wanted to work for myself, and for this I moved to Anapu, and live there through today. (Interview with author 2006)

The disappointments experienced by the once-intrepid colonists were numerous; malaria was rampant, the soil was difficult to work with, and the incentives seemed stacked against small-scale farmers. "We had nothing, we needed everything," one of the region's settlers described, remembering the hardship she faced. "Misery" and "stuck" were words commonly used to describe the settlers' experiences. The cash crops the Transamazon agriculturalists planted had poor yields,[10] and significant agricultural losses were also experienced because of grassland bird predation and rice crops rotting or getting eaten by pests before they could be brought to market (Smith 1978). In contrast, larger-scale ranchers received both subsidies and land, enough to hire day laborers to manage their properties from afar.

For many newcomers, the promise of free land in the Amazon never resulted in secure tenure through land titles. Expectations for social services were also unmet; the new settlers lacked knowledge of traditional medicines and had no local hospitals. They were understandably afraid of the enormous snakes and jaguars they encountered near their doorsteps. Even with the highway just steps away, they had few institutions to turn to for help and often were stuck along the road, rather than mobile. People living along the highways joked that the Amazon's two seasons are not the rainy and the dry season but rather the muddy and the dusty.

One longtime resident of the region described the hardship in tandem with the operative logics of labor exploitation that occurred as the region was colonized:

> These colonists were brought here and then were used . Principally in Anapu it was terrible, the government came in without organization, it [land] wasn't demarcated, and the objective was directly for the large landholders, since there wasn't energy, no electricity, and they [the ranchers] lived in São Paulo and the big [urban] centers, but sometimes brought their functionaries here to do slave labor, day labor, really slave labor as hired gunmen, and they didn't want to work here. (Interview with author 2006)

As the quote above makes clear, the difficulties of living and working in the region were formidable. There were health challenges and disappointments in terms of agricultural productivity. In addition, many people, especially young men, who came to the region induced to work as hired hands for bigger landholders would often find themselves in isolated circumstances where they were unpaid and tasked with "guard duties" to maintain the boundaries of the landholder's claim. Working as hired gunmen, given the absence of a trusted police presence in the region, their role was to threaten violence against other would-be claimants to the land, who themselves were frequently poor agriculturalists seeking land to farm. The struggle for land was linked to a host of social oppressions and was bound together by the inconsistent and generally insufficient presence of the Brazilian state.

The trajectory of many settlers along the BR-163 involved larger-scale land acquisitions and settlement that took place almost a decade after the Transamazon wave of colonization. One resident explained his family history: His father arrived to Castelo de Sonhos, in the south of Pará, in 1981, seeking to buy land and to "economize the road." They came with the good intentions of "integrating the Amazon to not surrender it" (*integrar para não entregar*), but there were many promises left unfulfilled. The populations along the highways continued to grow, though the colonization efforts were generally lacking in coordination and organization, and accurate data concerning how many people were settling in the region and where they were settling was nearly impossible to obtain. Table 4.1 shows the change in population in the major municipalities of pertinence to this discussion starting in the early 1990s, when such records became (somewhat) more accurate.

Along BR-163 in the early 1980s, colonists were asked to register themselves, and this helped encourage people that moved north into Pará along BR-163 to get designated as colonists so that they could qualify for land and agricultural credits. Still, the colonization was rather opportunistic, with settlers seeking out whatever livelihood paid the best income, as suggested by the interview excerpted below.

> We came to work on the land, the tillage was principally rice, but there was gold in the wildcat mining operations [*garimpos*] . . . I got about 80 different malarias, and ultimately this was the cause of my stopping work as a diver in the Curuá river *garimpo*; I had no money left to buy cattle, but also had a love for the land . . . like a bug! It gets into your system and you can't get it out!" (Interview with author 2007)

This interviewee laughed at his own predicament, wrapping up the telling of this brief history of his livelihood in the region. Along BR-163, property speculation was rampant, and social descriptors became clearly demarcated between the *pequenos* and *grandes*; that is, the smallholders that once were the peons (*peão*), and the large landholders and landlords who were once the patrons (*patrões*). Those terms "pointed to emancipatory futures," writes anthropologist Jeremy Campbell, "even as they retained a whiff of the clientelistic past" (Campbell 2015,

Table 4.1 Population of Municipalities near the Transamazon and BR-163 Highways

Year	Altamira	Anapu	Brasil Novo	Medicilândia	Novo Progresso	Vitória do Xingu	Pará (state)	Brazil (national)
1991	72,408	-	-	29,728	-	-	4,950,060	146,825,475
1996	75,384	-	13,940	30,858	14,647	12,778	5,466,141	156,032,944
2000	77,439	9,407	17,193	21,379	24,948	11,142	6,192,307	169,799,170
2007	92,105	17,787	18,749	22,624	21,598	9,693	7,065,573	183,987,291
2010	99,075	20,543	15,690	27,328	25,124	13,431	7,581,051	190,755,799
2016	109,938	26,271	14,834	30,315	25,102	14,566	8,272,724	209,567,920

Source: https://cidades.ibge.gov.br. For simplicity, several of the less-populated municipalities in the region are omitted.

50). While the social differentiation was common throughout the region, the meanings were often very context-dependent. The landholding sizes were much greater along the BR-163 than for settlers along the Transamazon; the *pequenos* along the BR-163 often held between 100–500 hectares, and the *grandes* more like 2,500 hectares (about 6,000 acres). The Transamazon settlers, in contrast, had around 50 hectares (124 acres) for a smallholder, and above 500 hectares (1,236 acres) were considered *grande* (Pokorny 2013). Many aspired to own cattle, as ranching is associated positively in Luso-Brazilian culture, and peasants tend to describe cattle ranching as involving less arduous and more leisurely work (Smith 1982).

The Rise of Social Movement Activism

In response to the challenges of settlement along the roads in the 1970s, colonists began to organize, at first through the Catholic Church and grassroots ecclesiastical communities. Through regular meetings between 1972 and 1985, a generation of activists became educated, gaining training within church groups and unions. The military dictatorship's repression left little room for protest and social movement mobilization. With the loosening of censorship and freedoms that were allowed as Brazil transitioned into democracy, the activists in the Transamazon region formed an organization called the Movement for Survival on the Transamazon (MPST). The MPST was an umbrella group for farmer cooperatives, labor unions, women's groups, and others in civil society living along the highway.[11] They became a political force to be reckoned with; some 300 activists in the movement marched the 1,891 kilometers from Altamira to Brasília in 1991 to make their demands for emergency medical assistance, educational support, agricultural credits, and improvements to the road (MMA 2006). Most MPST members also had ties to the Workers' Party (PT), and were able to leverage those ties as, gradually, communication channels with the government opened. Links with the rural workers' unions also helped to gain credits for rural agriculturalists and to launch programs for supporting housing credits, agricultural extension visits, and crop commercialization. The highway remained unpaved, however, and much was left to be desired, still, in terms of strengthening agricultural support, education, health care, and land tenure in the region.

In addition to the MPST's march to Brasília, local activists campaigned with the hope of drawing attention to the many needs of the people in the region. They advocated for schools, labor rights, health concerns, women's issues, and land reform. They also organized around some of the more horrific episodes of violence that marked everyday life in Altamira and elsewhere along the Transamazon highway. Most notably, the women's movement in Altamira was sparked by the brutal "emasculation case," which involved the abductions, castrations, and murders of over a dozen young boys.[12] Life on the Transamazon was brutally hard, both because it had been marked by incidents of social trauma and because of the sheer difficulty of living in such an inhospitable climate. While the international community voiced concerns about the links between road-cutting, colonization, and deforestation, the local conversations about what the region needed focused on requesting a greater governmental presence in the region in order to access basic services and have the rule of law upheld.

There was little to replace or transition out of the clientelist relations with patrons that often accompanied the experience of poverty in Brazil. Substituting the patron for the state, many frequently voiced the concern that "there is an absence of government," which, despite the past failings, was thought to be a presence bringing a greater level of rule of law and social and economic opportunities for the population. The sustainable development framework offered to invoke the renewed attentions of the state upon the region, doing so through renewed attempts at organizing land, generating economic productivity, and transforming the Amazonian territories.

Conservation, Land Reform, and Justice: Sister Dorothy's Mixed Legacy

Sister Dorothy's assassination in 2005 had some uncanny similarities to the land conflicts and environmental struggles that have persisted in the Amazon since the 1970s, when the region experienced a wave of newcomers including many people with interests in getting wealthy quickly through logging and cattle ranching. Beyond Sister Dorothy and Chico Mendes, there were the losses of Wilson Pinheiro, Father Josimo, and about forty other people advocating for land rights nearly every year for the prior two decades. When, if ever, would it end? In the immediate aftermath of Sister Dorothy's murder there was some reason to suspect that things would be different now, thought the people living in the region. Marina Silva, Chico Mendes' longtime ally, was in office as the Minister of Environment; Luiz Inácio "Lula" da Silva of the Worker's Party (PT), a longtime favorite of leftist activists, finally became President of Brazil in 2003, having run unsuccessfully for the position since 1989. Doors were more open to social movement activists than before, and many longtime activists were now in positions of political power. Things *had* to be different now, people frequently reassured themselves when I inquired along these lines.

The rest of the region, outside of Anapu, received significant attention in the aftermath of Sister Dorothy's death, although in highly uneven ways. In Altamira, the principal nearby city located about three hours' drive (137 km) away from Anapu, the government established a base for the Federal Police and established a federal public prosecutor's office. This served as a formidable resource for defending peoples' interests within the legal system. In response to the local and international outcry over the murder of Sister Dorothy Stang, the government took emergency actions to show the global public that it was able to maintain law and order in the Amazon. At the brink of making Amazonian logging concessions only one week before, the Brazilian Congress reversed its position and tightened restrictions on sawmills.

An immediate step was also taken the week of Dorothy Stang's death to spur environmental protection in the region. A series of conservation areas were created in the Terra do Meio (Lands of the Middle) area of the Xingu River basin, covering nearly seven million hectares (17 million acres) of forested lands. These areas are discussed in greater detail in Chapter 6, but a brief explanation is also merited here. The Terra do Meio region is a mosaic comprised of several different types of conservation areas that range in their degree of environmental preservation aims. The region is composed of indigenous reserves, fully protected ecological stations, and national parks, as well as areas where sustainable use of the forest is permitted for people with historical land rights in the area, such as the extractive reserves. To the north of the Terra do Meio, in addition to the RESEX Verde Para Sempre that had just been created, the government planned to create three additional RESEXs in the Terra do Meio along the Xingu and its tributary rivers, the Iriri and Riozinho do Anfrísio. By 2008, the official process of creating the Terra do Meio conservation area mosaic was completed. A total of 28 million hectares (69 million acres) were dedicated as protected areas, with some 215 riverine families gaining the formal protections and rights to remain on their lands (Schwartzman et al. 2013, Nepstad et al. 2006). Combined, the area was one of the world's largest contiguous conservation corridors.

Brazilian officials from all over the country attended Sister Dorothy's funeral. Locally, however, the land conflicts over many of the parcels continued to be disputed directly in the PDSs. The residents in the PDSs themselves saw little by way of local benefits or governmental attention. In the aftermath of her death, a local office of the federal land reform agency, INCRA, was opened in Anapu. That office was inadequately funded, however, and within two years shut its doors. For the residents in the PDSs near Anapu, very little changed in terms of land title disputes, and there was little new investment or support for the small-scale agriculture taking place there.

Sister Dorothy's death did put a spotlight on the question of impunity in the Amazon. The high-profile quest for justice as her assassins were brought to trial was a consistent national news story for about a year.[13] Many close observers, both internationally and in the region, held some hope that because Sister Dorothy was an American, international attention would help yield some quick action in the region and justice for the gunmen and those who ordered her assassination. Songs and even an opera were written in her honor, and a Hollywood film was made about her life and impunity in the Amazon. Locally, an annual pilgrimage involving a walk from her grave in Anapu to the site of her assassination inside PDS Esperança continues to keep the memory of her struggle vivid.[14] Sister Dorothy Stang's loss is a tragic one, but it is far from unique. The Pastoral Land Commission reports that since 1985, 975 murders related to land disputes have been reported in Brazil, more than 200 of which were in the state of Pará. Between 2002–2013, at least 908 environmental and land rights activists were killed worldwide, and 448 of them were in Brazil (Global Witness 2014). Of 1,115 homicides associated with agrarian conflicts in Brazil between 1985–2014, only twelve have been brought to trial (Pontes 2016). A twelve-year high of rural assassinations took place in 2015, with fifty assassinations and fifty-nine death threats recorded by the Pastoral Land Commission (CPT 2015). In early 2016, land conflicts were again so prominent in Anapu that locals requested a return of federal troops to help maintain peace in the region (Couto 2016). Impunity within the Brazilian justice system remains an ongoing challenge, and agrarian conflicts remain a point of serious concern.

The Sustainable Development Projects in Anapu

The Projects for Sustainable Development in Anapu represented a proof-of-concept for a model for merging environmental interests with agrarian reform. The vision for the PDSs entailed encouragement of agroforestry practices, achieved through active training and agricultural extension activities. The regulations for residents in the PDS involved stipulations that the community could collectively manage its forested lands, with strict adherence to the federal laws (often ignored and unenforced) that 80 percent of the land be set aside as a forest reserve. Farming livelihoods could be augmented through commercialization of forest resources, including fruits, Brazil nuts, and timber from designated forest plots, which would be sustainably harvested. Some forest products from the PDSs were meant to be processed and sold at a small-scale level, as well; a woodworking workshop trained PDS residents to produce artisan furniture from fallen woods in the forest, and women would sell their handicrafts—frequently, painted tea towels, magnets, or bead jewelry made from forest seeds—in local markets. The nearby fruit pulp processing plant established by Sister Dorothy and other activists had the capacity to process and freeze the fruits for commercial sales as fruit juice pulp, flavored yogurt, and banana chips. The agronomists and agricultural extension agents that worked with the PDS farmers were Sister Dorothy's longtime mentees, and they did regular outreach and support work in those communities. They offered the settlers seeds, transportation help, fruit commercialization, and advice on their farming practices, among myriad other forms of assistance.

Long vilified as culprits of Amazonian deforestation, small-scale migrants living along the Transamazon highway were once regularly blamed for the burning of the forest.[15] This impression was changing, however, and a more positive impression was bolstered by the PDS model. While colonists, especially historically, played a role on the front lines of deforestation, they were also victims of misguided political and economic systems that incentivized them to come to the Amazon and subsequently offered them no support. Relative to other types of activities such as cattle ranching, the contribution of the small-scale farmers to deforestation is in fact relatively minor (Barber et al. 2014, Binswanger 1991, Pfaff 1999, Godar et al. 2014, Schneider et al. 2015). Sister Dorothy and other activists in the region raised the prospect that the small-scale farmers of the Transamazon, like the *seringueiros* who had also once learned to live in the Amazon region through gathering Brazil nuts, tapping latex, and practicing small-scale agriculture, could make a sustainable livelihood through living on the Amazonian lands in responsible ways (Pacheco 2009b, le Breton 2007).

The PDS modality aimed to present an Amazonian land reform project that responded to critiques that smallholders were unfit for forest conservation.[16] In the PDSs along the Transamazon highway where Sister Dorothy worked, the goal of achieving an alternative development vision of small-scale family farming in conjunction with forest preservation is situated on an uneasy middle ground of identity articulation, wherein the newer settlers to the region must convincingly portray themselves as partners in conservation (Conklin and Graham 1995, Bratman 2011). Moreover, the PDSs are often in a liminal status between environmental and agrarian reform regulations because they are subject both to forest management regimes and stringent environmental protection laws, in addition to being beholden to the institutional oversight of the agrarian reform agency, INCRA. Community-based forest management is the primary means of generating a supplemental income to farming for the communities where Sister Dorothy worked. In the face of largely unviable slash-and-burn agricultural practices, no extra capital for investments, and low-productivity agricultural practices, the settlers in Projects for Sustainable Development require an extra degree of commitment to environmental protection, heightened community organization levels so that community-based forestry can take place, and significantly more bureaucratic interfacing than an independent small-scale farmer would require.

The challenges of achieving legalized community-based forest management as a viable income source in the PDSs was particularly vexing. A community association was formed in 2002 in PDS Virola-Jatobá, where Sister Dorothy worked, and in 2006 they opted to make an agreement with a private logging company to conduct community forest management on their lands. The outlook seemed optimistic at this point for many settlers:

> I used to hear the Sister (Dorothy Stang) say: "soon management will be in your hands, then you will be able to extract timber and it will help you to survive so you don't have to deforest the rest of the property." This was a distant dream! [. . .] But now I think it has worked! I think there is still a lack of organization here in the community, we should be on an equal footing with the company! (Settler in the Virola-Jatobá PDS, 45 years old, Anapu, Pará, quoted in Mendes and Porro 2015, 101)

Years would go by, however, before the community could ever viably manage its forest and gain profits from it, and meanwhile the temptation to log illegally permeated into the PDS as well. An institutionally vulnerable context set the stage for initial struggles within the community, involving both logging companies and rule-shifting of IBAMA and INCRA. The first logging company in the community made an agreement with the PDS, but subsequently closed due to financial insolvency. Soon thereafter, another private partner was found, but they had somewhat less rigorous standards in place for environmentally sound timber extraction, and this led to conflict and further delays. The unstable institutional context also contributed to the predicament. Until 2012, the government accepted a document called a Promise for Buying and Selling (PCV) that functioned as a legal right to land use, where certain plots of land could permissibly be used for sawmills even without the titling of that land being fully resolved. An abrupt shift occurred later that year under the newly rewritten federal Forest Code, however, which mandated that logging companies must hold full title to the land, not just usufruct rights.[17] This affected many of the logging companies operating throughout the region, halting most of their operations or at least throwing them back into the realm of illegal or semilegal status. For the PDS Virola-Jatobá residents, who were just initiating community forest management, the new law meant another upheaval. The government banned operations by the logging companies working with the communities. As these regulations changed, it became clear that in fact, no substantial community forest management practices could remain viable in practice, given the lack of economic capital and legal barriers to defend the smallholders' rights to use lands within the constraints of changing rules over land use, and the tandem looting of timber resources within the PDS areas by illegal loggers (Mendes and Porro 2015). No substitute means for capital and specialized services was arranged for the PDS residents, who had worked for two years to try to get their forest management plans approved.

The result of the several years work of formulating community forest management plans was a whole host of new conflicts that arose within the PDS. Between the rule-shifting of IBAMA and INCRA and the simultaneous absence of enforcement from those agencies to regularize land holdings and combat illegal logging, the families of the PDS were left in a bind: any logging would be considered illegal and face penalties, but waiting for legality to manage the forest led to a race to the bottom where rulebreakers benefited as rule followers became increasingly frustrated. Understandably, the PDS communities became demoralized in the face of these events. Allegations ran rampant of people cutting down their trees to prevent encroachments from other predatory loggers, and the community structures that had been in place for forest management on the collective lands began to implode with infighting and the frustration of legal paralysis. The PDS communities were unable to create new contracts for sustainably managing their forested lands, distrustful even of many of their own community institutions, and simultaneously unable to remove already-felled trees because of the regulatory regime in place.[18] As of this writing, the PDS residents and others in the region where family farming is taking place experience a bind, wherein the only feasible legal alternative left for farmers is that of burning any trees still standing in agricultural fields, and that is what frequently occurs.

In the year following Sister Dorothy's assassination, illegal land-claiming and deforestation abated somewhat in the municipality of Anapu. In subsequent years, however, it rose to being near the top of the list of Amazonian municipalities with the highest increase in deforestation (INPE 2012). Table 4.2 illustrates the substantial increases in deforestation in Anapu and surrounding municipalities.

As of this writing, some fifteen years after Sister Dorothy's death, the settlers continue to face internal disputes and institutional shifts about when and how to make use of the PDS land. These conflicts tend to impede their autonomy and fray the social fabric of the community, as rule-breaking, free-ridership, and the chaotic regulatory regime dishearten participation in community forestry and other initiatives (Mendes and Porro 2015). Analyses of frontier expansion concluded that there was so much illegal deforestation taking place in 2014 that PDSs were ultimately still a part of an expanding frontier, despite attempts over a dozen years to organize land uses to contain deforestation (Bringel 2014). In 2016, there were five deaths associated with agrarian conflicts concerning lot 83. This lot, which is still in legal limbo concerning its ownership as of this writing, was one of the main land parcels that Sister Dorothy had advocated to include in the PDS. It was claimed to be owned by Regivaldo Galvão, who was sentenced to 30 years in prison for ordering Sister Dorothy's assassination.

PDS Esperança and PDS Virola-Jatobá residents, who lived to the south and north of the Transamazon highway near Anapu, often reiterated that the main

Table 4.2 Deforestation in Major Municipalities Bordering Transamazon and BR 163 Highways (2000–2015)

	2000		2005		2010		2015	
	Deforestation (km^2)	**% Deforested**	**Deforestation (km^2)**	**% Deforested**	**Deforestation (km^2)**	**% Deforested**	**Deforestation (km^2)**	% Deforested
Altamira	2058.8	1.29%	5124.1	3.22%	6726	4.22%	8092.6	5.07%
Anapu	862.5	7.24%	1623.30	12.50%	2020.40	16.96%	2356.8	19.79%
Medicilândia	848.9	10.26%	1662.7	20.10%	1944.7	23.51%	2066.5	24.98%
Novo Progresso	1789.8	4.69%	4114.2	10.77%	5317.9	13.93%	5892.6	15.43%
Vitória do Xingu	943.7	30.09%	1772.1	56.51%	1843	58.77%	1974.1	62.95%

Source: http://www.dpi.inpe.br/prodesdigital/prodes.php.

lesson they learned from Sister Dorothy was cooperation—"We have to stand united, that's what Sister Dorothy always said!" residents expressed. It was not easy, however; the loss of organizational leadership and support was a significant void that Sister Dorothy left in the community. The resident's associations within the PDSs are often fraught with internal disputes and fracture among leadership. While the legacy of Sister Dorothy was one of regional progress toward conservation generally in the vicinity of Anapu and the PDSs, the specific localities and people that she strove to defend remain in a struggle over land, forest resources, and their very safety. While the Projects for Sustainable Development promised to offer a new and inspiring path for smallholder livelihoods along the Transamazon, in practice, the results of sustainable development planning involved continued social struggle, contradictory environmental outcomes, and considerable social and geographical unevenness in terms of the sites and populations that benefited from governmental action and civil society attention. Generally, it is safe to conclude that those living closest to the PDSs were those who benefited the least from the interventions that followed Sister Dorothy's death.

The BR-163 Forest District

Along the BR-163 highway, a contemporaneous effort to pave the road took place in conjunction with the Brazilian government's first-ever attempt to create a Sustainable Forest District. Improvements to the roadways would mean improved access to hospitals, markets, and greater interconnectivity. Yet the longer the populations along the roads remained in the region without pavement, the less imperative the matter seemed to officials (Barber et al. 2014). The region's residents had long demanded that the BR-163 highway get paved, but their requests fell on deaf ears until Sister Dorothy's assassination. A federal employee working closely on the BR-163 plan reflected:

> We were doing this work for years, and everything, but with her death [Sister Dorothy Stang's], there was really the necessity to respond. . . . There, the movement for land-claiming there is very strong. They insulted the residents, saying that Sister Dorothy was taking their employment away, and that the government isn't doing anything [to help or create jobs], and was just closing logging operations. So, they were trying to get the residents to think this way, but in reality, it wasn't that way. These were measures that had to be taken because the loggers were operating totally illegally, and various registers of slave labor with these loggers existed . . . The social measures that were taken were done without

> time to see the results, to have any impact for the population. It is a kind of illegal war. It's very difficult. (Interview with author 2006)

Starting in 2004, the lands surrounding both the Transamazon and the BR-163 highways began to be discussed in meetings about sustainable development zoning and changed land ownership plans. These meetings aimed to quell concerns that paving would lead to unmitigated forest losses and the heated conflicts of land speculation that often accompany development dynamics in frontier regions.

The planning process for the BR-163 highway entailed conducting ecological-economic zoning studies along the road and establishing corridors where national parks and national forest districts would buffer the remaining forest ecosystems that were still intact on either side of the highway. Widespread territorial zoning decisions would be made, environmental management programs instituted, and infrastructure development would all become simultaneously slated as urgent necessities for the region (SocioAmbiental 2007). The new Sustainable Forest District, created in March 2006, lauded its own potential as having "the possibility of creating 100,000 new direct jobs, generation of an annual production of 4 to 6 million cubic meters of logs and may generate from 200 to 800 MW of energy [from burning logging waste], without damaging the forest" (Ministério de Meio Ambiente [MMA] 2006). The BR-163 Forest District proposal principally derived from the Brazilian Ministry of the Environment. The Forest District was meant to offset the negative effects of road paving and sought to preserve the pristine forest along BR-163, which was 95 percent intact (Alencar 2005).

The conservation areas within the BR-163 Sustainable Forest District include national parks, extractive reserves, and, principally, national forests. The area of the Sustainable Forest District is huge; its area is 190,000 square kilometers, around the size of the Brazilian states of Rio de Janeiro and Ceará combined. In US terms, this is about 73,359 square miles, slightly larger than the entire state of Washington. This area is depicted in Figure 4.3.

On paper, at least, the Sustainable Forest District extended the total area of conserved forest in the region to 6.4 million hectares (158 million acres) and established seven new conservation areas, in addition to extending the Amazon National Park. With the newly established conservation lands, the government achieved a laudable 50 percent increase in areas designated for conservation. In only three years, the amount of conservation lands increased from 30,700,000 hectares (~76 million acres) in 2003 up to 45,800,000 hectares (~113 million acres) in 2006.

When the Jamanxim National Park (FLONA-Jamanxim) was first declared as part of the Sustainable Forest District, many of the people with land claims in the

The BR-163 Sustainable Forest District

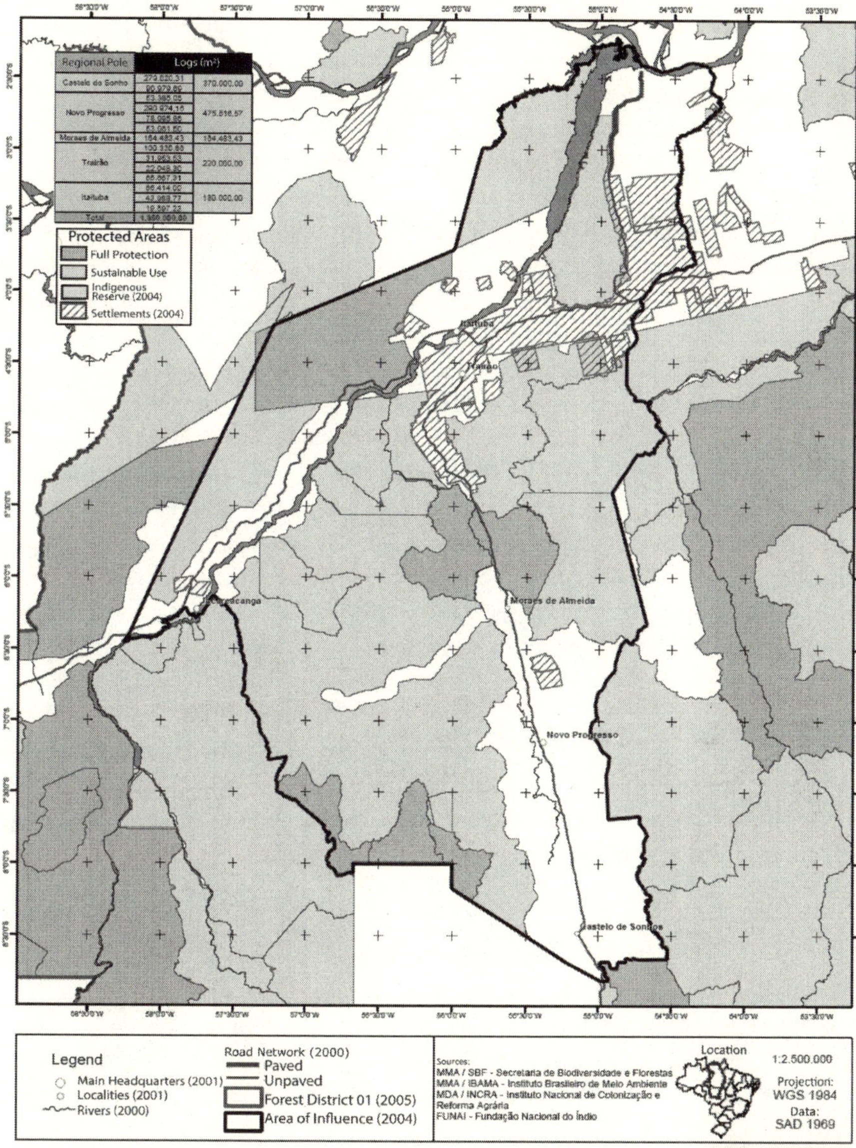

Figure 4.3 Map of the BR-163 Sustainable Forest District. Some of the boundaries shifted slightly after the district was created due to disputed landholdings, despite an extensive public involvement process and ecological-economic zoning meetings.

area had a reactionary response; they cut down and burned considerable parts of the forest out of anger, feeling that the government had ignored them in public meetings and that the forest boundaries had been determined more by looking at maps and flying over the area in helicopters than by anything said at the public hearings and consultations. Some of the most restricted types of conservation areas were located just outside of cities and were even overlaid with sawmill towns. Many local residents commented unhappily that this was indicative of a systematic disregard for existing residents' needs in the plans, and a privileging of "environmentalists' goals" which trumped local social and economic needs. Despite what was supposed to be a landmark public participation process about land uses, such privileging, in tandem with "participation fatigue," led many local stakeholders to be skeptical about the entire endeavor.

Along BR-163, environmentally concerned policymakers found an unusual partner in the timber industry. Cognizant of their inability to halt the road paving project altogether, the Ministry of Environment saw creating protected areas as a viable policy measure to buffer the region from new deforestation. In addition, an economic logic underpinned much of the strategic approach to forest management in the region for local citizens living along the road. It was hoped that these areas could become profitable centers of sustainable forest management and legal logging operations in the region. In the FLONA-Jamanxim, some 5 million hectares (12.3 million acres) would be opened to timber concessions, pending approval of the logging companies' forest management plans (Souza 2006). As part of the BR-163 Sustainable Forest District, the land was legalized for managed timber extraction but not for settlement by small- or medium-scale farmers. The result was that cattle ranchers, long affiliated with the logging sector, became politically ostracized, while many in the timber industry welcomed the creation of the new Forest District in hopes that their businesses could finally become legalized.

Yet the loggers and the government fell out of each other's good graces within a few years. In Castelo de Sonhos, at the southern end of the Sustainable Forest District, sawmill owners complained in 2014 that, over the past decade, many of their proposed forest management plans, once approved, had become illegal because of the shifting Forest Code laws and other constantly changing administrative protocols. It seemed to them that as soon as required documentation for operating was in place, the law would change again, making some other element of the lumber industry illegal. Although the national forests are supposed to permit forest management and sustainable logging practices, many of the sawmill owners expressed that it is "impossible to operate legally" in the region.

Extensive public participation processes in regional land use and conservation decision making were ultimately conducted with the aim of making forest protection possible at the same time as Amazonian road-paving projects. For the BR-163 (Cuiabá–Santarém) and the Transamazon highway (BR-230), paving entailed making modern engineering upgrades that promised to make the roads functional for year-round use. Yet, despite widespread public outreach, zoning efforts, and new legal frameworks that aimed to control land use and settlement patterns, illegal land-claiming and conflicts over land continued at serious levels in the BR-163 area of influence (Branford and Torres 2017, Torres, Doblas, and Alarcon 2017, Rocha 2015b). Despite the existence of the Forest District, deforestation increased substantially.

These roads once embodied the crude attempts by the military dictatorship to "develop" the Amazon. In contemporary times, the road paving projects—and their adherent plans for forest protection and land reform in the vicinity of those roads—are enacted within a performance of participatory, transparent governance which, when laid bare, reveal an underlying legal and bureaucratic framework that involves considerably more messiness. The outcomes of the protection plans and land organizing initiatives, moreover, ultimately did little to resist the encroachment of logging and land speculation, while promoting rational management as the public face of sustainable development.

Roads for Sustainable Development

As contemporary modernization projects, road paving in the Amazon is oriented by a foundational understanding that infrastructure improvements are necessary for bringing both "progress" and "sustainability" to the region (Campbell 2012, Baletti 2012). The symbolism of having paved highways through the Amazon was compelling for governmental officials and social movement activists alike. They represented infrastructure that would meet development needs and a completion of long-standing promises of government presence to help address the many needs in the region.

Road paving in the Amazon was a governmental priority that was just important enough to make it into local campaigns, and just low enough that the promises never manifested into realities because of funding shortfalls and inter-municipality coordination difficulties. Some cities along these two federal highways had a few meters of pavement, others up to a few kilometers into and out of town, and a few had none at all. In the 1990s, only about 90 km of BR-163 was paved, despite the passage of around twenty years since the road had first been cut. Along the Transamazon, even when contracts for paving were signed, the budgetary shortfalls were so huge that actual results were inconsequential. In the state of Pará, only 89 percent of federal and state roads were paved in the year 2000. These data are presented in Table 4.3.

Table 4.3 The Amazonian State and Federal Road Network (2000)

	Paved Km	% Paved	Unpaved Km	% Unpaved	Total Km
Acre	838	16	4,561	84	5,399
Amazonas	1,705	28	4,495	73	6,200
Amapá	223	10	1,915	90	2,138
Maranhão	5,407	10	47,840	90	53,247
Mato Grosso	4,509	5	80,046	95	84,555
Pará	3,840	11	30,735	89	34,575
Rondônia	1,417	6	21,016	94	22,433
Roraima	900	17	4,384	83	5,284
Tocantins	3,471	13	23,596	87	27,067
Total Legal Amazon	**22,310**	**9**	**218,588**	**91**	**240,898**
Brazil	**164,988**	**10**	**1,559,941**	**90**	**1,724,929**

Data from Vera-Diaz, Kaufmann and Nepstad 2009, based on 2005 GEIPOT data (GEIPOT is no longer in existence, and data from later than 2000 is not available elsewhere).

Vera-Diaz, M.d.C., R.K. Kaufmann, & D. Nepstad (2009). The Environmental Impacts of Soybean Expansion and Infrastructure Development in Brazil's Amazon Basin. *Global Development and Environment Institute,* Working Paper, 25.

It is important to remember the activism and organizing context that provided much of the social legitimacy for the road paving projects to move forward. The slogan developed by the social movements along the Transamazon highway was simple and compelling: "If it was a mistake to bring us here, to abandon us is a crime." The MPST and other social movements of the region became more politically engaged by the mid-1990s. They organized three marches to Brasília in the early 1990s, entailing a journey by foot of some 1,880 kilometers.[19] After that, the movement began supporting PT party candidates running for municipal, state, and federal offices. While no umbrella organization existed to unite civil society groups living along the BR-163 highway, the Transamazon social movement groups were especially well organized and politically active. They launched municipal-level development plans throughout the region and were active in making denunciations of illegal logging and heart of palm (*palmito*) extraction also occurring in the region. A proposal for regional land use and reform that the movement released in 1998 was called the "Cry of the Transamazon." The recommendations included creating significant new areas for environmental conservation, establishing new extractive reserves located both to the north and the south of the Transamazon highway near Altamira, and major crackdowns on illegal logging operations.

The Transamazon activists' longer-term strategy and demands also included building rural schools and making agricultural credit available for small-scale agricultural activities. They aimed to have the next generation of people living along the road become equipped to maintain sustainable agricultural practices while farming Amazonian lands. After having some successes in these initiatives, the social movement groups clearly articulated that they were seeking an alternative vision for the development of the entire region. The umbrella organization of the MPST even changed its name to the Movement for the Development of the Transamazon and Xingu (MDTX). Their mission, by this point, had evolved from advocacy for mere survival into a more comprehensive development agenda for the region. The MDTX functioned as an umbrella activist group of 113 locally specific organizations, and they also had a formal not-for-profit organization through which they could apply for grant and development funding and have formal representation at meetings. This organization was known as the Foundation for Life, Production, and Preservation, or FVPP. Geographically and socially their reach expanded as well, with the organization becoming an advocate for the river-based peasants of the Xingu river in addition to the small farmers who had settled along the highway.

The civil society groups were less active along the Pará stretch of the BR-163 highway. There was little by way of organized labor union or farmer groups in the southern sections of the road as it neared the border with the state of Mato Grosso.[20] Some people nicknamed the BR-163 corridor in Pará between Castelo de Sonhos (to the south) and Moraes de Almeida (to the north) "Quase Brasil"—meaning "almost Brazil"—because of its near-total vacuum of public institutions.[21] Generally, this part of the region lacked the strength of a coalition-based infrastructure, and infighting was common among the leadership of the few organizations that did exist.

In the early 2000s, the economic context radically shifted along the roads of Pará. Brazil had recently dropped its ban on growing genetically engineered foods, and the state of Mato Grosso was rapidly becoming the global leader in soybean production.[22] Cargill, one of the world's largest multinational agricultural companies, built a $20 million grain terminal in the city of Santarém in 2003. They did so on the bet that with eventual road paving, soybeans could be transported from Mato Grosso through Pará on BR-163 for exportation (mostly to China and European nations) via the Amazon River. Transportation was anticipated to be much more cost-effective if the commodities could be moved northward up the BR-163 to the new port, avoiding the congested roads and longer routes previously used in the port cities of Santos and Paranaguá in the south of the country.[23] When President Lula announced later that year that the paving of BR-163 would be official, other multinational companies got in on the opportunity. For example, Bunge, another major soybean export company, built an export terminal just south of Santarém in Miritituba, along the Tapajós river.

Bunge soon sold half its assets in Miritituba port to the Amaggi Group (Branford and Torres 2017).[24] Amaggi was another major agribusiness firm, owned by a powerful politician named Blairo Maggi. In 2003, Maggi, then governor of the state of Mato Grosso (and remaining in the governorship from 2003–2010), controlled over two million tons of soy destined for livestock in Europe and Asia. His company grossed a whopping $600 million, earning him the title *O Rei da Soja*—the King of Soy. As owner of the Grupo André Maggi, which is Brazil's largest domestically owned soybean producer, his stake in the road was both personal and political (Lilley 2004). The economic case for paving the highway was a significant one; the environmental impact assessment for the project suggested that the road paving would save BRL $20 per ton in soybean transport costs, yielding BRL $150 million per year more in revenues (USD $47.8 million/ year) (ECOPLAN Engenharia Ltda 2002).[25]

Similarly, the political landscape in the region began to shift, as the Worker's Party (PT) consolidated control through winning the presidency in 2003 under newly elected President Lula. PT leadership in the Pará state governorship followed, beginning in 2006. The party successfully united interests of both organized labor and the broader social bases by including environmental and social concerns prominently in their political agenda (Vanden 2012). The PT emphasized citizen participation in the execution of government programs, in decision making about how government spending should be allocated, and in the kinds of programs that should be implemented (Galvao 2014). Operationally, the PT emphasized democratic participation from the bottom up, in contrast to Brazilian and Latin American historical experience. Participation became a centerpiece of the asphalting project along BR-163 especially, although along the road the social movement organizations were neither very robust nor very coordinated, especially in contrast with the Transamazon highway civil society groups.

A Dream Deferred: Paving the Soybean Highway

In 2003, newly elected President Lula promised to pave the BR-163 highway. Most people in the region took the promise with a grain of salt, given that they had heard the story from innumerable other public officials in the several decades past, practically since the road was first cut. Highways, roads, and dam projects for the region, including BR-163 and the Belo Monte dam (discussed in

Chapter 6), had frequently been included in the federal government's pluriannual plan (PPA) for growth, only to be tabled. Under President Lula, however, the rhetoric seemed more serious because it was backed by public officials visiting the region and a process of extensive consultation.

The plan for paving BR-163 was further invigorated when the federal government adopted a multiyear (2004–2007) policy for large-scale development, the PPA, in which BR-163 and large hydroelectric dams were the main projects funded (Scholz 2006). Increased speculation along BR-163 drove up land prices by nearly tenfold in the course of a few years ("Asphalt and the Jungle" 2004). When the road's paving was announced, pressure increased substantially around land-claiming. In an already generally lawless region, even higher levels of violence and social upheaval became prominent (Grupo de Trabalho Interministerial 2005). The conflicts were especially between those who held land as ranchers and landless peasant farmers, although conflicts between wildcat miners were also common.[26] This also coincided with deforestation, which increased steadily in the south of Pará, especially along BR-163. The Instituto SocioAmbiental's deforestation point-person, Juan Doblas, observed: "The loss of forest in the region was so out of control that for every year between 2004 and 2013—except 2005—while deforestation in Amazonia as a whole fell, it increased in the region around the BR-163" (Branford and Torres 2017). Some internationally based environmental groups began decrying the road as a "soybean highway" that would spread monocrop agriculture through the heart of the Amazon. The concern also entailed the criticism that the road would repeat a long-established pattern of deforestation:

> The area in the state of Pará to be traversed by the BR-163 Highway is one of lawlessness and impunity in every respect, including the environment. This applies especially to the 646-km unpaved stretch from the Pará/Mato Grosso border to Trairão (26 km south of the junction of BR-163 and the Transamazon Highway). (Fearnside 2007a, 602)

Greenpeace activists loudly clamored against Cargill's port in Santarém, and protests over the port turned violent at times (Greenpeace 2006). Some researchers projected that 22,000–49,000 km^2 of forest would be lost within 35 years if the road were paved (Nepstad et al. 2000, Fearnside 2002, Laurance et al. 2004). Asphalt, at the same time, seemed to indicate progress to others in the country; the contrast between paved areas on the BR-163 highway in Mato Grosso versus the unpaved stretch in Pará was formidable and was perceived to be correlated to other indicators of development, including the quality of education, family incomes, and agricultural productivity.

In principle, the plans for road paving were designed to mitigate negative social and environmental consequences through creating the BR-163 Sustainable Forest District. The federal government's response appeared highly calculated, aiming to avoid a public relations debacle along the lines of that which it had experienced during the 1970s road-cutting efforts. The BR-163 highway was included in the pluriannual plan for growth, but it would be done as the "Sustainable Development Plan" for paving BR-163. Through creating a Plan for the Sustainable Development of BR-163, the federal government sought to instill the project with an unprecedented level of public participation and governmental engagement in the region. Through extensive mapping, zoning studies, economic analysis, soil studies, and the like, the region's productive potential was emphasized in community meetings, as was technocratic competency. But compounding road paving and other infrastructure projects within the framework of sustainable development was a contradiction to some close observers:

> Note that the object of the current [federal pluriannual] plan is "growth," not "development," much less "sustainable development." The term "growth" implies simply an increase in size, whereas "development" implies an improvement, whether or not size increases. The plans have, indeed, been focused on size rather than quality, each plan being essentially a long list of highways, dams and other infrastructure projects that the government regards as of high priority. (Fearnside 2016a, 29)

While public engagement and information dissemination was a main goal of these meetings, the government also attempted to leverage the platform to convey its seriousness about instituting the new forestry areas along the BR-163 corridor and asserting its commitment to infrastructure investments in the region.

The federal government cooperated extensively with civil society groups throughout the region, and the Ministries of Transportation, Social Development, Foreign Commerce, Justice, Education, and other agencies were all collaborating in a fourteen-ministry working group to bring in other projects, programs, and benefits into the region. The main goal of this interministerial working group was to minimize the impacts caused by the construction and paving of the highway.

The level of intragovernmental collaboration was an innovation unto itself, officials noted. Beyond the extensive bureaucratic teamwork, consultations with civil society were abundant. A public employee from the Ministry of Transportation described the consultations as extensive:

> This process was constructed, because when the idea was born to pave BR-163 . . . people said no, we want more than that. That's to say, "it's going to make things easier, but now, we need to establish a series of government instances, which are absent." These are fundamental parts of government, the question of education, health, social, and all the rest, so the decision was to include them. (Interview with author 2006)

Decision makers in Brasília looked to the local workers' unions and conducted extensive meetings and consultations with the social movement groups working in the region. Despite having a less robust civil society presence directly along BR-163 than on the Transamazon highway, the interministerial working group conducted numerous public hearings in the region and garnered significant turnout. While the forest area boundaries and the exact ecological and economic zoning for the region remained the source of frequently heated public debate, opinions among business and other nongovernmental groups appeared to be wholeheartedly supportive of road paving. One person involved with the working group described it this way: "At all the public consultations, we heard that everyone wanted asphalting on BR-163. Everyone wants asphalting . . . And the plan is moving along, because the effects [of paving the road] are already underway." While the social movement groups tended to be allied with the federal government, municipalities, which often had political leadership from more center and right-leaning political parties, differed over issues concerning how to go about doing the paving and about the extent of agrarian reform, social programs, and funding that would take place.

Despite this attempt at comprehensive ecological and economic regional planning, the operative logic at stake was still driven by the national macroeconomic growth agenda. Brazilian GDP was experiencing growth rates of an average of 5 percent between 2004 and 2008, and almost 25 percent of GDP came from agricultural exports (Geromel 2013). "The soy is just a motivation for the road to begin . . . The deforestation would happen with or without the road, and without the road you don't have the visibility to know what's going on inside the forest, because it is so dense" (Interview with author 2006). Following from this view, the highway paving is presented in the name of environmental conservation rather than destruction; conservation along the highway's margins could be an upshot of otherwise completely destructive frontier expansion practices, brought on by the irrepressible demand for the commodity of soybeans.

Beyond these motives there was also an underpinning hope, held even by governmental officials, that this time the state really could change something in a positive way for the local residents in the region. For the chief engineer working on the BR-163 project at the Ministry of Transportation, paving BR-163 signified helping the low-income people living along the road improve their conditions, beyond the macro-economic advantages of the soybean industry's growth:

> Evidently, the question of soy functioned as a motivator, and launched the intensified action in the region . . . In my way of thinking, soy is interesting, but not in the way that it can improve the lives of those who are there . . . Because if I make a road, I will permit the people who are there, if they produce whatever commercial article or thing for subsistence consumption in the municipality nearby, they will have a road to take the product which he produced to a consumer center. (Interview with author 2006)

He was not alone in expressing this view that paving ultimately was a path toward addressing a whole host of other social challenges in the region. An official at the Ministry of Social Development explained the imperative to pave the road in even more resoundingly social terms:

> So, with this, and since promise, promise, promise, to do the paving, for sure, the immigration was much more strong from there. What I think is that in these last few years, the last four, five years, the flux [of migration] went up a lot in the region. We are working because we were worried, because with this migration came prostitution, child labor, unemployment, all these things. Structural problems of lacking infrastructure, health, education, you know, there was nothing. . . . And they don't know our programs, which deal with the family grants . . . we think that all the people know about the family grant, already know about it and how to use it. But there, they didn't know how it worked, it was unpredictable to receive money, and there was information that was just not arriving in these places. (Interview with author 2006)

By engaging an exceptional level of broad-based public involvement and consultations, the federal government took a different tack into Amazonian environmental governance, offering the promise of regional support for the initiatives. They captured a certain vision of sustainable development as a "new paradigm for development in the region," one without considerable sacrifice of ecological concerns in the face of economic growth interests, or vice versa (Ministério de Meio Ambiente [MMA] 2006).

Without substantial governance reforms, however, skeptics argued that the project showed little credibility in terms of convincing people about the new seriousness with which rule of law would enter into the region (Fearnside 2007a). Critics were justifiably suspicious about the idea of how a highway that was motivated by greater soybean revenue and agribusiness interests could be conjoined with environmental concerns in the first place; the road instead seemed to reinforce an economic logic of resource extraction rather than conservation. In tandem with the interministerial working group's efforts, an NGO project led by the World Wildlife Fund[27] called the "BR-163 Dialogues" project involved four years of meetings and seminars in the region from 2005–2009. Their work centered upon the idea of "reducing impacts" of the road through having multisector discussions. The social rifts and arguments over how the future of the region should look became so contentious that some people who worked closely on the BR-163 "Dialogues" (*diálogos*, in Portuguese) nicknamed them by a Portuguese homophone, the BR-163 "Devils" (*diablos*). The idea of participation was presented by the government as a prefigurative way of achieving the best outcomes for the region, but, in many such meetings, NGO representatives argued that their participation was being used as a means of justification for the project to move forward rather than entailing more meaningful engagements.

A regional plan for land registration (the Program for Legal Land) aimed to crack down on illegal claiming and speculation of lands, a 2008 Plan for a Sustainable Amazon was written, and by 2012 the new Forest Code also established a national framework for registering lands under a policy called the Environmental Land Registry, or CAR. Despite the existence of all those well-intentioned plans, unequal development was an entrenched reality. While 90 percent of the population occupying public lands were smallholders, they were only claiming 19 percent of the relevant areas in question. Some 63 percent of those landholdings in question were held by around only a few (6 percent) large-scale land claimers. The historical concentration of land distribution patterns and rural violence persisted (Sauer 2005) and were even augmented by the opportunities that new governmental plans for registering and reclaiming land offered (Torres, Doblas, and Alarcon 2017).[28] In this way, the plans for sustainable development along BR-163 continued to entrench existing inequalities. Although earnestly undertaken by NGOs, the federal government, and meeting participants alike, those participatory meetings and the new forest boundaries that resulted from the Sustainable Forest District offered what ultimately was a thin veneer of environmental protection. The deeper structures of shifting forest policies, inconsistent environmental enforcement measures, and the difficulties of achieving land regularization impeded the efficacy and longer-term protections that such measures sought to address.

Despite the cooperation present between social movement groups and the government, some mistrust remained that the plans would ever go through and become reality. Along the BR-163 highway in Castelo de Sonhos, local residents were so frustrated with all the talk while nothing was put into practice that at one point, around 2004, a group of citizens kidnapped a team of officials who had come from Brasília for a public hearing. Unable to find much bargaining leverage through the tactic, the team was let go after two days, and officials were rather reticent to ever return to the place. Moreover, not all members of society were pleased with the multi-pronged initiative aimed at achieving governance in the region prior to having the road paved.

By 2005, there had already been multiple meetings along BR-163, and then Sister Dorothy Stang's death near the Transamazon caused repercussions throughout the region. When the Brazilian government cracked down on illegal logging in the spring of 2005, hundreds of people in Castelo de Sonhos along BR-163 were left jobless. The economic boom had been tremendous and rapid in Castelo: consistent electricity had only arrived to the town five years earlier, but by 2005 it was host to nearly fifty sawmills. Within a few weeks, shutting down the sawmills crashed the entire economy of the town. A Pastoral Land Commission (CPT) staff member who visited Castelo de Sonhos recalled:

> There were 300 families camped along the side of the road there, and they were waiting for food. The truck [carrying the food aid] took 44 days to come from Santarém to Castelo, because the road conditions were so bad. It was the rainy season. The road was mud, trucks get stopped for days on end. People were living in total misery.

The frustration voiced by the citizens in Castelo de Sonhos expressed concern that the government only bestowed attention upon the people of the region in order to stymie their livelihoods; paving the road in order to improve conditions appeared a distant prospect.

By 2014, less than 30 percent of the road from Castelo de Sonhos to the northern city of Santarém was paved, despite decades of discussion and planning for paving BR-163. Just 15 kilometers North of Castelo de Sonhos, the road once again becomes nothing more than carved earth, making way for a grueling, bumpy, daylong drive. The bridges are precarious, and buses frequently get stuck in the mud during the rainy season, often necessitating overnight delays for passengers while nearby tractors are brought in to rescue stranded vehicles. The federal government allocated BRL$220 million (USD $70.3 million) toward paving and road improvements on BR-163 in Pará between 2015–2017.[29] A 2017 memo from Maurício Quintella, Minister of Transport, Ports, and Civil Aviation, emphasized that paving BR-163 was still a top priority: "We will not allow the next crop harvest to happen like this one, so the Ministry of Transport has prepared its budget to once and for all solve the problem of handling Brazilian production via BR-163" (Ministério dos Transportes 2017). There are multiple reasons for the delays, some of which relate to budgetary shortfalls, licensing delays, lack of adequate institutional cooperation, access to long-term capital, and the difficulties of working on the roads during the rainy season. Compounding the frustrated efforts, Brazil's extensive corruption probe,

Operation Car Wash, showed that kickbacks and bribes were extensive between Brazil's largest civil construction firms and various politicians. The very firms responsible for completing road construction were ultimately brought to court, and many executives and politicians alike ended up with prison sentences as a result of the investigations, including President Lula. One study estimates that because of the money lost to corruption during the first PAC, from 2007–2010, railway construction could have increased by 525 percent, and road infrastructure could have been 124 percent greater (Amann et al. 2016).

The Sustainable Development of BR-163 Plan was approved in June 2006, providing for fifty-four priority actions including bringing social services to the region. It entailed conducting "territorial ordering" activities which would clarify the illegal land-claiming problems, beginning infrastructure work, creating new conservation areas, and supporting both research and law enforcement activities along the road. Meanwhile, environmentalists and government officials alike became concerned that the south of Pará would be completely dominated by soybean growing, cattle ranching, and logging, despite their own concerted efforts to establish rigid environmental protections and governance in the area. A consortium of nongovernmental organizations charged that it was "not clear that there has been any fundamental change in the federal Amazon policies," even though they had been in dialogue for two years with an interministerial working group to shape the plans (Scholz 2006). In practice, the hospitals remained without doctors and schools without children in attendance; sometimes, people protested outside of "participatory" meetings rather than appear to democratically acquiesce to their central assumptions by attending (Baletti 2014). After its eventual approval, the plan for sustainable development along the road was again criticized by NGOs for not being implemented.

Despite the creation of the Sustainable Forest District along the BR-163, those protected areas were not very effectively enforced as protected areas. Political debate continued for a decade over whether the Forest District should be maintained and what its exact boundaries should look like. Illustrative of this is that in 2017, the Federal Senate passed a proposal to significantly reduce the size of the Jamanxim National Forest and the Jamanxim National Park, after only seven minutes of debate on May 23, 2017 (bills 4/2017 and 17/2017) (WRI Brazil 2017, Braga de Souza 2017). The proposal was vetoed by President Temer, who faced the threat from the government of Norway that its Amazon Fund contributions to Brazil (around USD $1 billion) would be cut if it did not take measures to prevent deforestation. The local outcry from those who wanted to see the Forest District scaled back was significant, however; road blockade protests shut down the BR-163 highway, delaying grain exports (Teixeira 2017).

A Dream Come True? Paving the Transamazon

Paving the Transamazon highway through the state of Pará was an equally slow process, in spite of the fact that far less environmental regulation was necessary along the road for land tenure regularization and forest protections. Most of the forest had already been lost on the margins of that highway, given the earlier colonization patterns involving "fishbone" deforestation that most prominently occurred in the 1970s and 1980s.

Unlike along the BR-163, public hearings about the Transamazon paving were kept to a relative minimum; the highway paving was widely viewed as an obvious necessity, and environmental groups, at that point, were concerned far more about the likely devastation caused by the Belo Monte dam—also planned for the region—than the highway paving itself. Although getting the road paved was the long-standing and central demand of the social movements along the highway, locals strongly suspected that the Transamazon paving project was essentially a political bargaining chip. There were rumors that the Belo Monte dam's construction would only be possible if the road was paved. The dam would entail transporting several gigantic (18,624MW) Francis turbines. Transporting those huge turbines by boat was impossible due to waterfalls along the river. Those close to the hydroelectric project noted that paving the road was not really a product of the social movement's demands in any direct way; instead, it was a key piece of infrastructure that would allow the national priority of increasing energy capacity to be achieved.[30] Pragmatically, the federal government could rationalize road paving within the logic of getting its turbines, as well as thousands of construction workers, to and from the dam construction site more easily.

There was also less of a need for agrarian reform and new conservation areas to be established along the highway, except in the PDSs near Anapu and a handful of other locales. Discussion about completing the asphalt along the Transamazon highway lagged behind the process of the BR-163 highway. Instead, the Transamazon paving dovetailed the planning of the Belo Monte dam, which was not yet officially reactivated in governmental plans in 2006, although it was being discussed.[31]

For the social movement groups living along the Transamazon, paving the road was appealing. The road would be good for development; it would be "progress" according to the traditional notion of the term offered by General Medici and the original Transamazon settlers. Paving would show the local people in the region that the federal government cared about investing in the Amazon, and it would mean on a symbolic level that long-held dreams and social movement demands could become true. Most of the benefits to the region came in the form of a $2 billion (BRL $3.6 billion) regional "compensation" package known as the Xingu Regional Sustainable Development Plan (PDSRX). A major new hospital would be built as part of this compensation package, and funding would be increased for schools, agricultural credits, and a host of other demands made by local populations. Many of these social benefits from the PDSRX, however, did not yield lasting, if any, results. The hospital remained built but locked and without equipment due to a host of political and financial disputes between the state of Pará and the federal government, well after a year of its completed construction. Artists that were slated to receive grant-based monies to support the projects that they were approved for in the PDSRX never received payments. The impression of many people in Altamira, it seemed, was that the PDSRX was yet another broken promise of the government.

Conclusion: Faltering Through Rational Planning

The PT government's leadership represented formidable change in terms of the evolving plans for highway paving and territorial organizing efforts in Pará. Rather than being antagonistic toward the state or federal government's presence in the region, for the most part civil society, long accustomed to protesting the federal government, instead was allied with the PT and advocated for strong state action intended as a palliative presence to mitigate the effects of capitalist industrialization. Some of the social movement groups, such as the Rural Worker's Union, articulated a more traditionally Marxist approach to economic development. Others, such as the MDTX, more moderately articulated "another type of development" where small-scale farming would be valued and, largely, where neoliberal economic policies would be resisted. For all the insistence upon supporting small-scale farming and merging this interest with conservation-oriented goals, however, nearly every group active in the region supported the paving projects. Paving along BR-163 and on the Transamazon seemed to promise a means of achieving greater capabilities for health, education, information, environmental quality, and security for the people in the region.

By 2014, 44 percent of the Amazon was demarcated as lands for indigenous peoples or was protected as a national park, wildlife reserve, or an extractive reserve (Busch and Ferretti-Gallon 2017). This represents a significant step forward for conservation, since there is considerable evidence that suggests creating conservation areas offers a buffer against deforestation.[32] Enforcement of park boundaries and forest protection occurs as a cat-and-mouse game between logging interests and Brazil's environmental enforcement agency, IBAMA. By day, IBAMA conducted helicopter flyovers of the national forests, aimed at enforcing regulations and fining illegal loggers. By night, those living in the region claimed that guerrilla tactics were used to interfere with logging. People complain that sand is being put into logging truck engines, and several burnt trucks by the side of the road conveyed a clear message: the national environmental agency will shut your operation down. Locals would park the trucks on the side of the road for all to see, as a means of encouraging outrage against the regulatory agencies. When fines were issued by IBAMA for deforestation, they usually remained unpaid. Eventually, forgiveness of fines and institutional reforms would lead to a new set of rules, people argued. Generally, they were proven correct over time, especially with the Forest Code revisions of 2012.

Despite the best attempts at garnering participation in the regional planning initiatives and sensitively accounting for local development needs, the results are disheartening; the compromise of having sustainably managed forests along BR-163 seems to be an ever more distant possibility, as instead the reality of escalating conflicts between those endorsing environmental regulations in the region and those aiming to profit off of the forests—whether through legal or illicit means—becomes clear.

One section of the paved road located between the town of Vitória do Xingu and Altamira is so pothole-ridden that drivers engage it like a slalom course, weaving between bumps and holes. As one driver once aptly described the road situation there to me: "It gets better, just after the asphalt ends. There, at least, the bumps are more regular, the earth is more consistent." While the paved road is significantly better in other stretches, this little stretch of cracked up asphalt is what the future of the paved Transamazon may become. At present, that little stretch of road offers travelers and drivers alike a foreboding sense that the paving projects in the region may not necessarily help more than hinder in the long run. Júlio previously worked for the Catholic Church in Altamira as a driver and logistics manager. He knew every bump, mud-pit, and road stop point on the Transamazon highway. Nowadays, he works as a supervisor involved with the Transamazon highway paving project. I asked how it was going—had the asphalt arrived? He responded, "Have you ever seen a land tortoise? . . . Well, that's how we are with the paving; we are crawling towards progress like a tortoise." Gradually, the project is being completed, but whether or not the final result has durability and investment in maintenance is a lasting concern.

Domestic development in Brazil in the 1970s championed the notions of progress driven by such macro-economic growth, industry, and massive infrastructure projects, largely following from the modernization theory of development. By the new millennium, building highway infrastructures to further export-based commodity growth was seen as a strong means of furthering and strengthening GDP in Brazil, just as it was in many other developing countries (Lewis 2005). A less costly and easier-to-maintain road improvement could have been accomplished through a gravel-based project on BR-163, but paving was symbolic: asphalt would signify the government's long-term capability to build and maintain a major new infrastructure project while simultaneously encouraging a viable, legalized approach to using Amazonian forest resources through creating a Forest District along the road (Nepstad et al. 2004).

The road paving of BR-163 was intended to send a larger message to the world about the approach toward sustainable development that Brazil envisioned. Achieving (and maintaining) high economic growth rates was a top priority, while balancing infrastructure construction and preserving the nation's most treasured ecosystems could be simultaneously achieved. By the early 2000s, the vision for development articulated by the state took on the aspirations of the democratic era, aiming to correct some of the frontier dynamics marred by violence, illegal logging, and low-productivity agriculture. The notion of establishing stronger governance regimes, ideally though the coupling of satellite monitoring, strong public involvement processes, and clear and present environmental enforcement regimes, was captured in these plans. On paper, the plans all made sense; the process was solid, and the compromises made within those plans were understandable. Yet in practice, the results left nearly everyone involved disappointed and mistrustful. So fraught are forest management plans along both the BR-163 highways and in the Transamazon PDSs that the forest has become strikingly deforested in spite of the strict laws in place to avoid just this occurrence from happening. Why?

One important explanation entails institutional and policy implementation shortcomings. The contestation over land and resources taking place between local actors and the state has continued in the BR-163 and Transamazon highway region with little restoration of trust and confidence, which was augmented by shifts in forestry laws, forest boundaries, and never-resolved land claims. Without deeper and durable institutional reforms, sustainably managing the lands became impossible at local and community levels. Aside from the legal complexities in gaining permits to conduct logging and forest management activities (whether in a PDS community forest management plan or as a sawmill owner along the BR-163 highway), resistances were more subtle, along the lines of Scott's (1985, 1998) foot-dragging, argument, protest, boycotting, and other "everyday resistances."

Second, participatory planning efforts functioned to coopt and avoid resistance from social movement actors. As a manifestation of environmental governance, the territorial planning taking place along BR-163 and for the communities of the PDSs living along the Transamazon highway ultimately resulted in a changed relationship between the region's social movements and NGOs, and the federal government. Despite the claims of inclusivity, democratic engagement, and accountability that participatory governance strategies offer, in this case we see a manifestation of social movement and NGO groups positioned as allies rather than in resistance to plans. Instead, these groups became increasingly the agents through which participatory governance could take shape, and in this role gave sanction and legitimacy to the planning process for the region. Along the Transamazon highway, the dominance of a strong social movement and rather cohesive group of civil society actors allowed for an acquiescent and collaborative relationship with the state. In this instance, the vision of an alternative development for the region based in the viability of small-scale farming became subsumed within the logics of a modernization-oriented developmental state, focused primarily on fueling the economic growth of the nation as a whole. Along BR-163 the priority became encouragement of the necessary infrastructure for commodity-based exportation in the form of soybean agribusiness; in the case of the Transamazon highway it was to expedite the turbines needed for completion of the Belo Monte dam.

Among the host of concerns, creating the Projects for Sustainable Development, conducting an ecological-economic zoning, and establishing a Forest District emerged as a politically appealing response for the region because it appeased a range of interests and appeared to slow down the speculative frontier economy for land and resources that might otherwise have occurred. Perhaps most importantly, however, while the planning processes did not necessarily quell the scramble for resources, they did serve to create an impression of orderliness and logical, rational planning. Still, instilling environmental governance before the other sets of policies along the roads of the region were in place led to inevitably uneven outcomes. Despite the promises, road paving has barely occurred, and there has not been consistent enforcement of forestry laws or permissions allowing for economic viability of the BR-163 corridor or the Transamazon highway to come to fruition.

Last, an explanation rests upon a convincingly sequenced message about development that managed to override small-scale farmers' interests and ultimately privilege national infrastructures and macro-economic logics above other rationales. Between the policy and practice of plans conducted in the name of sustainable development, the federal government managed a certain "smoke and mirrors" sleight-of-hand trick regarding the vision for development being articulated through these plans. Reminiscent of the modernization-oriented policies of the past, Brazil's renewed developmentalist strategy oriented a shift that bolstered the region's status as a priority space for attention, where a strong emphasis on environmental management and land organizing would promote the green development goals central to the national development agenda. Simultaneously, maintaining confidence in participatory environmental governance as a means of preventing environmental destruction in the region offered a foundation through which the infrastructure-centered policy measures could take effect. While modernization-oriented plans of the past were seen as gross failures of lofty state visions for the region, the newer approach toward land organizing within the framework of environmental management served a subtler purpose. It legitimated modernization's goals to environmentalists, renewed attention on the importance of paving roads, and convinced people that more of a state presence in this frontier region was a good thing, despite all of its failures in practice and despite the many years where social movement activists strived to articulate an alternative development model for the region.

After thirty years of planning to pave the Transamazon highway and the BR-163 without seeing those plans through, it is important to acknowledge that even though many of the plans themselves have not come to fruition, the processes of planning in the region have led to salient outcomes in terms of social structures and forest management. Rather than being prosperity-generating, environmentally protective strategies for social development, these same projects can constitute a form of violence against people who lack the economic capital, educations, and social and political power necessary to secure their rights (Graeber 2012). The violence is a slow one (Nixon 2011) wherein, over years of mounting hopes, promises, meetings, and promotion of plans aimed at generating improvements, the casualties are often those people who effectively believed that participation would lead to beneficial results and who engaged in forest management plans hoping that these would ultimately yield positive, legal returns.

Under the vision for sustainable development, the unquenched demand for national economic growth was convincingly framed as being compatible with measures to mitigate environmental impacts. This idea of a harmonization of often-conflicting interests follows from an ecological modernization ideal that remains prominent in environmental governance in the Brazilian context. Present, albeit obscured somewhat by this same discourse, lies a core concern involving state planning, which emphasizes logistical expansion, agribusiness encouragement, and increasing energy production as a strategy for modernization. Through this transposition of renewed developmentalist concerns with ecological modernization, the experience of sustainable development is one where set of regulatory regimes and policy interventions lead to disappointments and perceptions of unmet expectations on the ground. Residents in the Projects for Sustainable Development and those living along the Transamazon and BR-163 highways are situated in contingent relationships to the state, often caught in a liminal space of regulatory restriction and, paradoxically, a vacuum of state presence.

5

The Land in the Middle

Conservation from Conflict

We have a moment which will be really tense, which depends on a politics of the government. This will be when the grileiros are taken off of their land in the Terra do Meio. They're in the Terra do Meio and in Verde Para Sempre. They're still living there, and they have no right to indemnification. There are people who have 20 or 30 km fenced in. They have paved roads and helicopter pads. They have 5,000 heads of cattle. Then, you imagine—the government takes them out and sends them away without any indemnification, because this was government land.

—Tarcísio Feitosa, Pastoral Land Commission Coordinator, Altamira. Interview with author, Altamira, 2006

On February 12, 2005, Brazil's environment minister, Marina Silva, stepped off a helicopter into a conservation area in the middle of the Amazon, near the confluence of the Xingu and Amazon rivers. She was there to attend a meeting about forming a residents' association in the Verde Para Sempre Extractive Reserve (RESEX Verde Para Sempre). The conflict between loggers and land claimers made the area a rather unfortunate focus of national attention. With the recent creation of the RESEX to protect the riverine peasants, or *ribeirinhos*, living in the area, the future looked brighter, more peaceful, and more verdant. The residents' association would provide the social structures for the community to represent its interests, to make decisions collectively, and to eventually develop plans for community forest management plans.

Marina, as she is affectionately called by Brazilians, had been close friends with Chico Mendes, the union organizer and rubber tapper whose assassination in December 1988 sparked the creation of the first extractive reserves. As a child, she herself had been a rubber tapper in the Amazonian state of Acre prior to setting her sights on politics. The RESEX is a unique type of conservation area. The designation allows the populations living inside of the reserve to engage in low-impact activities such as tapping latex for artisan rubber production, Brazil nut (*Bertholletia excelsa*) gathering, and fishing. The national environmental agency,

IBAMA, is responsible for making sure their land rights are secured and their forest areas protected from illegal encroachments by loggers or other intruders. In many ways the RESEX was a revolutionary model; in it, forest peoples were viewed as allies in conservation rather than as obstacles to forest protection.[1]

Marina Silva's presence was significant on several levels. Her visit signaled a triumph for the RESEX model as an important axis of Brazilian conservation strategies. For local residents, it also signified that their struggle was of national political significance. Moreover, Marina herself represented proof that even the most poor and isolated of rural Brazilians could become a well-respected national leader. By visiting, her story of struggle for land and the creation of RESEXs alongside Chico Mendes became linked in the historical legacy of RESEX Verde Para Sempre. The day seemed to symbolize a hopeful new era, and at the same time a pinnacle amid the longer history of achievements for forest peoples. In the words of one of the central community leaders, Idalino Nunes de Assis, "the struggle has now ended, and a story has begun."

The positive name of the RESEX Verde Para Sempre, meaning "Green Forever," however, was quickly becoming more aspirational than literal. Only a year later, when I visited the residents' association to commemorate the official signing of their community forest management plan, sardonic humor was expressed by allies of the RESEX in whispers at the back of the room: "Green Forever" should really have been called "Green Every So Often," since the area was so fraught with encroachments by ranchers and loggers. From the very day Marina Silva arrived in RESEX Verde Para Sempre, tragic disappointments were intermixed with tremendous successes in the new story that was unfolding.

Earlier that same morning, less than 300 km away near the town of Anapu, Sister Dorothy Stang, a 73 year-old American-born nun working for the Pastoral Land Commission (CPT) was assassinated in the rainforest while walking to a community meeting where she was organizing small farmers and working for forest protection (refer to Chapter 4 for a longer discussion). The news had not yet reached those in Verde Para Sempre, so the day of Marina's visit remained a joyous one, though the immediate aftermath of the meeting was replete with mixed emotions.

As people around the region grieved over the loss of Sister Dorothy, the Brazilian government responded by doubling down on its commitment to rainforest protection. The week following the assassination, the government created the Xingu River basin conservation area mosaic. Not only would RESEX Verde Para Sempre have protection, but an additional three RESEXs would be created upstream on the Xingu (and its tributaries, the Iriri and the Riozinho do Anfrísio rivers), along with a national park, an ecological station, an environmentally protected area.[2] Located adjacent to indigenous areas on the Xingu, the mosaic of conservation areas in the Terra do Meio region became one of the largest contiguous conservation corridors in the world, at just over 28 million hectares (around 69 million acres). It was a tremendous step forward for environmental conservation and was a significant measure aimed at quelling the encroachments of land claimers and loggers who had been threatening the populations in the Xingu River basin, which include 25 indigenous ethnic groups and about 12,000 people. Around 200 families in the region are *ribeirinhos*, a legally recognized traditional population of river-based peasants that mostly arrived into this part of the Amazon as rubber soldiers during the Second World War.[3] Figure 5.1 shows Marina Silva visiting Verde Para Sempre and the assembled crowd.

The creation of the Terra do Meio conservation area mosaic was a significant achievement for Brazilian land regularization efforts, in addition to environmental protection. Previously, accurate maps did not exist to clarify who legitimately held title to land in those areas. There was little to no ability for the government to distinguish what lands were the federal government's, the state government's, individuals', or were legally held in community-based arrangements. Creating the conservation area mosaic meant that an organized environmental and social protection approach would triumph over centuries of chaotic land regimes. The move was especially important because the Xingu basin was along the "arc of deforestation." This arc refers to the wide swath of frontier lands where, especially in the southern Amazon and also from the

Figure 5.1 Minister of the Environment Marina Silva speaks to a packed audience at the Verde Para Sempre reserve, February 14, 2005. (Photo: Alberto César Araújo).

southeast of Pará, pressure from agribusiness, logging, and road construction was causing forest fragmentation (Aldrich et al. 2012). The riverine peasants who lived in the newly created conservation areas were hopeful that the creation of the areas would mark an end to the forced expulsions from their homes that they were experiencing at the hands of the illegal land claimers, many of whom were associated with these forest losses. It was widely believed that establishing the conservation areas would help protect the forest and its peoples, quelling new deforestation and the further expansion of the frontier.[4]

The Terra do Meio conservation area corridor was not the first time a momentous triumph had arisen from a tragedy in Amazonia. In late 2002, near what was to become the RESEX Verde Para Sempre, 400 community members blockaded barges loaded with illegal timber, mostly hardwoods like mahogany, destined for export.[5] Rather than the typical practice of burning the apprehended logs so that they lost all commercial value,[6] civil society pressure combined with mediation from the Federal *Ministério Publico* (MPF) to allow the timber to be donated back to the communities from which they were taken. The result was a substantial fund that became managed by local civil society groups and dedicated toward supporting socio-environmental projects throughout the Transamazon and BR-163 region. The fund, called Fundo Dema, was named after Ademir Alfeu Federicci (nicknamed "Dema"). Dema was assassinated in 2001 in Altamira in front of his family. He was a much-beloved activist and leader of the Movement for the Development of the Transamazon and Xingu (MDTX). Despite such jarring incidents of human and ecological violence, the people of the region were showing the Brazilian government and the loggers and land claimers that they were far from helpless, passive victims. While isolated, very poor, and frequently illiterate,[7] the *ribeirinhos* were active agents in charting the course of their region's future. It was a path that involved both major ups and downs that were navigated through careful attention to discourses of sustainability, crafting of identities, and conscious construction of attention to the region.

This chapter tells the story how the world's second-largest biodiversity corridor was created. It concerns the sustainable development narratives articulated by the residents, intermediaries, private actors, and NGOs that worked in in the three RESEXs that were created in the Terra do Meio region between 2005–2009. It offers insight into processes in which impressions of legitimacy are created and reinforced through deploying a framework of sustainable development. Some authors have suggested that outside actors, especially anthropologists and environmentalist nongovernmental organizations, imposed alien conservationist frameworks on forest peoples to the detriment of both forest peoples and environmental conservation (Terborgh 1999, Redford and Padoch 1992). For others, the picture of how certain frameworks of identities and struggle come to be adopted is more about subverting identities into collective imaginaries held by others rather than a direct imposition of clashing values (Snow and Trom 2002). Ironically, the environmental movement frequently places Amazonians into a marginalized position, because their appeals often rely on the political effectiveness of widespread ideas about indigenous peoples that are ultimately homogenizing and disempowering (Fisher 1996, Hecht and Cockburn 1990). It is important to acknowledge these critiques while also appreciating that domestic and transnational networks involving social and environmental activism can provide beneficial political resources and meet mutual needs (Keck 1995, Keck and Sikkink 1998, Hochstettler and Keck 2007). Moreover, NGOs and other intermediaries can amplify the framework through which a movement conveys its identity, transforming the ways in which people think about an issue to shift discourse, perceptions of the mainstream, and extend concern to communities that would not otherwise become engaged.

This chapter reveals how subjects of sustainable development are constructed through different visions of state planning and control of space. The *ribeirinhos* of the Terra do Meio region and the NGO and governmental actors who interacted with them engaged in a process of gaining legibility for the boundaries of the land and the identity of the communities themselves as they became newly recognized as citizens and landholders. This process of gaining legibility involved clarifying who was considered a legitimate RESEX resident, consolidating a unified historical narrative of sustainable practices in the region, and delineating the region as a common geographical entity. In so doing, they conformed to expectations established by the state that they would be partners in the process of governing the region, through acting as sustainable users of the forest's resources. The imaginary of sustainable development that is present in the case of the Terra do Meio conservation areas involves creating and contesting various visions of what "nature" and human/nature relations should look like.

As with other conservation areas, these contesting visions often take shape in idealized, imagined, and virtualized forms. The imaginary also delineates the prospects for the possible (West, Igoe, and Brockington 2006, West 2006, Carrier and Miller 1998). Culture, politics, economics, and a variety of social relations together co-constitute socio-nature, a non-dichotomized approach to human/natural relations (Lefebvre 1991 [1974]). Governing for sustainable development in the region involves identity construction in ways that are both spatial and social. Attempts to gain recognition and legibility are substantially influenced by the role of intermediaries, and they involve grassroots actors' own dynamic ways of engaging with intermediaries and with regulatory institutions.

This chapter begins by portraying the Terra do Meio region as a site where sustainable development is invoked and articulated by a range of actors, including both nongovernmental organizations and private firms. Their presentations of themselves and their respective projects under the umbrella of sustainable development are based upon concerted efforts to draw attention to conservation efforts as well as conflicts, and simultaneously to create a sense of urgency for governmental recognition of and attention to the region. The chapter highlights how processes of sustainable development governance unfolded by examining the positioning of peasant identities, geographic imaginaries, and the important roles played by intermediaries, who negotiate regulations between the state and those local populations. These intermediaries, whether environmental NGOs or business operative agents, act to portray legitimacy—both of themselves and those they purport to represent—and in so doing, aim to establish resonant frameworks through which to obtain power, usually manifested through territorial control and influence. At the same time, the Brazilian state wields influence over sustainable development planning largely according to logics of macro-economic interests and reactions to public relations, making a tapestry of policies that are contradictory in terms of their goals and frequently unequally distributed in terms of their benefits.

Fighting for the Land in the Middle

The residents of the Terra do Meio region are the riverine peasants who live several days' journey by boat from the nearest town (for most in the region, Altamira). Their experience is one of substantial isolation from the rest of Brazilian society and, often, each other: each family often lives several hours' paddle by dugout canoe from one house to the next. Save for the occasional community party, short-wave radio communications, and the gossip mill of river-based travelers and traders, contacts are infrequent between the *ribeirinhos*. The populations in the Terra do Meio survived for generations living in the rural area along the Xingu, Iriri, and Riozinho do Anfrísio rivers without birth certificates, voter registration cards, and work records for social security benefits. By all standard measures, before the RESEXs in the region were created, they were a population that was invisible to the state.

Most of the riverine peasants of the Terra do Meio had settled there three and four generations earlier, when their grandparents moved to the region during the first rubber boom, between the 1850s and the first decade of the twentieth century. They worked as "rubber soldiers" for the land-owning rubber barons, who, in the tradition of plantation owners, bought their rubber, provided their housing, and controlled both healthcare and educational functions within each rubber plantation (Harris 2006). As rubber tappers, the river-based peasants and the landowners upon whom they depended were marked by patron–client relations. Even several generations after the end of the rubber boom, clientelism was a central means of winning loyalties as the riverine peasants later sought out protection and support. After the rubber boom ended, the peasants stayed on the lands that the rubber barons had generally abandoned, living predominantly from subsistence fishing and farming activities. They had little by way of formal education, and for years their main contact with the outside world happened through visits from the local priests, who would travel down the river as part of their ministry. The land was the *ribeirinhos'* not because they had papers to prove it but because they had been living on it and making it productive continuously for several generations. Still, the *ribeirinhos* went unrecognized by the authorities, without identity cards, land titles, or even participating in the national census.

As illegal land-claiming and deforestation increased in the mid-1990s, the *ribeirinhos'* livelihoods became threatened; some had their thatched-roof houses burned down, others were forced to leave their lands at gunpoint. Beyond the challenge of catching the attention of decision makers, this population of mostly illiterate farmers and fishermen were up against formidable odds. One major obstacle was the physical control of the region that was maintained by a firm owned by an individual known as the "biggest *grileiro* [illegal land-claimer] in the world" (de Barros 2005).[8]

Cecílio Rego de Almeida (hereafter, C.R. Almeida) was one of the hundred richest people in the world according to *Forbes* in 1992, through a fortune he amassed from civil construction projects in Brazil during the 1970s and 1980s under Brazil's military leadership. The enormous quantity of land Almeida claimed to own in the Terra do Meio region was the magnitude of whole countries. The territory he had bought (although illegally) was referred to by some as if it was a kingdom, called "Cecíolândia"—Cecioland—after Almeida's own first name). It was about 6 million hectares (about 14.8 million acres), the equivalent size of Belgium and the Netherlands combined (de Barros 2005, Greenpeace 2003). The land claim consisted of five rubber-growing areas totaling 1.2 million hectares (nearly three million acres).[9] On maps, the lands claimed by Almeida overlapped with the Terra do Meio Ecological Station (a conservation area) and several indigenous territories.

The New Baron of the Terra do Meio

C.R. Almeida started investing in Amazonian lands beginning in the mid-1990s. In the Terra do Meio region, his claims included an extensive portion of land along the Xingu River (1.2 million hectares, about 3 million acres), which, when cross-referenced with government maps, revealed locations that were positioned over the territories of Arueté and Paracanã indigenous peoples as well as the Xingu National Forest.[10] The other main lands that he claimed were along the

Curuá and Iriri Rivers, comprising 4.7 million hectares (11.6 million acres).[11] When he purchased the lands, none of the longtime residents had any idea about what had occurred. This was not particularly unusual, however; illegal land-claiming in Amazonia has a long history involving improper maps, improperly documented sales, falsified titles, and superimpositions of property lines. At 125 million hectares (309 million hectares), Pará is Brazil's second largest state and one of its worst centers for illegal land-claiming. Approximately 70 percent of the land in the state falls under the federal government's control. Some studies estimate that in the state of Pará, well over 60 percent of lands have false titles or no titles at all. In Amazonia, around 45 percent of lands have no owner or legal title (IPAM 2006). Several important tactics were used by Almeida's companies in the attempt to portray these investments both as sustainability-oriented and to convince the local populations that the landholdings were legal; these included attempts to gain the loyalties of the *ribeirinhos*, promotion of regional conservation and ecotourism development initiatives, and mirroring the discourses of environmentalism through the creation of NGOs. These techniques will be detailed below, following a brief explanation that illustrates the issue of land-claiming in greater depth.

The problem of illegal land-claiming in Pará can be traced back to complications starting in the Republican Constitution of 1891 in Brazil, which transferred unused lands into states' dominions. This created a legal lacuna, complicating the question of which lands were the federal government's and which were the state governments' to control. From 1891 on, a majority of lands were registered as possession-based holdings, but these were never measured and demarcated. The full legal procedure for achieving land ownership, rather than just possession holdings, would have involved entering into a process wherein the land becomes "legitimized" and in which possession becomes registered as land under the holder's dominion. In other words, a prospective owner would have to prove ownership of the land itself, not just the labor put into the land. Normal acquisition of land purchases and sales were also legalized on conditions of "effective occupation and habitual residence"; as a result, there was substantial confusion over who rightfully owned parcels versus those who were merely working the land with usufruct rights. The scale of C.R. Almeida's claims was enormous, but because of these long-standing historical and current realities, the fact that such substantial legal chaos existed over land titling was not particularly unusual.

C.R. Almeida's firms, Incexcil and Amazônia Projetos Ecológicos Ltda., initially established a benevolent presence when they arrived in the region in 1996. Incexcil at first aimed to position itself in opposition to illegal loggers, exerting rigid control of the lands by keeping a base of armed guards in the area. They occasionally ousted illegal loggers from the area to build their security bases, but largely left the *ribeirinhos* in the region alone. Several of the predatory logging companies were extracting mahogany from the forests without compensating the *ribeirinhos*, whereas Incexcil offered to pay some peasants to merely stay on their land and protect it from incursions. Through this approach, the firm began credibly presenting itself as forest protectors, filling the void of environmental enforcement that IBAMA had left through its absence in the region. Figure 5.2 portrays one such security base, along with a sign that mimics the IBAMA protected area signage, such that it might be easily confounded for a federal property rather than a privately owned parcel.

At the outset, few Terra do Meio residents were troubled by "The Firm";[12] at the very least, Incexcil was bringing them some basic food assistance, and occasionally they brought doctors and dentists to the region, whereas previously the population had no such care. "The firm was very good to us; they gave us all sorts of assistance," said someone in defense of Almeida's enterprise. But others were not so trusting of the handouts:

> The firm . . . the proposal that they had was that for every person who was in favor of it [Incexcil], that we would take care of our own place, and they would pay a salary, for the guy, and give everything . . . but in trade for what? . . . what

Figure 5.2 C.R. Almeida's firm uses a sign similar in format and style to that of the federal government to deter other would-be land claimants and convey an impression of legality to the local population, most of which is illiterate. Photo: Tarcísio Feitosa

> is the interest you have to help me in my place? . . . in three or four or five years, he'd [C.R. Almeida] come and throw the guy out, and show the documentation, that he had been paying the citizen in exchange for them to take care their place, but really their place would turn into being the firm's place, C.R. Almeida's. And there are a lot of people that don't understand this. (Interview with author 2006)

Almeida's companies sought to use sophisticated propaganda and public relations attempts to present a convincing vision for the sustainable development they hoped to achieve in the region. Initially, Incexcil and Amazônia Projetos Ecológicos were involved in discussions about funding and establishing scientific laboratories in the Terra do Meio in order to explore the forest for its biodiversity and potential medicines. Under the name of the "Amazon Dream" project, Almeida proposed a future of large-scale ecotourism for the region, involving the construction of luxury hotels, forest trails, and an airport. Included in the project was a proposal for generating more than 3,000 jobs in Altamira and investing $100,000,000 in infrastructure. Altamira's squatter-housing settlements would be transformed into public housing, benefiting some 2,000 families living in the shacks over a stream which floods homes annually during the rainy season. Aside from a sleek brochure and a short video promotion about the project, no one close to the project ever saw anything more specific in terms of formal documentation. The brochure, entitled "Project Amazon: Forest Forever" emphasized preserving cultural values, providing social services without becoming either a development agency or duplicating the government's responsibilities, and safeguarding the forest in a non-predatory way, such that its ecosystems would remain preserved and in balance (Almeida 1999).

C.R. Almeida also proposed a philanthropic idea modeled after carbon offsetting, involving selling parts of his land or individual trees over the Internet so that well-meaning contributors could buy them to save a piece of the Amazon for permanent conservation purposes. Almeida personally ran the idea past Raul Jungmann, who at the time was the president of IBAMA, the national environmental protection agency. Jungmann was enthusiastic: "I thought the idea was so good that I even proposed that the government should do something similar" (Junior 1999). Altamira's mayor at the time, Claudemiro Gomes, also got on board with the project. By 1999, Almeida's vision for the Terra do Meio entailed a privately owned forest protection initiative which was a viable alternative, of sorts, to the social movement's regional conservation proposal, which was called the Lungs of the Transamazon (discussed below). However, many of Altamira's more active civil society voices remained skeptical about C.R. Almeida's intentions and the companies he established. They suspected bio-piracy, or that he must have ulterior motives for using the land.

The framing of Almeida's intentions as environmentally friendly also took institutionalized forms. In Altamira, an NGO called Bio-Ambiente was founded by Incexil to devote itself to environmental conservation. In the eyes of most of Altamira's activists, Bio-Ambiente was a "pseudo-NGO" which served as an environmentalist front for what were really the firm's capitalist interests. Still, to many *ribeirinhos* the Bio-Ambiente logo looked official, reminiscent of a police shield. To the untrained eye, Bio-Ambiente would appear to be a prominent and upstanding local environmental organization, as much as any other.

This tactic of mirroring established NGOs which had longer track records of credibility reveals the power of how environmental frameworks served to legitimize a vast range of interventions on Amazonian lands. Moreover, the presence of NGO intermediaries between the grassroots actors and the state played an important role in making such arguments convincing. The firm's tactics were two-fold: gain land by force, if necessary, and meanwhile set up goodwill agencies to gain loyalty and support as a benefactor in the region. While the violence was not as bad in some parts of the Xingu River, elsewhere in the region, especially along the Curuá, Riozinho do Anfrísio, and Iriri Rivers, Incexcil had "security guards" who were waging a low-level war against the *ribeirinhos*. Stories were commonplace of shootouts and grievous acts of violence.

> I had a lot of fear living there, since people were forcing others to leave. That is the only reason I left. I lived alone, and only trusted in God, because I was working completely alone in the fields, and then they got the idea that I should leave, to avoid something happening to me like this other case that I saw. There was this other thing happened [upriver], where they took and killed people . . . When we got to Ilha da Rocha, above Novo Linda, they had already killed one, and there were still two people . . . After two or three days they killed him at about five o'clock, and covered him with sticks. They tried to set fire [to him] to it but it didn't catch. We all saw this situation. (Interview with author 2006)

One person's house was burned down by people who worked for the firm; this was explained to other community members by the firm as necessary so that they could establish a guarded "monitoring point" on the same strategic location, at the mouth of the Rio Pardo, where many other land claimers were entering. Still, even there, several people had disagreements over getting paid for services rendered to the firm. The environmental and beneficent roles that the firm was taking appeared a thin veneer to some residents, but some loyalties were torn among the *ribeirinhos*.

Almeida's company and Bio-Ambiente organized some members of the Terra do Meio communities to form into community associations, whereas local social movement activists from the Pastoral Land Commission (CPT) and the

Foundation for Life, Production, and Preservation (FVPP) began helping the *ribeirinhos* do the same, with the intention of doing community organizing work to strengthen their advocacy for the creation of new extractive reserves as a solution to the region's problems. The CPT in Altamira, which at the time was led by a particularly talented and engaged coordinator named Tarcísio Feitosa, especially came to be perceived as vying with C.R. Almeida's firm for influence with the *ribeirinhos*. "Whose side are you on, Tarcísio's or the firm's?" residents of the Terra do Meio asked each other with some frequency. "Tarcísio's side" signified an allegiance with the NGOs like the FVPP and Instituto SocioAmbiental (ISA), as well as support for the creation of the extractive reserves.[13]

The C.R. Almeida case illustrates several important dimensions of the struggle over land rights in the Terra do Meio region. Environmental concerns were articulated by C.R. Almeida's companies in a manner that illustrates the pragmatism of adopting environmental positions, whether or not a deeper set of conservation-oriented values was put into practice. By seeking to portray their aims in the Terra do Meio as beneficial actions, powerful allies could be won over, land could be managed, and Almeida's firms could present themselves as filling a governance void instead of inviting more of a state presence. This functioned, at least for a time, to consolidate their power in the region, and built upon the existing histories of the *ribeirinho* population as relatively subservient populations, maintaining much of their dependency upon Almeida's firms as caretakers. The discussion which follows focuses on the role of the local civil society groups that acted as intermediaries for the riverine peasants of the Terra do Meio area. It examines the power dynamics of those intermediary groups, and explains the transitions that took place as sustainable development visions for the region's future competed with each other. These organizations campaigned for the conservation areas of the Terra do Meio mosaic to be created using a very different strategy from the high-investment, singular-organization, and sometimes violent model that C.R. Almeida's firms adopted.

Negotiating Conservation

Ousting control away from Almeida's firms in the Terra do Meio took considerable time, effort, and risks. These were faced by both the *ribeirinhos* and a host of NGOs of longer standing that were working in the region. Their pressure and proposals were especially important given the competition they faced from C.R. Almeida's firms and associated NGOs and his counter-proposal for the lands to become a privately held protected area. The first step for these local NGOs involved an attempt to gain the attention of the federal government to the plight of the Xingu's riverine peasants.

The first legal filing against C.R. Almeida came in August 1996, soon after the lands were originally purchased. It asked for the annulment and cancelation of Incexcil's land holdings with the Pará state land reform agency. It was a very slow legal process of adjudication of the land claims; parcel by parcel, the holdings that Almeida claimed had to be tracked down in the notoriously corrupt offices of notary publics, and then each parcel went through a legal review of its history, boundaries, and land titles. Further complicating the process, at the local level the notary offices in Altamira were known as some of the most corrupt in the whole country, and this is where many of the land titles would need to be tracked down before Almeida's claims could be legally expropriated (Thadeu 2007, Esterci 2003).[14]

Efforts renewed during the 1998 campaign called the *Grito da Transamazônica*, "Cry of the Transamazon," when thousands of people from the Transamazon highway and Xingu River basin traveled to Brasilia to demand better infrastructure, rule of law, and social policies for the residents of the Transamazon highway and the Terra do Meio region. Their plan was known as the Lungs of the Transamazon proposal. It aimed to stave off unchecked roadcutting, land-claiming, and to quell deforestation rates in the area (Souza 2006, Toni, Santos Souza, and Porro 2006). The Lungs of the Transamazon outlined a nascent proposal for creating the conservation area mosaic in the Terra do Meio region and for organizing land titles of small-holder farmers along the Transamazon highway. It suggested ways to quell rampant illegal land invasions by giving land titles and legal protection to the hundreds of *ribeirinho* families who had lived on the Terra do Meio lands for generations, unrecognized by the government. Specifically, it proposed creating three main blocks of conservation areas in the regions to the north and south of the Transmazon highway in the Xingu River basin, in Porto de Moz (the area that now is the Verde Para Sempre Extractive Reserve) and in Renascer. The necessity for action seemed an urgent imperative:

> . . . we saw at the time that the forested areas, they were becoming degraded—illegally . . . and after the exploitation of wood, the areas were left for *fazendeiros* to put in pasture . . . and we understood that at the same rhythm that was happening, we saw that in only five years all of these areas would be totally destroyed by the logging functions, and everything would be in the hands of the *fazendeiros*, and soon we wouldn't have these places, nor more space for any families to live on the land and work, we just wouldn't have it anymore . . . . (Interview with author 2006)

The proposal derived from initial outreach to the Terra do Meio populations, conducted by a Catholic priest from the Xingu diocese, Padre Angelo, who traveled the region from 1983–1985 and conducted an initial survey concerning the families living along the rivers. By the mid-1990s, peasants from the Terra do Meio started arriving in Altamira in consternation. They sought help after their homes had been burned down, the wood from their forests had been taken, or when newcomers seemed to be putting up fences and claiming lands that had traditionally belonged to their families. They sought out the CPT, which was affiliated with the Catholic Church, and began talking with an organization that was then called the Movement for Survival on the Transamazon (MPST).[15] Starting in 2002, as the land-claiming and logging in the region was increasing, the populations of the *ribeirinhos* began to be shepherded on multiple trips to government offices at the urging of dedicated staff at Altamira-based NGOs, the CPT and the FVPP. These groups were the first to inform the local populations that if they wished, they could ask the government to create conservation areas in the Terra do Meio. Doing so, they explained, was the permanent way to solve the insecurity they faced. The short-term strategic step of conducting research about the area also appeared pragmatic to everyone. Documentation and inventory of the social and ecological significance of the area would show that the *ribeirinhos* were longtime Brazilian citizens who had rights to this land, and that the land had an ecological importance for the entire nation. This was a necessary first step along the path toward ending the violence afflicting their community, which was a primary motivation for *ribeirinhos* and local activists alike.

A positive initial response to their request for action and attention to the area came from the Amazon Secretariat of the Ministry of the Environment. The office commissioned a study by the ISA, a national environmental organization. The study aimed to assess the ecology and potential viability of creating conservation areas in the Terra do Meio region. This study was the first active collaboration between the local activists and national-level partners in relation to the Terra do Meio area.[16] The study was thorough, but several years passed without further governmental action. According to some close to the social movement efforts, the proposal "accumulated dust in Brasilia." Back in Altamira, and largely thanks to the nationally and internationally networked ISA activists, the local social movement organizations, led by the CPT and FVPP, formed broader activist alliances. They brought in the WWF and the Environmental Defense Fund as allies to help write grants and develop projects for the region. While the proposal for the "Lungs of the Transamazon" languished in Brasilia, local peasants were organized into residents' associations, largely also resulting from the CPT and FVPP's community organizing efforts.

Leaders from the local communities continued to call attention to the problems of illegal logging and encroachment upon their lands. At the request of the Terra do Meio residents, a report was commissioned by the federal House of Deputies which entailed a federal investigation into illegal land-claiming in the region. It began to reveal the magnitude of C.R. Almeida and others' landholdings and false land titles throughout the area (CPI 2001). In addition to the seven million hectares of forest lands (about 17.2 million acres) claimed by C.R. Almeida, the investigation revealed that an entity representing a consortium of land claimers used false documents to seize twelve million hectares (30 million acres) of land under the fictitious name of Carlos Medeiros. With some of the land claims still ambiguous, the report noted that the amount claimed by Carlos Medeiros could be up to 35 million hectares (86.4 million acres), which would total up to 30 percent of the land in the state of Pará. (CPI 2001, Greenpeace 2003) Much of this land was sold to third parties, many of whom took on fictional identities of their own. A Greenpeace report sums up the history of these illegal titles:

> Lawyers claiming to represent him stated that Medeiros, in the 1970s, received land from the heirs of two Portuguese settlers who had claimed ownership of large sections of Pará. A Pará judge in 1975 recognized the legitimacy of the claim of Medeiros, but was later removed from office for irregularities. Carlos Medeiros has never come forward. His lawyers said they could not locate him to bring him to the CPI investigation. His existence has never been confirmed. He is almost certainly a 'ghost.' (Greenpeace 2003, 10)

Given the magnitude of these chaotic land claims, advocacy for land titles and legal protection for the hundreds of *ribeirinho* families who had lived in the Terra do Meio region became an important agenda item for Altamira-based activists. Many *ribeirinhos* had left their homes on the rivers due to intimidation or violence, and others were afraid to support the proposal, given the violence that still afflicted those living in the midst of the land conflicts and the competing pulls from Almeida's own NGOs for their allegiance.

As one person from the Xingu River recalled:

> Five years ago, there were a lot of people here, and on the *beiradão* [river banks] today, it's only abandoned places. People went into Altamira, or into São Felix . . . really, for these *grileiros* who began to arrive, many people sold [their lands], and began to leave. And then, too, C.R. Almeida came, and has been messing in the Xingu for five or six years, and they arrived, and said the land was his, and even though today we know that none of it was really his, a lot of people got scared by the pressure from them. And so they started to look for a way to leave, to go live in Altamira or to São Felix. (Interview with author 2006)

Increasingly, the people of the Terra do Meio region sought out allies outside of C.R. Almeida's firms and employees. They turned to the CPT and the FVPP, both based in Altamira, for help. The CPT office had short-wave radios, and became a hub for the city residents to communicate with their friends and family members living along the riverbanks. The local organizations also offered support to the *ribeirinhos* by accompanying them to government offices and hospitals when necessary, writing up denunciations against the illegal logging in the region and striving to maintain some political pressure on the federal government so that they would address the situation in the Terra do Meio.

One resident from Riozinho do Anfrísio communicated the story of their community's struggle through a ballad. It described how the *ribeirinhos* experienced threats, shootouts against the firm's hired gunmen, and long community meetings where money and boats were promised to the peasants in exchange for their loyalty. The ballad praises the assistance of the IBAMA representative in the region for helping secure an eventual Federal Police team to come to the region to reestablish the land as the *ribeirinhos'* own. One of the few literate *ribeirinhos* living on the Xingu wrote letters himself:

> I am writing only to ask you to do something for me, since I have no transport, and not even communication here with me.... People from Serra [*sic.*, meaning C.R.] Almeida are cutting strips of land in front of my house and I can't do anything so I ask you to please go now to IBAMA and ask [the officials] to take these people out of here.., only IBAMA can correct it, and I can't keep making these commentaries.... (Interview with author 2006)

Countervailing pressures came from the Incexcil representatives and the other people paid by C.R. Almeida, who did their best to undermine support for the extractive reserves and the other conservation areas. They spread misinformation among the *ribeirinhos*, claiming that the government would no longer permit people to farm on their lands within the reserve and that gardening, fishing, and raising chickens would also be prohibited once the RESEX was created. Aiming to convince the *ribeirinhos* that the status quo was preferable to any changes, they also argued that people would be forced to leave their lands if the land became a reserve. Correcting these untruths became a time-consuming obstacle for the activists at the FVPP and CPT, as they worked to establish support for and greater awareness about the benefits of creating conservation areas for the local populations. Generating effective public participation and engagement was similarly a significant challenge. In one particularly charged situation in 2005, multiple employees from C.R. Almeida's companies came to the initial public hearing about the creation of the RESEX along the Xingu dressed in uniforms very similar to those of the military police. The company men had to be removed from the meeting on the basis that they intimidated the *ribeirinhos*. Despite their removal, they succeeded in achieving their aims; several families chose not to participate in this all-community meeting, out of a mix of intimidation and mistrust. Others decided that abstaining from participation in meetings was the best, and safest, alternative. In interviews, the Brazilian environmental agency officials present at those meetings expressed that they felt the situation too conflict-prone and the community too disunited to establish the RESEX that year, despite the fact that meetings had happened already on the Riozinho do Anfrísio and Iriri Rivers nearby, and those areas had already become RESEXs immediately following Sister Dorothy Stang's death in February 2005.

Gradually, the government was able to pass an order that forced C.R. Almeida's companies off of the lands in the Terra do Meio and then, parcel by parcel, canceled their false titles (Mendes 2006). The last piece of the Terra do Meio conservation area mosaic, the RESEX Xingu, was established on June 6, 2008, about two years after C.R. Almeida's land claims were legally canceled in the region. This was a major legal victory, as one of the greatest difficulties in establishing protected areas is resolving the legal claims surrounding particular land parcels and then physically removing the illegal actors from the area.[17] This is also the stage in conservation area creation that involves notably higher risks for conservation protagonists and for illegal deforestation in the areas to take place, as the quote at the very beginning of this chapter illustrates.[18] It is noteworthy, too, that in addition to the land title questions that delayed the RESEX Xingu creation, the federal Ministry of Mines and Energy also stalled the proposal from 2007–2008 because of concern that establishing the extractive reserve might have presented a stumbling block for the Belo Monte dam, which was proposed for construction further downstream (ISA 2008). The Belo Monte project and the activism surrounding it is the subject of Chapter 6. Considering the magnitude of geographic expanse and the powerful interests involved, ousting Almeida and creating the RESEX was a substantial achievement for activists, the *ribeirinhos*, and the government. Figure 5.3 illustrates the area where the Terra do Meio conservation area mosaic was created.

Even after its official creation, the fate of the RESEX Xingu remained in some limbo. It narrowly escaped being vetoed by President Dilma Rousseff in 2010 on the grounds that it might interfere with licensing for the Belo Monte dam project.[19] For some other extractive reserves in the Amazon, however, presidential vetoes did go into effect; dams planned for the Tapajós and Madeira Rivers have caused reductions in the conservation areas that were once established, on the grounds that having the conservation areas in place would be an impediment to achieving the environmental licensing necessary for the hydroelectric projects to move forward (Miotto 2011). As one local activist who was closely observing the politics of conservation area creation recalled:

> The same government that authorized millions of hectares to be protected has also authorized the construction of hydroelectric dams in Rio Madeira and Serra do Pardo. At least, we knew the line of Fernando Henrique [Cardoso], we

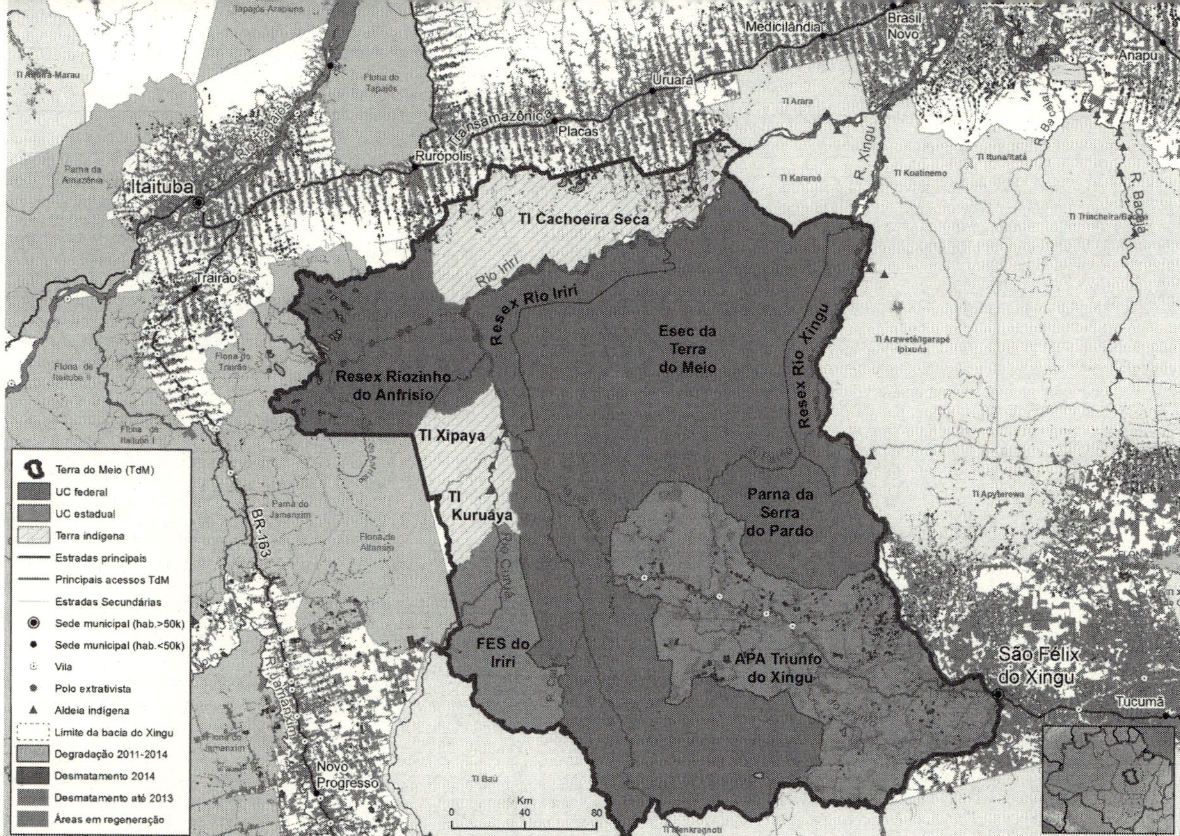

Figure 5.3 A map of the Terra do Meio conservation area mosaic. This huge biodiversity corridor of 8.48 million hectares includes three extractivist reserves (Riozinho do Anfrísio, Rio Xingu, and Rio Iriri), an ecological station (ESEC Terra do Meio) and environmentally protected área (APA Trionfo do Xingu), and the Serra do Pardo National Park. It is contiguous with the earlier-established indigenous lands of the Cachoeira Seca, Curuaya, and Xipaya. To the west of the Iriri River is the BR-163 Sustainable Forest District, and to the north along the Xingu River is the Verde Para Sempre extractivist reserve. Map Credit: Instituto Socioambiental

> knew that the avenue was development at whatever price. Under Lula, I think, in truth, that he doesn't have a plan for Amazonia. He's shooting in every direction. (Interview with author 2006)

This observation suggests that activists perceived the policies for Amazonian development to be contradictory under President Lula. While collaborating with the government in creating the conservation areas, some were already wary that in the bigger picture, such close alliances could involve significant compromises. The delays of the RESEX Xingu's creation compared to the other extractive reserves in the region, as well as the distinctive struggle to mobilize the community there compared to the demographically similar and geographically proximate communities in the rest of the region, is illustrative of the unevenness of sustainable development plans as they are put into practice.

From Invisible to Environmental Citizen

The process of creating the conservation areas in the Terra do Meio involved many *ribeirinho* communities gaining citizenship rights and responsibilities for the first time. In addition to the need for communities to gain security to live safely on their lands in the conservation areas in the Terra do Meio, free of the threats from illegal land claimers, part of their experience was one of gaining recognition as citizens, often for the first time. Most of the people living along the rivers in the Terra do Meio region had never before possessed birth certificates or identity documents, thus making them invisible to the state. Without work cards or their voter registrations, the Terra do Meio *ribeirinhos* did not receive any sort of public benefits nor congruent abilities to have their land or labor rights secured. While they received no benefits of citizenship, they also were not obliged to undertake correspondent rights and responsibilities of citizenship, such as voting[20] and schooling. Sustainable development provided a framework for land use plans, and also community organizing. In this way, modernization in the form of health care, educational access, identity documentation, and commercially based economic livelihoods all became more commonplace.

As riverine peasants that descended from rubber tappers, the Terro de Meio residents are considered traditional populations under Brazilian law. Under this designation, the *ribeirinhos* receive special attention from the Environmental Ministry, including having particular protections and collective land rights.[21] Decree 6040, the National Policy for Sustainable Development and Traditional Communities (February 7, 2007) establishes the rights of these traditional populations to live in conservation areas and defines them as those who are culturally distinct, have some form of social organization, and use territory and natural resources for their religious, cultural, and social reproduction (Bolaños 2014). While the category of a "traditional" population is deliberately broad, it explicitly entails an exchange-based relationship with the federal government. The premise of the arrangement is that the traditional populations, if given adequate conditions, would manage the conservation areas, entering into a covenant with the government for the guarantee of land rights, and which requires making alliances with nongovernmental organizations, academics, and governmental institutions in order to gain recognition (Carneiro da Cunha and Almeida 2000).

It is significant to note that in this type of exchange relationship, the designation as traditional populations living in extractive reserves reinforces the historic clientelism that those populations experienced, replacing the patron figure of the *seringalista* with a new patron: the state. The federal government takes on the role of a protective and powerful benefactor in the relationship, and the *ribeirinhos* are responsible to them as the eyes and ears of environmental protection on the ground. In return, they are expected to perform as the state would hope good conservation actors *ought* to behave—bringing illegal activities inside of their areas to the attention of government officials, participating in meetings to form community associations that install democratically elected representatives, and conforming their land uses and livelihoods according to the logics of the state's guidelines. Ironically, these logics at times diverge from the very traditional practices that the state purports to protect; democratic elections, for example, were never a part of the traditional life of the *ribeirinhos* and instead had to be taught by the NGOs facilitating their community organizing endeavors.

As the *ribeirinho* communities and the government entered into contact with each other, much of their traditional lifestyles and practices would begin to change. Traditionally, women along the Xingu, Iriri, Curuá, and Riozinho do Anfrísio rivers gave birth with the help of midwives, not doctors or hospitals. Commerce was done locally with river-based traders who brought in supplies for the people of the region most often in exchange for fish, which was sold in the city upon the traders' return. Most of the families along the riverbanks lived in considerable debt to these traders, who kept the books and charged more for the cost of oil, sugar, and coffee supplies than the families could repay through weekly fish yields. There was no expectation of social security or retirement benefits, nor schools or health care facilities. Sometimes people learned the basics of reading and writing from semiliterate family members. Barter was the predominant mode of exchange between families. With the creation of the extractive reserves, while the traditional economic livelihoods of fishing and Brazil nut gathering and other small-scale extractive activities were encouraged, other elements began to change.

Increasingly, both with the assistance of NGOs and because of governmental requirements, community health agents became health interlocutors and began seeking out hospital-based prenatal (and sometimes birthing) care for their fellow community members. Schools—although often left unstaffed due to the difficulty of finding and funding teachers to live in the isolation of the region—became a part of the children's upbringing, along with increased attention to literacy. Similarly, the economic livelihood of the traditional communities began to change with the advent of forest management plans and new community boats that could facilitate the transportation of fish and Brazil nuts out of the remote region. These would be established and led by community members in conjunction with governmental officials and NGOs. Such changes yielded positive metrics by all the conventional measures of development. The *ribeirinhos* were healthier, more literate, and financially stable. Conditions improved, by most accounts, for the Terra do Meio populations. Sustainable development was not without its benefits, although all these changes remained centrally rooted within the modern development paradigm rather than the metrics and conditions those populations had lived in during previous generations.

Gaining Recognition

Seeking out the government's recognition was something that became widely desirable for the Terra do Meio populations. The river-based peasants knew all too well that without some sort of relationship to the state, they were "*nem Indios*"—not treated even as minimally as the indigenous peoples—by the government. This assumption was not without reason; when federal funding for rural health care service trips to attend to the area fell short in 1999, only the indigenous tribes in the Terra do Meio benefited. The indigenous populations' budgetary allocations were allotted under FUNAI funding rather than the federal environmental agency. An outspoken public health advocate based in Altamira remembered, "indigenous people are the faces that Brazil wanted to show the world," while "the poor *ribeirinhos*, they look like other *caboclos* [peasants], they were not colorful or exotic enough" (Interview with author 2007). As a result, she assessed, the government did not allocate funding toward the *ribeirinhos*, although the population was written into health-related grant proposals alongside the indigenous groups. Amazonian populations struggled since the early 1970s to show the authorities that the region was not just "one big empty jungle" (Mendes 1989, 37). Especially for the non-indigenous populations of Amazonian residents, having meetings in Brasilia, gaining media attention, and drawing both research and the public eye to the multiplicities of Amazonian residents were important steps toward breaking down such overly simplistic representations. Long-standing conflicts between rubber tappers and indigenous peoples would gradually transform into alliances as, beginning around

1986, indigenous groups and rubber tappers began participating in organizing meetings, making joint proposals, and collaborating against illegal land speculation, road paving, and logging in the region (Mendes 1989).

The process of gaining formal government recognition entailed strategic narration of the *ribeirinhos'* recent history. The process of obtaining these identity documents from the government was often slow and bureaucratically complicated, but was a necessary step to both prove one's legal land claim as a legitimate resident of the RESEX. Given the movement of people between the Terra do Meio and houses in the city of Altamira, and their conflicted loyalties with regard to C.R. Almeida, it was important to clarify exactly who had a legitimate claim to land as a *ribeirinho*, and why that person was well-suited for the area. The CPT and FVPP contributed in this arena as well, making new frameworks possible for thinking about the history of the region's people. They did so to emphasize to a wide audience that the *ribeirinhos* were capable of being good environmental stewards. Further, they aimed to convey such a compelling story about the region that it would generate sufficient political pressure to spur the government to recognize the rights denied to the people of the Terra do Meio for decades. In so doing, the process of subjectivity formation in the Terra do Meio involved not only establishing legibility of the population through documentation but also the development of a set of discursive categories to describe the population's character and geography.

One such discursive shift was the characterization of the Terra do Meio populations as *ribeirinhos*. Initially, the river-based populations in the Terra do Meio did not adopt a self-identification as *ribeirinhos*. In describing and introducing themselves, most would say they were simply *beiradeiros*, meaning people who lived along the banks of the river. One of the oldest residents of the Xingu told me, to the agreement of several other longtime residents of the area: "I'm confused, I don't know a *ribeirinho*. I'm a *beiradeiro*, I am a *seringueiro*. . . . everyone all along the Xingu was a *beiradeiro*, and they come these days saying '*ribeirinho, ribeirinho*' so people use it today." For some of the *beiradeiros* of the Xingu, the term *ribeirinho* was not an immediately embraced identity category. For them it connoted people who live predominantly through fishing activities, but given that most fishermen were indebted to the *regatões*, or fluvial traders[22] who worked along the rivers of the region, *ribeirinhos* evoked debt and extreme poverty. It also tended to erase the memory of rubber tapping, which many of the older residents of the region especially felt connected to. While *ribeirinho* was used by a broad base of governmental and civil society actors, for many of the former *seringueiros* being called a *ribeirinho* was new and somewhat discomfiting. The *ribeirinho* term was aimed more at making their community legible to outside actors than attuned to their own narrations.[23]

For the NGOs and political actors who helped to promote the discourse, however, classifying the population of the region as *ribeirinhos* was logical, considering the term's political instrumentality. *Ribeirinhos*, as a traditional population, would be recognized for their environmental stewardship: "Traditional populations are also defined by their connection and relative symbiosis with nature, by their deep understandings of nature and its cycles, and by the notion of a territory or space where they socially and economically reproduce" (Santilli 2005). Especially compared to the term *caboclo*, the term *ribeirinho* would allow greater potential for political and social recognition, which, to a degree, meant achieving greater security, health care, and education.[24]

> In the case of a word with the sense of exclusion, like *caboclo* (in many ways the pariah [*sic*] of Amazonian colonial society), the name attributes an identity that catches the group and its subjects in a social immobility. The permanence of the name restricts the possibilities for emancipation. It's not by chance that in political movements, especially those linked to environmental problems, they are presented with new social identities, whether it is as 'People of the Forest,' Traditional Populations, Artisanal Fishermen, or Women of the Forest, but not as *caboclos*. (de Magalhães Lima 1999, 28)

One of the earliest evidences for applying the term *ribeirinho* to the Terra do Meio populations is found in a 1996 civil society letter to the governor of the state of Pará. "*Ribeirinho*" is used consistently throughout subsequent official documents, such as the Congressional investigations against illegal land-claiming and when referring to the local communities in the Terra do Meio. By classifying the societies of the Terra do Meio region not as peasants—akin to *caboclos*—but rather as a type of widely recognized traditional population, the population would become fixed in a different way. Instead of continuing in ignominy, the *ribeirinhos* could instead become recognizable through the common and legally recognized identity categories. As a result, they could easier fit into roles as co-caretakers of the Terra do Meio alongside the environmental agencies that would regulate and oversee the areas (Nugent 1993).

While these discourses helped to establish their legitimacy with governmental decision makers, the population's own denomination emphasized their rubber-tapping history and deemphasized the livelihoods they had practiced in more recent memory.

> It was always a full table there, you never went hungry, because you could work the fields, you could fish, and have Brazil nuts when they were in season . . . life on the *beiradão* [riverbanks] is so good, you sleep well at night there. Working

with rubber is the best work a man can do. I would go back to rubber tapping immediately, if there were incentives for it. (Interview with author 2006)

By the 1950s, the rubber industry had fallen substantially and left the region without an economic substitute. Consequently, the *ribeirinhos* began basing their livelihoods on other things. One former rubber tapper from the Xingu pointed out: "It wasn't until 1962 or 1963, when rubber ended, that we really started earning" (Interview with author 2007). Many of these new economic bases were far less appealing to the sensibilities of today's environmentalists, in both local contexts and international ones.

When rubber tapping became nonviable as an income source, many people living along the Xingu River turned toward work in *garimpos*, or artisanal mines (generally for gold, although bauxite is also present in the region) and toward hunting for pelts of wild cats as new income sources. In addition, logging activities and the encroachment of illegal land claimers in the area became frequent. The history of the region was often told by the *ribeirinhos* in terms of the various economic sectors that predominated in the region, harkening a new present age—that of conservation, where the RESEX would be created. "When rubber stopped, pelt hunting, [known as the *época de gato*, or "time of the cats"] started. When that was prohibited, logging came into play, and then came C.R. Almeida. And now, today, we have no patron. We need this reserve to be created" (Interview with author 2007). The pelt-hunting era was also deemphasized, which was a common way for former rubber tappers to continue making a living along the rivers in the post-rubber era. Extremely high prices could be gained through selling the pelts of spotted jaguars, black panthers, giant river otters, and other animals, which would eventually be sold for even higher prices by fur traders in urban areas, who would export them to North America and Europe to be sold as fanciful costumes and décor for the rich. It was during this stage that the jaguar reached near-extinction, and with awareness-raising and outcry from the international community, the "cat skin" economy quickly disappeared. For the majority of people living along the Xingu, who worked in both the mining operations and in large-game hunting, the money earned through these endeavors was spent just as quickly. For those working in *garimpos* and as pelt hunters, a get-rich-quick mentality generally dominated their earnings, such that fortunes would be gained but just as quickly lost in superfluous spending in nearby towns (Schmink and Wood 1992, Branford and Glock 1992). Indeed, the livelihoods of the *ribeirinhos* from the 1960s through the mid-1990s became virtually left out of the narratives the *ribeirinhos* would later tell. These less environmentally friendly activities had been the primary means of sustenance in the region for a generation, but since those livelihoods were so dissonant with the environmentalist identity, a certain elision was important to maintain.

Using these activities as the basis for their livelihoods, the *ribeirinhos* labored more autonomously than they had previously during other economic stages. These livelihoods did not neatly conform to a collective narrative of a shared past, despite being profoundly important to people's continued and changing relationship with their land. Moreover, emphasizing the *ribeirinhos*' history within these economies did not fit with the image they were striving to cultivate as sustainable extractivists. Environmentally oriented NGOs and the media alike would not particularly benefit from the more complex narrative of the forest's protectors as small-scale miners and jaguar hunters. The more the population articulated clear desires for being a part of the proposed RESEX, the more they had to present themselves as good stewards in order to be convincing.

In surveying the area's residents, government questionnaires and NGO research emphasized the sorts of extractivism people in the region relied upon; specifics of the prices, quantities of resources extracted, species cultivated, and hunting practices were central to interview questions. Perceiving this emphasis, *ribeirinhos* responded accordingly, giving only brief mention to those times where natural resource extractivism was not practiced with the same regularity. The illegal logging and rampant land-claiming in the region led to a strong emphasis on the violent conflict that has afflicted the *ribeirinhos*. The violence was highlighted by governmental officials and *ribeirinhos* alike, as illustrated in this excerpt from a government survey about social conditions along the Xingu River:

> They left in 2000 because they were scared of the invasions. People were killed on the Igarapé Primaveira in 2003. There were shots exchanged at Anastásio. At the mouth of the stream, they tied up some *beiradeiros*. The gunmen (5 gunmen) didn't want anyone to enter. The names of the gunmen are: Rabbit, Goat . . . [name omitted] thinks that they will till the fields so that they can plant. Planting in the winter and burns in the summer. (Interview with author 2007)[25]

Another mention also from these surveys supports this point, and implicitly positions responsibility upon the federal government through noting its absence:

> The *ribeirinho* residents of the Médio Xingu, in the Terra do Meio region, are being expelled from their houses and lands, threatened by gunmen and police, intimidated, humiliated, and cornered, at the mercy of invading land claimers that act as feudal barons in the absolute absence of the State. (Sauer 2005)

The conflicts were often driven by land claims but were also frequently related to illegal loggers who extracted mahogany from the lands. The fight over land played into the *ribeirinhos'* narrative of their history in the place and is suggestive of a conscious attempt on the population's part to spur the government into taking rapid measures in the area. In one sense, the emphasis on violent incidents and on the fishing and rubber-tapping economies that characterized people's narratives stands in contrast to an alternative interpretation of the population as pelt hunters and gold miners. Further, it positioned the *ribeirinhos* as environmental stewards and victims rather than people who at times collaborated with loggers in perpetrating deforestation, or wildcat miners who exploited the resources in the area in less-than-sustainable ways.

Organizing Out of Dependency

The denunciations of violence and the allegations against the illegal loggers of the region were made directly by the river-based peasants. At the same time, however, the patronage relations that historically marked the community had transferred toward Almeida's firm, which for a time won their affections through providing some services and sometimes income supplements to the community. As a short-term means of winning affections with the *ribeirinhos*, this patronage seemed to need substitution rather than total abandonment, according to many narratives from the *ribeirinhos* themselves. The local NGOs in Altamira obliged. Led by the CPT and FVPP, they wrote grants and organized boat trips in support of the communities' needs, sending in teams to do medical and dental work, advocating for the issuance of identity cards and documents for the peasants, and sending basic food support packages to the people living in the region.

Gaining this allegiance through patronage was not an expressed strategy or long-term goal of the local NGOs, but they did aim to fill the void of governance as a stopgap measure while the conservation area creation process stalled in governmental offices. As the NGO representatives called the communities together in meetings, the *ribeirinhos* practiced the basic skills of meeting in groups, voting for leadership, and expressing opinions in a public forum. Especially initially, meetings frequently involved everyone speaking at the same time. There was little by way of education for emancipation along the lines of Paulo Friere's popular education models taking place in the Terra do Meio communities. Instead, the basic starting point for work was about cultivating two or three main leaders among the community, generally those who were already the most literate or well-spoken. Subsequently, training people in the basic skills of listening and speaking among each other in a way conducive to decision making was a focus in community meetings that occurred on NGO-led trips into the Terra do Meio region. Chico Mendes, the assassinated leader of the rubber tapper's movement, wrote in his 1989 memoir that "The rubber tappers have been here for more than a hundred years with no schools, nothing, while at the same time being brainwashed by the rubber estate owners. People tend to keep that slave mentality and therefore do not involve themselves much in the struggle" (Mendes 1989, 33). Gaining basic involvement in community meetings was less of an issue when the meetings were held in the local communities and without the threats of Almeida's companies intimidating people. But breaking the "slave mentality" was a more difficult and long-term challenge. In a meeting I attended along the Iriri River, led largely by Tarcísio Feitosa of the CPT, people regularly talked over each other, as loud talkers were chided to instead listen. Tarcísio and other leaders who organized the meeting permitted only one person to speak at a time. Later, I asked Tarcísio how long it might take for the community to be able to lead itself, without the CPT or anyone else organizing meetings. "Fifty years, at least," Feitosa replied. "Fifty, really?" I asked, taken aback by the estimate. "Yes, they're a long way off," he said, shrugging. The development of organized associations within each community in the Terra do Meio took time, but also involved a process of transforming long-standing social relations, Feitosa explained. The CPT and FVPP were so important to the population, at that point, that when Tarcísio left the CPT in 2006 to find other work in the state capital of Belém, many of the *ribeirinhos* asked "who will take care of us?" Many still looked to the CPT office, and Tarcísio personally, as a base for receiving social services in Altamira. The NGOs in Altamira filled an important void and strived to gradually empower the local populations to become their own advocates, though this was long and slow work and often was significantly hampered by the very structures of dependency those groups were aiming to break down.

Community organizing became situated against the very institutional logics of empowerment through the establishment of NGO leadership and organizing of meetings, agenda setting, and project proposals. While there was a need for community meetings and organizational structures to exist if the resident's associations were to be recognized by the government as viable residents, those same structures—with democratic voting processes, leadership hierarchies, and the like—were largely the result of the frameworks conveyed by NGOs and academics rather than by the determination of the community members themselves.[26] The government, for its part, only gave sporadic attention to the *ribeirinhos* of the Terra do Meio. Vulnerable to the institutional shifts of personnel changes, institutional reorganizations, and funding variability, the governmental guarantee of land rights was important, but their contacts with the Terra do Meio populations were more limited. Over time, people living along the rivers of the Terra do Meio region began interacting in parties and other social settings, and getting to know each other through face-to-face contacts and relationships of mutual support.

Illustrative of the increasing economic empowerment and self-governance of the *ribeirinho* communities was the purchase of the RESEX Iriri community boat (see book cover image). The boat was purchased shortly after the creation of the reserve itself, and it immediately offered economic and transportation advantages to the residents, allowing people sell goods like Brazil nuts directly in Altamira and thereby giving them a greater return on their harvest. The acquisition of the boat enabled the community to attain greater transportation mobility and economic autonomy from the river-based traders that had previously predominated in the region. They no longer solely depended on these middlemen for the transportation of basic necessities, which often came with high mark-up costs attached. Slowly, economic life began to transform for most of the residents toward greater self-sufficiency, and it also involved more regular trips into Altamira. These developments were not without challenges along the way; on a few occasions, people suspected their community association leaders of hoarding food assistance packages or distributing food unequally, or disagreed about boat management questions, with little process in place for conflict resolution. Gaining a greater ability to rely on their own community structures rather than the Altamira-based NGOs to become the arbiters of disputes remained a longer-term challenge.

Over the next several years, a greater number of projects would help to fund and support the *ribeirinhos'* extractive activities, giving the populations more self-sufficiency and thrusting participants in those projects into self-governance roles more directly. In addition, the community was legally bound to formalize forestry management agreements with the government, such that monitoring of natural resource stocks and reporting of any suspicious illegal logging became part of the partnership agreement that the populations of the region had with the government. In subsequent years, the residents began to form additional associations for fishing and Brazil nut gathering, and the commercialization of other forest products became a newly notable dimension of *ribeirinho* life. The process of making the *ribeirinhos* legible to the people living outside of their communities entailed shifts in the language of their self-identification, strategically narrating the community to fit the frames of environmentalism and traditional populations that were recognizable and amenable to NGO allies and the government. It also involved a slow transformation in their relationships to NGOs and the government away from the long-standing clientelism that marked the population's history.

Making the Middle Lands

An additionally important dimension of constituting an environmental identity in the region involved consolidating the geographical imaginary surrounding what and where the "Terra do Meio" was. Especially led by intermediary NGOs, regionally based community meetings and maps of larger territories of conservation served to create a greater sense of geographic cohesiveness in talking about the strategies for sustainable development in the region. This also functioned to create a politically identifiable unit that could be measured, monitored, and marked by those with an interest in making the region visible to the outside world.

According to most accounts, the descriptive category of the Terra do Meio only arose as a common use when people from IBAMA, ISA, the CPT, and the FVPP started visiting the area in 2002. The geographic region of the Terra do Meio—the Middle Lands—is delineated by a ring of indigenous lands found in the south, north, and northeast, which were established through land demarcations in the 1980s. The Xingu, Iriri, and Riozinho do Anfrísio rivers provide additional territorial boundaries to the east and west. While the indigenous reserves buffered the new waves of land occupation coming from the center-west region of Brazil, the Terra do Meio was frequently portrayed as a hollow core inside. While the indigenous lands provided some security from encroachments, impunity reigned so long as land titles remained unorganized, and new threats to the forest were continuously arising. One road that stemmed from São Felix do Xingu through the middle of the Terra do Meio was becoming visible in satellite images around 2005, threatening to extend as a connection point to the BR-163 highway. Once such roads connected, the rest of the region would quickly become accessible and hence deforested, many close observers feared.

Terms such as the "São Felix do Xingu/Iriri front [of incursion]" described the same area earlier than the adoption of the *Terra do Meio* term in documentation by Padre Angelo from the 1980s. Those lands were mostly located within the Xingu Diocese of the Catholic Church and could have been described purely on the basis of their geographical location in the center-west of the state of Pará. Identifying the lands as the Terra do Meio, identifying the 'middle' within the geographical context of indigenous areas and rivers, promoted a conceptualization of the region as one where conservation activities were taking place. Beyond the politics of institutional influence and these broad geographic descriptors, establishing the notion of the Terra do Meio as a region helped to underpin a different conceptualization of the space, one based upon the vision of creating protected areas there, rather than deforestation incursions or in reference to the historical rubber plantations.

Establishing the cohesion of the region geographically also served to reinforce a common portrayal for the outside world of who the region's residents were. Through doing so, the NGOs could conduct broader regional work and provide an impressive base of geographical and environmental statistics through which to make more effective arguments (Escada 2005). As federal officials and NGO partners planned their course of action in the region, issues of illegal land-claiming, violence, and deforestation in the area could be addressed in a more holistic manner if, in addition to refined local strategies, a regional perspective was adopted. Establishing the boundaries of the region had significant financial and political ramifications for the civil society groups who worked to consolidate the Terra do Meio geographic imaginary; claiming larger victories for impacts upon a whole region, and focusing on larger numbers of acres protected and beneficiary populations, gave civil society groups abilities to claim larger successes than if they had only worked within individual areas.

This geographical discourse of the Terra do Meio region as a whole contributed to the consolidation of identities among *ribeirinhos* that involved greater recognition and identification within a newer collective geographic imaginary of place. Frequently, for example, I heard the people of the region identify with their specific river of residence, or other specific geographical markers: "I live on the Xingu," "I am from Riozinho" [Riozinho do Anfrísio], or "I live at the foot of Morro Grande" were common descriptors. The geographical specificity generally accorded to identification of territory within this vast space is logical, given the movement of the populations in the region up and down a single river, and only rarely between rivers. The *ribeirinhos* used significantly more specificity to characterize their home locales, based on the historical boundaries of different rubber plantations:

> My father is from the riverbanks of the Xingu, he was born and raised there. My grandfather was Maranhense [from the state of Maranhão], he came as a young man, and married my grandmother, and went on constructing a family. My father was born near a stream known as Estragado. The same as the *seringal* location. It's near where I live, below [downstream from] where I live. Today I live at Morro Grande, I was born at Jatobá, and grew up between Murici and Porte de Almeida. It's inside the area that today would be where the reserve is going to be created. In the same place. (Interview with author 2006)

With the new categories for the space in which they lived, histories and identities became increasingly distanced from specific locales and instead folded into broader imaginings of shared histories and places.

Unless one had worked on a trading boat or in *garimpos* in the region, it is highly unlikely, for example, that someone from the Xingu River could articulate differences and similarities between the local cultures, communities, and rivers of the Riozinho do Anfrísio or the Iriri. Instead, most would know their own river area in substantial detail but with little knowledge or conception of the vast geographical expanse of the region as a whole. The idea of the Terra do Meio fostered a sense of solidarity and identification with the area as a singular place—for those working within the area, for the media, and for the *ribeirinhos* of the three rivers running through the region, who increasingly were meeting each other in Altamira's offices and in NGO-led meetings concerning the future of the region.

Before the consolidation of this particular geographic imaginary, however, the geographic boundaries of the Terra do Meio were also subject to some debate by civil society organizations. Because of such territorial uncertainty, some NGO groups voiced discontent about how territorial overstretch by other NGOs occurred, diluting the regional recognition and clarity that the concept of the Terra do Meio aimed to establish. For two of the organizations working in the region, the Terra do Meio includes around eight million hectares (22.2 million acres) in the state of Pará between the Xingu and Tapajós Rivers, with its frontiers at the indigenous territories of the Arara, Kararaô, and Cachoeira Seca do Iriri to the west, and the Xingu River to the east. The southern boundary is the Kayapó indigenous lands, and the northern tip is where the Xingu and Iriri Rivers part (Feitosa da Silva 2005). The map of the conservation area corridor produced by the ISA emphasizes the Terra do Meio's location as part of the Xingu River basin, which, notably, is a region where ISA works extensively, from the Xingu's headwaters in northern Mato Grosso all the way North to Altamira. Emphasizing the Xingu River as the heart of the territory adds extra significance to their works. The WWF's concept of the Terra do Meio, however, emphasized the region's location as a "conservation block" of eleven million hectares (27 million acres) including a northern margin along the Transamazon highway (BR-230) and a western margin at BR-163. Excluded from the Terra do Meio geographical reconfigurations were the extensions of the conservation areas in the RESEX Verde Para Sempre, located where the Xingu meets the Amazon River, and the Projects for Sustainable Development (PDS) along the Transamazon highway near Anapu. Originally, these were part of the "Lungs of the Amazon" proposal for how the Terra do Meio would fit into a regional plan for creating conservation areas envisioned by the MDTX.[27] The conservation areas in the BR-163 corridor, moreover, were generally treated separately from the Terra do Meio region on maps, though they bordered the region to the west. Not only was the discursive identification of the region as the Terra do Meio an important construction, so too was the clarification over the physical territory itself that these various maps captured, because they signified a way to account for regional conservation work to the funders and governmental decision makers.

Metaphorically speaking, the rhetorical grout of the Terra do Meio mosaic was the establishment of a cohesive discourse about regional interests and collaboration. The very "mosaic" character of the Terra do Meio conservation areas opened the possibility for civil society actors to create disjointed policies and separate land uses that did not gain traction with policymakers as a cohesive regional strategy. Conceivably, NGO actors could easily have divided their work in the Terra do Meio, based on their different expertise in dealing with conservation areas allowing for human use or, on the other hand, complete ecological protection.[28] While civil society efforts were divided so that various organizations could work cooperatively and address the needs of the entire region, all of the NGO actors consistently used the discourse of the Terra do Meio to talk about the area and couched the problems they were addressing within this particular regional context. The loose understanding of boundaries in the Terra do Meio functioned to bring the activist networks together for communication and collaboration, fostering their abilities to participate jointly in planning meetings and sharing information about what was happening in the general vicinity.

Other important geographic consolidations that took place in the region involved how the *ribeirinhos* related to property rights and how they narrated their own transiency on particular lands along the riverbanks. Having lived in the region under *seringueiros*, the riverine peasants in the Terra do Meio did not understand the concept of private property and did not have much (if any) of a framework for attributing value to the land itself. Beginning in the 1970s many peasants in Amazonia were duped into selling their lands and were often evicted from those lands (Branford and Glock 1992).

However, after nearly a decade of work toward ousting illegal land claimers and creating the conservation areas there, the people in the region came to know well that selling land was illegal and that encroachment on their lands by outsiders was unfair. "Everyone here has sold their land, everyone. Many people deny it, but they all did . . . " one resident of the Xingu explained to me in a defensive tone. I hadn't asked about his land claims or anyone else's, but it didn't matter. The informant continued on about how he was the only one in the community who, in fact, had never sold lands in the Xingu. I began asking people directly about this in interviews; by most people's accounts, no one had ever sold *their* particular lands. Through piecing together the stories that the *ribeirinhos* told of each other, it became clear that the vast majority of the population had at some point in time sold at least some rights to loggers so that they could earn a bit of money in hard times, at other times sold lands to other *ribeirinhos*, and even occasionally to outsiders who wanted to settle (and potentially raise cattle, speculate on lands, or grow cocoa) in the region. Between land sales, violence from *grileiros*, and the appeal of the Altamira as a place to access health care and education, population losses throughout the region were significant between 1984 and 2002, as shown in Table 5.1.

The negative implications of having sold lands within the region were obvious to the *ribeirinhos*; being distanced from any association with land selling helped guarantee a more convincing claim to their rights to remain in the area. While the NGOs were making lists over which residents were legally allowed to remain in the RESEXs, it was strategically important to make sure that a person

Table 5.1 Population Change in the Terro do Meio Region (1984–2002)

	Number of families living in each area	
	1984	**2002**
Riozinho do Anfrísio	N/A	24
Rio Curuá	25	12
Rio Iriri	200	55
Rio Xingu	80	27
Total Population (2002): 740 inhabitants		

remained in good standing as a *ribeirinho* associated with a particular area in the region. For the would-be official members of the RESEX, cultivating an identity as a good land steward was important as a means of gaining legitimation from the NGOs. Conversely, accusing others of improper behavior was a way to explain some of the confusion over land rights in the area and to get a leg up in what were often long-standing disputes between neighbors.

A certain geographical fixity also informed this process of claiming long-standing possession of the lands in the region. In practice, the RESEX land designation does not involve individual property titles but rather is a form of collective landholding. This arrangement was in keeping with the traditional settlement patterns of the *ribeirinhos*, who commonly moved between multiple sites on the same stretch of the riverbanks, establishing their homes and practicing swidden agriculture. The populations were not necessarily settled in one particular location along the river, and people often maintained a house in the city as well. In some cases, children in a family would move to their own lands, settling as adults on the opposite bank of the river or on lands adjacent to their siblings.[29] Sometimes people along the river would decide they liked a different location better and construct their home in a new location, claiming it as their own. At other times, a piece of land would be sold to other families or people interested in establishing a land claim in the area. On occasion, family members would sell the land to someone, while meanwhile their other relatives would sell it to someone else or claim it as their own. These incidents were often the source of extensive roils and antagonism, particularly as doubts arose among the populations about who would be permitted to live in the lands once the extractive reserves were created in the region.

While many people living in Altamira had family ties to the region, those considered by the government as the rightful population for the RESEX were the people who continued to stay there and work the lands as best they could. "Ninety percent of the people in the periphery of Altamira are descendants of the Xingu and Iriri," one interviewee claimed. Getting counted as a legitimate *ribeirinho* became desirable for the people who had moved to the city at some point between 1984 and 2002 but wanted to move back, especially once they saw the potential for gaining secure land in the region. By law, Extractive Reserves are areas where collective management of natural resources is mandated, and individual property titles do not exist. Given this stipulation, the *ribeirinhos* could have usufruct rights and engage in community-based forest management, but the land itself is the property of the federal government. This land use stipulation made considerable sense in light of the population's varying land use and ownership ideas, which are considerably more flexible and dynamic than traditional private property regimes would allow. Land conflicts could cause substantial discord among the children of *ribeirinho* parents over who had rights to return to the area. It frequently fell to the local NGOs, specifically using the lists made by the CPT and the FVPP from their visits to the region and interactions with the *ribeirinhos,* to determine who was allowed to move back into the areas on the basis of their perceived dealings over land and with regard to their alliances with C.R. Almeida.

One close local observer critiqued: "The problem is that these organizations are treating the *ribeirinhos* as if they were land reform clients, and not traditional populations, but it's not that way; a RESEX is like indigenous land—the population has a right to live there because of their history and culture there, that goes beyond whether they stayed and fought for the land or not" (Interview with author 2007). Claiming residency as something authentic, in the sense of having never sold one's land in the region and maintaining ties to family and land there, was an important feature in the struggle for land rights. Once the *ribeirinhos* sufficiently convinced the NGO intermediaries that they were credible as longtime residents in the area, they were able to return to the lands without a problem. Individuals at the CPT became powerful arbiters of such decisions, but as soon as the reserve was legally created, those arguments over who had rights to live in the area became moot points. As social theorist Henri Lefebvre has noted, authority is what "produces" space (Lefebvre 1991 [1974]); in this case, the authorities were intermediary NGOs, who functioned to represent both the people and the place of the Terra do Meio so that it could become a visible territory, viable as a space where governmental arbitration of land rights and forest management could take shape.

A Completed Mosaic

Achieving environmental conservation after the conflicts the Terra do Meio region faced could read as the tidy happy ending to this chapter, suggesting that sustainable development plans *worked*. In this rendering of the story of the Terra do Meio, the *ribeirinhos* can be seen to have peacefully returned to the lands that were once threatened, and they now contentedly steward the forests and protect it through thriving on Brazil nut collection and small-scale farming. All the while, they are protecting the forest from the encroachments of would-be loggers and ranchers. Such is the encapsulation of a sustainable development vision that emphasizes the feasibility of strengthening poor people's livelihoods while protecting the rainforest. Indeed, this is also largely how those plans did eventually function, when examined from a time horizon of several years and from some distance from the locales. The creation of the conservation areas on the Xingu River, and more broadly in the Terra do Meio region, was a remarkable achievement. Bit by bit, most indicators of economic and social conditions seem to be improving for the Terra do Meio *ribeirinhos*. Hopeful though it is, this idyllic conclusion might lead readers to conclude that RESEXs or the Terra do Meio case is a perfect illustration of how to salvage sustainable development and manifest an idealized target of conservation and human development.

Despite the great promise of creating of the Extractive Reserves as a viable long-term strategy for promoting sustainable livelihoods and environmental protection, many serious challenges and concerns remain. First, while creating extractive reserves and other conservation areas can be a strong strategy for reaching conservation goals, doing so does not always yield remarkable results. Studies show that actually achieving lowered deforestation rates inside park boundaries takes monitoring, strong community institutions, and active enforcement of regulations (Bruner et al. 2001, Morton et al. 2006, Nepstad et al. 2014, Nepstad et al. 2006, West, Igoe, and Brockington 2006). Given the depletions to IBAMA staff and funding in recent years, most prominently under President Jair Bolsonaro, there is little reason to believe a consistent enforcement approach will remain in the long term.

At present, the tongue-in-cheek joke about the "Green Forever" extractive reserve only being "green every so often" serves as a warning for the vast region that is the Terra do Meio area. Despite its immense size and ecological richness, there are only about a handful of environmental agency staff charged with monitoring and responding to the needs, both social and ecological, in the enormous expanse of the Terra do Meio protected areas. Deforestation in the Terra do Meio declined significantly between 2007–2012. After that point, between 2013–2015, environmental enforcement funding was cut and the Belo Monte dam was constructed, and the Terra do Meio region as a whole suffered from three consecutive years of increasingly large deforestation rates (Braga de Souza 2016). Some of the close observers of Brazilian conservation policies note that a tenfold increase in staffing by IBAMA and ICMBio would still be insufficient to implement and maintain these reserves over time, and prospects are distant for any substantial increase in governmental attention to the area. The immensity of the Terra do Meio region is both its greatest strength and its greatest challenge. There are only a handful of staff tasked with enforcing the park boundaries and regulations. While studies show that creating protected areas in the Amazon largely serves to mitigate the negative effects of deforestation, there remain questions about the extent to which some of the avoided deforestation is just displaced to other, still unprotected areas that have become the new frontiers of the region (Barber et al. 2014).

It is more productive and more widely relevant to take the stories offered in this chapter as illustrative of the power dynamics and tensions that take place amid sustainable development land use planning efforts. This chapter showed how conservation-oriented narratives were co-created by NGOs, local residents, land claimers, and the government. These narratives and their associated discourses about the people and territory of the Terra do Meio region are an important part of governing. They constitute the frameworks through which particular histories, aspirations, and social ties are established. It is also important to recall that the process of fighting for the Terra do Meio conservation areas entailed achieving structures for environmental governance to take place out of what was both a vacuum of state presence and a long-standing historical trajectory of ambiguous land titling and land use regimes. The sustainable development strategy traced here was far from a proactive initiative of state-led planning, nor was it one of equal treatment for all the affected members of the geographical region desiring such plans. Instead, some RESEXs were created sooner than others, with definitive land titles and benefits reaching some of the Terra do Meio communities faster than others. It is also worth remembering that establishing rule of law and basic security in the face of violent conflict was an urgent necessity for the people of the region from the mid-1990s, but it took nearly a decade to achieve—and only then was achieved through a framework involving other constraints, which especially privileged environmental protection above other social concerns.

The unevenness of sustainable development planning, moreover, is highlighted by recalling how Sister Dorothy Stang's legacy played out in the Terra do Meio. While she had never worked closely with the *ribeirinho* population and instead worked with the small-scale farmers of the Transamazon highway, it was in the Terra do Meio region that the most lasting land use changes took place. The plans to create the Terra do Meio conservation areas emerged through concerted and longer-term advocacy but came into governmental practice rather spontaneously, presumably as a reactive response to show progress in the region while media attention was still focused on the Amazon. The benefits the *ribeirinhos* gained were those of visibility to the state, essentially becoming environmental citizens with special responsibilities for protecting their areas. The physical protection they initially sought was achieved, but the longer-term desires for health care, education, and economic improvements were slower in coming.

The role of intermediaries was central in creating certain articulations of identity about conservation-oriented behavior and framing the history of the local population as one of *ribeirinhos* as legitimate partners in conservation. Establishing common narratives of struggle and a cohesive set of political demands centered around the creation of the extractive reserves functioned to make the case more compelling to those in power. These identity creations were co-constituted in people's own lives, too, as a reconfiguration of their history and personal narratives emerged that emphasized extraction of renewable natural resources above other, less sustainable means of generating livelihoods used in the past. These articulations made the population visible as an identifiable community from a specific region, and hence allowed them to gain political resonance as they advocated for their needs. Moreover, the disingenuous narrative of conservation was unsuccessful: C.R. Almeida's attempts to construct a positive environmental image failed on the basis of the violence and threats that underpinned the work of his NGOs and the firm that he ran in the region. This observation indicates that consolidating environmental subjectivities takes repeated iterations of practice that conform with discourses. Actions do not alone speak louder than words, in this instance; it is not sufficient through discourse—or practice—to be convincing if they operate independently of each other.

The construction of identities in relation to land use plans is neither the result of imposing conservationist values from outside organizations nor the result of innate understandings and sets of values or geographic spaces. The creation of a recognizable historical narration of the *ribeirinhos*' relations to place and livelihoods helped to legitimize the inhabitants of the region as subjects that the state could then deal with as partners. The naming and formulation of the concept of the Terra do Meio region as a geographical territory also perpetuated the narrations of success for those nongovernmental organizations operating in the region as they described their work for audiences with particular interests in containing deforestation in the region and protecting its natural resources.

Through these examinations, we are witness to a process whereby actors subtly shift and reconfigure their articulation of identities and allegiances in relation to the power structures and political control. The *ribeirinhos* are not purely adopting identities as powerless subjects of the state, nor are they disempowered subjects of more powerful NGOs. Instead, at times they are more assertive in demanding rights, strive for legibility, and gradually gain more empowerment as they interact with those groups. This is one illustration of how the modern state exerts authority over land and space as part of its governance, much akin to anthropologist James C. Scott's discussion of state control (Scott 1998), although here the peasantry in question is more quiescent than resistant to the authority of state control. While the official papers and policies are in place, the relative absence of state engagement leaves the *ribeirinhos* of the region in a position of making demands for more functions of governance by the state rather than less. Intermediaries function to translate their articulations of identity to find resonance and to gain traction with more powerful audiences (Scott, Kaplan, and Keates 1997, Tsing 1997). Those who would seek to obtain the most secure ground in relation to the state are pushed to articulate their own history, identity, place, and values based on their perceptions of what the state and various powerful intermediaries embrace as legitimate, which is a set of ideals that are both dynamic and inconsistent.

Ironically, while the Brazilian government is largely responsible for granting some political power to the residents of the region, in this chapter, the state is far from homogenous. One of the contradictory motives embedded behind the vision of sustainable development that it chose to promote in the Terra do Meio region was that creating the reserves could function to appease environmental interests, having the effect of taking significant wind out of their sails when it came to the later contestation over the Belo Monte dam that was proposed for the Xingu River. The apparent contradiction between environmental preservation and development goals that delayed the creation of the RESEX Xingu, as the Ministry of Mines and Energy evaluated its potential to derail the planning of the Belo Monte dam, marks one of the tensions of governing in the rainforest. While the sustainable development framework argues that we might marry conservation and development goals, this often entails satisfying oppositional and frequently contradictory visions. The next chapter focuses on the case of the Belo Monte hydroelectric dam to illustrate these tensions in greater detail.

6

The River

Contesting Clean Energy

It's because of these constructed fantasies that we should not be afraid of debating. It's because of these constructed fantasies that we need to say: the state of Pará and the Xingu region cannot give up Belo Monte, there's no way to go without it.

—President Luiz Inácio "Lula" Da Silva, Speech in Altamira, 2010

In 1989, an indigenous Kayapó warrior named Tuirá gave a moving speech. Brandishing her machete in an auditorium filled with public officials and thousands of indigenous people from around the Xingu River basin, Tuirá confronted the president of the Eletronorte electric company, José Antônio Muniz Lopes. She held her machete up to his face as he sat behind a table with other dignitaries at the front of the auditorium. Her impassioned statement sent a strong message: the indigenous peoples reject the hydroelectric dams being proposed for the Xingu River. The high-profile meeting included about 1,200 people from all over Brazil and the world, among them 500 indigenous people. The group came together in Altamira for an event known as the First Encounter of the Xingu, where they planned to discuss the proposed dams and the future of the region (Carvalho 2006). The Encounter marked the culmination of the early organizing against dams on the Xingu River, which were proposed under the title of the Kararaô project. In addition to its objectionable social and environmental costs, the name Kararaô itself was an affront to the indigenous populations. The word is a war cry in the Kayapó language and is referent to another Amazonian tribe that was proselytized to extinction (Arnaud and Alves 1974, Diversi 2014).

The proposed project, which began with initial surveys in October 1975, entailed multiple power generation stations and would eventually include five upstream dams. To produce the anticipated 20,000 MW of electricity, a reservoir of 22,000km^2 would span the entire area of an indigenous reserve called Paquiçamba, and approximately 6,000 people living along the river would need to be relocated. If the early proposals went through, at least twelve indigenous tribes would be directly affected. Indigenous activists and several anthropologists met with World Bank officials about the dam in Washington DC in 1988. They returned to Brazil facing criminal charges, indicted as foreign aliens for involving themselves in Brazilian political activities (Rabben 1998).

The First Encounter of the Xingu presented a strategic moment for those opposing the Kararaô dam. In addition to the record-setting number of indigenous peoples present, the Encounter of the Xingu in Altamira, Pará was also attended by the rock star Sting, a Canadian supermodel, and a host of other nationally and internationally famous people who found appeal in lending celebrity clout to the cause of saving the Amazon. Moreover, the gathering marked an important stage for activists from both the indigenous rights movement and the environmental community, who united to focus attention against the project and to pressure its funders to withdraw their financing. Tuirá's gesture was not lost on those who witnessed it at the meeting, and it quickly became a famous act of symbolic protest. Her message was clear: there would be strong opposition to the dams on the Xingu, and this form of development was unacceptable to those living in the region. Tuirá's message found resonance with those she aimed to influence. The project was tabled indefinitely when the World Bank withdrew its financing to Eletronorte, which had little success in finding other creditors. The Brazilian government itself was in a debt crisis during most of the 1980s, making domestic funding a distant prospect. The victory by environmentalists and the indigenous activists against the project seemed to be lasting, at least for the next fifteen years.

Still, the project remained of interest to technical personnel at the Ministry of Mines and Energy (MME) as well as to Eletronorte, which proposed a substantially revised version of the project in 1998. What became called the Belo Monte project consisted of two smaller dams on the Xingu and a canal to divert water from a smaller reservoir toward a generation plant. This design, frequently known as a run-of-river dam, is commonly accepted as a hydroelectric dam model which is more environmentally benign than the massive impoundment dams commonly used in the past. Even as a run-of-river dam, however, Belo Monte remains a mega-project; The diversion of the water and related earthworks are akin in scale to constructing the Panama Canal.

Under the revised proposal, no indigenous areas would be flooded by the dam's reservoir, which was much smaller than the reservoir of earlier proposals. A significant area of flooding would still occur at around 516 km^2,[1] and many indigenous populations would be affected by lower water levels elsewhere on the river. Brazilian officials defended its utility based on its high energy yields, which derive primarily from the geomorphology of the Volta Grande, or Big Bend, of the Xingu. In a unique series of turns, Volta Grande involves a 90-km stretch of river that makes three consecutive 90-degree bends. Belo Monte was slated to become the fourth most productive dam in the world, producing around 11,233 MW at its peak capacity during four to eight weeks of the rainy season every year.[2] The project would cost some USD $14.4 billion to construct, though the initial estimates were significantly lower (Moya, Franco, and Rezende 2007).[3]

Although the dam was forecast to yield a substantial amount of energy when running fully, its economic, environmental, and social viability was vehemently questioned by those who opposed the dam, as well as scholars, who argued that many of the economic and ecological costs were inaccurately represented (de Sousa Júnior, Reid, and Leitão 2006, Jaichand and Sampaio 2013, Berchin et al. 2015). The same physical geography of the Xingu which makes it appealing for the dam's construction, with its complex channels of rapids with considerable fluctuation in water levels, also make it a unique site for Amazonian biodiversity (Sawakuchi et al. 2015). The argument that run-of-river hydroelectric dams are environmentally benign is also questioned by researchers, who point out that the greenhouse gas emissions involved with tropical hydropower[4] likely exceed emissions from fossil fuel–based electricity generation (Fearnside 2016b).

The Brazilian government financed the project almost entirely through the Brazilian National Bank for Economic and Social Development (BNDES). The Chinese government would invest in building cross-country transmission lines to get the energy distributed across the national grid. A drought in 2001, coupled with a rise in Brazilian energy consumption, made the demand for new energy sources appear increasingly pressing as a political issue. A fear of national energy shortages became a common concern again in 2010, when numerous serious blackouts affected the country (Hall and Branford 2012). The Belo Monte hydroelectric project soon appeared inevitable as a solution to the energy-hungry, economically thriving nation.

Stable, positive rates of economic growth from 2003–2008 indicated to investors that Brazil was a hot market, and the nation's Accelerated Growth Plans (PAC I and II), stipulated that new infrastructure projects—including Belo Monte—would offer a backbone for sustained growth. Locally, the project was slated to yield considerable job growth; 18,700 direct jobs and, during construction stages, an additional 23,000 indirect employment opportunities. The businesspeople and real estate speculators in Altamira saw opportunity: "It will bring development for the city" was a sentiment expressed loudly and frequently at public meetings, without regard for the sort of unchecked growth implied by the notion of development.

This chapter will show how the sustainable development discourse functioned to legitimatize the Belo Monte dam project, and it illustrates the Brazilian state's power in framing the debate surrounding what development should entail. It responds to the following questions: Why did building a mega-dam become championed as a national priority, achieved under the discourse of renewable energy and the green economy? What changed for activists, who once so strongly opposed the project, as their numbers dwindled and the dam became a fait accompli? On the broadest level, these questions also force into focus an understanding of how power relations shifted within the framework of sustainable development being used to justify the project's construction. Whose interests were reinforced through the politics of building the dam, and to what end? I argue that the discourse of sustainable development, when coupled with strong national development financing and close ties between economic and political actors, played a central role in reinforcing the feasibility and need for the project. The results of this constellation of power dynamics functioned in some degree to undermine the norms of environmental protection and participatory democratic engagement that underpin Brazilian environmental laws. The net result, too, was that at the same time as the dam was constructed in the name of sustainable development, it reproduced and reinforced unequal social relations and environmental harms in some significant ways.

Belo Monte presents several paradoxes concerning how rainforest ecosystems are marked by pragmatic and political constraints within the sustainable development framework. Evaluating the credibility of the competing narratives about Belo Monte and passing judgment about the worth of the dam is ultimately is not the purpose of this chapter, nor, in the end, is it an endeavor likely to yield political traction. Time will tell just how productive, efficient, devastating, costly, or useful the dam will be. What *will* become clear from this chapter are the ways in which the Belo Monte project effectively serves as an example of how sustainable development was deployed as a hegemonic discourse, which promoted the continued dominance of the renewed developmental state over those that voiced alternative visions for development and people's empowerment. To understand this relationship, we must endeavor to understand what the effects were of sustainable development discourses on power relations, and how the Belo Monte project encoded those relations upon society.

This chapter proceeds with an overview of the project and the key actors involved in promoting and resisting it. It then discusses the history of contestation over the project, explaining how and why the mega-dam became politically acceptable and was articulated as a lynchpin of Brazilian sustainable development strategies. In order to structure this chapter's exposition of what is one of the world's most controversial dams, the discussion is organized around three central axes, all of which contributed to the creation and perpetuation of the sustainable development narrative surrounding Belo Monte. These areas concern the legal disputes, civil society activism, and global-level policies over hydroelectric dams. The chapter concludes with a critical analysis of the divergence between articulations of sustainable development in its idealized form and the mismatched shortfalls that were present.

The Belo Monte Hydroelectric Project

The Belo Monte project was given new life under the Growth Acceleration Program (PAC), which was launched in 2007 under President Lula. The electricity generating capacity from Belo Monte was asserted as an essential means of reaching Brazilian goals "to achieve some of the fundamental objectives pursued by the Brazilian Federal Constitution, such as the promotion of human dignity, national development, eradication of extreme poverty, and the reduction of social and regional inequalities" (Brazil 2011). The Brazilian government considers the Belo Monte project to be especially essential for meeting its energy demand, given forecasts that the nation needs to increase energy supplies to keep pace with rising consumer demand that accompanies the nation's burgeoning middle class (US Energy Information Administration 2015, Luomi 2014).

Renewable energy is a central component of Brazil's energy portfolio, with more than eighty percent of the nation's produced electricity coming from hydropower. Brazil is a net exporter of energy, with a huge amount of bioenergy from ethanol production complementing its strength in the hydropower sector. Brazil's energy sector is currently among the world's lowest in terms of carbon-intensive forms, with renewable energy sources comprising 45 percent of primary energy demand (International Energy Agency 2013). A huge, albeit underutilized, store of oil wealth exists in the Pre-Salt reserve, giving Brazil the potential to rival Venezuela and Saudi Arabia in oil production if the stores can effectively be captured (Duffy 2007). Still, in terms of energy production, the common assessment among Brazilian and international energy experts was that Brazil was underperforming and needed to significantly ramp up domestic capacity in order to keep pace with economic growth rates and increased demand. The International Energy Agency assessed the importance of Amazon hydroelectric generation especially:

> The search for a model for Amazon hydropower that can command social acceptance is important for Brazil. If the potential in the Amazon River basin proves to be off-limits (beyond those projects already under construction), then the hydropower resource picture changes considerably. Without the Amazon, over 50% of the total hydropower potential in Brazil (including operational and under construction) has already been harnessed, leaving less than 70 GW untapped. (International Energy Agency 2013, 385)

Dam building in the Amazon is viewed by many energy planners as an essential means of achieving Brazilian energy production goals. If Amazonian hydropower can be captured, the logic goes, then other, likely more carbon-intensive, energy sources need not be tapped. Questioning the demand-side estimates, which are based on the logic that more energy is a necessary correlate to economic growth, rarely figures into such calculations.

Brazil also financed the construction of dams in Peru, which were aimed at providing energy back to Brazil (Nelsen 2012). Domestic energy increases were perceived by government officials as necessary not only because Brazil's energy capacity was significantly below similarly large nations such as the United States and South Africa, but because the country had experienced significant blackouts. In addition, an economic boom between 2005 and 2010 sent prices soaring for iron ore, as well as commodities like soybeans and beef (Cunningham 2014). Much of the energy from hydroelectric dams would go toward the aluminum smelting industry, which is a highly energy intensive industry and relatively strong export sector of the Brazilian economy, although it is predominated by multinational companies (Fearnside 2005, Bermann and Martins 2000). A good portion of Belo Monte's energy was slated for the explicit use of the bauxite and iron ore mines present in the state of Pará.[5] Hydroelectric energy was especially anticipated to sustain the economic growth trend, and seriously revisiting plans for building the dam took place during an economic upturn, making construction appear a reasonable expense.

The Belo Monte dam was estimated to produce a whopping 11,233 megawatts of electricity when operating at maximum capacity, with around 440km^2 of flooded area (Hall and Branford 2012, Fearnside 2005). Policymakers tended to see this as a remarkable achievement; earlier versions of the project involved a reservoir more than seven times that size. The official government announcement about the Belo Monte's inauguration harkens to the 1970s versions of the dam, portraying its completion as a long-deferred dream becoming realized:

> The construction of Belo Monte attends to the interests of the Brazilian government to produce clean, renewable, and sustainable energy to secure the economic and social development of the country. The first studies began in the 1970s and since then, the original project suffered various modifications so that there would be reduced environmental impacts from the power plant. (Government of Brazil 2016)

The word *suffered* in the text is illustrative of a perception that environmental protection functioned in detriment to the original vision for the dam. Despite stating the rationale based in Brazil's need for clean, renewable, and sustainable energy, the fact that environmental protections are positioned as a negative thing involving suffering rather than an improvement or complement to the goal of sustainability presents an important contrast. Such compromises, which the announcement subsequently goes to great lengths to detail, entail significant investments in social and environmental protections, with high costs. The announcement is defensive in asserting that in comparison to the 1970s project proposal, no indigenous areas will be submerged by the dam. Even as the hydroelectric project was inaugurated, the shadow of the past and the apparent contradiction between development goals and environmental and social protections loomed large over the present.

The Controversy over Belo Monte

Belo Monte was so hotly debated among researchers, celebrities, and political leaders that it was seen as "just as controversial, or more, than soccer or religion," as one government official described to me in an interview. Anthony Hall and Sue Branford, two longtime Amazon researchers, described the Belo Monte dispute similarly: "... rather like a medieval jousting tournament, the battle lines at Belo Monte have been firmly drawn" (Hall and Branford 2012, 852).

Belo Monte has been a keystone project for Brazilian energy planners since the 1970s. Dam building in the Amazon would provide what planners called energy complementarity to the nation's electric grid, such that the existing and proposed dams in the north would provide electricity during precisely the months when the dams in the south were less productive (See Figure 6.1). As a renewable energy source based on a run-of-river dam, Belo Monte was viewed by many engineers as a new way to build clean energy into Amazonian futures, and it presented an alternative that was distinctly different and better than the region's dams of the past (Mendonça 2011). The most notable historical precursors to Belo Monte are the Tucuruí, Samuel, and Balbina dams, all of which are Amazonian dams constructed under Brazil's military government. Those dams are widely regarded as environmentally problematic, if not also disappointing in terms of their energetic yields (la Rovere and Mendes 2000). Defenders of the Belo Monte project argued that as a democracy, Brazil would heed the imperative for sustainable energy production. They contended that hydroelectric generation was a clear necessity, and with more and better public consultations the mistakes of the dictatorship years could be avoided (Pinto 2012, Hernandez 2012). At around USD $14 billion (BRL $31 billion) in construction costs,[6] Belo Monte was certainly expensive, but the promise of meeting up to 10 percent of Brazilian energy demand was compelling (Ministério de Minas e Energia 2011). In the region, many people looked to the additional USD $2 billion (BRL $3.6 billion) allotted to the Plan for the Regional Sustainable Development of the Xingu (PDRS Xingu) with optimism that substantial social and environmental support would reach the people of the region.[7]

For most anti-dam activists, Belo Monte was perceived as a gateway project, leading to a new era of Amazonian dam construction. It would facilitate the other

Figure 6.1 This map of electric transmission in Brazil reveals the importance of linking northern hydroelectric production to the south and east of the country, where demand is highest. Credit: ABRATE (http://www.abrate.org.br/)

dams proposed in PAC I and II as well as projects in Bolivia and other parts of South America proposed in IIRSA (Initiative for the Integration of Regional Infrastructure in South America). Their general concern entailed reservations about the social, ecological, and political consequences of Brazil's state-led drive to install massive infrastructure in fragile ecosystems. While earlier Amazonian dams were widely recognized as disappointments (or outright disasters) for their low energy production and severe social and environmental consequences, over 34 sizeable dams were slated for construction by 2021 in the Amazonian basin ("The Rights and Wrongs" 2013). Figure 6.1 conveys the extent of electric integration and importance of hydroelectric grid connectivity between the north and south of Brazil. Figure 6.2 shows both planned hydroelectric projects as well as those

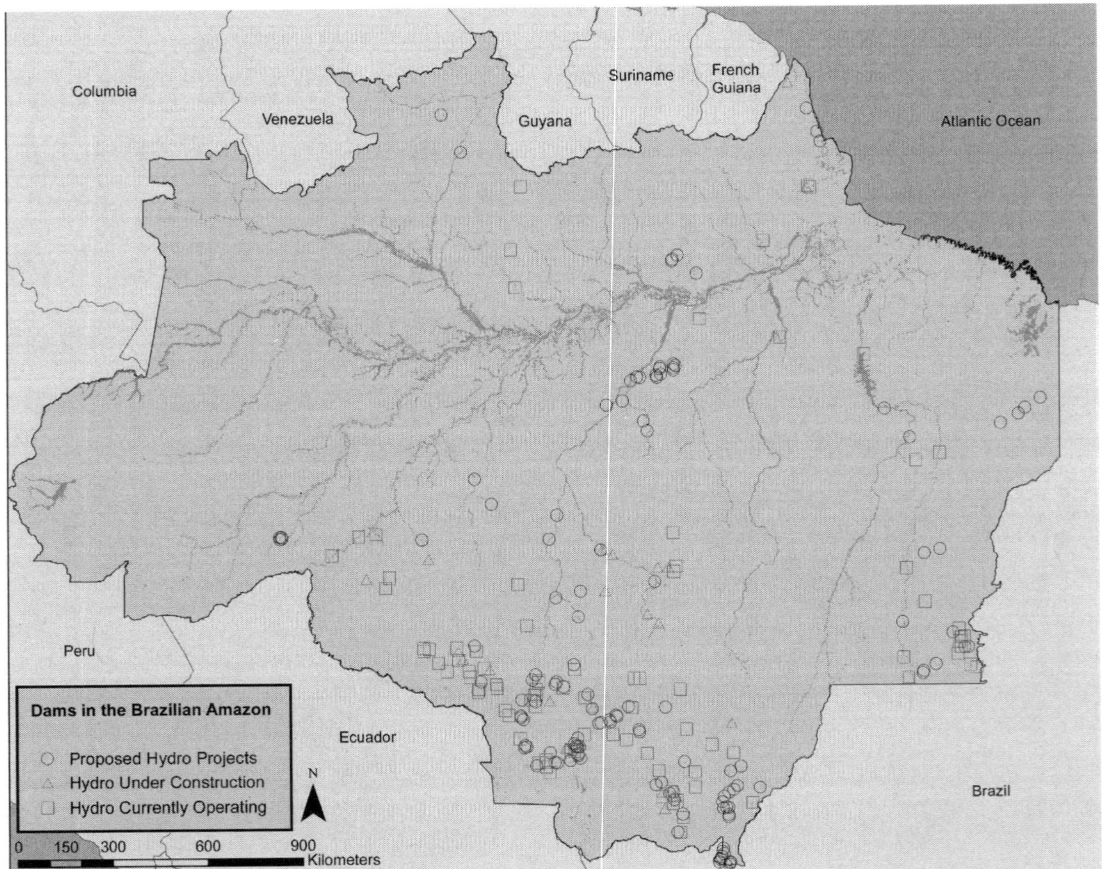

Figure 6.2 This map indicates the extent of hydroelectric dams that are built, under construction, or planned for the Amazon region, as of 2016.

currently under construction and in existence. Taken together, they reveal the magnitude of the Brazilian hydropower system, and help to convey the geographical expanses that are marked by dam-related infrastructures throughout the country.

Some scholars expressed concern about the ecological and social costs of the Belo Monte dam, and about the energetic feasibility of the project itself (Bermann and Martins 2000, de Sousa Júnior and Reid 2010, de Sousa Júnior, Reid, and Leitão 2006, Fearnside 2005). President Lula quipped that Belo Monte would be constructed "by fair means or foul" (*na lei ou na marra*) (Hall and Branford 2012, 853), a statement that caused considerable consternation among activists. It suggested that despite Brazil being a democracy, the project was going to be approved, and it would likely steamroll over social and environmental concerns.

Around 24,000 people, mostly from in urban Altamira, were displaced by the Belo Monte in the course of its construction (Elizondo 2012).[8] Most of the affected communities were compensated by the construction consortium. The few who refused to give up their houses had little recourse when the government claimed "public interest" rights for the construction site and the surrounding areas, but for the most part the dam-affected migrants' aspirations were met (Randell 2016). While technically no indigenous lands were flooded or indigenous people displaced by the project, those displaced from the flood zone were mostly poor, urban residents in Altamira. The primarily fishing and river-based livelihoods of indigenous people and *ribeirinhos* of the Xingu River were also affected, but by lower water levels along many parts of the Xingu rather than by flooding. Left high and dry, the indigenous groups were also severely affected. They experienced severe and negative impacts upon their fishing-based livelihoods and river-based transportation, as well as other ecosystem-wide and cultural impacts ("No Pará, Morte de Peixes" 2016, Ministério dos Direitos Humanos 2017).

There have been many additional indirect social consequences wrought by the construction. The urban conditions in Altamira seemed to worsen considerably for the city's residents. Most locals use the term "chaos" to describe the changes. Induced by the 20,000 construction jobs associated with the dam, people moved into the city, especially young men. In two years, the population of Altamira increased by 40 percent, going from around 100,000 to 140,000 between 2010 and 2012.[9] While income and employment rates rose within the Altamira population, prices also skyrocketed for food and rent, traffic was out of control, malaria outbreaks increased, and violent crime became a persistent concern ("A Batalha de Belo Monte" 2013, "Para Moradores de Altamira" 2013). The chief of the Altamira police force stated that "trafficking of drugs and bank robberies have intensified in the Xingu region because of a higher number of people and the movement of resources generated by the construction project" (Costa 2011). A host of other problems were experienced in the city, including higher traffic accident incidents, health problems, and significantly higher costs of living. Residents complained mightily about these challenges. Nevertheless, public opinion surveys indicated that in 2013, while construction was still underway, a 57 percent majority of Altamira's residents remained in favor of the dam ("Para Moradores de Altamira" 2013). By the time the dam's construction was almost entirely completed, in 2017, Altamira earned the dubious distinction of being Brazil's most violent city ("Altamira Lidera" 2017).

In addition to the social concerns about the project highlighted above, the economic viability of Belo Monte was also questioned. Several studies raised doubts about the economic rationale of the project by offering competing analyses and contending that the costs of the dam itself were too substantial to be effective, particularly when environmental considerations were taken into account (de Sousa Júnior, Reid, and Leitão 2006). Private-sector bidders pulled out of the auction for the project the week before, leaving the contract to be won by Norte Energia, a state-owned consortium of pension funds and firms. This not only raised suspicions that the other bidders had lost confidence in the project, it also raised fears that Brazilian taxpayers would shoulder the costs. Norte Energia is state owned, and the financing for the Belo Monte project would come from the BNDES. Ultimately, this arrangement meant that cost overruns would be backed not by Norte Energia but by Brazilian taxpayers ("The Rights and Wrongs" 2013). Upon exiting the auction room, the team representing Norte Energia was met by protesters, and they were showered in three tons of pig muck. The message was effectively delivered that the project was a literal shit show.

During Brazil's rainy season, when water levels are high, Belo Monte functions at maximum capacity with substantial energy production. Belo Monte is also unproductive for about four months of the year, as it produces only a small trickle of energy during the dry season. On average, the dam produces only 40 percent of its capacity, yielding an annual mean of 4,500 MW (MMA 2011).[10] Given the cost overruns on the project, plus the complicated legal arena in which Belo Monte was licensed, *The Economist* magazine voiced concerns about the accuracy of calculations of cost-benefit analysis; "These failures mean that the most important question—whether Belo Monte is really cheaper than the alternatives—has never been satisfactorily answered" ("The Rights and Wrongs" 2013). Many studies pointed out that less costly and more efficient ways of capturing energy could be achieved through reducing transmission line losses, building small-scale hydroelectric dams, and investing in wind energy and sugarcane residue co-generation (Carvalho 2006, Experts Panel 2009, de Sousa Júnior and Reid 2010). Alternative proposals included both reducing energy demand and emphatically pushing for aggressive solar, wind, and natural gas investments in Brazil. Still, concern remained that Brazil's energy grid needed a certain surplus in reservoirs that can only be effectively harnessed through dams, as these reservoirs would provide a backup supply of energy for times when demand spikes and production is low ("The Rights and Wrongs" 2013). Some scholars raised the concern that more dams would ultimately need to be built on the Xingu so as to make the Belo Monte project more viable in terms of energy production (Fearnside 2005). While the government did issue a legal resolution providing that Belo Monte would be the only dam built on the Xingu (MMA 2011), the Brazilian environmental and judicial system is so full of loopholes and reversals that such promises do not evince confidence.

Additional concerns involved the public engagement process and the ecological consequences of the project. While reams of paper—a document of some 20,000 pages—was generated through conducting the Environmental Impact Assessments, they amounted to few tangible modifications to the plans. The studies raised major concerns about species losses, rapid deforestation, and increased greenhouse gas emissions (Hochstetler 2011, Sevá Filho 2005, Jaichand and Sampaio 2013, Vieira 2013, Magalhães 2002). During and after construction, the dam impacted around 6,140 square kilometers of the unique and fragile ecosystems of the Xingu River. The upstream reservoir alone was slated to generate familiar impacts as other mega-dams, given that approximately 440 square kilometers was flooded—an area equal to the size of the city of Chicago (Hochstetler 2002, de Sousa Júnior and Reid 2010, Experts Panel 2009).[11] The impact on biodiversity includes the likely extinction of migratory and endemic fish species on the Xingu River, including the dwarflike cichlid and the zebra pelco. The National Amazon Research Institute calculated that during its first ten years, the Belo Monte dam complex would emit 11.2 million metric tons of carbon dioxide (CO_2) equivalent, and an additional 0.783 million metric tons of CO_2 equivalent would be generated during construction and connection to the national energy grid (Fearnside 2012b). Furthermore, vegetation destroyed as a result of the land use changes involved in constructing the dam would release excessively large amounts of methane, a greenhouse gas that is 25 percent more potent than carbon dioxide (International Rivers 2012, Fearnside 2012a).

The Belo Monte hydroelectric complex was built by a consortium of companies known as the Belo Monte Construction Consortium (CCBM), which included the giant civil construction firms Andrade Gutierrez, Odebrecht, and Corrêa Camargo, as well as a number of state-owned and state-run companies and pension funds that hired contractors to complete the work. Local municipal governments, consultants, and prominent business interests in the Transamazon highway region formed pro-dam advocacy groups, who organized around the message "I want Belo Monte, with social responsibility."[12] The electric authorities (Eletrobras at the federal level and Eletronorte at the regional level) also hold major stakes in the dam's construction. In addition, the international aluminum mining industry has vested interests in Belo Monte.[13]

The Belo Sun Gold Mine

In addition to all the construction along the Xingu River associated with Belo Monte, a newer proposal for a massive gold mine was also slated for the area. Located on the land along the Volta Grande, or Big Bend, a Canadian company, Belo Sun, holds mining rights to a huge gold deposit (see Figure 6.3).[14] Slated to be the largest open-pit gold mine in Brazil, Belo Sun involves a $380 million investment, slated to operate for twelve years.[15] The Belo Sun company began acquiring mining concessions between 2010 and 2013. Artisanal gold mining occurred in the region for decades, but the Belo Sun mining interests in the Volta Grande, and their adherent environmental impact assessment and licensing processes, generally coincided with the Belo Monte hydroelectric licensing and evaluation processes.[16] Because of this project, Brazil would accrue royalties and taxes totaling approximately $270 million (BRL$850 million), over the course of the mine's installation and operation.[17] The Belo Sun corporation would earn $7.98 billion over this same time period. The Belo Sun mine involves 2,100 construction jobs and 526 longer-term employment positions. While the Canada-based Belo Sun corporation does not hold significant interest in the Belo Monte hydroelectric project itself, the fact that the mine is located so near to the dam is illustrative of a territorial investment strategy that shows both heavy levels of state investment and international capital in the region.

The Belo Sun mine is feasible because the Xingu River along the Volta Grande was diverted due to the Belo Monte dam, leaving the area both drier and more physically accessible. Despite the coincidental timing of the two projects and their overlapping geographies, the two were never considered for their combined impacts and synergistic effects during the licensing procedures (Bratman and Dias 2018). The absence of indigenous consultations in the Belo Sun case also indicates strikingly similar tendencies to the Belo Monte construction. The Brazilian National Human Rights Commission, which visited the Volta Grande region in October 2016, observed: "indigenous and riverine peasants who live in the region and who are potentially affected by the impacts of the project do not have the most basic information related to the project that is slated to be installed in that area" (Ministério dos Direitos Humanos 2017). While public participation did occur in both the Belo Monte and Belo Sun cases, the processes of engagement remained so flawed that in both instances, Brazil was found guilty of violating international human rights commitments because they lacked consent from affected groups (Borges 2017). Figure 6.3 and Table 6.1 illustrate the

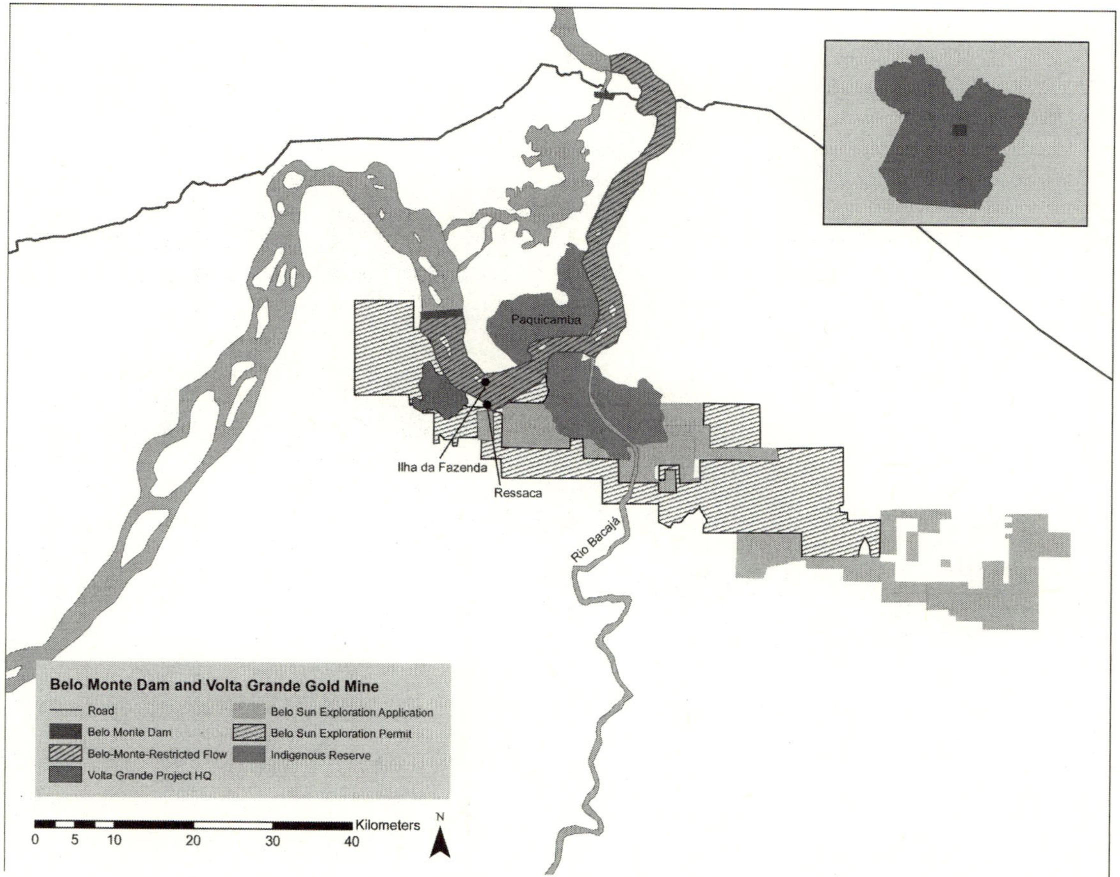

Figure 6.3 The Belo Monte dam and the Belo Sun mining area are both located adjacent to indigenous lands. The Belo Sun mining concession lands were also made significantly more accessible due to the rerouting of the Xingu River for the Belo Monte hydroelectric project.

Table 6.1 An Overview of the Belo Monte and Belo Sun Projects

	Belo Monte Hydroelectric	Belo Sun Gold Mine, Volta Grande
Cost	$14 Billion USD (approx.)	$ 380 Million USD
Employment	18,700 Construction jobs 90,000 New residents from indirect employment 32,000 Longer-term regional population increase (approx.)	2,100 Construction jobs 526 Longer-term jobs
Financing	Brazilian Government (BNDES), Vale	Belo Sun Mining Corp. (Canada)
Size	516 km^2 (reservoir)	1033.5 km^2
Production Yields	4,637 MW annual avg.	205,155 oz. gold/year over 10 years
Construction Time	1975: Initial proposals 2007: Inclusion in PAC I 2007–2016: Licensing and permitting 2011: Construction starts 2016: Inaugurated 2019: Full capacity operation	2010: Acquisition 2010–2017: Licensing and Permitting 2017: Construction starts 2019: Commercial Production

Data: Belo Sun Mining Corporation. 2015. Feasibility Study on the Volta Grande Project; Eletronorte (2002) Complexo Hidrelétrico de Belo Monte—Estudos de Viabilidade- Relatório Final. 1 and 2.

specifics of Belo Sun and Belo Monte in terms of both projects' general contours. They also portray the relation of the two sites to each other geographically and with respect to locally affected indigenous areas.

The Belo Sun mine is illustrative of the broader state-led approach to this region as a zone of resource extraction, where heavy investment is planned as the backbone of harnessing energetic and economic potential for the nation. In keeping with the renewed developmental approach, in this case, international investments in the mining operations are a significant part of the larger Brazilian push to use nationally built infrastructure as a vehicle for spurring international investment. Given how the Belo Monte dam's construction geographically functions to beget to the Belo Sun mine, and how the Belo Monte project is related to much more widespread planning for energetic interconnectivity and power generation in the Amazon, the projects are indicative of a much broader shift taking place in the region toward larger-scale investments and infrastructure development, which occur based on an emphasis on economic rationale.

State Capital and the Car Wash Scandal

The linkage between state funding and private corporations was formidable in the Belo Monte case, and tied to complex networks of bribes and political kickbacks. The lion's share of financing for the Belo Monte project (BRL $22 billion) stemmed from the BNDES, and the majority state-owned electric company, Eletrobras, predominated amid the investments in the project. In the case of the Belo Monte project funding, Brazil's BNDES approved loans of $11.3 billion (BRL $22.5 billion) for the project in 2012. This was a massive sum, considering that the BNDES' funding for the entire energy sector (including transmission infrastructure improvements improvements) in 2012 was $13.9 billion (BRL $27.7 billion).[18] Moreover, attaching social and environmental criteria to its loans was something that only began in 2009, and these were not enforceable or stringent enough to cause a withdrawal of financing from a project (Branford 2016).[19]

There were several strong criticisms launched against BNDES as it ramped up its spending on the Belo Monte project and other major Brazilian infrastructure initiatives. First, the bank was lending at much lower rates to companies than commercial bank loans, and second, the BNDES was consolidating power among large companies "friendly" to the government through its lending practices. By December 2010, the BNDES was the largest development bank in the world, and Brazilian investment abroad totaled $190 billion, quadruple the amount the government had directly invested abroad in 2001. The benefits on those investments, even those made abroad, were ultimately reaped by Brazilian companies. In 2010, 57% of BNDES loans went to twelve companies, including two state companies (Petrobras and Eletrobras). The national firms that BNDES financed were principally Odebrecht, Camargo Corrêa, and Andrade Gutierrez, and some giant Brazil-based multinational corporations (Vale, Votorantim, JBS) also held prominent places in their lending portfolio (Zibechi 2014). Many of these were also the largest corporations involved with constructing the Belo Monte dam: The list involved notably included Brazil's five largest infrastructure firms, specifically Odebrecht, Camargo Corrêa, Andrade Gutierrez, Queiroz Galvão, and OAS.[20]

During most of the activism and debate over the Belo Monte dam, these firms were not known to be directly involved in any political kickbacks. While the initial auction for the Belo Monte construction in April 2010 did raise some questions for close observers about fair process, the levels of concern surrounding corruption were at relatively normal levels by Brazilian standards; corruption was assumed to be present in some degree but was not a central point of contention or debate. Skepticism over the auction process arose because the proposals appeared economically infeasible, and the largest companies pulled out of the auction at the last minute. As a result, the federal government spurred formation of the construction consortium, with a 49% share held by Companhia Hidro Elétrica do São Francisco, a subsidiary of the state-owned Eletrobras group.[21] The other companies involved with the CCBM did not assume substantial risk in the endeavor, as they themselves considered the project "economically unviable" (Zibechi 2014, 145). The revelations of high-level bribes and campaign funding kickbacks coming from Belo Monte contracts only became public in 2016, once the Belo Monte dam was already partially operational.

Lava Jato, or Car Wash, corruption investigations began in Brazil in 2014 and initially focused on Petrobras procurement and construction overcharges. The investigation soon expanded into other projects, however, and Belo Monte became centrally implicated as a source of the bribes and kickbacks that were taking place between politicians and Brazil's major firms. There were USD $41 million in campaign donations made by Andrade Gutierrez, Camargo Corrêa, and Odebrecht that stemmed directly from Belo Monte construction bids (Sabatini 2016). Between 1–2 percent of the project's total costs went into the campaign coffers of Brazil's major parties (Haidar and Gorczeski 2016). The Car Wash investigations have led to the political demise and actual imprisonment of over one hundred corporate and political leaders, and the scandal is centrally implicated as a factor leading to the impeachment of Brazilian President Dilma Rousseff in 2016.

A whole host of factors—energetic, economic, and long-term Amazonian land use planning related—explain the Brazilian government's eagerness to build Belo Monte. To attribute corruption solely or even primarily to the financial incentives associated with the Belo Monte construction funding would be a mistake. Anti-corruption investigations showed that corruption was so widespread that it was associated with nearly all of Brazil's major construction projects, including Belo Monte, and also World Cup soccer stadiums, the Comperj oil refinery, and a host of other projects. It is nevertheless important to remember that Belo Monte dam was strongly linked to corruption, even as the dam was built, by many public officials' account, under what was announced as an exemplary participatory and democratic process. Brazil's ambassador to the United Kingdom narrated success in the Belo Monte case, and has argued that more dams in the Amazon should in fact be constructed because of their efficient electric generation potential and because Brazil has corrected for its past mistakes: "Based on lessons learned, Brazil has developed a comprehensive legal, technical, environmental and social consultation process, including on terms of compensation, safeguards and corrective measures, aiming to guarantee that social, economic and environmental benefits are enjoyed by all, particularly local communities, fauna and flora" (dos Santos 2017). The crucial role of state financing and the strong will of political leaders at the federal level ultimately made the Belo Monte project possible. The corruption associated with the dam is now also a part of the enduringly tarnished reputation of the project.

Central Actors in the Belo Monte Hydroelectric Debate

Among the Brazilian governmental agencies, the MME was the most vocal in supporting the Belo Monte project. Notably, some of the officials working within the ministry had supported it since the original surveys began for the Kararaô project in 1975. The main actors involved in opposing the construction of Belo Monte include a range of NGOs, celebrities, and the Catholic Church. Some are motivated by an ideological position which sees large infrastructure as inimical to sustainable development. Others, especially at a local level, have presented a not-in-my-backyard perspective on the dam, rejecting the project on the basis of its local impacts. Those with more moderate perspectives demanded that the planning and construction process integrate safeguards of environmental, economic, and human rights protections for affected populations. Of this group, some negotiated over regional benefits packages and participated in negotiations over the project, causing rifts with those opposed more vehemently to the dam on principle.

Local residents directly affected by the project lived in the city of Altamira. Nearly 24,000 residents were displaced[22] and relocated during the dam's construction. Many of these people did not mobilize against the dam, perhaps surprisingly. The bulk of the displaced population lived in the informal settlements along a streambank in Altamira, in ramshackle wooden houses. The newly constructed houses that the construction consortium promised they could own appeared to many to be of better quality than their current homes, which suffered from leaky roofs and flooding during the rainy season. The promise of new homes served as an enticement for many of those urban residents in Altamira to acquire formal property rights. For others, especially men, construction jobs at the dam site and in town also held appeal. Rural residents in smaller towns such as Vila Antônio and Vitória do Xingu, located along the banks of the river near the construction site were also displaced, and many of those tight-knit communities dissipated. A few holdouts, who stayed in their homes to oppose the dam's construction for as long as possible, benefited more handsomely than those who accepted the basic offer of new housing right away; some residents received much more in indemnification than others. In addition, numerous indigenous groups and *ribeirinho* populations living in the Xingu River basin, both upstream and downstream of the dam, became active in opposing the dam in a relatively united way. This was not the case with all the tribes, however; many groups splintered over whether to oppose or endorse the project. While some tribes, such as the Juruna and Kayapó were consistently and publicly outspoken against the dams, the Arará da Volta Grande do Xingu tribe and the Paquiçamba tribes, which live near the dams and are directly affected, were not actively opposed to its construction as the project reemerged around 2008.

A few international NGOs, such as Amazon Watch and International Rivers Network, vocally and steadfastly opposed the construction of the dam. Friends of the Earth—Brazilian Amazon, Greenpeace, and the Environmental Defense Fund were also involved in campaigns against the dam at various points. Most notable among the Brazilian NGOs involved are the Xingu Alive Forever Movement (Xingu Vivo), the Movement of People Affected by Dams (MAB), and the Instituto Socioambiental (ISA). Notably, too, the Catholic Church was politically active against the Belo Monte project since the Kararaô proposal of the 1970s. This was often through the personal leadership of the Xingu prelacy's bishop, Dom Erwin Krautler, who worked in the region for thirty-five years, until he retired in 2015. Pastoral organizations affiliated with the church were also influential; the Indigenous Missionary Council (CIMI) and the Pastoral Land Commission (CPT) actively interfaced with the affected populations and participated closely with the Xingu Vivo group, and shared office space with them.

Researchers also often participated in the debate over the dam; most notably, an experts panel of independent researchers was convened and published a book of studies that generally critiqued the Environmental Impact Assessment and instead, offered an alternative analysis of ecological, social, and economic viability of the Belo Monte project. Other professors and researchers have also written and joined in advocacy over the project, at times defending it. In one prominent case, a University of São Paulo engineering professor produced a popular YouTube video with his students countering many of the claims in an earlier video, which was made by celebrities who opposed the dam. The Movement for the Development of the Transamazon and Xingu (MDTX) held a more ambiguous position in relation to the project. One of the organization's central leaders, Ademir Federicci, known as "Dema" by his friends, was assassinated in August 2001, in what was thought to be a murder motivated by his butting heads with those that wanted to construct Belo Monte, as well as local loggers and land speculators. At the time, the MDTX strongly objected to the dam. The organization later vacillated in its stance and by 2008, when the project seemed to most people to be inevitable, the group did not participate in anti-dam resistance efforts. The oppositional coalitions weakened as this sense of inevitability became pervasive, both locally and within the political decision making surrounding the project's viability (Zhouri 2010, Hochstetler 2011).

The next section of this chapter details how dynamics of legitimacy creation and inequality operated through the process of proposing, constructing, and contesting the Belo Monte project. Centrally, the discourse of sustainable development played a role in maintaining a framework for policies that were aspirational, contradictory, and meaningless all at the same time. Nevertheless, the sustainable develpment narrative functioned to perpetuate the impression that due process and compensatory measures were being taken, and this created new dynamics of state control over the project's development.

Contesting Hydropower on the Xingu

Belo Monte was frequently in the international and national media spotlight, so officials were careful to establish strong protocols for participatory consultations, rational management structures, and governmental oversight. More than 39 bound volumes from public hearings and the environmental licensing process, each around 600 pages long, were being digitized at the offices of the federal environmental agency, IBAMA, in July 2012. The Norte Energia consortium proudly detailed their efforts between 2007–2012:

> There were 12 public consultations to discuss plant construction; ten workshops with the community that lives in the enterprise area; technical forums in Belém and in the Xingu; visits to over 4 thousand families; four public hearings in the Brazilian Institute for the Environment and Renewable Natural Resources (Instituto Brasileiro do Meio Ambiente e Recursos Naturais Renováveis/IBAMA), involving over 6 thousand people; and 30 meetings held by the National Indian Foundation (Fundação Nacional do Índio/Funai) in villages, with the participation of Eletronorte employees. (Norte Energia 2014)

In interviews, IBAMA agents spoke about Belo Monte as the project with the most paperwork and most extensive consultation in their memory. Yet "more" was not necessarily better participation, nor was it considered adequate by some accounts.

Legal and Procedural Disputes

During the licensing stages of the project, a 20,000-page study was completed, in 35 volumes. Yet, despite such apparent thoroughness, the studies also appeared inadequate: independent experts argued that the Environmental Impact Assessment (EIA) was an exercise in "attempting to hide its grave consequences . . . and attempting to repair technical problems in the previous project." Separately, the independent expert panel, which consisted of twenty-eight researchers, produced a set of additional studies, many of which recast the hydrological, economic, and ecological consequences of the project in far less favorable terms than the official EIA (Experts Panel 2009). When I spoke with IBAMA officials about whether these parallel studies had any influence in terms of the project evaluations and design, the response was lukewarm:

> It helped, a little, but then it was also clear how much some university professors are out of touch, using old studies and so on, especially as they questioned the energy viability and the economic dimensions of the dam. Some of the useful things that came up [during their studies] was about the indirect deforestation impacts from the dam; the heating up of the economy and how integrating that into our deforestation models would make a difference—we need new means of support for enforcement. (Interview with author 2012)

Protracted legal battles over the licensing of the dam caused the project to proceed in fits and starts since its revival in the early 2000s. A variety of NGO stakeholders occasionally did inform new project designs, although the exact nature of their influence is almost impossible to discern, given the many iterations of the project. The Nature Conservancy elaborated a hydrogram for the dam's diversion canals, for example, but it came in 2009 when other versions of the project were also being proposed within the MME and by Eletrobras. It is, at least, clear that between the 1988 Kararaô project (and subsequent alternative studies of Kararaô III and Koatinema II) and the ultimate project that was licensed, there were stark differences in design (Sevá Filho 2005). Even as the standard three-stage licensing process occurred for the Belo Monte project,[23] various stipulations continued to be negotiated and clarified, all of which also ultimately influenced the character of the project.

IBAMA granted the 2010 construction license for the dam along with two long lists of preconditions, which purportedly had to be met before the government would grant installation licenses. There were forty points on the list of environmental preconditions as well as thirty-eight indigenous preconditions (FUNAI 2009, IBAMA 2010). Attaching such preconditions to licensing was a relatively new maneuver, having only begun in 2003. Since they were first used, Brazilian environmental licensing increasingly incorporated these preconditions so that dam construction projects could remain on fast-paced timetables. The use of so many preconditions in the Belo Monte case was especially jarring to environmental lawyers. This legal workaround allowed for licensing and construction to continue despite numerous serious concerns about the project. Many of these preconditions remained unmet, although later licenses were also granted. In other words, since subsequent licenses were legally intended to be granted only upon meeting preconditions, "preconditions" became a relatively meaningless term. Fines for noncompliance were issued with hefty penalties, with the aim of incentivizing the project team to meet all of the conditions as quickly as possible, or else face a suspension of the project.

Arguing that the public hearings and licensing procedures were insufficient, a coalition of human rights and environmental NGOs asserted that "the number of public hearings was inadequate," that "location of the audience was inacessible for most affected communities," and that the lack of interpreters for indigenous groups who do not speak Portuguese, coupled with the presence of heavily armed Brazilian police, were all major deterrents to effective participation (SDDH 2016). IBAMA employees involved in the hearings recalled that most people did not fully understand the use of the public hearing. They described people showing up to state whether they supported or opposed Belo Monte. While the IBAMA employees wanted to use public input to inform which additional areas the government should study, or what considerations the agency should incorporate into the Environmental Impact Assessments or the draft Basic Environmental Plan, public engagement was used instead by the public as a forum for debating the dam itself. Despite the documentation and formal legal procedures being followed by the state, the mismatch between the intentions and the results of public engagement were clear. IBAMA officials did not gain useful information from the meetings to substantively alter their analysis, while the public that participated to express opposition to the dam was effectively coopted because any existential objection to the construction of the dam was ignored. Further compounding the procedural exercise, the sheer magnitude of documentation and paperwork became an impediment because it was so voluminous that only those with incredible patience and aptitude for navigating governmental records would find it useful.

Even as extensive public involvement was taking place, consent for the project was not granted, putting Brazil in violation in violation of Free, Prior, and Informed Consent laws that were part of Brazil's international human rights commitments (Timo 2013, Conectas 2011, Graeff 2012, Jaichand and Sampaio 2013). The Inter-American Commission on Human Rights (IACHR) applied precautionary measures to protect the affected indigenous peoples in April 2011, although Brazil essentially responded by ignoring those measures and affirming its commitment to build Belo Monte.[24] President Dilma Rousseff suspended the nation's payment of $800,000 to the Organization of American States (OAS), temporarily withdrew Brazil's ambassador to the organization, and publicly criticized the decision as "hurried and unjustified" (Jaichand and Sampaio 2013, Sotero 2012). The move was a blunt one, which was politically effective for Rousseff, though it diluted the impact of the IACHR and caused considerable strain within the Inter-American system. The OAS Secretary General made a public statement that the IACHR's precautionary measures were not compulsory for nations to follow (Salazar 2012). Exactly two months after the finding against

Brazil, on June 1, 2011, the installation license for the dam was approved by the government.

Several other appeals were made by local activists and indigenous groups to international human rights organizations. One urged the UN Human Rights commission to take action: "The Brazilian government has systematically ignored cries from the scientific community, organized civil society, environmentalists, people that depend on rivers, indigenous peoples, the Public Ministry, and human rights organizations," said Roberta Amanajás, a human rights lawyer (Conectas 2011). The dam was nearly complete when FUNAI and the Federal Public Ministry advised against granting the operational license. By June 2015, an interministerial working group had identified 55 unmet conditions for environmental and human rights compensatory and mitigation efforts. By 2015, when the UN Working Group on Business and Human Rights made a visit to the Belo Monte site and Altamira, many earlier social concerns were echoed. These included that residents in neighborhoods about to be flooded lacked information on where they would be relocated and what compensatory measures they would receive; some riverine people whose livelihoods depended on the river were relocated far away from river access; temporary schools built were inadequate; consultations had not occurred, and Norte Energia lacked even the basic means of assessing what human rights risks their actions might cause (UN Working Group on Business and Human Rights 2015).

While the opposition groups were unsuccessful in stopping the dam altogether, protests, court injunctions, and labor strikes intermittently slowed the Belo Monte dam's construction both in licensing and construction stages. Injunctions against the project were primarily filed by the Brazilian Prosecutor General's office, or *Ministério Público Federal*, with legal claims based on both social and ecological impacts. In total, eight court-mandated stoppages and over twenty lawsuits were issued by the *Ministério Público* regarding the Belo Monte case. These included injunctions after the operating license was granted and further injunctions after the dam's first turbines were already installed. The injunctions were issued because of fish kills in the Xingu River[25] and because the city of Altamira's basic sanitation system was never properly installed and operational, which was one of the preconditions of the licensing.[26] Environmental impacts such as fish kills continue to affect local fishing communities. These impacts were the source of repeated fines for Norte Energia and caused substantial concern for local residents (G1 2016). When licensing injunctions were overruled in higher courts, the government used a legal instrument that was established during the Brazilian dictatorship, involving a rationale based on security interests (*suspensão de segurança*). This instrument allows an injunction to be overturned based on a rationale that the injunction could pose a threat to national security, health, and the economy (Justiça Global 2014). Several legal reviews of the case suggested that the government's judicial branches were insufficiently independent from influence by the other branches (Graeff 2012, da Fonseca and Bourgoignie 2011).

> Beyond the question of the pertinence of the project in terms of environmental protection, social development or economic profitability, the Belo Monte project raises a much more fundamental issue about the independence of the Brazilian judicial system and the national institutions protecting the public interest. Such a project should simply have been withdrawn or fundamentally reviewed after it was made clear that compliance with the constitution of the country or the existing legislation had been jeopardized. In this case however, none of these arguments have been followed by the courts in the first instance. (da Fonseca and Bourgoignie 2011, 107)

Despite more than ten different legal actions, and notably strong claims, legal analyses suggest that the project moved forward more for political reasons than based on legal rationale.

In addition to these concerns, several high-level resignations marked the project with suspicion that legal protocols were meant as more of a rubber stamp than a serious process of regulatory oversight. In 2010, the head of IBAMA, Roberto Messias Franco, resigned over differences of opinion surrounding the Belo Monte dam, and again in January 2011, the next IBAMA head, Abelardo Bayma Azevedo, also stepped down, allegedly over pressures he faced to grant a full environmental license for the construction of the dam (da Fonseca and Bourgoignie 2011). An IBAMA licensing analyst explained:

> The way that it works is that with every license, you say what additional studies might be done, and what could have been better. If the directors decide that it's enough, you go forward with it, or do more studies; with this license, there were already thousands of pages of study, and FUNAI had given its approval on the indigenous conditions, so even if we did have some concerns, really this is under FUNAI's jurisdiction to decide.

This concise summary highlights the importance of interagency jurisdiction and the power of IBAMA directors' decisions. While lower-level IBAMA employees are buffered from political pressure because they take exams to enter governmental service, the directors themselves are far from immune from such influence.

The above discussion of the legal and procedural disputes surrounding the dam suggests a politics taking place that privileges the interests of the federal government and local businesses, and consolidates around the logics of national security and energy demand. While human rights and environmental impact concerns figured prominently into the legal and procedural debates over the dam, many of these concerns were ultimately sidelined or postponed so that the planning and construction of the Belo Monte project could proceed. Anthropologist David Mosse argues that development projects become successful when proponents are able to persuasively articulate and represent "success," which is achieved through conveying participatory engagement and community benefit (Mosse 2005b). In the case of Belo Monte, this appears a trenchant observation. The project appeared to be extensively studied and legally contested, which tended to add weight to a public narrative that the dam conformed to legal procedures and norms even when it did so in ways that involved some legal maneuvering, or smoothed over contradictory and competing institutional assessments concerning the project licensing.

Local Activism

Locally, activism surrounding Belo Monte was heated, then dissipated, and then rather sporadically flared up again. In June 2006, as President Lula was considering adding Belo Monte to the PAC, a march by the local pro–Belo Monte alliance[27] was organized in downtown Altamira to demonstrate in support of the dam's construction. Well over 2,000 people participated. Many of the banners indicated that the logging and downtown business sector were well represented; signs also criticized the creation of the Terra do Meio conservation areas, the Catholic Church, and the crackdown against illegal logging in the region. Still, activism on either side was rather quiet regarding Belo Monte after that march, especially as the licensing and studies were underway. The Eletronorte consortium maintained a presence in the city of Altamira, with a staffed information center about the dam project. The company also ran a cultural center along the riverfront that was an important space for arts events, *capoeira* classes, and occasional meetings.

Nearly twenty years after Tuirá's symbolic gesture at the First Encounter of the Xingu, a second protest involving a reworked Belo Monte proposal took place in May 2008, at which point the proposal to construct Belo Monte was firmly established on the national agenda. Tuirá, along with several thousand indigenous peoples from around the region, united in Altamira for another major protest. An engineer from the electric company Eletrobras spoke to the assembly, inciting the outrage of the indigenous peoples present at the meeting ("Índia Repete" 2008). Tuirá again held her machete up in protest, confronting the engineer standing up and face-to-face. This time, the gesture of the raised machete was not planned, and the symbolic protest repertoire was ineffective. The engineer then became surrounded by a whole group of angered indigenous people and ended up with a shoulder wounded by a machete. He was whisked away to the local hospital. Activists were more embarrassed by the gesture than anything else. As with the 1989 protests, many of the same tactics and transnational activist strategies that had been successful in the past were deployed again (see Figure 6.4). Despite using every trick in the playbook from 2008 onward, anti-dam activists faced formidable obstacles to having their "stop Belo Monte" demand become reality. By 2008, most observers were skeptical that the anti-dam movement would be able to effectively stymie the dam's construction; despite a strong international activist coalition, the organized pro-dam forces both locally and nationally had political will and public funding as leverage (Hochstetler 2011).

Social media and celebrity activism were also deployed as tactics to change public opinion surrounding the project. A web video, called Drop of Water (*Gota D'Agua*), was made in 2011 involving Brazilian celebrities criticizing the dam, and was coupled with a petition asking for the project's suspension. It garnered over two million signatures in just a few days and was one of the

Figure 6.4 Top left: Tuirá Kayapó at the First Encounter of the Xingu, 1989 (Photo: Paulo Jares). Top right: Tuirá Kayapó at the Second Encounter of the Xingu, 2008. Bottom left: The rock star Sting with chief Raoní Kayapó in 1989 (Photo: Sue Cunningham). Bottom right: Actor James Cameron with chief Raoní Kayapó, 2008.

most viral campaigns in Brazil's social media history. But politically, it yielded no immediate change.[28] Nationalist rhetoric was used to rail against the video, characterizing it as a "calling of nutty environmentalists" because it was made in the style of a Stephen Spielberg "Get out the Vote" video (Azevedo 2011). The year before, in 2010, celebrities from North America got involved in opposing the dam, including James Cameron and Sigourney Weaver. They framed the project as a real-life version of the rainforest destruction at the hands of cruel corporations, based on their wildly successful fictional film *Avatar*. Many of the historically successful tactics that worked in stalling the late twentieth century Kararaô and Belo Monte proposals did not play out nearly as well when they were echoed at the 2008 protest gathering and in the early twenty-first century, although celebrity activism certainly did build pressure and help keep the debate over the dam under public scrutiny (Jampolsky 2012). While international attention was brought to bear on the case, the emphatic response from many Brazilians was that other countries, and especially TV and movie stars, should mind their own business and leave Amazonian politics to Brazil.

Locally, people held marches to protest the dam, which were organized by the Catholic Church, the MAB, and Xingu Vivo Para Sempre. Dozens of legal actions were filed, which slowed and at times halted work completely on the project. However, there was also a strong local push for the dam to move forward. Many people in Altamira, as well as most of the municipal governments in the region surrounding the dam, saw the opportunity for urban growth, jobs, and investment to come to the region if such a massive project were to take place there. For some of the NGOs working in Altamira, collaboration with the government and the dam-building consortium paid off. Organizations that agreed to negotiate over the social benefits package gained more influence with state and federal officials, participating in meetings with them and positioning themselves as allies in local development projects. In so doing, they were better able to consolidate their base of funding and gain project support. In contrast, organizations that took a more hard-line stance and opposed the dam remained marginalized and increasingly suffered repercussions for their views. In the case of property damage caused by indigenous groups against the CCBM offices during the June 2012 protests, for example, local police targeted anti-dam activists as the culprits of the crime. Given that indigenous groups who had committed the offenses were offered special protections under Brazilian law, using known anti-dam activists as the scapegoats for the crimes was one manifestation of this persecution. Numerous other manifestations of state surveillance and control were reported by local activists who opposed the Belo Monte project (Xingu Vivo Para Sempre 2013). In addition, their ties with other, more moderate local organizations were over surrounding disputes about the dam (Bratman 2014). This isolation of opposition groups functioned to promote the state's own legitimacy and control, as those who objected to the project appeared to be increasingly marginalized and relied on more radical tactics of resistance.

President Lula visited Altamira in June 2010, marking the first major rift among the coalition of activists who opposed Belo Monte and those who remained amenable to the project. Individuals and NGOs who were more loyal to the PT party tended to acquiesce to the project at this point, induced by the wedge issue of seeing their long-standing demand to have the Transamazon highway get paved due to the dam's construction. Moreover, party loyalty played out as another fracture point. The activists who defended President Lula and rallied with him during his pro–Belo Monte speech were pitted against their once-close allies, who showed up to the rally as anti-dam protesters. Longtime friends and collaborators found themselves on opposite sides of a barrier fence, shouting at each other, with the anti-dam activists blocked from entering the arena where the speech was taking place (Bratman 2014).

The peaceful demonstrations turned into increasingly radical actions and protests involving civil disobedience by 2011 and 2012, as opposition groups held slim remaining hope of stopping the dam. During the Occupy movement protests in 2011, there was a four-day occupation of the Belo Monte construction site, and again, in 2012, indigenous groups from around the Xingu River basin occupied the site. They camped at the construction site often for several weeks at a time, stopping all trucks from moving along the Transamazon highway and preventing work from taking place. Their opposition was adamant:

> Before they wanted to make Kararaô, I was a very small child, but I remember that for many years, my grandmother spoke in our village of a monster that would come and would destroy the indigenous nation. During that time, no one knew what it was about, but now we all know what it is. This monster is called Belo Monte!
>
> It is destroying our dear Xingu River, doing away with the woods, the fish, and, most painful for us, the indigenous people. And our resistance, our struggle, is not showing any value at all.
>
> I am feeling very sad to know that the Brazilian government wants to see all of us dead, because this is what is going to happen to us. Without the river, there will be no fish, and so what will we eat? How will we survive?
>
> There are several questions, and we don't want to be quiet. Belo Monte is a monster, really, of ambition and destruction. I ask that the world listen to the cry of all of the indigenous peoples, and that we stop Belo Monte while there is still time.
>
> —Jayra Juruna, Indigenous Occupation,
> Worksite at Belo Monte, July 7, 2012

Through equating the dam to indigenous folklore about monsters, the indigenous groups offered a discourse which was easily dismissed by the state; deep and seemingly irrational fears of ancestral knowledge could be pitched against the rationale of state planning, which is scientifically informed and where costs are economically calculable. Indigenous knowledge articulations were more successfully received by the Kayapó tribe decades earlier, on the basis that their claims could be scientifically proven (Posey and Balick 2006). Yet despite the presence of dozens of academic experts, technical reviews, and legal claims that frequently served to respond to and translate indigenous concerns in this instance, those concerns became distilled into an older trope evoking the ignorance of their perspectives. Former President Lula da Silva's speech from his 2010 visit to the region is illustrative:

> I think it's important that the press register this democratic act that we're doing here. Certainly, a half-dozen well-intentioned young people . . . If they had the patience to listen, they would learn what I've already learned all this time.
>
> When I was their age, they [the opposition] used to say . . . that Itaipu would change the whole climate of the region. And they used to say even more: that the water would leak out beneath the Earth and it would change the Earth's axis, the Earth wouldn't be the same anymore . . . And they went with other arguments: the weight . . . isn't that true? The weight of the water would change the Earth's axis. (da Silva 2010)

Here, the president represents a positivist ontology of knowledge from the state itself. Within this framework, predictable change may be measured and assessed, adequate monetary compensation will be offered for those displaced, and scientific studies will provide truthful, accurate, and adequate assessments of ecological impacts. The activist efforts are acknowledged, but they are presented as inconsequentially small in numbers, naïve, and resistant to an otherwise democratic process of state decision making. While the indigenous objections to the project value traditional knowledge and encode emotion upon the landscape, these values are easily dismissed by the paternalistic rhetoric of superior claims to evidence and legitimated governance processes.

Another statement by indigenous protesters, issued at the beginning of the 2012 occupation, was more explicit. It presented a list of demands, with specific attention to environmental impacts. It is worth quoting at length, as it details their main concerns in a form much more akin to the language of the planners and bureaucrats supporting the project:

> The Xikrin people of the Bacajá Trench Indigenous Lands would like to emphasize the environmental impacts:

A document was written containing such information, which must be attached to the studies, in the final report.

- Just a year of the Bacajá River Complementary Studies are not sufficient to know how the river operates and what the impact will be on the river from the construction of the hydroelectric plant.
- The Complementary Studies should continue to learn about the cycles of the water's flood and lowest levels, ebb and flow; fish that arise from the Xingu and species may be affected.
- There needs to be monitoring of the amount of clay that the Bacajá River carries, of water velocity, of the deforestation of the headwaters and tributaries of the river, of water quality, of water temperature and algal blooms and mosquitoes as malaria, diversity and size of fish goes up the river and reaches the region of the villages, of backwater effect changes in the spawning season, the sailing conditions for transport of people and for the transportation of production, mainly of the Brazil nut that is made during the flooded season, and occupation of land in the vicinity of the Indigenous Lands due to mining, water pollution, deforestation, hunting and fishing practices and activities.
- It is necessary that the following immediately be done:
  - Implementation of Monitoring and Surveillance Stations;
  - Definition of Basic Environmental Programs (PBAs).
  - Definition of a transition program after the Emergency Plan.
  - Definition and presentation of transposition system in the villages.
  - Definition of staff for monitoring, with people who are trustworthy community.

—Posted 25th June 2012 by Xikrin Xingu (Xinkrin Xingu 2012)

In this instance, indigenous protest captures a precise set of claims against the government, articulated as critiques that the government has not met the very same regulatory regimes, plans, and scientific studies upon which the state claimed legitimacy. The complementary studies for the Bacajá River are argued to be superficial; the monitoring and surveillance plans are not implemented; basic definitions are lacking for transition plans, environmental programs, and staffing needs. In making these claims, the indigenous populations adopt the language of the state, aiming to discredit the rigor of the scientific studies that took place.

Eventually, these occupations would disband, and the statements garnered little by way of response. Sometimes after only a few days, the indigenous groups would be split into smaller negotiation groups and would have received promises of motorcycles, faster motorboats, and other material goods. At times, their demands were met for more emergency protocols and transition plans to be established. While compromises would be reached, none of these measures would significantly slow or stop the pace of construction. More often than not, temporary stoppages served as a tactic that yielded short-term gains for the affected communities. Brent Millikan, the International Rivers Network Amazon Program Coordinator, observed that "It seems like the indigenous groups are hedging their bets, that they don't really think they can stop this, so they are waiting for better benefits, health care and so on" (Interview with author 2012). The "emergency plan" for delivering benefits that the indigenous communities originally asked for—schools, land demarcations, and health clinics—instead gave way to goodies that placated the opposition. From 2011–2013, each village was given a monthly budget of BRL $30,000 per month. "Centuries of a subsistence lifestyle gave way to instant gratification in the form of food, laptops, new vehicles, freezers, motorbikes," reported *The Guardian* (Watts 2014). With goodies instead of more serious concerns being met as the results of negotiations, halting the project altogether was not a credible goal of the opposition, but nor was even addressing the most pressing social concerns of the communities themselves. Despite the material goods they were receiving (or more likely, *because* of those material goods), the Federal Prosecutor in Altamira, Thais Santi, concluded that an ethnic genocide was taking place for some of the indigenous tribes affected by the dam. In the recently contacted Arará do Cachoeira Seca village, Santi described how under the Emergency Plan, resources were given to the indigenous people that were meant to empower and strengthen their communities. Instead, her visit found a scene of a comatose society:

> I saw the quantity of garbage that they had in the village, I saw their destroyed homes, with broken tiles, raining inside. And they were sleeping there . . . it was a post-war [scene], a holocaust. The Indians did not move. They just stood there motionless, stuck, asking for food, asking to have homes built for them. There was no more traditional medicine. They had stopped talking and meeting each other. The only time they met was at night to watch a telenovela on a plasma TV. It was brutal. And the garbage in the village, the garbage was stunning . . . The Emergency Plan had created an absolute dependence on the company. (Brum 2014)

Santi described her impression that Belo Monte was reminiscent of the totalitarian states described by Hannah Arendt, where anything is possible and in which Belo Monte represented "the most extreme example" of flexible legal frameworks present that allowed the dam in the first place (Brum 2014).

While some indigenous tribes in the Xingu River basin were unsuccessful in sustaining their opposition to the project and ultimately gained resources from CCBM's beneficent role, other tribes expressed opposition based on the regional hydroelectric construction efforts taking place. The Munduruku tribe, which lived along the nearby Tapajós River, saw the construction of the Belo Monte dam as portending the construction of other dams throughout the region. The Teles Pires dam proposed for the Tapajós River, they feared, would wreak havoc and disaster upon their territories. Notably, as earlier mentioned, at the June 2012 Xingu +23 gathering at the Belo Monte site, which took place in June 2012,[29] some Munduruku people looted the Belo Monte Construction Consortium offices. Outraged that dams throughout the Amazon basin would become all the more feasible if Belo Monte was approved, they resorted to property damage, smashing computers and windows as a means of conveying both outrage and desperation. No one was injured (Haidar 2012). Hydroelectric dams would affect their livelihoods and landscapes in the near future, and no amount of resistance, peaceful or otherwise, appeared to be a workable means of opposition (Bratman 2015).

Indigenous groups have legal protections from prosecution under Brazilian law, which meant that they were less a focus of prosecutorial attention than other local anti-dam activists. Given local pressure and considerable police funding from the CCBM, the police turned their gaze onto local activists, pressing them with criminal charges for the property damage. Eleven activists were charged, including a priest, a nun, a documentary filmmaker, and the well-known leaders of the Xingu Alive Forever and Indigenous Missionary Council groups (Bratman 2015). The charges were later dropped, given that none who were charged in fact participated in the looting. Still, merely pressing charges against those known anti-dam organizers seemed to be a case of legal persecution intended to intimidate and further marginalize and inconvenience the leaders of the opposition movement.

The legal discord over the dam also spilled onto the international stage. At the Rio +20 Earth Summit in Rio de Janeiro in June 2012, Izabella Teixeira, the Minister of Environment, engaged in a 10-minute shouting match with anti-dam critics, and a video of the incident was then disseminated on the Internet (Bratman 2014). Concurrent with the Rio +20 conference, protesters gathered in Altamira and near the dam construction site to protest the project, making a human banner that read "Stop Belo Monte" (*Pare Belo Monte*). In a symbolic liberation of the Xingu River's water, the protesters dug a small canal out of the clay barrier that had been built on the Xingu, letting the water flow freely. This image was a powerful symbol and, combined with flyover photographs taken by Greenpeace of the massive construction site and the ecological devastation, the poignant set of opposition images conveyed the project's destructive potential.

Regardless of the public outcry, the government's assertive defense of the project was unsurprising, as President Dilma Rousseff was formerly minister of Mines and Energy from 2003–2005. One of her first actions as president was to give the official "green light" for the project to proceed. Still, she had a history as a revolutionary activist with the PT party, defining herself as a socialist. By some of her long-standing allies, she was endearingly thought of as a "guerrilla president," having spent time imprisoned by the military regime (Diversi 2014). President Rousseff had spoken in her inaugural address about the importance to "respect and develop the biodiversity of Amazonia in the North" and of her "greatest commitment to honoring our women, protecting our most vulnerable people, and governing for everyone." Still, the president was unequivocal about her commitment to "greatly encourage" ethanol and hydro-energy sources, championing clean energy (Rousseff 2011).

President Rousseff's position appeared disingenuous, but on technical grounds the government had a relatively strong legal basis upon which to defend its claims. The protections for indigenous peoples had received approvals from FUNAI; because no indigenous villages would be flooded, conducting consultations there was not required under Brazilian law. The government had conducted 30 visits and explanatory workshops to indigenous villages between 2007 and 2010, and had also conducted four public hearings and twelve public consultations about the project (Brazil 2011). The CCBM, meanwhile, became a de-facto patron of many of the indigenous communities where compensation measures had been granted. While the federal agency tasked with managing indigenous affairs, FUNAI, is supposed to have primary responsibility for providing assistance to the indigenous tribes under Brazilian law, the assistance from the CCBM took the form of effectively saying to tribal leaders "you can have anything you ask for." This resulted in black markets for goods, dietary shifts (including significantly greater consumption of sugar-filled and highly processed food products), and an immense amount of tribal fragmentation, conflict, and diminishing of local productive capacities inside indigenous communities. Moreover, it diminished the capacity for FUNAI be trusted and to fairly address the needs of the indigenous populations following from their mandate (Brum 2014).

In distilled form, two basic and idealized narratives can be told about the Belo Monte project. First, in a negative light, it is a repetition of the age-old story of colonial imposition and exploitation of people and the environment, wherein indigenous peoples are hurt, and the state repeats the wrongheaded and massive projects of the past, driven largely by financial gains for politicians. It does so projecting confidence that this time things will be different, and that democratic systems, participatory engagements, and the existing laws in place are more than adequate to ensure citizens' well-being and successful project outcomes. On the other hand, the more positive perspective on the Belo Monte story is that of a renewable energy project, producing substantial energy for Brazilians without contributing significantly to climate change. In the revised project of Belo

Monte, consultations have been extensive; locally, the populations benefit from the hospitals, roads, and economic growth that they have long demanded from the government, and considerable investment pours into the region to meet social needs and address the ecological concerns involved with the project.

Both of these narratives are situated within a politics of sustainable development, wherein new approaches are taken to address long-standing challenges. Those challenges entail achieving economic development goals on the one hand, and on the other protecting people and the environment from harm. Through democratic processes of consultation and rigorous scientific assessment, as well as engineering changes, the project is positioned as a distinctly different one from that of the past. In practice, as much of this section has shown, both of these idealized perspectives lack nuance in representing the more complex realities, tradeoffs, and social movement dynamics that took place as the dam was contested.

The Global Debate over Dams and Development

While the Belo Monte project shifted substantially over its thirty-year history as a proposal, so too did the baselines for what clean energy looked like in environmental governance. These shifts meant that large hydroelectric dams found renewed favor on a global level, with the basic shift toward run-of-river design as a solution. Large dams went from being considered environmentally problematic (on the whole) to instead becoming embraced, at least cautiously if not even more actively, as an important component of renewable energy portfolios. Having long relied on environmental arguments to maintain opposition to dams, much of that same environmental discourse was instead used to justify the project, leaving no one with a discernibly clear claim to the discourse of sustainability.

In the early 1970s, large dams were being built at a rate of nearly a thousand per year. The World Bank supported an average of twenty-six dams per year between 1970 and 1985, but during this same time, hydroelectric energy projects became notoriously controversial (Leslie 2005). By 1997, the depth of disagreement between private companies, environmentalists, and government officials was severe, with close observers characterizing a meeting in which the groups came together as a momentary "truce" within a "battle" (Flanders 1997).[30] The World Commission on Dams (WCD) was established around this time, in an attempt to position itself as an international arbiter of the dispute over the efficacy and benefits of hydroelectric projects.

The WCD hoped to "change the tenor of the debate [on large dams] away from lack of trust and destructive confrontation and towards co-operation, shared goals, and more equitable outcomes" (2000, 310). The WCD was an independent international body composed of representatives from pro-dam, anti-dam, and mixed positions, with considerable participation by NGOs. It aimed to suggest a framework through which to evaluate the merits of future dam projects, balancing between the economic and environmental considerations surrounding them (Leslie 2005). Meetings continued for two years, leading, ultimately, to a 400-page report that established guidelines for future dam projects and suggested ways to benchmark their efficacy.[31] The report highlighted many concerns about large dams and historical failures of such projects, including cost overruns, devastating poverty experienced by many affected communities, and enormous social and ecological costs. Rather than being firmly oppositional toward large dams, the commission established a list of twenty-six guidelines meant to make the decision-making process involved with dam building more rational and transparent, and to help avoid disastrous consequences (Conca 2006). Establishing the unprecedented levels of collaboration over dam construction and evaluations was a significant contribution of the WCD, but the actual recommendations and final report still did not satisfy policymakers or technicians' expectations in terms of establishing strong global-level guidelines regarding dam construction issues (Fujikura and Nakayama 2009). While the report's guidelines were salient on a global level, the recommendations were intended for national-level implementation and adoption according to sovereign jurisdictions (Dingwerth 2005). Both in multilateral lending institutions like the World Bank and in national contexts, the WCD report meant that big hydroelectric projects were back on the table as a potential renewable energy source, despite the fact that the report's recommendations were substantially more cautious and tenuous about their construction (Khagram 2004, Fujikura and Nakayama 2009, 180).

Developing nations like Brazil tended to be wary of the WCD's recommendations. They argued that their national procedures held greater legitimacy and accountability than the internationally established standards present in the WCD report. China and India, respectively the world's leading and third-largest dam building countries, explicitly opposed the recommendations, while Brazilian officials voiced concerns off-record to the World Bank (Fujikura and Nakayama 2009). Brazil's BNDES, which is largest lending bank in Latin America and one of the largest banks in the world, was barely swayed by the WCD report.

For Brazilian energy planners, large dams appeared a much more viable renewable energy alternative even than sugarcane biofuel, which involves extreme territorial and labor impacts. Brazil's ten-year energy expansion plans essentially offered an all-out approach toward hydroelectric, wind, and bioethanol energy generation (IRENA 2015). Capturing hydroelectric potential, as well as opening up new ports and waterways to improve upon other regional transportation connectivity, is a significant component of IIRSA. Brazil's heavy investments in energy infrastructures, especially along the Madeira and Beni rivers, are also a part of Brazil's geopolitical westward expansion in the Amazon region (Zibechi 2014). Energy officials defended Amazonian dam building on the basis that relative to the Amazon's territorial expanse, dam reservoirs were quite small. One MME official contended in an interview with me that the total reservoir area covered by dams was only 0.5% of Amazonian territory; seen in this perspective, a hydroelectric reservoir was just a tiny amount of flooded area. Moreover, the same official argued, there was little value in the argument that the Amazonian ecosystem was too fragile or pristine to merit an intervention such as the Belo Monte dam.

> What most people don't understand is that Amazonia has already been inhabited by people, you've got houses constructed there that have always been of a temporary sort, and there was an extra impact in cities that never existed before. So yes, the dams may take away the houses that were there, constructed in this temporary way, but it is not a significant environmental difference on what already was an altered ecosystem. (Interview with author 2012)

This rationale permeated other parts of the planning process as well. When faced with critiques that the dam would displace people, Norte Energia and public officials were quick to emphasize that no *indigenous* people would be flooded out. The urban population who would be displaced from Altamira was a less compelling and media-savvy group. They were already living in unsuitable informal housing conditions and might be better off if removed from that area, officials argued.[32] Such assertions dually served to emphasize that Amazonia was not really a pristine nature that needed protection, and functioned to undermine the claim that vulnerable populations were being harmed by the interventions. Dams would offer both social benefits and make energy production possible on an otherwise relatively unproductive territory, they argued.

Hydroelectric construction in the Amazon was also a key component of Brazilian pride in its energy matrix. Despite the rising rates of energy consumption, Brazil's energy matrix is one of the cleanest in the world, with 43% of its energy supply coming from renewables.[33] The country is nearly self-sufficient in terms of energy production, largely thanks to increases in large hydroelectric capacity in addition to its supplies of oil and ethanol production (Luomi 2014). Both large and small hydroelectric projects are described as having low greenhouse gas emissions, and, therefore, they contribute toward energy portfolios that are considered clean in the face of climate change (World Bank Group 2011).

The New Development Bank, established by the BRICS nations (Brazil, Russia, India, China, and South Africa) in 2014, would also begin financing major energy and infrastructure projects. By 2016, the New Development Bank screened projects for their social and environmental impacts and developed more assessment criteria for these impacts in their lending frameworks.[34] In addition to the New Development Bank's $100 billion commitment in authorized capital, investments from foreign direct investments in Brazil were also substantial. In 2010, Brazil ranked fifth in the world as an attractive destination for foreign direct investment, with $48 billion poured into the nation, largely from Chinese and Spanish investments in the Amazon region. Brazilian assets also swelled thanks to capital accumulation from pension funds, which went from 12% to 17% of Brazilian GDP contributions between 2000–2010 (Zibechi 2014). While the late 1980s and 1990s activism focused on pressuring the World Bank's operations in the region, the present political economy of investments in Amazonian infrastructure involves a much more dynamic and complex constellation of finance, investment actors, and multilateral institutions.

As Table 6.2 shows, the World Bank's lending for hydropower over the 2003–2012 interval is dwarfed by the BNDES lending for that sector, whereas their alternative renewable energy funding is considerably greater.[35] Table 6.2 also highlights a contrast between spending on large hydroelectric projects and funding for wind and solar energy. The World Bank's shifts in relation to renewables funding is also illustrated in Figure 6.5, wherein the data shows that World Bank funding for large dams especially exceeded allocations for other

Table 6.2 World Bank and BNDES Lending for Major Renewable Energy Sectors, 2003–2012

	World Bank	BNDES
Large Hydropower Funding (billions USD)	7.21775	33.08488
Large Hydropower Projects	55	47
Renewable Sector Funding (billions USD)	17.81272	7.190366
Renewable Sector Projects	169	174

World Bank vs. BNDES funding for Large Dams vs. Alternative Energy, 2003–2012. Alternative energy includes solar, wind, biomass, and co-generation. Small hydropower and thermal energy not included. Calculations for BNDES funding based on exchange rate of .554 BRL - USD average rate. Data from World Bank Projects and Operations, and BNDES (https://www.iea.org/media/workshops/2013/scalingupfinancingtoexpandrenewables/6BNDESMariaHelenaIEARenewableEnergy09.04.13.pdf)

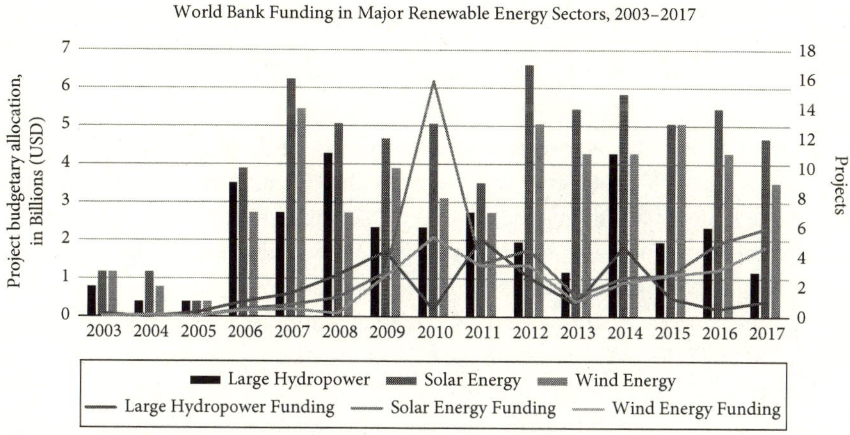

Figure 6.5 World Bank funding in hydroelectric, wind, and solar sectors. Data from World Bank Projects & Operations, http://projects.worldbank.org

types of renewables until 2009, though since then has tended to decline in relation to wind and solar funding. Notably, this data shows the relatively high allocations of funding for a relatively small number of hydropower projects. The greater numbers of solar and wind projects being funded typically involve smaller amounts. It can be inferred that there is higher-stakes investment occurring in the large hydroelectric dam projects instead of the more diversified projects funded in the solar and wind energy sectors.[36]

The global trend back toward financing large hydroelectric projects has salient ramifications, both in the Belo Monte case and more broadly. On a global level, the acceptance of the claim that large hydroelectric dams qualify as clean energy function to substantiate the idea that however large they may be, hydroelectric projects have strong green credentials as sources of renewable energy. This legitimizes their presence within sustainable development strategies, although the ecological consequences of the projects are frequently severe (Finer and Jenkins 2012). The Kyoto Protocol's Clean Development Mechanism financing, which has the aim of incentivizing development of minimally damaging energy sources, has also been applied to such projects despite their dubious track record ecologically (Fearnside 2013, Sutter and Parreño 2007). Some of the most distinct environmentally rooted criticisms of large dam projects contend that they inevitably entail greenhouse gas emissions and biodiversity losses. Yet in contrast, the discourse supporting dam construction that stems from multilateral institutions adopts a similarly environmentalist stance but making opposite claims: Rather than being significant emitters of greenhouse gases, dams (especially if constructed as run-of-river dams rather than large reservoir dams) offer carbon-efficient and renewable energy provided in a cost-effective manner.

Given the centrality of the environmental critique against dams, the shift instead toward an explicit environmental rationale for embracing them functioned to undermine the anti-dam environmental critiques. In Brazil, despite the myriad objections that activists raised against the project on environmental grounds, the federal government was able to successfully frame the Belo Monte project as part of its clean energy strategy. Positioned as a major contributor toward the nation's sustainable development, advertisements at the Rio +20 UN Conference on Sustainable Development promoted Belo Monte as "clean energy for Brazil." Airing on both national television and on airport display monitors during the conference, the ads aimed to convince conference-goers that the Belo Monte project did, in fact, capture the best of the sustainable development goals that were being discussed at the conference.

In the global arena, large dams were once popular, and then during the mid-1990s their construction was virtually a political nonstarter. After an extensive worldwide debate over large dams, however, they were back on the table and ultimately held a central place in articulations of sustainable development and renewable energy. The BNDES doubled down on hydroelectric investments with a relative lack of concern for international lending norms and the findings of the WCD report. By 2012, Belo Monte, and more broadly hydroelectric energy from large dams, was framed as a necessary good for Brazil and compatible with the global sustainable development agenda.

Disputes over a Completed Belo Monte

On the short flight into Altamira from the Pará state capital, Belém, a middle-aged man in a pressed shirt and with new-looking hiking shoes sits next to me. He is chatty and clearly excited for the trip, talking also with other nearby passengers who appear to be his colleagues. His name is Rodrigo and, like me, he too is a professor and is going to "the field" near Altamira. Rodrigo asks me a question that I had heard variations on for the past ten years of working in Altamira, as the Belo Monte hydroelectric project was being proposed. "On the balance, do the positives outweigh the negatives?" How does one even begin answering that question? I wondered to myself, for at least the hundredth time. Rodrigo offered his evaluation in my brief moment of hesitation, sparing me from having to reframe and dissect the issue. He was convinced that the positives did, in fact, outweigh the negatives, because of the "organization" of the city, the reconstruction of the palm-thatch roof houses that had once housed people "living in terrible conditions." And, he noted, the social benefits that are coming to the communities in the region are formidable. Rodrigo and his team's work was funded through the Plan for the Regional Development for the Xingu (PDRX). His program—and dozens of others like it aimed at improving housing, education, health care, and more in the region—are all a result of the money that came as part of the benefits package for the region. But even the benefits package was the subject of much frustration, as many project initiators never received reimbursements, or made proposals that never materialized because of financing and oversight problems.

The regulatory framework surrounding the Belo Monte project was couched in participatory consultations, rational management structures, and governmental oversight. These structures ultimately reinforced a politics that privileged local business interests and consolidated the power of the governmental officials who had initiated the project. Incentivized by the promise of jobs and an economic boom, a rush of newcomers arrived in Altamira and the Transamazon highway region, but those who maintained most influence locally were the same business owners and politically elite families who had long held control in local politics and real estate. Consider this description of the unevenness of urban development in one of the Altamira relocation settlements, São Joaquim, narrated by a 32-year-old resident of Altamira who had been displaced by the dam: "There are four water tanks that need to be filled up for all of São Joaquim's 4,500 or so residents. The villa houses [in a gated community just below São Joaquim, where many engineers and other higher-level Norte Energia employees live]—which are maybe 200 in all—have four water tanks as well." In São Joaquim, water trucks come to supply those four giant tanks. The families then get the water pumped into their homes' water tanks. For various reasons the tanks ran dry for about fifteen days in 2016. For the most part, without adequate backup water supply, São Joaquim's poorer families were forced to purchase water or go totally dry. Those in the villa houses, just a few blocks away, remained with their water access, and some houses even kept full swimming pools. Another Altamira resident summed up the changes: "This is not the progress that people imagined it would be" (Interview with author 2016).

Several key components of licensing conditions remained unmet, even as the dam became operational. As of 2017, these included a regional hospital that still lacked fundamental operating equipment, and connections for Altamira's long-awaited sewage treatment and drinking water treatment systems. Today, "there's nowhere for people to show up and make their demands, and the company is in retreat mode—this is the way that they will slink off and let the municipality and the people fend for themselves" (Interview with author 2016).

The Belo Monte dam was slated to be a new model for Brazilian success, offering a centerpiece of sustainable development achievement for the Amazon, as Brazil's booming economy and vibrant democracy under the new leftist leadership was at its strongest. The "pink tide" receded, however, and the Belo Monte dam is symbolic of something else altogether. The detritus left behind by the tide involves a democracy that is significantly frayed, manifestly corrupt, and an ecosystem that is largely unrecognizable. The discourses of sustainability and social development that were championed and celebrated at the Rio +20 summit, and which marked nearly every dimension of the Belo Monte project's rhetoric, instead ring hollow for those Brazilians most closely affected by such plans.

It is worth recalling that the overarching economic and political approach during the time that the Belo Monte dam was being proposed and constructed involved renewed developmentalism. Under this model, corporate and state actors—most prominently the construction companies involved, as well as PT and PMDB party loyalists, utilized frameworks of democratic consolidation and appearances of public consultation to present themselves as reformist and the Belo Monte project as responsive to long-standing critiques. At the same time as these heavy-handed state influences presented opportunities for investment and some social benefits, new socio-natures emerged within the region.

The sustainable development processes discussed in this case study reveal transformations of physical areas: riverbeds became derivation channels, riverbanks became the site of a massive gold mine, and new urban resettlement communities were constructed. Socio-nature is also co-constituted by the broader social processes of transformation in the region, including changes in activist alliances and tactics, demographic shifts into and out of certain locations, and changing rates of violence, health care, and urban service delivery. Underpinning such processes, the discourse of renewable energy and energetic growth imperatives in the country functioned to entrench the perception of necessity surrounding the project and sustainable development arriving in the region more broadly.

Technical elements such as the public participation that was engaged amid the years of debate over the dam helped establish a basis for the argument that legitimate procedures and legal actions being followed. While many development projects are labeled as being community-based, concerned with indigenous practices, and participatory, this "does not reverse or modify development's hegemony so much as provide more effective instruments with which to advance external interests and agendas . . . behind the beguiling rhetoric of 'people's control'" (Mosse 2004, 643). Numerous public hearings and consultations were built into the process, but at the same time a remarkable lack of transparency took place as the project was developed. The PT party, whose leaders were largely responsible for reinvigorating the Belo Monte project, championed participation and public involvement in decision making as part of the fundamental uniqueness of their political identity. While officials from the federal environmental agency noted that consultations over the dam had involved record-setting amounts of public hearings and engagement, these were more procedural than intended to influence the project. Within the energy sector a clear inner circle persisted, which shared decision making among themselves and based their plans on assumptions of unmanaged, and generally unlimited, expansions in demand. Despite an emphasis within PT party discourse on social inclusion and transparency, only certain agencies closest to the energy production system were included in energy planning.[37] Other related agencies, such as the National Water Agency, who should have a remit over hydroelectric energy, had very little input into Belo Monte or any of the other hydroelectric dams planned in the Amazon basin (de Sousa Júnior and Reid 2010). While participatory forums took place, technocratic decision making predominated over participatory practices, making those forums look more perfunctory than genuinely consultative forms of public engagement.

Being opposed to the dam's construction was also framed as fundamentally unpatriotic and as involving an unreasonable stance against Brazilian development. "Even inhabiting the regions earmarked for the implementation of these plans can be considered 'blocking the road to development,' and the punishment of those who stand in the way is generally severe, as the indigenous peoples themselves discovered" (Timo 2013, 140). The former minister of Mines and Energy, Edson Lobão, characterized those opposing Belo Monte as "demonic forces" (Elizondo 2009). While Brazil's Ministry of Mines and Energy has a far from stellar record with indigenous peoples (Zhouri 2010, Jaichand and Sampaio 2013, Bingham 2010, Garfield 2001, Kimmerling 2013), comments such as these function to conclude that the state's priority was one of development at any cost, rather than one of development wrought from deep democratic practice and objective evaluations of project efficacy (Timo 2013).

As earlier noted, Belo Monte's implications for the human rights of the indigenous peoples of the region are significant. In addition to violations of the International Labor Organization's Free, Prior, and Informed Consent stipulations, additional concerns include the violations of Brazilian domestic laws concerning protections for land and cultural rights of Brazil's indigenous populations (Jaichand and Sampaio 2013). While some groups negotiated and saw substantial material gains, other groups, such as the Arará do Cachoeira Seca, experienced a total cultural transformation as a result of the project. Nationalist rhetoric was used to justify the construction of the dam and to slight the international human rights institutions that otherwise critiqued Brazil for its track record.

Paradoxes of the Green Economy

This chapter advanced the argument that sustainable development functioned as a mobilizing discourse to encourage spatial transformations, which created highly uneven results for the local populations. Henri Lefebvre argues that space serves to perpetuate the existing mode of production through underlying knowledge, technical expertise, and ongoing action (Lefebvre 1991 [1974]). In this case, spatial transformations entrenched the modernist paradigm through the logics of energy deficits, rational infrastructure planning, and harm mitigation for local populations and the environment. In so doing, state power and influence over the Xingu River and its nearby residents became consolidated, reinforcing Brazilian neodevelopmentalism in Amazonia.

Through embracing the common language of sustainable development and the logics of clean and renewable energy, the Brazilian state was able to influence the development trajectory of the region and to maintain a paradoxical mix of high regional investment along with minimal support. Its use of Belo Monte as a celebrated example of public participation and planning served as a discourse that concealed the contradiction inherent in the embrace of large dams as a part of sustainable development, and which undermined the critiques against how participation and consultation had been handled (Bratman 2015).

The incremental and rather slow process of creating a sense of inevitability and acquiescence surrounding the Belo Monte project also meant that large dams in the Amazon became emblematic within Brazil's embrace of sustainable development. Through a series of minor legal changes, environmental and human rights norms began to be repositioned and no longer carried as many stringencies surrounding licensing preconditions and informed consent stipulations as they once did. Facing no significant opposition from the strong and politically connected national lending institutions, and little grounds for objection in international environmental policy, constructing the dam became inevitable. Once constructed, the objections to the dam, and the continued lack of implementation of some of the social safeguards and benefits that were supposed to have been established all along, became moot issues. Sustainable development justified the dam for higher levels of management but was conveniently elided from discourse once the dam was already built and the on-the-ground realities diverged from the intended outcomes.

Through claiming legitimacy by engaging in the international community's and the Brazilian domestic legal expectations of local consultations, environmental assessments, and open bidding, the state gave all appearances of having effectively changed from the military government and short-sighted modernization efforts of the past. The reimagined Belo Monte project involved articulations of procedural adherence and extensive public consultation, in addition to an overarching framework presenting the project as one promoting clean energy, ultimately with little cost environmentally or socially. Belo Monte is revealing of how the baseline of environmental standards and public consultations shifted over time, both inside Brazil and globally. Globally, the logic of sustainable development is almost entirely championed as the world embraces large hydroelectric projects in the name of clean energy, legitimized under the framework of sustainable development. In many cases the notion that economic productivity does not necessitate environmental sacrifices, and that environmental losses are not a necessary byproduct of economic growth, is indeed credible. But when applied to Belo Monte and other dams in the Amazon basin constructed in the name of sustainable development, the same logic does little to acknowledge the actual social, environmental, and economic losses that are more prevalent.

7

Conclusion

Weighing Environmental Governance

People are evidently inclined to grant legitimacy to anything that is or seems inevitable no matter how painful it may be. Otherwise the pain might be intolerable.

—Barrington Moore Jr., *Injustice: The social bases of obedience and revolt* (1978)

It is worth briefly remembering the scene from the 1979 film *Bye Bye Brazil* that commenced this book to set the stage for reflection on changes to the Amazon region in light of the sustainable development framework. The film, in this brief scene, suggests that the elderly woman's own life and livelihood are threatened by a host of national policies that denude the landscape and leave the nation's fragile indigenous populations without support or protection, often in harsh urban settings. For many, the Xingu River basin continues to be a site where projections of big dreams for attaining wealth and opportunity simultaneously collide with cultural losses and landscape transformation. The story of transitional times in the Amazon did not begin with globalization, nor is neoliberal capitalism a particularly useful lens through which to make sense of Amazonian rainforest politics. Influential roles are played by a variety of other political institutions, earlier ideologies, locally powerful economic forces, and civil society actors in the region.

Since colonial times, Amazonian history has been torn between different, often competing views on how the forest and its resources should be used. It is frequently viewed as a pristine rainforest whose stewardship-oriented peoples are threatened by an opposite extreme, that of a terrain vast in natural resources that can (and should) be made productive through major investments, infrastructures, and resource extraction. Today, along the Xingu River where the scene from *Bye Bye Brazil* was shot, there is a concrete dock that was built for some of the region's riverboats. At the quay where some boats used to park, there is a new, but tiny, man-made sandy beach area. The beach is located only a few meters from where a city sewage drain pipe spews into the Xingu. The beach and the drainage are separated by a low rock wall—one that does not convincingly appear to shield any prospective bathers from the effluent. A few new bars and restaurants enliven the waterfront, which remains a popular destination for nightlife. The Espaço Eletronorte, where the energy company housed some information about the Belo Monte dam project and the local non-profit *capoeira* group used to train—is now a private gym.

Sustainable development arose as a global policy paradigm in the late 1980s, almost a full decade after *Bye Bye Brazil* was released. Since that time, various attempts to achieve economic growth in the Amazon region and for Brazil as a whole have been more tightly connected to concerns over deforestation, environmental protection, and conflicts over land rights and social inequality. At the level of activists and institutions, important changes took place as sustainable development plans and policies were made, often involving new oversight and enforcement regimes as well as different constellations of social movement alliances. These tended to vary widely in relation to the political and economic opportunities that Brazil experienced during the past three decades.

The pages of this book have detailed numerous anecdotes of assassinations, death threats, and conflicts amid plans to improve the region through sustainable development. These help illustrate how in actual practice, the struggle to achieve different (and often competing) visions of sustainable development are a far cry from a smooth process of weighing out scientifically neutral evidence, making disembodied choices over land use, or evaluating the most efficient economic outcomes. Sustainable development is political, and it involves messy politics at that.

It is tempting to conclude a study of sustainable development by tracing the various social, economic, and ecological phenomena in the Amazon today—deforestation rates, new conservation areas created, human development indicators, literacy, and so on— and to offer up a neat prognosis for the socio-ecological future of the region. On the balance, a brief synopsis would likely lead readers to the rather unsatisfying conclusion that the sustainable development framework in the Amazon is a mixed bag. It would also suggest that sustainable development is likely to persist as an orientation in Brazilian policy—this despite rival fad words and alternative paradigms being evoked in other parts of the world such as *resilience* and *buen vivir*. In the Brazilian Amazon, sustainable development still rules the day when new plans are made or visions espoused for a brighter future, and the idea has not lost much of its luster as a policy-orienting discourse. An exercise of stock-taking surrounding sustainable development will not, however, lead students, scholars, and practitioners into a deeper set of understandings about sustainable development's role, either in the short or the longer term.

Beyond evaluation of whether sustainable development on the balance has been good or bad for the Amazon, it is important to understand more about where the messiness of sustainable development comes from and how it plays out in people's experiences, as the framework is so often used to guide and orient the processes of governing the region. Henri Lefebvre asserts that our theorizations of socio-nature must encompass dynamism and fluctuation in how we understand human relations to nature (Lefebvre 1991 [1974]). This book extends Lefebvre by contributing to an understanding of the contradictory and pluralistic experiences that are constitutive of the socio-nature experience of sustainable development. On this level, the contradictions of sustainable development are often masked by the conceptual foundations of the idea itself, which posit that frequently competing interests can—and must—be balanced when sustainable development is used as a policy discourse.

The historical overview of sustainable development that was presented in the first chapters of this book suggested the theoretical and political undercurrents of tension between environmental conservation and economic growth. The social and natural spaces of the region were deeply shaped by modernist conceptualizations of nature as something outside of human control, but needing to be tamed and brought into productivity through land settlement and infrastructure interventions. This occurred in early colonial history and in the later history of Amazonian-directed colonization efforts. The rift between humans and nature, deeply embedded in modernist thought, informed the goals of Amazonian development insofar as they positioned the rainforest as a potential source of wealth and at the same time as a problem, needing to be brought into contact with the rest of the nation, tamed and controlled. The Amazon region embodied a tension as the region was imagined by explorers, naturalists, and developers alike to be a place of precious and pristine nature and at the same time a place that required capitalism and colonization for human and economic well-being to flourish. This ideational orientation was carried forward through developmentalist economic approaches in which alignments of state and capital accelerated in the 1950s, shaping the Amazon region with a stronger emphasis on its potential economic contribution to the nation through agriculture and industrial development.

Subsequently, the settlement of the Amazon and massive investments in the region catalyzed rapid social and ecological changes. These programs accelerated the transformations to Amazonian nature and society, driven by spatial imaginaries of the Amazon as "empty" and by physical planning efforts to organize urban centers, build roads, and incorporate the Amazon into the national development and security agenda. By the late 1980s, the sustainable development idea arose as a measure to break the standoff between the frequent contradictions between economic and environmental protection goals and to escape the seeming contradictions that appeared between economic and conservation goals. The Brazilian political landscape was often contradictory in response to the idea of sustainable development, and policy efforts to achieve the framework were far from cohesive. The concept of sustainable development did not erase the debate between economic and environmental goals, or between articulations of human settlement as oppositional to the pristine nature of the Amazon, at the same time as some policy measures suggested, through ecological modernization and later neoliberal conservation models, that such goals could be satisfied.[1] The socio-natures brought together through the lived experiences of these often competing aims yielded spatial productions that were understandably fraught with contradictions and social strife.

The case studies presented in the latter half of this book show how sustainable development is carried out in lived experiences in ways that diverge significantly from the harmonization and balance between goals that comprise the mainstream understanding of the concept's meaning. For the would-be foresters and settlers along the BR-163 highway, the uncertain legal frameworks of forest protection involved a backlash against conservation-oriented policies; years of economic planning, meetings, and ecological zoning resulted not in stable structures of institutional regulations but rather in a long-term reality of shifting institutional rules and sporadic enforcement. The Projects for Sustainable Development (PDS) residents in Anapu, similarly, experienced a tandem desire to gain full legalization of their areas, but mixed with a strong degree of frustration and alienation when such incidental attention to their areas took place in the wake of Sister Dorothy Stang's assassination. Under sustainable development land use plans, the Terra do Meio *ribeirinhos* become bound to new forms of social organization, and new understandings of their place and history became enwrapped in processes of adapting to the state's constraints and interactions with intermediary agencies. In the case of the construction of the Belo Monte dam, articulations of sustainable development involved numerous conflicts, including the contradictory insistence on a desire for the state to assert its influence in the area and a simultaneous resistance to the presence of the state by civil society actors. The Belo Monte case also reveals the challenges of public engagement, in which adherence to many environmental licensing principles such as public participation and documentation take place while simultaneously, other arms of governmental institutions may flaunt the nation's human rights, participation, and licensing commitments, undermining or working around them altogether.

At different scales of political action, environmental governance takes shape. Governing the rainforest involves articulating convincingly conservationist identities to ward off further violence and help spur the creation of new protected areas; it involves social movement contestation and participation over new infrastructure projects; it means struggling between national and international pressures while shaping the future of Amazonian infrastructures and land uses.

That is, from the level of the United Nations down to municipal committees, and also by international NGOs and private sector actors, there are myriad attempts being made to address the environmental challenges in the Amazon. Understanding how sustainable development is articulated by these various actors can inform how scholars and the public think about the process of governing land and people. Interrogating the role of state institutions and civil society actors in light of sustainable development articulations in the Amazon is an important theme of this work, which merits discussion in light of how power dynamics of influence take shape between these scales.

The Sustainable Development State

Thinking of competing visions for Amazonian sustainable development offers insight into how contemporary Amazonian spaces are produced in light of modernity. As Anthony Giddens has suggested, the institutional dimensions of modernity entail four key dimensions: capitalist accumulation in the context of private markets; surveillance, which involves control of information and social supervision; military power; and industrialism, in which nature is transformed and replaced with a human/nature "created environment" (Giddens 1990). Bringing the Amazon into the modern world entailed coalescing around making economic production in the region increasingly industrialized and interconnected with the global economy, as well as connecting Amazonian society to the rest of the Brazilian state through interventions that made the space more legible to outsiders, increasingly dominated by a military presence, and frequently unequal as capitalism expanded along Amazonian frontiers. The ecological modernization embedded in the notion of sustainable development, similarly, involved a managerial impetus, largely driven by the state, that further entrenched the dualism between humans and nature and reinforced the presence of the state and capitalist expansion. This was achieved through historical examples of road cutting, land organizing, and dam building in the Amazon, as well as more contemporary efforts along similar lines that have been detailed in this book's case studies.

Research on Brazilian water institutions by scholars Rebecca Neara Abers and Margaret Keck suggests that a major difficulty for Brazilian environmental governance lies in the divergence between a national policy of integrating natural resource management principles and the configurations of bureaucracies that hinder their effectiveness. Their research describes how water basin organizations and rules are entangled between state government, federal politicians, corporate interests, and other actors which stymie effective implementation. In a few cases, these "institutional entanglements" and their roadblocks can be overcome through the work of savvy brokers who work actively both inside and outside of government to innovate and mobilize informal networks (Abers and Keck 2013). The role of intermediaries, whether as gatekeepers or as interlocutors between grassroots-level actions and national policies, is influential in shaping the local legitimacy of certain land use and infrastructure plans, and can be centrally important to shaping how grassroots actors portray and narrate their own histories and identities as viable stewards and rights-holders in the region. Political scientist Craig Kauffman's observation, derived from a comprehensive study of Ecuadorian experiences with sustainable development, is that if global governance for sustainable development is to become effective, influential domestic actors are necessary in order to guide the national contexts of implementation (Kauffman 2017). Amazonian sustainable development policies are illustrative of the conflicts experienced, at times, between institutions; the Ministry of the Environment frequently conflicts with the Ministry of Mines and Energy, for example, or INCRA's land organizing initiatives conflict at times with IBAMA's enforcement regimes. Certainly, too, intermediary actors, such as the Altamira-based NGOs who guided the Terra do Meio *ribeirinhos* into being able to return to those areas as an extractive reserve, functioned to make a more efficacious outcome for land use in the region. In practice, too, however, it is important to note that sustainable development policy outcomes are unevenly distributed, often privileging people, interests, and geographies that are distant from those people who are living in the physical spaces where such plans take shape.

At a granular level, the case studies in this book reveal the unevenness of governing for sustainable development, manifested in how the state is both present and absent, while desired and alternately resisted by local populations who are the subjects of state plans. The state-led finance and planning of mega-projects, such as the Transamazon and BR-163 highway paving, the creation of a mega-corridor for biodiversity in the Terra do Meio, and the construction of the Belo Monte dam, all generally offer examples of strong assertions of state power. Those cases are illustrative of the state's tendency to base plans on assumptions that strong and continuous improvements in bureaucratic efficacy, enforcement, and accountability will be possible, and further, that those processes will yield positive results for the Amazon and for all Brazil. In practice, however, the state is not monolithic, and its institutions are frequently at odds with each other. The remarkable level of interministerial coordination present in the case of the BR-163 highway showed the potential for integrated work between agencies, but at the same time, the fact that over ten years have gone by since those agencies began working on the highway and the road still remains lacking in basic services and pavement, suggests a remarkable level of bureaucratic lack of co-ordination. Similarly, the concerns over creating the RESEX Médio Xingu illustrate conflicts between the Ministry of Mines and Energy and the Ministry of

Environment. The Belo Monte dam case is replete with institutional competition and entanglements between the federal and state *Ministério Público*, the federal ministries, and IBAMA. Moreover, as the Car Wash scandal shows, significantly vested interests between politicians and construction companies contribute significantly to suboptimal decision making. The institutional entanglements in these cases are illustrative of the challenges of policy implementation, and the general lack of brokers who can smooth over institutional hurdles in projects as substantial as those that have been detailed here.

The cases also highlight the tension between the desire for a strong state role in places where it has been notoriously absent, and the disappointments that sometimes occur when the state subsequently does insert itself into ordering socio-nature in the Amazon. For the BR-163 and Transamazon highway paving plans and land organizing initiatives, the federal government aimed to address long-standing demands of civil society, yet despite participatory engagements and years of planning efforts, the results frequently left community members at odds with the policies that were developed, and sometimes those policies were only marginally implemented. Shifting legal frameworks and enforcement regimes also caused chaos in terms of environmental governance, rather than offering the stability of a stronger state bureaucracy. In the Belo Monte case, many local leaders and some civil society groups expressed support, but subsequently found themselves disappointed by a federal government role that remained staunchly blithe to local concerns, corrupt in its motives, and ignoring of its own social benefits, human rights, and environmental commitments as the project took shape. The engagement of civil society actors themselves involved transformed roles in relation to the state, especially as the PT party rose to power.

The result of such modernist orientations in planning and policy, captured through these projections of strong (though frequently inadequate) state intervention, is frequently that such governance attempts disproportionately affect people who are already disadvantaged and struggling to make livelihoods out of adverse circumstances that are largely historically circumscribed. Overly simple abstractions of state-led planning frequently result in failures because the local social and ecological realities on which those plans are imposed are often far more nuanced than big bureaucracies can ever adequately plan for (Scott 1998). This was especially the case in the Amazon during the years of Brazil's military leadership. The more participatory agenda of the PT party did tend, overall, to lessen the magnitude of such failures, and established expectations that mitigated the experience of abjection that occurred in other cases. Ferguson notes that this experience of abjection is an important consequence of modernity-driven development interventions, through his research on Zambian copper mining (Ferguson 1999, 1994). In the case of the Terra do Meio *ribeirinhos*, for example, sustainable development plans yielded attention to communities' needs in a way that allowed them greater access to social services and economic livelihoods. Intermediaries and community organizing among the populations most locally affected did make a difference, leading to more equitable outcomes. Those outcomes were also not possible without the beneficent partnership role played by state agencies, which created and maintained the conditions for such possibilities through its designation of the conservation areas and through maintaining an enforcement presence in the region.

A cynical conclusion one might draw from this research is that social policies, and even some of the environmental and social protection measures taken to defend the people closest to sustainable development plans, are merely token gestures, implemented without a degree of depth that might suggest a sincerity of motivations toward actually achieving sustainable development. "For the English to see"—*para inglês ver*—is a common Brazilian expression. It refers to times when certain behaviors are presented that conform to others' desires, more for the purpose of conveying an impression than for making any substantive change.[2] Doing something "for the English to see" means that one takes action to give an impression of abiding by certain norms of good behavior more to appease outsiders, whom one might at the same time resent and depend upon, than to actually show changed behaviors. It is important to recognize that the Brazilian state has shown a certain willingness to bend to international pressures and transnational environmental movement activism, even if it initially resists such pressures (Hochstettler and Keck 2007, Keck and Sikkink 1998, Rudel 2013). But it is also important to remember that the relationship between the outside seer and the seen is not a fixed position. During the 1980s and 1990s Brazil was more sensitive to outside pressure from environmental and human rights groups, and more in need of international finance. Yet by the mid-2000s, national development funding and a renewed state–private enterprise constellation of investment structures fostered a more independent, go-it-alone approach in Brazil. This dynamic is again shifting in light of Brazil's economic downturn, and the enthusiastic Chinese investments entering the nation and the Amazon in particular. Scholarship on Brazil is duly challenged, since there is neither a clear set of political opportunity structures to look toward, nor a predictive model available that adequately captures the dynamics of the assemblages of political relationships that are present in the Amazonian realities.

Instead, a generous view of the state might suggest that its ambitions do not match its capacities. In this interpretation, the Brazilian state is holding on to lofty aims of sustainable development policies as an aspirational set of goals, and then falls short of those goals. Ineffectiveness in achieving a perfect triangulation of the goals merely indicates that the state has overreached its capacity to deliver on the expectations it has set forth. Rather than ulterior motives or competing goals undergirding sustainable development, the disappointing results instead may merely be the product of a certain amount of incompetence. Such failures may stem from a host of factors such as corruption, lack of technical coordination, financial challenges, and competing institutional interests in domestic policymaking, among other variables. Seen in this light, Brazil is striving to have it all ways; it aims to meet economic goals through modernization-oriented policies, as well as to do right by the people living in the Amazon, all while still meeting national and global ecological commitments.

Taken on the whole, the Brazilian federal government has maintained a longstanding emphasis on its national sovereignty over the Amazon and has not substantially shifted in its desire to make the Amazon a productive region which bolsters national economic growth. Instead, as Brazil creates new conservation areas or reduces deforestation, the achievements of the environmental movement are commonly heralded as effective. The Brazilian state, meanwhile, is positioned as a reluctant but still willing international environmental leader. Indeed, accusing the Brazilian state of consciously pursuing strategic economic interests at all costs may ascribe too much agency to state institutions. Conversely, being too desirous of a "have it all" approach may inappropriately assume a uniformity and institutional consistency within the planning processes that are taking place in the Amazon. Instead, I posit, certain underpinning logics of state and economic strategic interests are adopted for Amazonia because there is a predominant expectation, established under the discourse of sustainable development, that the state can appease its critics while still clinging to the rationale of modernity. Under sustainable development, the credible possibility of meeting a broad range of goals persists as a hopeful ideal which can be accomplished, without adequate recognition of the process that sustainable development politics requires of people and asserts over landscapes as a form of environmental governance.

Before any litmus test is applied to assess sustainable development's merits, analysis of the concept should incorporate consideration for how the discourse and practice of sustainable development embodies ongoing processes of contestation and attempted resolutions that take form in socio-natural spaces.

Unevenness and Entrenchment in Amazonian Sustainable Development

Those living more distant from sustainable development plans will tend to celebrate the "arrival" of forms of environmental governance such as sustainable development. After all, for the most part the concept is positive, and remains something that represents an improvement upon development-as-usual. Even if these sustainable development initiatives are only marginally successful, or if they come as belated, remedial measures for previous mistakes, sustainable development is a discourse that holds appeal. Deployed as a discourse through which the state (or any number of actors) can achieve such a broad host of objectives, sustainable development becomes a shape-shifter. The problems with sustainable development are not limited to inadequate technical considerations, nor implementation flaws in well-intentioned policies. They are flaws of conceptual omissions and wishful thinking, which are embedded within the discourse itself.

It is important to remember that most of the accomplishments of sustainable development planning should be evaluated in light of their historical contexts. The idea of progress that is captured within the sustainable development idea is something that tends to be imagined as linear, and on an upward trajectory, following from a modernist orientation. This notion follows from Hegelian concepts of historical forward movement toward stages of increasing human freedom. Relevant to the problems associated with this view, it is worth engaging the notion that sustainable development does not necessarily operate in a linear way, but in one that is perhaps more involving nonlinear, spiral, or repetitive processes across space. Marx and Engels famously corresponded about the repetitive nature of history: "causing everything to be re-enacted twice over, once as grand tragedy and the second time as rotten farce." In *The Eighteenth Brumaire,* Marx observes that as history unfolds, there is a "grotesque mediocrity that plays a hero's part." This, according to Marx, is largely as a result of ideas and possibilities becoming transmitted over time, through a process wherein history and historical relations of inequality actively conscribe the circumstances of the present day and delimit the boundaries of political imaginations and possibilities (Marx 2004 [1818–1883]). Lefebvre's dialectical materialism contends that space is constructed not as much through Marxist dialectics of history and economic spaces but rather through a dialectic of space itself. Drawing upon this notion of spatial dialectics over time, examinations of the regional history of the Brazilian Amazon offer some empirical evidence to support an understanding of spatial dialectics.

Some of the historical repetitions presented in this book include the construction of giant edifices that aim to show Brazilian importance to an international audience, as exemplified in the Manaus opera house and soccer stadium, as well as repetitions of symbolic tropes used by individuals, such as Tuirá's gestures with machetes at the Encounters of the Xingu to express outrage over the Belo Monte project. There are also historical echoes that remain tragic, no matter how many times they repeat in historical context. Most notably, Chico Mendes' and Sister Dorothy Stang's deaths are illustrative of this. The historical farce, in the latter case, is not the assassination of Sister Dorothy Stang herself but rather the fact that her historical legacy has yielded so little by way of meaningful changes for the PDS lands and residents. In the case of the PDSs where Sister Dorothy worked, planning toward sustainable development was desultory, experienced as little by way of tangible local actions benefiting the small-scale farmers of the PDSs and only fitful attempts to foster legalized, managed forest systems in their communities. In the aftermath of Sister Dorothy's death, it was the *ribeirinhos* of the Terra do Meio region who ultimately received the most attention through sustainable development governance efforts, rather than the settlers of the PDSs where Sister Dorothy worked. For the *ribeirinhos*, the creation of extractive reserves provided substantial physical security and began a series of changed social and economic relations that fostered a more coherent sense of community identity, place-based affiliation, and increasing economic freedom. The introduction of a stronger state presence in the region allowed for new relations of protection and trade for the *ribeirinho* populations to take shape, ultimately leading to divergence from the historical trajectory of clientelism and dependency that the population had experienced for generations.

For its part, the governmental agenda for the region has remained surprisingly consistent in historical perspective. The modernization-oriented policies of the past sought to make the Amazon an impressive asset for national economic growth, and the neo-developmentalist Brazilian state has adopted a parallel stance. Infrastructure initiatives such as road paving and dam building are state-led projects involving global economic interaction and substantial private investment. Consistently, they are driven centrally by the impetus of a strong national government motivated by macro-economic priorities, and they are predicated upon resource extraction from the region as a driver for such economic growth. The most notable example of this highlighted in this book is the Belo Monte dam, where the government showed itself able to successfully deploy wedge issues and engage in political horse trading over projects as it engaged civil society. This result is that of a hegemonic power in action, passively exerting influence over opposition by soliciting public participation in meetings about the plans for the region, while simultaneously actively performing exertions of control over more oppositional civil society actors. When strong central state and global industrial capital interests align, people are hard-pressed to resist such plans. There is still a role for international pressure and norms to exert influence but largely, domestic politics will tend to triumph. As one Brazilian scientist observes: "... in terms of national policy, the Brazilian government is consistently making decisions that go against the global policies it ratifies" (Loyola 2014, 1365). Moreover, the will of the state, especially when expressed through the executive and judicial branches, retains considerable power in Brazil today. The Brazilian state is not an unchanging monolith asserting hegemonic control over land and people, but it remains an important hegemonic actor in terms of regional influence, even as it is at times constrained by foreign economic influences. Domestic legal and financial pressures, exemplified in recent corruption crackdowns such as Operation

Car Wash (*Lava Jato*), may also function as braking mechanisms upon the assertiveness of the state.

James C. Scott posits that peasants will always find ways to withstand and resist the powerful presence of the state (Scott 1990, 1985), but in the cases presented in this book, the peasants, landless farmers, and *ribeirinhos* are often themselves seeking out the presence of the federal government and welcoming the notion of sustainable development, much more than resisting it. They do so as a means of counteracting their long-standing suffering from the absence of a state presence, which frequently leads to experiences of violence at the hands of illegal land claimers or deforestation from the encroachments of illegal loggers. The peasantry is, in a sense, following Barrington Moore's description at the epigraph for this chapter (Moore Jr. 1978). They legitimize and perpetuate environmental governance both because it appears to be an inevitability and because it is less painful than the alternative of having a continued vacuum of state presence in the region.

There are three factors which together support this granting of legitimacy to sustainable development as an orienting framework for governing the region. First, the Amazonian socio-environmental movement has traditionally viewed people's needs in tandem with environmental priorities. As a result, articulations of a governance framework were not interpreted as a particularly foreign imposition for many in the region. Ideationally, too, influence can be exerted through persistent news stories invoking various scenarios for regional change, promoting impressions of project inevitability, and hosting public meetings and activism oriented around specific demands as a strategy for consolidating shared values. Second, in physical forms, concrete proposals for creating new conservation areas and protected park lands, in addition to highways and dams, reinforce the values and discourses of state intervention in particular spaces. The previously polarized debate over whether the forest would be entirely conserved or, alternatively, sacrificed to promote economic aims instead, found a middle ground through the notion of environmental governance, which promised management, legalized timber extraction, and a more active state presence. Finally, in everyday lives, the spaces of environmental governance interact with these ideational and physical forms as people make decisions about where to settle, what to plant, how to approach managing one's forested area, inform who should get included in a reserve or kicked out of it, and so forth. The material dialectics of space, in other words, play out through sustainable development governance in ways that are often embodied both in lives and landscapes.

As a mechanism of environmental governance, sustainable development asserts a set of political necessities for action in the Amazon, as it does all over the world, in hopes of saving rainforests, creating a more balanced global climate, and preserving the earth's biodiversity. The tendency to use sustainable development as a legitimizing discourse for all sorts of plans that may only be tenuously connected to the values the concept purportedly contains is also, understandably, difficult to resist. The concept contains transformational possibilities in its conceptual and discursive form, even if in practice it at times does just the opposite, masking more substantial changes (economic, political, social, cultural, or environmental) that could be possible while still capturing the reformist aspirations of "development."

Stepping back to examine the everyday lives and landscapes described in this book in light of the idea of sustainable development, it becomes clear that there is considerable distance between those hopeful realities and the transformative potential ascribed to the notion by its champions. In practice, sustainable development is a process rather than a fixed point; understanding how it shapes and is shaped by different interests, values, and land use possibilities helps us to see why, in practice, it is so fraught with unevenness and contradiction.

Sustainable Development: Visions, Policy, and Practice

Contemporary Amazonian development is deeply marked by attempts to organize territory toward goals of achieving national growth and security, while at the same time facing an imperative to preserve what remains of the standing Amazonian rainforest. It is difficult to escape the economic, political, and cultural markers of the other dominant ways of viewing the region which continue to mark its present realities. Early visions promoted by the Brazilian state and powerful private enterprises involved making order out of a wild nature, encouraging settlement, and embracing the influence of capital in the Amazon. Subsequently, the vision for sustainable development involved similarly rational, organizationally oriented ideals concerning how the region's natural resources and populations should be managed. These involved establishing a greater degree of rule of law, and attempts to establish competent institutional presences in the region. It also entailed a vision that encouraging newer migrants to the region could be a source of labor to help populate the forest in support of security, economic, and territorial control interests.

Largely, these visions involve Brazilian attempts to have it both ways; conserving the region's natural resources through conservation-oriented environmental policies takes place at the same time as the nation envisions doubling down on infrastructure investments in order to achieve ambitious economic growth goals. This position is actually congruent with the global governance framework of ideas about sustainable development, which similarly do not acknowledge that trade-offs between these goals must be made (Robinson 2004).

The instances of sustainable development plans and the ongoing reverberations of those plans do function as an essentially conservative articulation of a utopia, which persists even in the face of its failures and tends to reproduce the same logics and shortcomings. In order to more fully explore the transformative potential of sustainable development as a utopic idea, below we examine several different manifestations of sustainable development utopic ideals, and situate each case study chapter in relation to those ideals.

The Modernist Utopia

Scholars Johan Hedrén and Björn Ola-Linnér suggest that certain central elements of modernity are present in sustainable development utopic "blueprints." Hedrén and Linnér's framework offers a useful means of assessing contemporary Amazonian experiments with sustainable development. They suggest that modernity's influence on sustainable development is especially prominent in three ways: where fixed final goals for politics are present, when fixed truth concepts that are rooted in science are entrenched, and when fixed territoriality notions, rooted in nationalism, take shape. Specifically, these elements may differentiate between manifestations of the utopic idea of sustainable development as either involving totalitarian prospects or holding transformational potentials. If a break from these three key areas of modernity's influence can be established, sustainable development can assume its transformative political potential rather than repeating its more conventional iteration as a modern utopic blueprint for totalitarianism (Hedrén and Linnér 2009a, b).

There is some evidence to suggest that from all three case study chapters presented here, sustainable development walks a fine line on all three of these key dimensions of the modernist utopia idea. Chapter 4, which treated highway development in the Amazon, is the most marginal case of those presented in this book as an illustration of sustainable development's transformative potential. In terms of fixed final political goals, the evidence suggests that the major infrastructure programs of *Avança Brazil* (Brazil Forward), PAC I and PAC-II, and IIRSA, all of which involved plans to cut and pave roads that ran right through conservation areas and where civil construction firms stood to profit mightily, suggests a fixity of political goals. The active engagement of civil society institutions along the Transamazon highway, however, suggests a more flexible politics of contention were at play. The shift of perspective that these social movement actors achieved toward being considered by the government as viable partners in conservation also indicates a less-than-firm position regarding science, which was predominated by careful studies and engagement with several seminal Amazonian research organizations. Territorial notions were at once nationalistic in their attempts to defend Brazilian economic growth through the development of infrastructures that had been originally planned under the military dictatorship, but at the same time were less fixed in nationalist rhetoric and values than previously, instead relying on rationale involving regional development. The more consultative iterative process of delineating the boundaries of the BR-163 corridor, moreover, suggests greater territorial flexibility than fixture.

The evidence from Chapter 5 concerning the Terra do Meio region is the most illustrative of sustainable development's transformative potential, though it is by no means complete. For the *ribeirinhos* of the Terra do Meio region, the creation of Extractive Reserves—one manifestation of environmental governance and sustainable development politics—not only provided substantial physical security, it also began a series of changed social and economic relations that, while still a work in progress, is largely conducive to the population's abilities to continue to live on those lands in the long term. The case is also one where sustainable development discourses oriented the political objectives of quelling illegal roads, settlements, and incursions into the rainforest, but there was little political gain or fixed goals pertaining to how the particular land uses should take shape. The very idea of scientific truth was also subjected to scrutiny in the case, especially as historical narratives of the region's people and history were constructed and consolidated by intermediaries and by the *ribeirinhos* at a grassroots level. The region's plans were also not nationalistic in their conceptualization or their implementation, aside from a general ambition articulated to reduce deforestation and illegal land claiming in the Amazon as a product of state control.

A fixity of political goals, truth narratives, and nationalistic territorial control does appear predominant in the Chapter 6 exploration of the Belo Monte dam case. The consistency of insistence on constructing the dam over a thirty-year history and the Brazilian government's response to criticism over violations of the indigenous Free, Prior and Informed Consent laws in the case of the Belo Monte dam point to a clear and fixed political objective of making massive infrastructure-oriented interventions in the region. The evidence suggests that the state's plans were motivated by a deeply entrenched conviction that the Belo Monte project was essential to national energy infrastructure development, and that the estimates of increased energy consumption in the country were a fixed truth. A pervasive high tolerance for the environmental and human costs of economic progress appears to predominate the Brazilian political landscape of sustainable development, especially evidenced in moments of resistance to international environmental influences, international laws, and international concern over Amazonian deforestation. Despite some of the participatory character of the Belo Monte project, it does not satisfy anything remotely transformative as an approach, and in fact leans much closer to the risks of alignment with a more totalitarian model.

The Social Justice Utopia

Another important theme present within understanding sustainable development involves considering how the practice of sustainable development stacks up against the utopic idea of creating a more just and equitable society (Harlow, Golub, and Allenby 2013). In earlier chapters, this book described some of the persistent social challenges that remain somewhat unsatisfied in Brazilian articulations of sustainable development. Boom-and-bust cycles from commodities marked the Amazon's history of socioeconomic inequality, and the region continues to be marked by stratification in labor relations and landholdings, despite the various initiatives taking place to engage in ecological-economic zoning, RESEX creations, or to achieve land reform through Projects for Sustainable Development.

Further, despite a predominant framework for sustainable development, impunity for serious crimes often prevails. In the case of the Projects for Sustainable Development PDSs in Anapu, where Sister Dorothy worked, planning toward sustainable development was desultory, experienced as little by way of tangible local actions benefiting the small-scale farmers of the PDSs and only fitful attempts to foster legalized, managed forest systems in their communities. In the Terra do Meio region, social relations are far from equitable, and the success of the intervention remained contingent upon government enforcement and considerable intermediary support. In the case of the Belo Monte dam, too, the social strife is obvious; while there are certainly some advantages that have accrued for regional growth, several important social conditions that were supposed to be met prior to even beginning the dam's construction remained unmet. Even two years after the construction was completed, the Arara do Cachoeira Seca tribe experienced an "ethnocide," and violence rates in Altamira are the highest per capita in the country.[3] Concepts of intergenerational equity are similarly ignored by the general lack of attention given to investments in schools and hospitals throughout the region, while the concomitant emphasis on resource extraction in the form of deforestation and mining operations continues relatively unchecked in the region.

The Pastoralist Utopia

Finally, sustainable development utopias also involve conservationist and more ecocentric or pastoralist values. This vision dates back to Rousseau and ideas about environmental ethics that are rooted in Enlightenment thinking, wherein values of cooperation and empathy are championed (La Freniere 1990, Harlow, Golub, and Allenby 2013). On this count, while more nuanced ecological analysis is largely beyond the scope of this work, a few basic conclusions can also be made. First, there is little evidence that sustainable development plans since the late 1980s in the Amazon have yielded transformative changes in terms of environmental conservation. Conservation area totals have increased, and deforestation rates have generally declined throughout the region. More rivers are dammed, and there are fewer remaining areas of native forest than previously. In terms of the overall trajectory, these efforts amount to a harm reduction strategy rather than a healing-oriented one. There are some initiatives taking place that seek to couple forest conservation, agro-ecology, and reforestation efforts with economic incentives for forest protection in the Amazon region, which generally operate in a land-use ethic orientation rather than through an orientation of ethical cooperation and reciprocal good that might be achieved by a more symbiotic repositioning of socio-natural relations.

Following from this discussion on the different utopic visions behind sustainable development, it is clear that salvaging the transformative potential of the concept or invigorating alternative utopic conceptualizations of the concept along the lines of a more ecocentric or a more socially just orientation could help steer the Amazon region toward a more emancipatory realization of sustainable development. Sustainable development shapes both lives and landscapes in lasting ways, which become reinforced and reproduced in nonlinear forms over time. As with so many other types of policy and programmatic interventions and discourses, sustainable development routinely entrenches the limitations of the very programs it sought to replace. Below, I review some of the ways in which sustainable development functions as a reproductive technology of unequal power relations.

The Uneven Geographical Terrain of Governing for Sustainable Development

The Brazilian translations of sustainable development visions into practice are uneven, not necessarily because of a lack of dynamic or influential intermediary actors and implementation gatekeepers, though having a stronger presence of such individuals might well help to establish a more consistent set of articulations surrounding what, ultimately, is meant when the discourse of sustainable development is used. Rather, it is important to recognize that there are some inherent contradictions embedded in the notion of sustainable development itself, and that these contradictions are not erased but rather become reinforced through the Lefebvrian trialectic relationships between planning for Amazonian land uses, conceptualizing the Amazon as a pristine nature and other times as a space for resource exploitation to fuel national growth, and the lived experiences of spatial production that are manifested as these ideational and physical concepts of space come into practice.

The geographical and temporal unevenness of sustainable development is seen in these cases to sometimes involve land use policies being made in one location, like the Terra do Meio region, which have little to do with the original struggles or populations that sparked attention, as with the PDSs in Anapu. The temporal delay of the Médio Xingu RESEX relative to the other Terra do Meio conservation areas, too, was a result that stemmed more from the internal politics of state priorities than the communities' organizational strength and self-determination per se. The Belo Monte dam's construction was framed around not displacing any indigenous peoples, but tens of thousands of urban Altamira residents did experience displacement from their homes. Because of the energetic complementarity logic that underpinned the Belo Monte dam's construction, furthermore, other dams in the Amazon may well be constructed, as the larger energy grid planning hinged on the creation of the Belo Monte project in Altamira in order to continue to be worth hefty investments of transmission line construction and electric grid integration for the nation as a whole.

The advent of the Belo Sun gold mine at the Volta Grande site on the Xingu River, furthermore, offers an illustration of the uneven temporal frameworks in which the socio-natural world is envisioned within the sustainable development framework. The Belo Sun company does not make any pretenses of producing a "sustainable" gold mine, but the concurrent planning of the mine at the same time as the hydroelectric project is certainly a central component of the developmental planning taking place in the region. The isolation with which those projects were treated in terms of the environmental licensing and project assessment makes clear that the time horizons for licensing and planning of the longer-term developmental futures have little to do with fostering and maintaining an environmentally and socially stable region for the longer term. The time horizons at stake are an estimated twelve years for the gold mine's viability, and around fifty years for the Belo Monte project's likely lifespan. The dearth of plans for what happens during those years of viability, as well as after, are illustrative of key political moments for shaping projects. This was the case for the Manaus World Cup soccer stadiums and is also illustrative of the approach taken to construction and infrastructure during the rubber boom, as illustrated by the Madeira–Mamoré railway. Perhaps, too, it is the predominant reality of the present-day orientation toward soybean exportation, with concurrent plans for road paving and port construction without longer-term attention to the social and ecological ramifications of such developments. While licensing and construction delays certainly are part of the temporal slowness of such substantial projects becoming implemented, the licensing and conceptual orientation behind such projects tends to give sparse attention to their longer-term utility and social implications in medium and longer-term time horizons.

The Embroilments of Sustainable Development

A final few observations regarding reclaiming the transformative potential of sustainable development are merited. First, sustainable development can be, and is actively, already being reclaimed, usually by the people living closest to those plans as they play out on the ground. These individuals and communities face iterative challenges of making their places more livable, more viable, bounteous, safer, and more beautiful. They—as well as many readers of this text –may believe the worst is inevitable, as Barrington Moore suggests. Reclaiming sustainable development may mean confronting that fear of perpetuating, at worst, blueprints for totalitarianism and other forms of exploitation that sustainable development itself purportedly seeks to correct. The struggle *against* sustainable development is as important as the struggle *for* it. In resisting and grappling with the concept, it can become embodied as a process, which itself represents a step toward understanding it as a dynamic, contestable, and mutable discourse through which emancipatory futures can become embodied.

A reclaiming of sustainable development might begin with attention to the ongoing, iterative dimensions of developing sustainably. When conceptualized as a process rather than a goal with a fixed endpoint, sustainable development becomes one of a work in progress rather than a vision for progress. This is a relatively obvious observation, but it seems to fly in the face of a number of attempts to measure the "success" of sustainable development projects, which tend to posit a certain finality in their outcomes.

The philosopher Richard Rorty suggests that discourses can drive cultural change, far more than merely making compelling arguments (Rorty 1979). Environmental politics scholar Thomas Princen similarly suggests that we need new metaphors in order to change how people think and behave in facing sustainability challenges. Princen writes: "metaphors guide action appropriately to the extent they are grounded in experience, direct and indirect, and fit the purpose at hand—here, getting on a sustainable path." (Princen 2010, 60) Rather than imagining accomplishment of perfect, balanced triangulation between equity, environmental, and economic goals, recognizing sustainable development as an embroilment might be a more appropriate metaphor for understanding the practice of sustainable development as a lived experience. If the balancing metaphor that predominates in our current conceptualization of sustainable development is akin to balancing while walking a tight rope, then it is also worth remembering that even *balancing* involves an ever present shifting and manipulation of weight. A tight rope, after all, has a fixed final goal, a destination at the other side, where one can get off and breathe a sigh of relief. Again, however, in this sense, balancing for sustainable development problematically implies stability, finiteness of achievement, and linear directionality. These premises are part of the worldview that perpetuates unsustainability, rather than offering proponents of sustainable development an alternative that is more dynamic, infinite, embracing of complexity, and self-generating. The tight rope metaphor deceivingly conjures up a beautiful circus act, whereas the difficulties of balancing faced by a first-time slack line user may be more apt a characterization for how sustainable development is experienced in practice. Tempting as it may be to throw the term out altogether, its power is so prevalent and compelling that a total discarding would be impossible, if not counterproductive. Instead, a different metaphorical conceptualization is required for sustainable development to address these shortcomings.

As a new orienting metaphor for sustainable development, the metaphor of embroilment presents an exciting possibility for offering a transformative politics of sustainable development. The word *embroilment* derives from French, *embrouiller*, meaning "to muddle." Muddling through the challenges of climate change, rainforest losses, and social conflict is messy. It's not *neat*, nor *easy*. Embroilment involves mistakes, creating entanglements, and, centrally, recognition of dynamic, interconnected problems. Being embroiled implies being ensnared in a deep struggle. There is not necessarily a way out, an endpoint, or a clear objective. Confronting this messy, hard, and conflicted reality as we engage in sustainable development politics may help disabuse the discourse of the false crutch of perfect balance among its various goals.

Embracing the idea of embroilment as a way of thinking through sustainable development could inform our understanding of how different interests compete and contradict each other in different spaces. Recognizing that sustainable development may be better suited to address the fluctuations and diversity of capital, consumption, and resource flows across space, especially in today's age of globalization, may lead toward a conceptualization of sustainable development which better accounts for the unevenness of geographical impacts and contingencies of human populations which those plans are aimed at benefiting. It may reorient discussion around the conflicts and struggles that arise when sustainable development is articulated. At present, as much of Amazonian history reveals, planners and developers are easily steered toward lofty plans involving grand symbolic and practical attempts at territorial organization that seek to crystalize the sum of masterful planning in what are ultimately destined to become shortsighted attempts.

Confronting the tensions between the economy and nature, humans and other humans, and humans and their environment are some of humanity's most eternal and profound struggles. They are unlikely to be overcome anytime soon.

Given the magnitude of our planetary ecological troubles, giving up on the idea of sustainable development hardly seems a moral choice. Instead we might take guidance from the idea expressed frequently by environmental educator and writer David Orr that "*hope* [*sic*] is a verb with its sleeves rolled up" (Orr 2010). We might start by recognizing that there is no simple answer to such profound struggles, but that a moral response to the magnitude of Brazilian—and planetary—social and ecological challenges involves action, hard work, and acknowledgment of conflict. Like them or not, the discourses and frameworks of sustainable development permeate global politics.

Scholars and practitioners engaged in "doing" sustainable development have plenty of choices concerning how they adopt discourses of sustainable development: They may embrace the term, while recognizing its opacity; they may opt out of using the notion altogether, perhaps substituting a few stale discourses for newer terms (green economy, resilience, for example); and they may adopt it, further imbuing the concept with newly envisioned happy endings of harmonization and idealized triangulations of goals. Perhaps, instead, recognizing both that sustainable development is here to stay, and that it is problematic, could mean that scholars, practitioners, students, and concerned citizens all over the world will choose to aspire to become embroiled in sustainable development, and to think of sustainable development work as a process of muddling through. In so doing, we will root sustainable development in place, recognize it as an ongoing process, and grapple with the messiness that it inescapably entails as a form of struggle. Charting a new path will entail a clear-sighted recognition of the conflicts which certain discourses conceal, and will be mindful of the transformative potential of the powerful discourses underpinning them. Paying closer and more critical attention to the power dynamics and transformative possibilities that emerge between states and local communities, and between internationally held norms and national priorities, is a good starting point because it offers a deeper understanding of the ways in which individuals navigate tensions and contradictions in their lives. Perhaps, then, embracing the embroilments of sustainable development will allow for a closer and more nuanced understanding of the transformative potential of the people and places of Brazil, the Amazon, and the rest of the world.

Methodological Appendix

The research presented in this publication is the result of living and researching in Brazil over more than a decade. I first visited Altamira, Pará in July and August of 2005, and began with an interest in activism and civil society coalitions that were involved in creating the conservation area mosaic in the Terra do Meio region. I returned to Altamira to conduct twenty months of more extensive research between 2006 and 2007. During this time, Altamira was my home base for field research, and I frequently traveled and stayed in the Projects for Sustainable Development (PDSs) in Anapu, the city of Castelo de Sonhos along the BR-163 highway, and did two trips to the extractivist reserves in the Terra do Meio region. Usually these trips involved three-week visits, with a schedule of at least two interviews per day. While in Altamira, I was usually working from the offices of the Pastoral Land Commission and occasionally from the Fundação Viver, Produzir, e Preservar. There, participant-observation was my primary research method, and I was tasked with a mix of office-related support tasks that brought me into close contact with *ribeirinhos*, rural workers, and many local activists. Additionally, interviews with public officials were conducted in Brasilia and Belém. Subsequent field research in Brazil took place in 2008, 2009, 2012, 2014, and 2016, which allowed for more continuous accompaniment of events in the region, such as follow-up research on the Belo Monte dam and the activism contesting the project.

The initial field research from 2005 and 2006–2007 was the basis for my doctoral dissertation. Subsequent fieldwork informed the publication of several related journal articles, including one about the Transamazon highway settlers (Bratman 2011) and three about the Belo Monte hydroelectric project (Bratman and Dias 2018, Bratman 2014, 2015). Translations in this text are my own, unless otherwise noted. Out of sensitivity for the human subjects involved in the research, most identities of interviewees have been left anonymous or names have been changed, with the exception of public figures and elected officials.

Case study research generally offers a contextually rich basis for understanding developmental phenomena (Gomm, Hammersley, and Foster 2000, Yin 2003, Baxter and Jack 2009). Around a hundred in-person interviews took place with various civil society activists and key informants in Altamira, along with participation at meetings, marches, and forums concerning a host of development initiatives slated for the region. Among many, these meetings included public hearings and both pro- and anti-dam marches concerning the construction of the Belo Monte dam; social movement–organized seminars concerning the creation of the conservation areas in the Terra do Meio region, and subsequent government-led meetings where those conservation areas were made official; accompaniment of the Ecological-Economic Zoning meetings along the BR-163 highway; attendance at health council and Agenda 21 meetings in Altamira; and community meetings in the PDSs in Anapu, where everything from community forest management plans to the formation of women's groups were subjects of discussion. Additional ethnographic accompaniment of the Belo Monte case took place in Washington DC as opportunities arose in the intervals between trips to Brazil, including meeting with the Brazilian Ambassador to the United States with Sister Dorothy Stang's family members over their concerns about impunity for her assassination, and meeting the Brazilian indigenous visitors who represented the affected tribes to the Inter-American Commission on Human Rights. Between the three case studies presented in this work, participant-observation occurred at approximately 50 NGO-led local meetings and approximately twenty government-organized public hearings, meetings, and forums.

When available, transcripts and notes from public hearings and other meetings were obtained and read carefully, with important themes, quotes, and relevant facts highlighted. The interviews were recorded when interviewees granted permission to do so (91 interviews total) and were subsequently transcribed directly from Portuguese into English. Notes were taken during and after every interview, both recorded and non-recorded. Following ethnographic research methods, I wrote field notes on a daily basis from 2006–2007. Drawing upon the practices of writing effective ethnographic field notes detailed in Emerson, Fretz, and Shaw's work (1995), these notes recorded my observations while participating in daily life in my field sites, and focused on the social and interactional processes I was observing in daily life, my own observations, and the indigenous meanings and concerns of the people I was studying. All field notes were compiled and coded, based on ethnographic methods, with an aim of identifying key themes through an inductive logic of data acquisition relevant to the research questions. Initially, those questions focused on what brought such a wide variety of social movement actors into collective activism, and, over time, the questions evolved into a focus on how sustainable development was being articulated among different types and scales of actors.

Predominantly, the interviewees informing this research were the local stakeholders involved with the public hearings and indigenous organizing surrounding each case study, specifically, the individuals living in the PDSs, in the FLONA-Jamanxim and along the BR-163 forest corridor, and in the Xingu River basin's Xingu and Iriri RESEX communities. Additionally, interviewees included a broad range of NGO activists working at regional, national, and international levels. The centrally involved federal, state, and municipal employees doing work pertinent to each case study were also interviewed. Participants included local NGO organizations in Altamira, Anapu, Castelo de Sonhos, and various locations along the BR-163 and Transamazon highways. I also sought out and interviewed employees of Norte Energia, individuals who had worked for C.R. Almeida's firms, and ranchers along the BR-163 highway, though my access to these populations was significantly more limited than the contacts I had with NGO representatives. Additionally, interviews were conducted with individuals from the national governmental ministries as well as national and international NGOs and research institutions.[1] The aim of engaging such a broad base of interviewees was to triangulate among different sources in order to get more cohesive senses of events and different viewpoints. Working with partner organizations can accentuate problems of subject bias and consensual, informed participation, but it also can be a key way to access participants, gain trust, and support security of both research subjects and participants in conflict-prone areas (Paluk 2009). In interviews, I focused on separating my researcher identity from the groups with which I was doing my participant-observation, introducing myself as a student and (after finishing my doctoral studies) as an American researcher.

The general order followed for identifying and speaking with interviewees was based on a "snowball" approach. I began with conversations with other researchers, identified key informants from government and civil society for each case, and subsequently, based on key informants' areas of expertise, asked for suggestions on who else I should contact for interviews. After several months following this approach, I also became more of a known entity, and some interviewees reached out to me and accompanied me directly into the case study areas of focus. At this point my interviews proceeded generally based on house-to-house visits, thanks to introductions from the community residents that were my de facto guides. For various reasons of access and safety, it was important to gain trust of the participants in the research, in addition to their informed consent as informants. Because I began with interviews of social movement activists involved with creating the new conservation areas locally, my loyalties were somewhat associated with the political leanings from the very start. As I came to appreciate the distance between those who were deeply embedded in social movement activism and the ranchers, public officials, and logging sector businesspeople I also hoped to understand, I made more concerted efforts to get to know those groups, which I felt were underrepresented. I began having routine conversations with the regular clients and employees at a gossip-filled local barber shop where I became one of the only regular female manicure clients. In addition to forming a close friendship with my manicurist, this was a venue through which I was able to gain trust and overhear the gossip of a wealthier class of well-connected urban business people who were mostly middle-aged men. Among other endeavors, I also joined the local *capoeira* group, meeting youth and adults there from nearly all walks of life.

Understandably, given the legacy of mistrust of outsiders, biopiracy, and violence that have marked social relations in the region, gaining candid responses and forming trusting relationships were ongoing concerns. This was especially the case within the social movement groups most active in the region. Among many other important lessons I learned doing such field research, and one of importance for the Amazonian reality, was that while being boisterously loud in public and at home was par for the course in Brazil, it was important to speak softly in interviews, no matter their location, so as to build trust and a sense of safety for my informants. Another helpful tactic for getting into open conversations, I found, was to avoid perpetuating the expectation that, in line with other foreigners, I cared more about trees than people in the Amazon. I quickly learned that if I gave an impression of being an "environmentalist," conversations would rapidly deteriorate regardless of whether I was speaking with an NGO activist or with a cattle rancher. From the very start, articulating the importance of *socio-environmentalism,* or the Brazilian equivalent of the "social green" perspective (Hochstettler and Keck 2007), was often a necessary protocol to keep an interviewee willing to meet. As a young American in the Amazon, I was frequently negatively associated by my research participants with the environmental organization Greenpeace. This association was equally (or more) negative and probably more commonplace than being associated with the Central Intelligence Agency, as *gringo* researchers in Latin America so often experience. Foundationally, the socio-environmental perspective takes a human-centered approach as legitimate and valued. Acknowledging this position signaled a certain amount of acceptance of the fact that the people of the region, living as they were, had a rightful place in the Amazon.

Not uncommonly, social movement activists and leaders would become the targets of death threats and assassination attempts. "Asking too many questions" could result in a strongly worded threat. I once found this out directly after visiting some caretakers on a large piece of land (around 15 km^2) that had a clandestine airplane landing strip and boundary stones intended to mark where the land would be split up and sold into six parcels. The area was being illegally claimed and speculated along the Xingu River, within the area that was imminently slated to become part of the RESEX Xingu. I left the interview carrying gifts of magnificent pumpkins and a handsomely large chicken, pleased to have had such a candid recorded interview with the land's caretakers about the intentions that the *grileiro* had for subdividing the land. While there, at the request of the *ribeirinhos* who were my hosts and who lived elsewhere along the river, I also photographed evidence of the illegal land-claiming taking place in the area. At their behest, and with the counsel of other trusted locals, I was encouraged to send this evidence on to IBAMA officials as part of a trip report. A week later, just as my report was getting finalized, I received a message from the *grileiro*, delivered through one of the same *ribeirinhos* from the region who had escorted me on my trip. The warning was this: if I continued asking questions and visiting along the Xingu, I might "end up like Sister Dorothy" [Stang]. Given that Sister Dorothy was assassinated about eighteen months prior, and also an American, the threat hit a nerve. A human rights lawyer friend quipped that I should take the threat as a compliment: "You know you're making a difference if you piss people off," he reassured me. Many of the colleagues I had been working with in the local nongovernmental organizations, and many of the *ribeirinhos* themselves had experienced such threats for years. Still, once was enough, for me. I decided to take a step back. For about two months, I set aside my interview schedule and stepped away from working as a volunteer at the CPT in Altamira. Before leaving Brazil to begin analysis and writing up my field work, I spent a month co-coordinating and facilitating a grant-supported project from the Davis Projects for Peace that helped form and train a women's cooperative group in the PDS Virola-Jatobá in Anapu in making bead jewelry from *açaí* and other forest-based seeds. This was one important and practical way of giving back to the communities that had helped my research so significantly. I have since stayed in touch with many of my informants and have visited the region on several return trips to Brazil, especially to confirm key pieces of data and to follow historical events more closely on the ground during the time that the Belo Monte dam was being contested and constructed.

Among other insights I gleaned from my research was a deeper appreciation for the importance of being both compassionate and critical as a political ecologist (Jarosz 2004). My research ethic aimed for rigorous and multifaceted analysis of local realities through being balanced and reflexive in my approach toward engaging analytical constructs and thick interpretation. My affiliations with supporting organizations and also my ontological interests in socioeconomic and environmental justice came along with a recognition that "disinterested positivistic objectivity is a grail that we might strive for but never achieve" (Zahar 2009, 193). While imbued by a strong sense of research ethics and impartiality in the search for knowledge and meaning, the research presented here is situated by my own subject position of researching and working as an outsider in the region. While inescapably colored by my own perceptions and experiences, it is my fervent hope that the stories shared within these pages are accurate, and moreover, that they go some degree toward making the world a better place through the lessons that they offer readers.

Notes

Chapter 1

1. The soundtrack to the film captures something of the changing social context and tenuous, stifled atmosphere present during Brazil's military dictatorship in the early 1980s. A brief excerpt from Chico Buarque's introductory song to the film (also entitled *Bye Bye Brazil*) is illustrative:

Oi, coração	Hey, darling
Não dá pra falar muito não	I can't talk very long
Espera passar o avião	Wait, there's a plane flying over.
Assim que o inverno passar	After the winter's gone
Eu acho que vou te buscar	I think I'll come get you.
Aqui tá fazendo calor	It's so hot here
Deu pane no ventilador	And my fan just broke
Já tem fliperama em Macau	There is already a game arcade in Macau
Tomei a costeira em Belém do Pará	I sailed on a boat in Belém
Puseram uma usina no mar	They built a power plant on the sea
Talvez fique ruim pra pescar	And the fishing is terrible here
Meu amor	My love

2. Known as Fundo Dema, established in 2003 and named in recognition of a Transamazon highway activist named Ademir Federicci (whose nickname was Dema), who was assassinated in 2001, the fund was unique because its finances stemmed from a donation of the 6,000 or so apprehended mahogany tree trunks. Those logs were then sold by the fund's civil society management committee in order to redirect resources toward socio-environmental projects and organizations working in the region. Typically, illegal logging is punished with fines collected by IBAMA, the federal environmental protection agency, and the illegally logged trunks are burned to stop further black market activity.
3. Political ecology emerged in the 1970s, when there was an attempt to apply dependency theory to the environmental crises (Robbins 2004). The field, much like environmental studies and development studies, makes claims across disciplines and within its own field of discussion and drawing upon traditions in geography, anthropology, environmental sociology, and political science of the environment (Blakie 2008). Political ecology gained more widespread recognition following the publication of

Piers Blakie's *The Political Economy of Soil Erosion in Developing Countries* (1985) and Blakie and Brookfield's edited 1987 volume *Land Degradation and Society*. Blakie and Brookfield describe the field as follows: "The phrase 'political ecology' combines the concerns of ecology and a broadly defined political economy. Together this encompasses the constantly shifting dialectic between society and land-based resources, and also within classes and groups within society itself" (p. 17). Sympathetic critiques from the field suggest that political ecology could be both more political and, on the other side of the coin, more ecological in its focus, but opportunities for social justice–oriented environmental epistemologies are certainly abundant within the approach. See, for example, Forsyth 2008, Peet and Watts 1996.

4. For Hempel, students of political ecology employ the organizing principal of *asymmetric interdependence* to integrate both global and local political relations into their analyses; he also provides two definitions of political ecology. On the one hand, it is "the study of interdependence among political units and of interrelationships between political units and their environment" (Hempel 1995, 150–151); on the other hand, political ecology shifts emphasis toward the "physical environmental consequences of political decision-making" (pg. 151). For Robbins, political ecology has four main theses, namely degradation and marginalization, environmental conflict, conservation and control, and environmental identity and social movement.
5. For more on critical approaches in environmental studies, see Wapner 2008.
6. See also: Swyngedouw 2006, 2015, Levins and Lewontin 1985.
7. For David Harvey, urban areas are "created ecosystems" which are established through the power relations that are infused into different assemblages of socio-nature, historically and in perpetual recreations of the socio-natural world (Harvey 1996).
8. The list of potential oppositions is long; one of the more prominent contradictions, for example, concerns the "parks vs. people" issue over the extent to which conservation areas can be inclusive of residents. The embeddedness of development as a concept that is positioned against any number of other objectives may also be seen as inherently contradictory, given the post-development critiques that note how often the very idea of development itself runs against peoples' interests, self-determination, environmental protection, traditional knowledge systems, and local economic strength. For more, see e.g., Esteva 1992, Sachs 1993.
9. The WCS tended to emphasize environmental losses that were the result of poverty, rather than the pollution and resource consumption wrought by the developed nations. Relatively little urgency for addressing the problems of genetic diversity losses and ecosystem conservation was attributed to the developed nations. "People whose very survival is precarious and whose prospects of even temporary prosperity are bleak cannot be expected to respond sympathetically to calls to subordinate their acute short term needs to the possibility of long-term returns. Conservation must therefore be combined with measures to meet short term economic needs. The vicious circle by which poverty causes ecological degradation which in turn leads to more poverty can be broken only by development. But if it is not to be self-defeating, it must be development that is sustainable-and conservation helps to make it so. The

development efforts of many developing countries are being slowed or compromised by lack of conservation" (IUCN 1980, 2).

10. Brundtland was the first female Prime Minister in Norway. She held office as Prime Minister in 1981, and again from 1986–1989, and 1990–1996. In addition to her work as chair of the Brundtland Commission, she later went on serve as Director-General of the World Health Organization, from 1998–2003.
11. The implementation of an "environmental" fund was a response to environmental pressure taking place through major events in the mid-1980s. In 1989, the IMF and the World Bank signed a treaty in France to create an international financial mechanism for environmental issues (Streck 2001). As part of implementing environmental aspects into their database, the OECD started to track country-wide measurements of green growth that go back to the early 1990s for OECD, and the BRICS countries. In the meantime, the World Bank has created much environmental research, culminating in the creation of the Global Environmental Facility (GEF) in the 1992 Rio Earth Summit to help finance clean growth initiatives.
12. Agenda 21 is a voluntary and nonbinding commitment signed by 178 nations including the United States in 1992, relevant to nearly all areas of human impacts over the environment. The topics treated include smart growth, transportation planning, limiting rural development, and local efforts to curb greenhouse gas emissions. Despite surveys that find that around 85% of US citizens have no opinion about Agenda 21, a vocal sector of the conservative political movement in the United States began opposing it actively through introducing local legislation aimed at undermining Agenda 21 plans. A similar trend exists in Brazil. See, e.g., http://www.reuters.com/article/us-usa-campaign-teaparty-agenda-idUSBRE89E04J20121015.
13. The *green economy* term was used in a report to the government of the United Kingdom in 1989 concerning whether there was consensus definition over the term *sustainable development*. The report barely mentions the green economy aside from its title, but it does argue that economic leverage should be applied in order to benefit the global environment (Pearce, Markandya, and Barbier 1989).
14. At times the green economy definition closely mirrored that of sustainable development: The UN Water for Life decade defined the green economy as "an economy that results in improved human well-being and reduced inequalities over the long term, while not exposing future generations to significant environmental risks and ecological scarcities." At the UN's Rio+20 conference, the green economy was explicitly characterized as a tool to achieve the broader goal of sustainable development and poverty alleviation. Still, the difference between the green economy and the original Brundtland Commission sustainable development definitions were murky, at best. The working definition of the green economy put forth by UNEP was "one that results in improved human well-being and social equity, while significantly reducing environmental risks and ecological scarcities. In its simplest expression, a green economy can be thought of as one which is low carbon, resource efficient and socially inclusive."
15. Signed by all 189 UN Member States, the Millennium Development Goals established commitments that world leaders would strive, between 2000–2015, to halve

extreme poverty, eliminate hunger, stop the spread of many diseases like HIV/AIDS, provide universal primary education, slow environmental degradation, and combat discrimination against women. Target 7 A explicitly treats sustainable development: "Integrate the principles of sustainable development into country policies and programmes and reverse the loss of environmental resources."

16. The SDGs are distinct from the MDGs on a number of additional levels, including the more participatory and inclusive process through which they were composed. Both because of their expansiveness in breadth and their emphasis on local implementation, the SDGs are in many ways more reminiscent of the 1992 Agenda 21 than they are of the Millennium Development Goals.
17. Buttel's synthesis of the ecological modernization literature notes that its sister concept of sustainable development has "slowly but surely begun to recede from the social-scientific radar screen" (Buttel 2000, 61). While many social scientists did indeed lose interest in sustainable development theorization, the concept of sustainable development has gained far more prominence and staying power than ecological modernization in terms of policies and discursive traction.
18. Liberalism, of course, takes on many variants, and I refer to it here in the general sense, without delving into the nuanced debates concerning social contracts and moral principles that have been so richly discussed centuries ago by Immanuel Kant, Jean-Jacques Rousseau, Thomas Hobbes, John Locke, and John Stuart Mill. In more recent years, those same debates have been taken up by John Rawls, Martha Nussbaum, Karl Popper, and Michael Sandel, as well as a host of other political theorists. For our purposes, a sufficient understanding of liberalism is that it is centrally concerned with ideas about individual liberty, private property, and the distribution of wealth within markets. Generally speaking, a predominant liberal ethical approach emphasizes that the good life is a freely chosen one, where each person develops their unique capacities, though often according to social contracts.
19. For a Marxian and Gramscian approach to the process of development in the Amazon, see Stephen G. Bunker's *Underdeveloping the Amazon*. Bunker argues that the economic outcomes of development in the Amazon "[. . .] are likely to flow to other areas of the nation where the raw materials are transformed and revenues are directed to more productive enterprise" (Bunker 1985, 30).
20. There are 107 known uncontacted tribes in the Amazon basin. These uncontacted tribes remain intentionally uncontacted as a legal protection instituted in 1987 by the Brazilian government, which maintains a "leave alone" policy because of a history of attempts to contact tribes which frequently introduced viruses and diseases to those tribes, killing instead of protecting them. Debate about policies that leave the tribes uncontacted was recently renewed as some tribes experience threats from loggers and drug traffickers encroaching upon their isolated territories. Two American anthropologists called in a controversy-sparking 2015 op-ed in *Science* for the Brazilian government to take protective actions by planning and initiating controlled contact with the tribes (Walker and Hill 2015).
21. While the rates of new deforestation precipitously dropped during this time, it is still important to note that deforestation in aggregate has continuously increased over

time (unless reforestation activities occur). Deforestation is typically measured based on year-to-year comparisons during fixed time periods. A historic low rate of deforestation was achieved in 2012, with an 80% decrease between 2004–2012. In 2013, however, deforestation rose by 29%, and continued with upticks in deforestation rates between 2013–2017. See, e.g., http://multiple.rainforests.mongabay.com/amazon/deforestation_calculations.html.

22. The situation of rural land conflict is gravest in the Amazon, and worst specifically in the state of Pará. Of these 2003–2013 death threats, 692 took place in the state of Pará. The Pastoral Land Commission, which collects data on these death threats as well as related slave labor conditions, also reported in 2011 that twelve out of twenty-nine assassinations in the country occurred in Pará.
23. The International Labor Organization estimates suggest that there are over 25,000 people experiencing slavery at any given time in Brazil, although no one has been to jail for perpetrating such oppression. See: (Human Rights Watch 2014, Bevins 2012, Human Rights Watch 2017).
24. Scholarship focused on Amazonia as a frontier from the early 1980s and into the 1990s, focusing on political economy critiques and the relationship between capitalist expansion and settlement. A conference held at the University of Florida in 1982 called "Frontier Expansion in Amazonia" launched much of this scholarship, which culminated in an edited volume by the same name (edited by Marianne Schmink and Charles Wood, University of Florida Press, 1984). A previous conference (and later book) held in 1972 was entitled *Man in the Amazon*, and tended to focus on human ecological impacts and indigenous peoples in the region. Many publications from the 1970s took a similar emphasis on the relationship of the new colonists to soil quality, forest loss, land rights, agricultural production, and so on. For more on frontier scholarship, see, for example, Foweraker 1981, Schmink and Wood 1992, Moran 1981, Schmink and Wood 1984, Almeida 1992, Sawyer 1990, and Furley 1994.
25. The Amazonian frontier has been usefully described as involving a dynamic set of economic interventions, in which a sparsely populated and relatively disorganized or unrepresented population experiences rapid economic, cultural, and population shifts. The Amazonian frontier is generally thought to have evolved in three major waves, consisting first of the colonial experience, then the rubber boom of the late nineteenth and early twentieth centuries, and finally, a massive wave of planned settlement which began during the 1970s under Brazil's military dictatorship (Pinto 2002, Almeida 1992, Léna and Oliveira 1991, Sawyer 1990).
26. North American frontier writer Frederick Turner's 1894 description is illustrative: the frontier involves the free lands that are the "meeting point between savagery and civilization" (Turner 1894). Much like the same frontier vision that shaped the exploration into the North American West, the Amazon as a vast territory will, according to this view, gradually become part of a landscape that is influenced, studied, and made productive according to humans' needs.
27. The Amazon is remarkably sociologically diverse, and the frontier literature notes this fact but often neglects the populations of *quilombolas*, riverine peasants, rubber tappers, and *caboclos* that are long-standing residents of the region. In this use,

I refer to Amazonians in the broadest sense, including both indigenous peoples and first, second, and third-generation Brazilians living in the region that migrated and immigrated there.

28. The origins for this view stem from the early twentieth-century writings of the noted Brazilian writer Euclides da Cunha, who wrote about the Amazon as a "dangerous adversary" and that nature was a "sovereign and brutal nature" (Paraíso, 125). His friend, Alberto Rangel, wrote that the region was a "green hell" in 1908. For a detailed discussion on different visions of the Amazon, see Slater 2002, Cunha 2000, Rangel 2008 [1908].
29. The popular imagination figures prominently into narratives of good and evil actors, and the imagining of the Amazon is certainly well known to involve a conceptualization of pristine and untouched nature rather than an ecosystem of long-standing human manipulations, as more recent archeological and landscape evidence suggests. When feature films such as Avatar came out, links were immediately and explicitly made to Amazonian deforestation and referenced the Belo Monte dam as an Avatar battle happening in "real life." See: https://www.theguardian.com/world/2010/apr/18/avatar-james-cameron-brazil-dam. In describing the Dema Fund, Paulo Adário, Greenpeace's Amazon Coordinator, alluded to the scene in the Lord of the Rings where trees go to battle to save the Middle Lands region. See: https://site-antigo.socioambiental.org/nsa/detalhe?id=2337.
30. The term *caboclo amazonense* refers to peasants of mixed ancestry living in the Amazon region. It is used more frequently to signify peasant farm labor than tribal ancestry for the population. Amazonian *caboclos* have been significantly underappreciated in terms of their contributions to Amazonian society in most of the scholarly literature and social imagining of the region. See, for example, Nugent 1993, 2002.
31. Most notably, the *Ministério Público*, or public prosecutor, is key here, because this office can back up the force of Brazilian law with requests for information and can file public interest lawsuits. All economic agents, governmental agencies, and civil society groups are required by law to respond to the *Ministério Público*'s requests for information. Just in the state of São Paulo, the *Ministério Público* functioned as a law enforcement agency and conducted more than 21,000 investigations between 1985 and early 2000s. At the national level, 2,000 workers at the *Ministério Público* specialize in environmental law, and 200 of them work solely on environmental cases (Hochstetler and Keck 2008, 181–182).
32. The most significant example of this is the market-based approach toward protection of existing forests that is a part of climate change financing. In 2007 Brazil began pilot experiments with finance for the stored carbon in forest stocks, accounted for through REDD+ programs. Through REDD+ and other programs, where funding comes from the United Nations as well as other international organizations, markets are established which pay people for protecting ecosystem services. These payment-for-ecosystem-services programs value the protection of streams, forests, and other ecosystem functions through economic incentives. Launched in the early 2000s, they aim to offer adequate accounting and compensation measures through

financial payments that ultimately are intended to reach local residents. While such projects offered the potential of reversing the long history of perverse incentives in the Amazon, in practice funding often falls short or is not adequately or consistently delivered (Cromberg 2014). See also: Cromberg 2014, Le Tourneau et al. 2013, Zarin et al. 2004.

33. The funding included $1.1 billion in donations from Norway between its establishment in 2008 into 2016. By 2017, however, under the rules of the fund, Norway's contributions became halved because of rising rates of deforestation in the Amazon.
34. With road paving projects taking shape in the Amazon, leaders applauded how "much [has been done] to end the historic isolation of Amazonia from the rest of Brazil and has opened previously inaccessible areas to productive use . . . many of the mysteries surrounding the region's stock of resources are now being dispelled . . . many viable alternatives to traditional extractive agriculture [are evident]" (Giaimo 1988, 544).
35. In general, resource extraction through cattle ranching, agriculture, and mining were seen as a means of rapidly fomenting national economic growth (Bunker 1985, Hecht and Cockburn 1990).
36. A notable example of this is the response to high-profile assassinations such as the rubber tapper Chico Mendes' case. Mendes gained international attention by traveling to the United States, and when he was assassinated in early 1989 the response was swift. In 1988 and 1989 a national environmental policy was signed, and the national environmental and resource management agency (Brazilian Institute of the Environment, Natural and Renewable Resources—IBAMA) was established.

Chapter 2

1. An account from the Agassiz voyage up the Amazon is one illustrative example of the high aspirations projected upon the region: "when the banks of the Amazons will teem with a population more vigorous than any it has yet seen—when all civilizations will share its wealth, when the twin continents will shake hands and Americans of the North come to help the Americans of the South in developing its resources." José Palacios offers another illustration: "Immense woods, fertile valleys intersected by important streams are everywhere to be met with. The encircling air is perfumed by various flowers. How close must be the vegetation, where one sees everything, from the bulky cedar and the lofty palm to the lowly moss! Where many precious and valued cabinet-woods are found, such as mahogany, tirbeti, lignum vitae, jacaracandá, the strong chonta, the bibosi, the famous rose-wood so esteemed in Europe, various resin-yielding trees. The india-rubber tree grows abundantly, and proves of great value, being employed for manufacturing purposes, and even for ships" (Palacios 1869, 87).
2. The baron of Rio-Branco, José Maria da Silva Paranhos Júnior (1845–1912), helped to negotiate boundary disputes with Argentina in 1895. By 1900, he successfully negotiated to establish Brazil's boundary with French Guiana; the northern borders were negotiated with French Guiana in 1900, in a treaty with Venezuela in 1905, with Brazil and the Netherlands in 1906 determining the limits of Surinam, and in 1907

establishing the frontier between Columbia and Brazil. It added 101,000 square miles to Brazilian territory. In 1903 an acrimonious dispute emerged over the territories in the state of Acre, where Brazil and Bolivia experienced border tensions. The Treaty of Petropolis was signed in 1903, giving Brazil an approximate 73,000 square miles of rainforest land rich in rubber. In the treaty, Bolivia was given a stretch of land that gave it access to the Madeira River, a gateway to the Atlantic Ocean, as well as ten million dollars and the promise of a railroad that would connect the Madeira to the lower Madeira, bypassing rapids. The Treaty of Petropolis established Brazil's westernmost borders, although disputes continued with Peru until September 1909. These were also negotiated by the Baron of Rio Bronco, and Brazil was awarded an additional 63,000 square miles (Burns 1993).

3. Acre would eventually declare itself an independent state in 1899, on a date intentionally meant to coincide with the 110th anniversary of the storming of the Bastille. Acre was declared an independent republic founded on the same principles of liberty and equality that informed the French Revolution, but only a few years later, in 1903, it became a Brazilian territory. It was not incorporated fully as a state within the Federative Republic of Brazil until 1962.
4. In 1880, British investors controlled nearly 80 percent of the railroad enterprises in Latin America as a whole (Rippy 2000). Other scholars offer a perspective on the participation of the Latin American states in the construction of railroads during this period, stating that the states created measurements to facilitate the flux of foreign capital as well as control them. For an example, see Lewis 1983.
5. Fights roiled among the workers; German and Irish workers were getting paid higher wages than the Italians. Many walked off the job, disappearing in the general direction of Bolivia and some, traveling beleaguered and impoverished by boat, into Belém (Neeleman and Neelman 2013, Hecht and Cockburn 1990).
6. Percival Farquhar's investment in Latin America included a railway in the eastern side of the Cuban island, an electric power system in Rio de Janeiro, and the Grand Hotel de la Rotisserie Sportsman in São Paulo. In total, Farquhar controlled thirty-eight businesses and was famous for amassing huge portions of capital to mega-projects (Gauld 1964). Susanne Hecht writes that "at his apogee in 1912 he had a paper fortune worth $25 million and in that year controlled much of the economic activity of Brazil in railroads, ports, river traffic, utilities and cattle ranching" (Hecht and Cockburn 1990, 88).
7. A number of additional nicknames were given to the railway, including the popular "Mad Maria."
8. A 1931 federal decree (Decreto N°. 20.200) nationalized the management of the railway aiming to revitalize it, but by 1972, rail service was deactivated for lack of use and profitability.
9. Though it is also true that the remains of many of the locomotive parts rest peacefully in ignomy, not far from a cemetery in the city.
10. Many other mega-projects were undertaken in the region. Praising the conquest of man over nature in 1913, Isaiah Bowman addressed the *American Geographical Society*. He wrote: "[. . .] in the heart of a river system long closed by imperial edict

we have a railroad, a wireless service [between Porto Velho and Manaus], a telegraph line, steam launches, a pier for ocean-going steamships, and a great commercial future. The mystery of the Amazon basin diminishes" (Bowman 1913, 281).

11. The fascination with the Brazilian Indians was eclipsed by the accounts of the Maya, Aztec, and Incan civilizations. But descriptions praising the virtues of indigenous populations was not uncommon in North America, either; Hugo Grotius praised the communal life of American Indians in the seventeenth century, and Thomas More's vision of utopia was largely oriented around similar simple social models of communalism. Pufendorf, John Locke, and Baruch de Spinoza all wrote praising the nobility and grace of indigenous Americans' society and ways of life (Hemming 2006).
12. The specific geographic focus of their attentions was not on the western Amazon, but rather on the more easily navigable eastern part of the region. At that time, the Portuguese crown governed two independent states—the state of Brazil, whose capital was Salvador, and a northern region including the Amazon basin, then called Maranhão-Grão Pará. The latter region was comprised of two captaincies, then referred to jointly as the East-West Coast, in contrast to the North-South Coast the Portuguese controlled in Brazil. The captaincy of Maranhão was comprised of the present-day states of Ceará, Piauí, and Maranhão, while Grão Pará was comprised of Pará and Amazonas. Both were annexed into Brazil in 1772. Despite early missionary outposts and explorations, a royal decree by the Portuguese in 1733 banned contact in the western Amazon regions in an attempt to avoid clashes with the Spanish mission outposts.
13. In the middle of the seventeenth century, Jesuit missionaries conflicted directly with Portuguese colonists over their treatment of the indigenous slaves, but apparently those efforts were for naught, given the extraordinary death rates of the slaves. The importation of African slaves became more commonplace by the middle of the 1700s, while peaceful conversion was offered as an alternative to slavery by some of the traveling missionaries from Franciscan, Mercedarian, Carmelite, and Jesuit Christian orders that penetrated different parts of the region during their explorations. From settlements, expeditions would periodically venture up the Amazon and its tributaries in order to collect cacao, cloves, vanilla, cassia, and sarsaparilla from the dense jungle. While the Jesuits condemned slavery for indigenous people, they did not object to the enslavement of blacks, who worked preparing cocoa for export and processing firewood. The "free" Indians also performed forced labor, gathering spices and other goods from the forest and often working in exchange for payments that were not useful and which came in the form of goods that the Indians themselves had made (Boxer 1962, Harris 2006).
14. Interestingly, some of the earliest cattle ranching occurred in the Amazon when the Portuguese brought cows and water buffalo for milk and farm draught. The natural grasslands on Marajó Island and in Santarém were conducive to cattle ranching. Cf. Veiga et al. 2003.
15. *Indigenous groups* and *indigenous tribes* are used interchangeably here. The Portuguese term is *Índios* (Indians) or *indígenas* (indigenous).

16. This phenomenon made even well-intentioned and talented anthropologists, such as Claude Levi-Strauss and the Villas-Boas brothers, complicit in the human losses associated with contacting the indigenous tribes.
17. The indigenous population in Brazil has been rising since then; Nugent reported around 300,000 in 2002, and in the 2010 census the number was around 800,000. The majority of this population resides in the Amazon region. The Brazilian population as a whole is around 200 million. Cf. Nugent 2002.
18. The Portuguese made many distinctions among the general category of *índios*, or indigenous peoples. Most notable was the distinction between the "Christian" and "uncivilized" indigenous peoples, with *gentios* as those "ruled by the devil." Miscegenation between the indigenous populations and the settlers from elsewhere in Brazil that were of Portuguese descent occurred to a significant degree during this time. African and indigenous miscegenation occurred in the late eighteenth century. More recently, people of mixed descent have reclaimed and adopted the label *índio* upon identifying the names of the tribes of their ancestors (Harris 2006). See also: http://brasil500anos.ibge.gov.br/territorio-brasileiro-e-povoamento/historia-indigena/nomes-e-classificacao-dos-indios.html.
19. Maury wrote: "The Amazon valley is the safety valve for our Southern States. When they become overpopulated with slaves, the Africa slave trade will cease and they [Southerners] will send these slaves to the Amazon . . . It is becoming a matter of faith among leading southern men that the time is rapidly approaching when in order to prevent this war of the races and its horrors, they will in self defense be compelled to conquer parts of Mexico and Central America and make slave territory of that—and that is now free" (quoted in Hecht 2013, 146).
20. Other estimates suggest that from 1840–1900, over 700,000 people moved to the region. See Moran 1981, Santos 1980.
21. International investors often influenced the rise of these smaller commodity booms in the region. There was a gold rush in the Amazon from around 1857–1890, for instance, which attracted French investments in Guiana. Rubber interest and investments by the British were also substantial.
22. Rondón is often referred to as a military colonel; a marshal is the highest rank in the Brazilian Army, equivalent to a five-star general.
23. By the early 1980s and into the 1990s, political economy critiques and focus on the relationship between capitalist expansion and settlement was much more prominent in the frontier scholarship on the region.
24. For other commodity boom discussions, see, e.g., Hecht 2005, Dean 1987, De Onis 1992, Hall 2000.
25. Rubber was also produced in the Belgian Congo and in the Bolivian, Peruvian, and Colombian Amazon. Brazil dominated these other sources by far, however. The Belgian Congo was also growing rubber and exporting it as early as 1890, in highly abusive labor conditions. The Congolese latex derived from vines that are not able to be cultivated. See, for example, Powell-Cotton 1907. In Iquitos, Peru, the Anglo-Peruvian Amazon Company operated along the Putumayo River with some success from the late 1800s until the early 1900s, but it was exposed in British newspapers

for having abusive, slave-like treatment of its workers. The pressure on the company mounted between 1910 and 1913, eventually forcing its closure. See, for example, Hardenburg 1912, "Peruvian Amazon Company 1913.

26. Joseph Priestley, a British theologian, chemist (also credited with discovering Oxygen), and philosopher, noticed that the material effectively rubbed pencil marks off paper, and the word "rubber" was coined, around 1770.
27. The debt was both monetized, partially, and also non-monetized within the regional economy. It often moved seamlessly in these forms because of the interpersonal ties between debtors and creditors. The number of other products was usually small in both variety and quantity; there were, at various times, small markets for wild cat pelts, fish, turtles, turtle eggs and oil, and caiman skins. Cf. Cleary 1993.
28. There is relatively little research available on the role of the *regatões* that carried goods across the major river systems in the Amazon in their unique boats, called *gaiolas*, but many accounts from travel memoirs in Amazonian history suggest that there were many small traders that also covered long distances throughout the region. Cf. Cleary 1991, McGrath 1989.
29. In addition, the major industries that utilized rubber controlled the process of labor and land use taking place inside Brazil's national *latifundio* system, so in this sense, the *aviamento* chain of labor relations was marked also by even bigger linkages between providers and clients within the national and even international production and distribution process.
30. *Seringalistas* are frequently known as rubber barons, although not all of the "barons" were rich. *Seringalistas* were a varied group; some smaller *seringalistas* could be slightly better off in terms of living conditions, and they made the system viable by allowing their workers to buy tools, food items, and other goods on credit. Others were significantly wealthier, gaining reputations for living in opulence while maintaining servitude conditions for the *seringueiros*.
31. Despite such isolation, the *aviamento* system did allow for information exchange and for some travel between the rural areas and the urban centers. Still, when the rubber boom ended, the *seringueiros'* isolation was significant enough to preclude an exodus from the Amazon *seringais*. They remained on the lands, or *colocações*, predominantly practicing subsistence agriculture, fishing, Brazil nut gathering, and selling cheap rubber.
32. The suffering of indigenous peoples due to rubber tapping was likely worse outside of Brazil. Brazil relied more upon migrant workers for most of its rubber production. The most egregious indigenous abuses were found along the Putumayo River in Peru and Colombia where the Witoto Indians lived. This particular area was exploited by Julio Cesár Arana and his company, The Peruvian Amazon Rubber Company (see, for more, Tully 2011). So cruel was Arana's reign over the indigenous populations on the Putumayo that Sir Roger Casement, then British Consul in Rio de Janeiro, described what he witnessed as "not merely slavery but extermination" (Tully 2011, 99). Arana hired former plantation foremen from the West Indies who were experienced in managing slaves. The men routinely captured indigenous peoples to work as slaves, and then beat, tortured, and starved those who refused to work.

Young indigenous girls aged 9–16 years were turned into sex slaves by Arana's men and housed in a hut nicknamed the "Convent" (Tully 2011, 91). Moreover, many Indians succumbed to diseases including venereal disease contracted from their foremen. The real death toll remains open to speculation, but by Alain Gheerbrant's estimates, "for each ton of rubber exported, seven men, women, and children died" (Gheerbrant 1953). Indigenous leaders in Colombia estimate that the rubber boom in that country resulted in about 100,000 indigenous deaths. These deaths are linked to "forced labor, slavery, torture, and mutilation" of indigenous peoples during the rubber boom, a fact that caused then Colombian President Juan Manuel Santos to issue a formal apology to the indigenous communities in Colombia on October 12, 2012 (BBC 2012).

33. The *regatão* is a river-based traveling merchant who navigates the Amazon basin and exchanges products between regional centers, and was the middleman between the *seringalistas* and the *seringueiros*. The *regatão* typically travels in *gaiolas*—large, multilevel boats—and performs a key role as an agent of exchange in the Amazon through transfer of products, people, and information into the river systems of the basin (McGrath 1999). *O Globo* newspaper described the *regatão* as someone who "buys, sells, exchanges everything with everyone, but mainly with the Seringueiros that, running away from the domain of the owner of rubber estates, also feel the desire to hoodwink them, falling prey to those who suck even the last product of his labor" (O Globo, September 12, 1932).
34. In reference to the peasantry, this is the general term for the non-indigenous agrarian populations of the Amazon. A number of more specific terms, which evoke both specific racial descendants as well as labor and traditional practices, apply to the Amazonian peasantry. These include *caboclos, ribeirinhos*, colonists, *quilombolas*, and also other designations based on culture or national origin (e.g., Jewish, Japanese, French, Lebanese), none of which are seen as deriving from prehistorical Amazonians. Cf. Nugent 2002, 1993.
35. The Government of Brazil created a Rubber Defense Plan in 1912 in an attempt to forestall the crash in the rubber market that began once rubber was able to be substantially cultivated in Malaysia. The plan was rather limited in its actual support for the region, but did involve tax cuts and an array of investments in transport, education, health, and immigration policies (Feitosa and Saes 2013).
36. This sort of agricultural espionage was nothing new, although it was met with outrage and was certainly illegal. Brazil was the victim in the case of rubber, but its own strength as a coffee producer was derived from coffee beans that, as traditionally recounted, were taken from French Guyana in 1726 by a Brazilian sergeant major named Francisco de Melo Palheta. Prior, the coffee seeds had been adapted to the European climates in a botanical gardens in Holland, and from there were taken into France and spread throughout the French colonial territories. Wickam, for his part, encouraged the notion that the seeds had been smuggled illegally. He was later knighted by the British for "Services in connection with the rubber plantation industry in the Far East" (see Dean 1987).

37. The United States depended on Asian rubber plantations for approximately 98 percent of its rubber supply by the time it became involved in World War II. The Japanese invasion of rubber-growing parts of that region meant that the United States lost control of 92 percent of its rubber supply, a factor which played a strong role in motivating the them to strengthen ties with Brazil and encourage Amazonian rubber production (cf. Garfield 2013).
38. Another, significantly smaller natural resource boom over black pepper took place from 1933–1955 in the Amazon, especially in the state of Pará not far from the city of Belém. Pepper production was led by Japanese immigrants to the Amazon and was sparked by the arrival of only two pepper plants, imported from Singapore. Production volume grew to 630 tons by 1953, and black pepper prices were so high that the peppercorns became referred to as "black diamonds."
39. Called the "rubber soldiers," recruitment started around 1940 and lasted until the end of World War II. For this group of new "hillbilly" migrants from the northeast, the *aviamento* debt relations continued just as in the earlier rubber economy. Upon arrival to the rubber estates, the rubber soldiers found they were in debt for their journey out to the Amazon as well as for their clothing and equipment (cf. Rodrigues 2007).
40. Synthetic rubber production was developed during World War II as the price of rubber rose precipitously, and rubber was made synthetically and produced in over fifty factories by around 1944. In rubber production today, around 44 percent of uses involve natural rubber, most of which derives from Indian latex. A few artisanal latex production businesses survive in the Amazon, including a condom manufacturing facility in Acre, which utilizes rubber collected in the Chico Mendes Extractive Reserve and the Xapuri region, and "ecological leather" rubber bags made in the Maguary community in Pará in the Tapajós National Forest Protected Area (FLONA Tapajós). See, for example: http://www.endruralpoverty.org/, (2014).
41. Rubber was the central commodity in the Fordlândia plans, but Ford also aimed to use the land for timber and, ideally, gold mining, and even explore for oil. The main motive was a larger corporate strategy for vertical integration of the supply chain. Ford already controlled iron mines for steel, forests for lumber, and copper mines for wiring at the time he purchased the Amazonian lands (Grandin 2009).
42. Poetry by William Wordsworth and Henry Longfellow was celebrated especially, whereas the Brazilian folk and cultural traditions were almost entirely absent (cf. Grandin 2009).
43. A riot broke out when the food service policy was changed from one of table service with waiters to self-service in a cafeteria line. The Brazilian workers destroyed the cafeteria with their machetes, while North American employees waited out the riot from a distance on their boats. Another incident occurred over resentment about Barbados workers arriving at the plantation and allegedly earning higher wages. A West Indian was stabbed, and several Brazilians were injured, after which the Barbadians were banned from the plantation. For more, see https://www.thehenryford.org/collections-and-research/digital-resources/popular-topics/brazilian-rubber-plantations/.

44. Around 8 million trees were required for commercial production of the 38,000 tons Ford needed to produce annually, but between the two plantations the total was only around 3.6 million trees planted, and the first commercial tapping in 1942 yielded only 750 tons of latex. The trees were planted too close together, and suffered especially from agricultural pests including sauva ants, lace bugs, red spiders, leaf caterpillars, and a deadly leaf fungus. Eventually, saplings and seeds were brought in from East Asia, as the *hevea Brasilienensis* was yielding such disappointing results.
45. Another property owned by Ford, called Belterra, was a more moderate success in terms of the social experiment of the company town, although it was also a commercial failure. Today, Belterra has more of a resident population, a city government, and several festivals and beaches that attract visitors regularly.
46. The *seringueiros*, riverine peasants (*ribeirinhos*), Babaçu nut gatherers (*babaçueiros*) are now among many Amazonian groups recognized under Brazilian law as "traditional" populations, a category defined as "groups that are culturally differentiated and who recognize themselves as such, having their own forms of social organization, and who occupy and use territories and natural resources as a condition for their cultural, social, religious, ancestral and economic continuation, using knowledge, innovations and practices generated and transmitted by tradition" (Federal Decree N°6.040 of February 7, 2000). In addition to having at least some history of low environmental impact, the populations that are formally recognized as traditional populations are in a unique role as environmental stewards that experience national supervision. Essentially, these communities have agreed to sacrifice some of their territorial autonomy to the state, while agreeing to endeavor to provide environmental services for the land, including vigilance over its encroachment by illegal land claimers. A comprehensive discussion is in Carneiro da Cunha 2004.
47. Getúlio Dorneles Vargas led the *Estado Novo*, or new state, from 1937–1945. He was a dictator (officially titled Provisional President of Brazil) from 1930–1934 following a revolt in 1930, then became a congressionally elected president in 1934–1937, then again was dictator from 1937–1945 after he warned of a communist coup attempt. From 1946–1951 he was a senator and then served as president from 1951–1954 through becoming popularly elected to the position.
48. Perhaps the most famous part of the March to the West is the expedition of the Villas-Boas brothers, who subsequently played an influential role in the creation of the Xingu indigenous park. Echoing the era of westward expansion in the United States, the March to the West also built upon nationalist narratives of manifest destiny and frontier expansion to encourage new colonization efforts.
49. The policies and bureaucratic shifts that took place about a decade later, in the mid-1960s, revitalized the prospects for regional planning and private investments in the region.
50. The Manaus Free Zone, for its part, had no real administration and encouragement until 1967, when the Superintendency of the Free Zone of Manaus was established. Once the plan began administration, growth became evident both economically and in sheer terms of urbanization; the population of Manaus grew from 312,000 in 1970 to 633,000 in 1980, to over 1 million by 1990 (Mahar 1978).

51. The influence of the Economic Commission on Latin America and the Caribbean's economic theories, led by Arthur Lewis, Celso Furtado, Raúl Prebisch, and Gunnar Myrdal, among others, was prevalent. Conventional developmentalism posits that the state should play a leading role in forced savings and investment in firms; protectionism is prevalent; and there is some complacency toward inflation. See Bresser-Pereira 2009, Sikkink 1991.
52. The BNDE was the precursor to the BNDES, Brazil's National Bank for Economic and Social Development. The BNDE converted into a state-owned company under private law, through Law 5662, of June 21, 1971. It was renamed as the BNDES in 1982. There were eleven sectors of basic industry supported, including copper, aluminum, steel, sulfuric acids, fertilizer, heavy electrical machinery, railroad material, agricultural machines, and vehicles, though this was not a rigid definitional category (Sikkink 1991).
53. According to Benevides, cooptation of the military occurred under the Kubitschek government, as military leaders took on more prominent positions in the state. Still, the Brazilian economic ideas often overlapped in terms of which interest groups adopted certain perspectives; the industrialist views held by the military can be traced back to the leadership of Roberto Simonsen, who led the Brazilian industrial associations in the 1940s. The military leaders in Brazil during the late 1950s were well versed in economic issues, most notably through their training at the Brazilian Escola Superior de Guerra (ESG), which was strongly anticommunist and stressed a strong economic development agenda as inseparable from security concerns. See Stepan 1971, Benevides 1976, Sikkink 1991.
54. The Catholic Church was notably not complicit in this relationship, and most literature acknowledges that the Church played a strong oppositional role in relation to the military-led regime. The Church–state conflict during 1964–1985 evolved as a relationship of tense coexistence, however. Early on in the regime, the Catholic Church abandoned much of its tradition in its attempt to modernize and was courted by the military. The officer corps had little understanding of the process of religious change and the evolving Catholicism of Vatican II, but tended to emphasize to the clergy that the fight against communism was also a fight in defense of Christianity. State leaders promised the Church support and prestige if it worked to endorse and reinforce the status quo. While the Church found some of the hierarchy, discipline, and tradition of the military appealing, increasingly throughout the era of the military dictatorship the relationship deteriorated significantly, with conflict between the Church and state centering upon social justice and subversion (Serbin 2000).
55. Guillermo O'Donnell in *Modernization and Bureaucratic Authoritarianism* discusses recurring constellations of systems through which regimes, coalitions, and policies take shape in Latin America. O'Donnell is careful to distinguish between high modernization and socioeconomic "development," understanding modernization as a term most useful for studying changes within a socially rigid and highly differentiated national context where external dependence is present. The bureaucratic-authoritarian system he analyzes in Brazil in the post-1964 era is excluding and nondemocratic, but he emphasizes that it should not be confused with

the authoritarianism of nineteenth-century *caudillismo* or fascism, as in the cases of Germany or Italy. Instead, the high modernization in Brazil (and Argentina) involves the crucial component of technocratic actors within the national institutional context.

56. Deepening in this context means establishing backward economic linkages of intermediate production and capital goods industries once the latest-stage industries (which produce consumption or final demand goods) are established.
57. Illustrative of this nationalism is the following excerpt from a middle school textbook for the required Morality and Civics course, inserted after the 1964 coup: "The very map of Brazil appears in the shape of a human heart . . . The heart palpitates with future greatness for a powerful Brazil, seeking courageous solutions, fiery and spiritual, a country that brings to a tired and ageing world a new vision of strength. This is my country; I am proud to call myself Brazilian" (Shohat and Stam 2013, 59). On the rising giant idea, see also Momsen 1968.
58. The political challenge involved in this problem was notable because the majority of the governmental power structures were in the hands of sectors that lacked any larger interests in change. Within the state during the early 1960s, there was a certain resistance against the populist tradition, and this tended to create resistance to making gradual transitions within the agrarian sector. In fact, such political inclusion and broadening of representative government institutions would have been a much more difficult—and urgent—reform, allowing for the more gradual agricultural and economic reform to be able to take place (Neto 1997).
59. Most of the more revolutionary development paths were not taken into serious consideration at the time. The double articulation concept derives from Florestan Fernandes' 1974 work on the evolution of capitalism in Brazil. One side of the double articulation involves internal and external interests becoming united, and on the other side, the interests of the dominant elites articulate within the internal plan, trying to guarantee continuity in all sectors of the economy, from archaic to modern. The double articulation imposes a conciliation and harmonization of disparate interests (as much in terms of accommodation of internal economic sectors as in terms of accommodating the capitalist economy dependent on centralized economies); and, worse than this, carries a permanent state of conciliation between these interests. As such, they form a bloc that cannot be overcome from the perspective of a capitalist transformation, and turns an economic agent in the dependent economy into a position of being overly-powerless to confront the necessities of the dependency situation. They can, without a doubt, achieve economic revolutions, because they are intrinsically the various capitalist transformations. What they cannot achieve is to raise any economic revolution from the point of rupture with the very patron of dependent capitalist development (Fernandes 1975, 223).
60. The number of mining operations, and often their scale, continues to grow. In 1994, nearly 22,000 mining processes were occurring in Amazonia, and by 2006 that figure had doubled (Ricardo and Rolla 2006). This includes mining operations in areas that are environmentally protected. By 2030, mining is expected to have between

a threefold and fivefold increase in Brazil, largely driven by trade with the Chinese (Ferreira et al. 2014).

61. A distinction should be made between the early colonization efforts that mark the first arrival of European settlers in the region. Here, colonization describes the late nineteenth-century arrival of settlers, mostly from other parts of Brazil who came into the region. These new settlers are also often known as colonists (*colonos*) in Portuguese. There were two types of colonization during the contemporary period, directed and spontaneous. Directed colonization refers to the efforts led by the government to settle people in the frontier region on lands that then became into official government settlement sites, or private projects. Spontaneous colonization, as the name suggests, refers to the settlement of farmers that came without any form of guidance or incentives from the state or private entities.
62. It was not until several years later that revisionist scholarship questioned the classic frontier literature in relation to Amazonian development, and recognized the tendency for capital to retrench and for urban growth and informal mining sectors to coexist along with agricultural expansion. The newer literatures also acknowledged that petty commodity production not only persisted but sometimes expanded in the Amazonian frontier regions, and noted that the appearance of an inevitable expansion of capitalism was in fact attributable to enormous and short-lived inputs from state subsidies. See Schmink and Wood 1992, 1984, Sawyer 1984, Cleary 1993, Léna and Oliveira 1991.
63. The geography of Amazonian cities and small towns along these roads took on a rather unique form. Roads for "national integration" included the Transamazon highway, the Cuiabá-Santarém highway, the North Perimeter Road, and the Carretera Marginal de la Selva. Urban development and settlement plans focused on creating spatially consistent locations along roads for hub cities, or "poles," and satellite *agro-vilas*, or small towns that would be the initial depots for agricultural production. For an extensive discussion on the geography of Amazonian cities and towns, see Browder and Godfrey 1993.
64. Earlier attempts focused upon modernization in the agricultural sector, and the policies privileged economic sectors that produced for the external market far more than small-scale farmers. Many of these were halted in planning phases or never fully implemented, and the efforts focused especially on the northeast of the country. See Neto 1997, Alston, Libecap, and Mueller 1999.
65. From 1934–1969 various agencies for agrarian policies existed at the federal level in Brazil, with the first origins in 1934 under the Ministry of Agriculture's Irrigation, Reforestation, and Colonization Service. In 1938, they consolidated into the Division of Lands and Colonization (DTC). In 1954, the DTC was substituted for the National Institute for Immigration and Colonization (INIC), which lasted eight years and established eight colonization nucleuses in the northeast. The National Institute for Colonization and Agrarian Reform (INCRA), was established in 1970 under General Emílio Médici.
66. Several other financial instruments were also used at the time, creating further incentives for private capital investments. These included SUDAM, the 1967

legislation that approved special tributes to private businesses that established themselves in Amazonian Occidental Territories (Amazonas, Acre, Rondônia, and Roraima) and the establishment of the Free Trade Zone in Manaus. From 1974 on, as Operation Amazonia ended, new instruments were used, often in conjunction with the resources from the PIN. These included the Program of Poles for Agro-livestock and Agro-mineral Development of the Amazon (POLOAMAZÔNIA) and the Fund for Investment in the Amazon (FINAM), created by Decree Law 1376. Financially managed by BASA, income tax deductions could be taken with the criteria of investment for Amazonian-based projects; the beneficiary could negotiate exchange in special auctions for preferential stock with firms having SUDAM-approved projects. Through FINAM, there was less brokerage with enterprise investments in approved projects, making it easier for private investment to take place in the Amazon. For more on tax incentives in the Amazonian development programs, see Franco 1995.

67. A frequently unrecognized dimension of these migration patterns is that many colonists returned to their areas of origin once they experienced the lack of infrastructure for productive activity on many Amazonian lands. According to Emilio Moran's extensive studies of the Transamazon highway colonization and ecology, while some departing colonists were replaced by newcomers, many times the colonization was abandoned altogether, as the inhospitable soils, topography, malaria, and lack of markets posed significant impediments to long-term settlement (Moran 1993).

68. Data tracing farmer migrations in the Amazonian frontier regions of Pará show that individual migration from one frontier to another site within the Amazon decreases as assets or wealth accumulate, and this suggests that as development proceeds, formal titles are ultimately a deterrent to future moves. Land titles encouraged more permanent investments on land, and correlated strongly with increased land values. However, acquisition of such land titles was a slow, bureaucratic process given the inability of INCRA, the responsible governmental agency, to adjudicate and formalize land claims on pace with the rapid migrations (Alston, Libecap, and Mueller 1999).

69. President Fernando Henrique Cardoso subsequently abolished SUDAM in August 2001, in Interim Measure No. 2.157-5. Nearly $2 billion dollars in stolen monies were alleged to have been illegally appropriated through the organization. Cardoso created the Amazon Development Agency (Agência de Desenvolvimento da Amazônia, the ADA) in place of SUDAM. SUDAM was reinstated, however, in 2003 under President Luis Inácio "Lula" da Silva, and ADA was formally eliminated in 2007, with much of its structure incorporated into the new SUDAM.

70. The report, entitled "Studies of the Development Plan for the Amazon," was confidential but also was not an isolated example of internally produced government self-criticism. In 1973 the Minister of Planning, Reis Veloso, said that the planned colonization efforts were leading to "predatory occupation" in the Amazon. The report later led to new Amazonian development plans under President Geisel, who was critical of INCRA's resettlement schemes and small-scale farmers as being a drain on government resources and as being responsible for environmental devastation. See, for example, Hall 1989.

71. These were the Suiá-Missú ranch, held by the São Paulo–based Ometto family, later sold to Liquigás, an Italian company; a property called Campo Grande, owned by a São Paulo–based construction company called Catenco; the 600,000 hectare Codeara property, held by the National Credit Bank, or BCN; and the Vale do Rio Cristalino project, owned by Volkswagen. Over 469 ranching projects were incentivized by SUDAM financing by the mid-1980s, Cf. Hall 1989, 22; Cardoso and Müller 1977, Hecht, Norgaard, and Possio 1988.
72. The program was closed in 1989 but then reopened in 2003, and continues into the present.
73. A few additional laws to protect the rainforest did come out of the era of the bureaucratic-authoritarian regime, although many of these were skirted or ignored outright. Law 4.771, in Article 44 (1965) prohibited Amazonian landowners from deforesting more than fifty percent of their land. Ranchers found ways to distribute the uncut land to relatives in order to find a loophole in the law, or just ignored it outright; fines would sometimes be issued, but there was almost no penalty for not paying the fines. Established in July 1986, law 7.000 forbade the cutting and selling of Brazil nut and rubber trees, though since no other laws protected the forests surrounding these specific trees, the Brazil nut and rubber trees often died, standing in place, as their surrounding forests were turned into pasture.
74. The military training at the National War College (*Escola Superior da Guerra*, or ESG) centrally emphasized "development" in tandem with security. The ESG's scholarly journal is even called *Security and Development* (*Segurança e Desenvolvimento*) (Allen 2006).
75. Although the Amazon Cooperation Treaty (ACT) was signed by the Amazonian region countries in 1978, it was amended in 1998. In 2002, the Permanent Secretariat for the treaty was created. For the actual language adopted in the treaty as well as the signed documents from each nation state, see ACTO 2004.

Chapter 3

1. The stadium was approved for use as a 2016 Olympic soccer venue, but outside of mega-events such as this, only sparse utilization is expected. The costs of maintaining the stadium is around 780 thousand Brazilian Reais (BRL) per month (approximately $222,699.00 USD at 2015 exchange rates). The Amazon Arena cost 669.5 million BRL to construct (around $329 million US dollars, at a 2013 exchange rate).
2. The economic contraction rates in Brazil were between 3%–4% from 2014–2017, comprising eight consecutive quarters of recession. See: http://www.bloomberg.com/quicktake/brazils-highs-lows.
3. The Manaus opera house was also made famous in the early 1980s when it was used in the filming of Werner Herzog's film *Fitzcarraldo*. The film's production was perhaps more eccentric than the real-life story it told; in the film, an eccentric opera lover (with a crew composed of indigenous peoples) drags a 320-ton steamship over a hill without the use of special effects as part of his effort to shortcut between Amazonian

rivers to fulfill his mission to build a theater in the Amazon. The film is based upon the real-life persona of Peruvian rubber baron Carlos Fitzcarrald. In reality, he had a 30-ton boat disassembled, carried over an isthmus from one river to another, and then reassembled.

4. A survey from the magazine *Veja,* along with CNT/Sensus, was released in 2008 and showed that 82.6% of people in the Brazilian military believed that Amazonia faces the risk of a foreign occupation. A book called *Amazonia and International Greed* by Arthur Cezar Ferreira Reis details many of these arguments and has had five editions come out since its original publication in 1960. For greater discussion on the implications of these nationalist-driven concerns, see Sartre and Taravella 2009, and Mitchell 2010.
5. Federal Law 6.938/81, Articles 4, I and 4, VI.
6. "People of the forest" is a common term for the broad category of indigenous groups, *ribeirinhos, quilombolas,* rubber tappers, extractivists, smallholders, and other forest resources–dependent peoples (Conklin and Graham 1995, Allegretti 1990, Campos and Nepstad 2006a, Cronkleton 2008, Schneider et al. 2015).
7. The violence involved in the struggle for land was unsurprising, with an estimated 1,500 deaths over land conflicts by the mid-1980s. From 1971–1976, one out of every two reported Amazonian land disputes had victims, with more than half of those victims as deaths. There were some 6 million *posseiros*, or subsistence peasants who typically occupy land without having formally recognized titles to the property, in Brazil in 1980. The violence involved not only *posseiros* but also indigenous groups whose lands were not recognized. In the case of the Xavante Indians, occupation of big estates located in their territory was a strategy for driving away landowners and their employees and force pressure for the demarcation of those areas as indigenous reserves. The conflicts would be spurred when a would-be land trafficker, or *grileiro,* with falsified or incomplete land titles hired gunmen (*jagunços*) to keep watch over the land they were claiming. Often in conjunction with local police, the *jagunços* would pressure the *posseiros* to abandon the land, usually by burning their houses down, torture, or other forms of physical violence. For more, see Martins 1980.
8. *Extractivist activities* is the common term for the type of resource use that is based on renewable resource harvesting, such as rubber tapping or Brazil nut gathering. In contrast, extractive economies or extractive activities refers to nonrenewable resource use, such as mining.
9. Specifically, Mendes met with Senators Robert Kaspen and Daniel K. Inouye, the subcommittee co-chairs. His visit was facilitated by the National Wildlife Fund and the Environmental Defense Fund, with support from Mary Allegretti, a Brazilian anthropologist, Adrian Cowell, a British filmmaker, and Steve Schwartzman, an anthropologist affiliated with the Environmental Defense Fund.
10. An August 1981 meeting called the National Conference of the Working Classes (*Conferência Nacional das Classes Trabalhadoras,* CONCLAT) joined 5,000 delegates, although at the outset clear divisions were present between two major blocs. One was the *autênticos*—led by Luiz Inácio "Lula" da Silva (who later became president) and loyal to the PT party, the progressive Church, and holding Trotskyist

orientations. The *Unidade Sindical* (Union Unity) bloc was composed of those who benefited more from the status quo and was backed by the political parties PCB, PCdoB, and the PMDB. Both groups had equal representation in a commission that aimed to establish the Unified Workers' Central (*Central Única dos Trabalhadores*, or CUT). Because of disputes between the groups, however, CUT was not established until 1983, and a rival body was formed in 1986 by the *Unidade Sindical* which was first named CONCLAT and in 1986 became the General Workers' Congress (*Central Geral dos Trabalhadores*).

11. Marina Silva also notably left Catholicism and became an Evangelical in later years. She ran for president against the PT party in 2014 and 2018, affiliated with the Rede Sustentabilidade (Sustainability Network, or REDE).
12. In the 1960s and 1970s, the Church encouraged rifts between unions and local organized groups with the political groups that were being legitimized by the military regime. This was seen as a way of experientially concretizing the rupture with an older situation, conditioned by the subordination of the poor to the wealthy. The existence of the external group, those characterized as "evil" for the Catholics on the frontier, involved stark contrasts between "Us" (agriculturalists/poor people/smallholders) and "Them" (vendors/wealthy/big landowners). Of note, the Evangelical populations on the frontier were similarly focused on narratives of good and evil, though the idea of sinning for the Evangelical groups was far more a question of individual salvation, and in many of the Evangelical sects, illegal land claiming and work in certain sectors, like machinery importation, agricultural inputs, and cargo transport, were frowned upon (Araújo 1991). The Evangelical Lutheran Confessional Church in Brazil (IECLB) in 1981 and the Catholic National Conference of Brazilian Bishops (CNBB) in 1986 established annual themes concerning land questions, and turned their attention to building more robust alliances across civil society groups.
13. As the largest organized popular movement in the country, the MST played a key role in advocating for Brazilian agrarian reform. It was especially strong in the southern states of Rio Grande do Sul, Santa Catarina, and Paraná, and in the northeastern states of Pernambuco, Sergipe, Ceará, and Espiritu Santo (Carter 2010). The MST was only marginally present in many of the Amazonian land conflicts in the 1980s. More than 90% of the land distributed in Brazil since 1979 resulted from peasant groups that were not linked to the MST; this is largely because so much of Brazilian land redistribution has taken place in the Amazon, where huge amounts of land have been allocated for agrarian reform along an agricultural frontier. Aside from a few high-profile MST mobilizations and land conflicts in the Amazon, the groups of landless squatters on the front lines of agrarian reform were often independent, or organized by local activists in the CPT, the STR, or other groups. In later years, the MST took strong oppositional stances against genetically modified organisms and pesticides, which speaks to the ways in which their class-based struggle for land became tied to values of environmental protection and critiques of industrial, corporation-dominated agricultural systems.
14. Maybury-Lewis (1994, 119–120) notes that there were 2,275 rural unions in existence in 1979, all participating at this CONTAG congress in 1979 where the strategy

was elaborated. In 1964 there were 785 rural unions in existence, and by 1985 the number was up to 2,732.

15. For example, CONTAG was an active force behind the split that happened between CUT (the *Central Única dos Trabalhadores*) and the *Unidade Sindical,* and the creation of the CGT. The political rivalries and, at times, alliances that were formed between the various political parties that were linked to the union groups also played a significant role in these disputes.
16. A rich history of the environmental movement is offered in Hochstettler and Keck 2007. By contrast to the socio-environmentalists, conservationists maintained a more bio-centric stance, generally defining the environment and seeing the Amazon as protected only through scientific and technical expertise. For more on this history, see also Alonso, Costa, and Maciel 2005.
17. Earlier waves of environmental politics and activism had also been present, although not nearly so robust of a presence. The first Brazilian environmental institutions had already emerged between the 1950s and the 1970s and were mostly focused on linking scientific research to environmental conservation. NGOs such as the Brazilian Foundation for the Conservation of Nature (FBCN), led by Alceu Magnanini, and the National Campaign for the Defense and Development of the Amazon were some notable early examples. (For a detailed and thorough contemporary history of environmental activism in Brazil, see Hochstetler and Keck 2007).
18. This is sometimes referred to as the Alternative Nobel Prize. The award was established to "honor and support those offering practical and exemplary answers to the most urgent challenges facing us today" and was established in 1980 by German-Swedish philanthropist Jakob von Uexkull.
19. While the creation of the Yanomami reserve did mean notable progress for the protection of the group, the wildcat gold miners are still present in the area and continue presenting a threat to some of the indigenous peoples there; some Yanomami report seeing other uncontacted Yanomami, who they call Moxateteu in the reserve, and it is generally suspected that the Moxateteu live in the areas with the greatest concentration of miners. (For more, see: http://www.survivalinternational.org/tribes/yanomami.)
20. The central highway of concern at that point was the 900-mile BR-364 highway (Cuiabá– Porto Velho), which ran through Acre to the Peruvian border. It was supported through World Bank financing of Polonoroeste, the Northwest Brazil Integrated Development Program, and was the main impetus for the development of the state of Rondônia and ensuing environmental degradation there (Cf. Mendes 1989, Rodrigues 2004). The World Bank also withdrew its financing from the Belo Monte hydroelectric dam project soon after the 1989 meeting.
21. See, for example, Keck 1998, Rodrigues 2004.
22. Mary Allegretti is an anthropologist exemplary for being this sort of lynchpin between local activism, national politics, and international networks. Her 1979 thesis research about the rubber estates of Acre led to a 1980 cooperative and literacy program with the Xapuri *seringueiros.* By 1984 she was working as a lobbyist at a human

rights center in Brasília, and she later founded a Curitiba-based organization called the IEA, or *Instituto de Estudos Amazônicos,* which offered support for the rubber tappers and conducted research on Amazonian issues.

23. These parks were established in the early 1990s, although the National System of Conservation Units, or SNUC, which delineated various types of conservation areas serving different levels of conservation purposes (research, recreation, etc.) was only established officially in 2000 under Law No. 9.985/2000. SNUC was the result of a protracted set of debates among Brazilian environmental groups and the government, and was finalized after ten years of negotiations and revisions. See https://uc.socioambiental.org/en/o-snuc/what-is-the-snuc.
24. Even the word *enforcement* itself is somewhat alien in a Brazilian context; there is no literal translation of the word into Portuguese, although there are expressions that translate to following the law (*lei seja cumprido*), surveillance or inspection (*fiscalização*), and monitoring (*monitoramento*).
25. One flagrant example of this was the *Calha Norte* (Northern Trench) program, which was first approved by President José Sarney. It relied on the language of sustainable development but was mainly a program aimed at appeasing the military interests by establishing larger-scale operations in the name of national security, especially to the north of the Amazon River (cf. Espach 2002).
26. In 2003, Capobianco left ISA to become a high-level official in the Ministry of the Environment.
27. The total area of land placed under federal protection as national parks, ecological stations, extractive reserves, or other conservation areas nearly tripled from approximately 130,000 km^2 to approximately 440,000 km^2 between 1985 and 1997. This represents over 5% of Brazil's total land area; when indigenous reserves are included in that figure, the total land area is around 17% of national territory (Arrarás et al. 2002). The government estimated that in 1998, 16,800 km^2 was deforested in the Amazon, up 27% from 1997. Violent conflict in the Amazon region diminished during this time; there were around 40–50 reported cases of murder in land disputes each year in the 1990s, whereas in the 1980s the annual average was around 100 per year.
28. Some of the Portuguese literature describes this as *novo desenvolvimentismo* or "new developmentalism," and often the term used in the literature is *neodevelopmentalism.* As there is no scholarly consensus on the standard term as of this writing, I use *renewed developmentalism* throughout, suggesting the historical echoes of developmentalist strategies of the past.
29. Especially, BR-163. See, for details, http://rainforests.mongabay.com/amazon/2004_deforestation.html.
30. Three-quarters of the IIRSA Consensus Agenda was devoted to road infrastructure from 2005–2010.
31. Given the prescient concerns of environmentalists that deforestation would occur when the original Amazonian highways were being cut, protests and news stories followed about the encroachment of monocrop soybeans northward into the Amazonian forests from the state of Mato Grosso.

32. Costs far exceeded the $1.3 billion figure, however; the total cost was US $2.8 billion in 2014 (Reel 2014).
33. The $69 billion figure is for the 31 IIRSA projects completed by 2010. For more on IIRSA, see http://www.iirsa.org/ and http://www.bankinformationcenter.org/regions/latin-america/biceca/.
34. The transportation sector investments were among the most significant, aiming to allow goods to be more easily transported through other countries in South America and via the Pacific coast to China.
35. Indonesia, a country with considerable rainforests, similarly experienced significant deforestation increases as their economy grew during this same time period.
36. This is more than the entire country of Uruguay's GDP, for comparison.
37. The economic crisis was, of course, also made worse by the Zika outbreak and the lack of confidence in the nation's political system that was wrought by the corruption scandals. While the Petrobras scandal was a major factor in the economic crisis, the economic instability was in fact already afoot in 2011 when the Central Bank prematurely slashed interest rates, causing inflation to rise. Low industrial competitiveness coupled with red tape and high levels of public spending made matters worse for the Brazilian economy as well, and both were operative factors prior to the Zika epidemic and the apogee of the Petrobras scandal. See, for more detail, http://www.economist.com/blogs/graphicdetail/2016/04/economic-backgrounder.
38. An illustrative case is Marina Silva's tenure as Brazilian Minister of the Environment 2003–2008. A former rubber tapper, friend of Chico Mendes, and a founder of the rural worker's union in the state of Acre, Silva was a vocal socio-environmentalist. Her most notable contributions as Minister of the Environment were the creation of new parks and federal extractive reserves, which contributed to a substantial lowering of deforestation rates in Amazonia, especially from 2003–2006. Silva met resistance from the government over her positions on genetically modified organisms (GMOs), over finding alternatives to agrobusiness, and her opposition to certain large dam construction projects, including on the Madeira and Xingu Rivers. Ultimately, Marina Silva resigned on May 13, 2008, signaling her larger dissatisfaction with federal decisions that seemed too often to privilege development interests over environmental considerations.
39. Amid Brazil's generally stagnant economy during this period, agricultural exports were one of the strongest areas of economic productivity. This was a marked change from Brazil's 1970s and 1980s economic base (Barrientos and Amman 2015).
40. Those themes in the Amazon are centered over the political economy, the ideas of property rights, and of efficient production; these define the question of land tenure as the barrier to either maximum growth or effective conservation (Baletti 2012).

Chapter 4

1. This functioned to further local self-governance and to channel funding from the federal government more directly into the area. A 1996 constitutional

amendment prohibited the creation of new municipalities or modification of municipal boundaries, so there was a window where many new municipalities were created in the lead-up to the amendment being passed. A plebiscite, certain population minimums, and number of buildings are the main criteria for the creation of a new municipality. The Brazilian Senate has tried on at least three occasions to pass a resolution overturning the amendment, but there are serious fiscal implications to the measure given the anticipated high number of new municipalities (between 200–400). As a result, the resolutions have not gained approval from the House of Deputies and the president. A detailed discussion in Portuguese can be found at http://lucianarusso.jusbrasil.com.br/artigos/112329448/a-novela-da-criacao-de-municipios.

2. It became commonplace in the year before her death for the farmers living in the settlements to accompany Sister Dorothy as she walked between their homes, offering her a degree of protection. The Pará section of the Organization of Brazilian Lawyers bestowed her with a human rights award in 2004, for example, aiming to bolster her international reputation through the recognition, also with the hope that it would foster her security.
3. Even with the presence of the troops, several other individuals died in the week following Sister Dorothy's death, according to some residents of PDS-Esperança.
4. The death threats against Father José Amaro have ramped up in seriousness over the years and follow the same pattern of smear campaign and intimidation tactics that Sister Dorothy faced. He has been accused of numerous criminal activities, including conspiracy, extortion, money laundering, and trespassing. He was also arrested on sexual harassment charges in March 2018 that were subsequently dismissed, with his release from jail taking place in June 2018. The accusations against Father Amaro were leveled by the head of Anapu's Rural Association, Silvério Fernandes, who has business interests associated with the logging industry and is the former deputy mayor for the city of Altamira. Fernandes' brother, the rancher Luciano Fernandes, was assassinated in Anapu in May 2018, and Silvério has publicly expressed his own fears of being murdered. Father Amaro is under 24-hour protection by bodyguards and currently resides in Altamira.
5. The population of Anapu increased substantially between 2000–2016. The 2000 population was 9,407, and by 2010 the population was 20,543.
6. Between 2000–2010, BNDES disbursements grew by 470%, and its disbursements were around 7% of GDP (Zibechi 2014).
7. Plans originally involved settling over 100,000 families, mostly from Brazil's drought-ridden northeast region. But in practice, by 1977 (seven years into the Transamazon project) less than half of the families were from the northeast, and only 5,333 families were settled along the highway (Smith 1978).
8. For more complete descriptions and discussion about the correlations between road construction, logging, ranching, and deforestation, see Goodland and Irwin 1975, Godar, Tizado, and Pokorny 2012, Walker and Arima 2011, Fearnside 2008b, Barber et al. 2014, Walker 2000.
9. This slogan—and variants on it—are most commonly associated with Zionism, though its origins date back to the Christian Restorationist movement around the

mid-nineteenth century. Brazilian military President Médici borrowed the expression as part of the discourse that promoted the idea that settlement in the Amazon would lead to land ownership for the newcomers. The idea that the Amazon was devoid of people was patently false, because it denied the existence of the indigenous people that had lived there for centuries.

10. Rice was the predominant crop encouraged by INCRA, though it fared poorly, especially compared to manioc, which is a tuber and a basic staple in the regional diet. Sugar cane and coffee were also important cash crops. Manioc, beans, bananas, pepper, maize, cacao, and grasses were also planted commonly by agriculturalists, though generally with less commercial success (Smith 1978).
11. In late 1998 the MPST changed its name to the Movement for the Development of the Transamazon and Xingu (MDTX).
12. The actual number is unclear, as estimates range from seven (the number of victims handled in judicial processes and police investigations) to forty-four (the sum reported between cases in Altamira and the state of Maranhão). For more details on the emasculation case, see the excellent research of Paula Mendes Lacerda, 2012. "O Caso dos Meninos Emasculados de Altamira: Polícia, Justiça, e Movimento Social." Post-Graduate Thesis. Universidade Federal do Rio de Janeiro, Museu Nacional, Programa de Pós—Graduação em Antropologia Social. Available at http://teses2.ufrj.br/72/teses/784602.pdf.
13. The two gunmen that shot Sister Dorothy were brought to trial and convicted of murder, as was the middleman who had paid them on behalf of two powerful ranchers. At first, this seemed a rare achievement for the Brazilian justice system. Of the five people involved with Dorothy Stang's death who have been convicted in the past, not one is currently in prison. The only person ever convicted of ordering an assassination in the state of Pará is Regivaldo Pereira Galvão, but he was released by Brazil's Supreme Court in 2012.
14. The 2008 film is called *They Killed Sister Dorothy*, narrated by Martin Sheen. The opera, "Angel of the Amazon," was written in 2011 by Evan Mack. Several books also treat Sister Dorothy's life and work: *The Martyr of the Amazon* by Roseanne Murphy, and *The Greatest Gift: The Life and Martyrdom of Sister Dorothy Stang* by Binka LeBreton.
15. See, for example, discussion in Godar et al. 2014, Pacheco 2009a, Aldrich et al. 2012, Bratman 2011.
16. There is a significant body of literature addressing the question of to what extent smallholders can be viable partners in conservation. See, for Amazonian examples, Smith 1982, Bratman 2011, Fearnside 2008, Redford and Padoch 1992, Moran 1974, Moran and Ostrom 2005.
17. The forest code legislation also reduced the size of various environmental protection areas: the Amazon National Park by 437,000 km^2, the Tapajós environmental protection area by 200,000 km^2, and the Crepori National Forest by 8,561 km^2. See Decreto Federal 2011, No.542, August 12, 2011.
18. A legal restriction prohibits using felled trees for anything without proper authorization. Obtaining these authorizations is virtually impossible for farmers, given

the sluggishness of bureaucratic authorization processes as well as reluctance for authorizations to be granted out of suspicion that they will be misused and repurposed toward illegal logging activities.

19. The biggest of these marches involved around 300 participants.
20. At the northern border of Mato Grosso in the city of Sorriso, a Pro-BR-163 Committee was formed early on, but this small group was virtually the only manifestation of organized civil society groups campaigning for the northern section of the road paving. Within Pará stretch of the BR-163, there was a Rural Worker's Union, some presence of the FVPP, and occasional visits from the Altamira-based Pastoral Land Commission, but most of these organizations were either located in Altamira or were plagued with such inconsistent leadership that their activism did not amount to any significant presence.
21. The BR-163 highway never had a nickname that stuck, unlike the Transamazon. It was dubbed the "Soybean Highway" in the media in the early 2000s, but this nomenclature never held much traction locally.
22. Brazil was one of the last major countries to allow genetically engineered foods, with bans on growing in place in 1998 and 1999. Farmers continued growing GM soy, however. The bans were so lax and production so high that by 2003 GM soy constituted 80% of the crop in some of Brazil's soybean producing states (Ricardo Bonalume 2003).
23. Paranaguá was a particularly challenging port in 2005 and 2006 for agribusinesses betting on GMO production booms. In 2005, the governor of the state of Parana, Roberto Requião, who ultimately maintained political control over the port, resisted the national openness to GMOs by instituting a strong anti-GMO ban in his state and refusing to let GMO grains be transported out from the Paranaguá port. On April 20, 2006, a federal court ruled that the port must open all of its terminals to genetically modified soybeans or incur a fine of $R 5,000 ($2,400) per day, thus ending its ban on GMOs.
24. The deal also included assets Bunge had established at the Barcarena port, near Belém, Pará. This allowed soybeans to be loaded from trucks onto ships at Miritituba, which would then traverse the lower Tapajós, the Amazon, and then exit for transoceanic shipping via either the Barcarena port or the Santana port, near Macapá, Amapá.
25. The inadequacy of roads as well as other freight infrastructure in Brazil is a widely recognized problem. The World Bank estimates that operational costs are between 10%–30% higher than necessary because of the logistical difficulties of transportation infrastructures, cf. World Bank 2012, Amann et al. 2016.
26. Elsewhere in Brazil the Landless Worker's Movement, or MST, is the most widely reputed organization that leads land occupations and is frequently associated with rural land rights conflicts. Along the BR-163 corridor, however, the MST was not active, and the violence involved in these confrontations was not associated strongly with any particular organization or social movement.
27. These included the Belém-based Institute for Amazonian Environmental Research (IPAM); the University of Brasília's Center for Sustainable Development, the Center

for International Coordination and Agronomy Research for Development (CIRAD), and the Center for Life Institute (ICV).

28. The World Bank also attempted a more neoliberal agrarian reform in Brazil, which by several accounts had poor redistributive results as well. Cf. Sauer 2009, Wolford 2005, Jr. Borras 2003).
29. Data from http://dados.gov.br/organization/ministerio-dos-transportes-portos-e-aviacao-civil-mtpa.
30. The goal of increasing Brazilian energy production was perceived as necessary especially in light of economic growth; estimates from 2006 forecasted an 80% energy production increase to keep pace with rising consumption and GDP. Between 1990 and 2012, Brazilian energy consumption doubled. See Al-Saffar 2014.
31. *Not yet reactivated* here refers to the fact that various versions of the Belo Monte dam were floated with various levels of seriousness beginning in the late 1970s. The fuller history is discussed in Chapter 6.
32. There is some debate about the efficacy of conservation areas as a means of preventing deforestation in frontier regions, if those measures are not paired with adequate enforcement. The data from 2012–2015 suggest that protected areas had higher rates of deforestation than the parts of the Amazon that were not protected, which is generally thought to be the result of cuts to environmental protection and enforcement agencies in the country at the same time as growing investments in infrastructure and agribusiness. Deforestation also frequently increases in conservation areas during the first year after their creation, and generally only begins to decline in subsequent years. See Araújo et al. 2017.

Chapter 5

1. Extractive reserves became incorporated into the National Agrarian Reform Policy in 1987, and by 1989 were included the National Environmental Policy. They allow for traditional populations to be safeguarded in their rubber tapping, Brazil nut gathering, and other low–environmental impact activities on protected lands, and to be supported in those activities as economic livelihoods.
2. Specifically, these were: the RESEX Riozinho do Anfrísio (736,340 hectares), created November 2004; The Terra do Meio Ecological Station (ESEC), (3,373,110 hectares), created February 2005; the Serra do Pardo National Park (PARNA), (445,392 hectares), created February 2005; The RESEX Iriri (398,938.112 ha), created June 2006; the Triunfo do Xingu Area of Environmental Protection (APA) (1,711,147 hectares), created January 2006; the Altamira National Forest (FLONA) (689,012 hectares), created January, 2006; the Iriri State Forest, (5,449,888 hectares), created January 2006; and the RESEX Xingu (303,841 hectares), created June 2008.
3. In a few exceptional cases in the region the *ribeirinho* families arrived earlier, during the late nineteenth-century rubber boom. The population has considerable ethnic miscegenation, with a mix of indigenous, black, and northeastern Brazilian ancestry.

4. Deforestation rates in conservation areas generally drop significantly after the first year of their creation, though the rates of deforestation sometimes do increase during that first year, as there is frequently a delay between the creation of an area and the removal of illegal land claimants within it. Most scenario-based modeling of Amazonian deforestation suggests that the creation of indigenous areas and conservation areas are a strong policy option to slow and mitigate deforestation. That said, creating conservation areas is no panacea. Enforcement, road and other infrastructure developments, climate change, and consistent land rights and environmental policy regimes also are significant factors which can cause variability in the link between conservation area creation and slowed rates of deforestation. See Nepstad et al. 2014, 2006, Araújo et al. 2017, Davidson et al. 2012.
5. A similar action against illegal logging took place upstream on the Xingu, near Altamira and São Felix do Xingu in 2003, with IBAMA, the federal environmental enforcement agency, apprehending six thousand trunks of mahogany.
6. 95% of Amazonian wood exports during this time period stemmed from predatory logging, according to a study by IMAZON. See Arima and Veríssimo 2002.
7. The CPT estimated that 90% percent of the Terra do Meio populations in the three RESEXs were illiterate. As the reserves were being created in 2006, there was no existent plan from the municipality of Altamira to attend to the educational needs of the population. When *ribeirinho* children got schooling, it was through the city schools in Altamira rather than along the river. Some consultants hired by IBAMA did conduct a basic adult literacy short course in the region in February 2006, in preparation for the community members to be better capacitated to function in the management councils they would later form.
8. *Grilagem*, or illegal land claiming, is a phenomenon of land-grabbing which has resulted in significant social upheaval, causing population migrations and social conflict in Brazil. The origins of the term reflect a century-old practice of making false land documents appear old by putting them in a box with crickets (*grilos* in Portuguese), which soil the papers and chew at their corners sufficiently to make them look plausibly old. While this simple trick sometimes is the way *grilagem* occurs today, other more sophisticated schemes for illegal land claiming also take place in the state of Pará. In its most brute form, land may be claimed by force; if people are occupying the land a claimant claims for himself, it is by no means atypical for a *grileiro* to hire gunmen to threaten occupants and force their evacuation. More often than not, the land occupant will obey, especially if they are a *camponês* rather than a rival *grileiro*. Sometimes a small amount of money is offered for the land; other times, a *camponês* who has a field planted will be allowed to stay to collect his harvest. In this last case, not only does the *grileiro* gain possession of the land, but also the labor that went into clearing the land in the first place, and sometimes a portion of the harvest, since he claims to own the land. Most typically, people who work in government notary offices will be involved in fraudulent land title transfers, often changing the dates of purchase or the geographic coordinates of a landholding such that it is granted to the *grileiro*. When the land-acquisition process does not follow appropriate government procedures, the land may also be considered an "irregular" or illegal landholding, as titular status is the last step

in a series of administrative procedures necessary to legally acquire land. In addition, land may be fraudulently demarcated such that its geographic coordinates on paper do not match the topographical coordinates. Maps can be altered such that a false land title can be overlaid with lands that exist as previously declared land settlements, indigenous reserves, or conservation areas. Complicating the picture, *grilagem* can also occur as a third-party measure, where illegitimate land titles will be bought and sold, making illegal lands pass hands in what otherwise appear to be legal transactions.

9. For scale, a hectare is roughly equivalent in size to a soccer field. The specific holdings claimed were the areas of Mossoró, Belo Horizonte, Caxinguba, Humaitá and Forte Veneza.
10. These were the indigenous lands of the Igarapé Ipixuna and Apyterewa, respectively.
11. C.R. Almeida and his company, called Incexcil (Indústria, Comércio, Exportação e Navegação do Xingu Ltda.), achieved this through complicated shifts in ownership and illegal land claiming. Incexcil became a subsidiary firm to a preexisting business owned by Almeida called Rondon Projetos Ecológicos. Then, Incexcil was bought in the name of C.R. Almeida's son, Roberto Beltrão Almeida, as well as by Rondon Projetos Ecológicos. This purchase was made on June 13, 1995, when Incexcil's former owner, Umbelino de Oliveira, was already deceased. The business at the time claimed to have bought ten gigantic land parcels, totaling 4 million hectares all along the Iriri River. In the first count, the land became illegally held when the four original *seringalista* owners neglected to renew their contracts to it with the state of Pará. In 1923, at the time of their original leasing of the lands, it was stipulated that this be done annually. The land concessions, according to this original contract, were also not allowed to be passed to third-party names. In 1984, however, the lands were transferred to a single owner by a notary's office (*cartório*) in Altamira. The land changed hands again in 1993, purportedly becoming Umbelino de Oliveira's through paperwork filed at the same notary's office in Altamira. At the same time, a false map was made of the area, which extended the property by another 773,000 hectares.
12. Here, "the firm" refers to Incexcil; Amazônia Projetos Ecológicos operated predominantly in the Apyterewa indigenous area and was less a focus of attention from the *ribeirinho* population.
13. Given the historical understandings of patron–client relations in the region, however, loyalty was understandably personalized.
14. In the local notary offices, there was little to no evidence of digital records. In visits to several notaries in Altamira, I was witness to piles of dogeared papers that were stacked floor to ceiling, without any apparent organizational system or computerization. In these offices, necessary stamps and signatures and hand-copied records could be purchased for seemingly any sum (no prices were posted or listed visibly), and service appeared to be biased in favor of wealthier clients before others like the *ribeirinho* peasants I was accompanying there. The Altamira notary offices are known to be the most fraudulent in the nation.
15. The MPST became the Foundation for Life, Production, and Preservation (FVPP) a few years later.

16. Though the Instituto Socio-Ambiental did have a long track record of well-respected work further upstream the Xingu River basin.
17. The complications of establishing the RESEX Xingu were technical and personal as well as political. The president of the Xingu resident's association spoke at a public meeting in June 2006 about the necessity for the government to reassess the willingness of the Xingu area *ribeirinhos* to create the RESEX, because the government had earlier stalled when Almeida's firms intimidated the local population from participating in the meetings:

    > I vehemently endorse the creation of the RESEX Xingu, mentioning that the presence of C.R. Almeida and his people is very strong in the contracting of people and through food assistance. Aside from the threat to families that want the creation of the reserve. They are also spreading negative information about the transformation of the area in to an extractive reserve. I say for this reason that some residents were confused about the idea of the RESEX, but now, with more time and information, the situation has changed and the community has decided for the creation of the area. We continue to support receiving emergency auxiliary assistance for health and education for children. (2006, 17)

    The result was that the RESEX Xingu was designated over two years after the other pieces of the Terra do Meio conservation area mosaic were already in place.
18. Illustrative of this challenge is that once a *grileiro* is actually removed from their lands, there is frequently a further "heating up" of conflict as they retaliate for losing their land claims (and not receiving indemnification) with violence against activists or the local populations.
19. It was reported in the *Folha de São Paulo*, October 10, 2010, p. A-15 that the reserve was in fact vetoed, but there is no other evidence to support this.
20. Voting is compulsory in Brazil for citizens who are literate and between the ages of 18–70 years old. Illiterate citizens do not have compulsory voting, but still must file a justification form to not vote at election centers or post offices. Noncompliance can yield fines and other penalties.
21. Traditional populations also include rubber tappers and Brazil nut gatherers in the Amazon, crab fishermen, *quilombola* (maroon) populations, *babaçu* nut gatherers, and other relatively isolated communities found throughout the country. The needs of traditional populations living in conservation areas were formerly handled by the National Center for Traditional Populations (CNPT), which was a department within the Ministry of the Environment. In 2006, the CNPT was turned into the Directorate of Socioenvironmental Development (DISAM), remaining within IBAMA, the national environmental agency. Administration shifted again in 2007, however, when federal administration of environmental issues was restructured into two units. These were the Brazilian Institute for the Environment and Natural Resources (IBAMA), which became responsible only for handling environmental permitting, licensing, and enforcement, and the Instituto Chico Mendes de Conservação da Biodiversidade (ICM-Bio), which was tasked centrally with the social and ecological management of conservation areas. Indigenous people's issues fall into a separate legal category, under the administration of the National Foundation for the Indian (FUNAI).

22. The *regatões* and *ribeirinho* interaction followed a trade-based model that was common at the end of the nineteenth century. They generally traded industrialized or processed products (sugar, cooking oil, etc.) for the extracted natural resources of the region (fish, Brazil nuts, manioc flour, rubber, etc.). The exchange was often unequal in favor of the *regatões*, but debt collection was rarely enforced. The largely illiterate *ribeirinho* population allowed the *regatões* to keep accounts, so often the exact amounts of debt owed was only a general idea rather than a precise number.
23. On occasion, I also heard Terra do Meio residents describe themselves as "white Indians," also a somewhat self-deprecating identity category. Being a *ribeirinho* was perceived as more positive than being termed a *caboclo*, a more general term for a Brazilian peasant. The *caboclo* denomination ignored their history as rubber soldiers and was also perceived as derogatory (Zarin 2010). See also de Magalhães Lima 1999, Nugent 1993.
24. It is interesting to note that a related question of nomenclature and introduced terminology took place for the rubber tappers and riverine populations in the Amazon during the late 1980s, when the term *tropical rainforest* was introduced to rubber tappers like Chico Mendes and, conversely, the rubber tappers led by Chico Mendes and his organization introduced journalists and scientists to the idea that rubber tappers and other peoples of the forest were the people at the front lines of rainforest conservation.
25. Nicknames are commonly used among most residents in the region and are especially predominant among gunmen, who for obvious reasons value a degree of ambiguity concerning their identities.
26. After Feitosa left the CPT, for a time the *ribeirinhos* relied more on staff at the FVPP for assistance. By 2008, the Instituto SocioAmbiental (ISA) set up a local office in Altamira that offered additional support and locally based advocacy on behalf of the Terra do Meio populations, along with a greater degree of partnership with the local populations integrated into their approach.
27. Additionally complicating matters, the smallholder colonist farmers who were the PDS residents were often characterized and conflated in media accounts with the struggle in the Terra do Meio. The confusion was bolstered by the government creating the conservation areas in the Terra do Meio area in response to Sister Dorothy Stang's assassination, even though Sister Dorothy's primary work had been in solidarity with the PDS residents in nearby Anapu, along the Transamazon highway.
28. Under the National System for Conservation, areas intended for human use and residency comprise a category called "sustainable use areas" which include Extractive Reserves and Environmental Protection Areas. Those not intended for human residents are "integral protection areas" and become designated as Ecological Stations and National Parks.
29. Families in the region typically have between four and eight children, though upwards of ten children is also not uncommon. Younger families in the Terra do Meio region are more recently having fewer children, thanks to greater access to medical facilities and birth control methods.

Chapter 6

1. The exact amount to be flooded, according to the website of Norte Energia S.A., is 516 km^2. Some versions of the project had reduced the flooded area as low as 440 km^2, while others estimate that the real flooded area is actually closer to 600 km^2. The ratio of flooded area to the generation capacity is one of the best in the world, according to the BNDES (see http://www.bndes.gov.br/SiteBNDES/bndes/bndes_en/Institucional/Press/Noticias/2012/20121126_belomonte.html).
2. This figure is variable based on the energy productivity at different times of year; peak capacity is limited to only one or two months of the year, whereas in the dry season the guaranteed minimum capacity is only 4,571 MW. The capacity is calculated on a per-hour basis. The largest hydroelectric dam is the Three Gorges dam in China, at 22,000 MW, followed by Itaipú, at 14,000 MW of installed capacity. Belo Monte was initially slated to be the world's third largest dam, but the Chinese Xiluodu dam, proposed in 2013, was constructed first and has a capacity of 13,860 MW, taking third place instead. The Grand Inga hydroelectric project on the Congo River, if constructed as is currently proposed, would dwarf all these dams with 39,000 MW of installed capacity.
3. The project was initially budgeted for BRL$16 billion, with auction bids at BRL $19 billion and up to $28.8 billion in financing. But the costs doubled to around BRL $31 billion by 2013, and by 2016, amid clear signs that the project was also implicated in the Lava Jato (Car Wash) corruption scandals with kickbacks from construction firms to politicians, the cost overruns were even higher.
4. These emissions are based in carbon dioxide equivalents, and stem mostly from the methane released as vegetation decomposes in flooded areas and as soil carbon is lost through land conversions.
5. Indicative of this is that majority holdings (50.02%) in the project are controlled by the Norte Energia consortium, which is composed of energy and mining companies, namely, Neoenergia, Cemig, Light, Vale, Sinobras, J. Malucelli, along with the pension funds from Petros (Petrobrás) and Funcef (Caixa). The nationally owned Grupo Eletrobrás owns 49.98%.
6. This is the conservative figure of construction costs, approximated based on data from Eletronorte, CCBM, and the Ministry of Mines and Energy. Other estimates commonly found in journalistic reporting on the project suggest total costs between $16.52 billion (BRL$38 billion) and $25.21 billion (BRL $58 billion). See, for example, Rapoza 2014.
7. BRL $3.6 billion, at 2011 rates. Of this, at least USD $68 million was directed toward the indigenous communities in the Belo Monte zone of influence, consisting of approximately 3,000 people in 34 villages and 11 indigenous territories. For more on the PDRS, see https://www.planalto.gov.br/ccivil_03/_ato2007-2010/2010/decreto/d7340.htm and http://www.pdrsxingu.org.br/.
8. The Ministry of Mines and Energy notes specifically that 4,300 urban families and 800 rural families will be affected (Energia 2011), although other studies show the families affected estimate to be closer to 6,000, and some estimates are as high as 40,000 people in total displaced.

9. This number derives from municipal estimates rather than the federal census, which gives a significantly lower count.
10. This statistic is the source of some dispute as well. Other independent studies suggest that Belo Monte would need more dams to be constructed along the Xingu River in order to reach this operating capacity. One study, conducted as a doctoral dissertation, suggests that Belo Monte operating alone would only have an average capacity of 1,172 MW due to a lack of reservoir capacity and the need for interconnection with the national system (Cicogna 2004, de Sousa Júnior and Reid 2010).
11. In relation to other Amazonian dams, this amount of flooded reservoir area is relatively small, and is possible because Belo Monte is a run-of-river dam instead of a gravity dam. The size of the lake created by the Itaipú dam, for comparison, is 1,350 km^2, and the Tucuruí dam reservoir (along the Tocantins River, and completed in 1984), is 2,875 km^2. Norte Energia, the company responsible for Belo Monte, notes that the national average of flooded areas for hydroelectric plants is .49 km^2/ MW of installed capacity, whereas Belo Monte will impact .04 km^2.
12. In nearly every piece of written material, the "with social responsibility" part of the slogan was written in smaller print, below the main message, "I want Belo Monte." The truck driver's union, the association of stone masons, electricians, painters, and carpenters, and the business syndicate were also strong supporters on the pro-Belo Monte side.
13. Alunorte, a Japanese–Brazilian firm, as well as a Chinese–Brazilian alumina plant, operate at nearby Barcarena (Pará). The US-owned company Alcoa is currently building a plant at Jurití, also for aluminum mining. Additionally, Albrás, a Japanese–Brazilian aluminum smelting company, is expanding operations given the more abundant electricity supplies (Fearnside 2005).
14. Belo Sun estimates that there are upwards of 7 million ounces of gold that can be extracted at Volta Grande, located near the power plant at Belo Monte in areas that were largely exposed and made more accessible due to the rerouting of the river for the Belo Monte dam construction.
15. The total lifespan of the project is 17 years (including construction and shutdown operations) according to the Belo Sun materials.
16. The environmental license for Volta Grande was granted in 2015, and the construction license for the Belo Sun project was granted on February 2, 2017. The Belo Monte project was relaunched in 2007 under President Lula's Growth Acceleration Program (PAC), although it was not until 2009 under President Rousseff that the first licenses for construction began being approved. For more details, see http://www.belosun.com/_resources/170203_Belo%20Sun_Corporate%20Presentation.pdf and Bratman 2014.
17. The royalties estimates are BRL$5 million per year, totaling around BRL$60 million over the twelve years of operation. In taxes, there is an estimated BRL$130 in national, state, and local taxes that will be collected during installation, and thereafter BRL$55 million per year. Based on my own calculations derived from Belo Sun corporate data, over twelve years the Brazilian government (state and federal) would thus receive USD$270 million in taxes and royalties from the Belo Sun project. For

the Canadian Belo Sun company, the estimates are a twelve-year yield of $7.98 billion based on earnings of $665 million USD per year in NPV value, post-tax, with an IRR between 20%–32%. See Belo Sun Mining Corporation 2016, Melo 2017.

18. The largest energy infrastructure investments during this time period from the BNDES came at the start of the PAC, in 2010, with energy sector investments totaling $BRL 37 billion (USD $20.36 billion in 2010 USD). Data from the BNDES annual reports, available from: http://www.bndes.gov.br.
19. Such criteria began within the cattle and sugarcane commodity sectors. The BNDES's social responsibility commitment was approved in 2010 and updated in 2014. These are general guidelines and principles more than sector-specific recommendations. The BNDES was reticent to sign on to other social and environmental lending criteria, most notably diverging from the other major Brazilian banks by not signing on to the Equator Principles, which were a set of criteria coordinated by the multinational International Finance Corporation that established socio-environmental assessment of $10 million-and-over projects. The same year that the IFC withdrew $90 million in funding to a company called Bertin that was involved in the Amazonian beef industry after outcry from Greenpeace and other watchdog groups, that company was acquired by the Brazilian meatpacking firm JBS. Between 2007–2011, over $4 billion in loans occurred between BNDES and JBS, and these are currently the subject of investigations surrounding the Brazilian corruption scandals of Operation Car Wash (Réporter Brasil 2011, Paraguassu and Fonesca 2017).
20. Five smaller companies were also involved in the construction.
21. See http://www.chesf.gov.br/Negocios/Pages/default.aspx.
22. Again, the numbers here are contested and vary widely, and I have used the conservative estimates in text; the upper estimates of displaced people from the dam are around 50,000 according to the anti-dam activist group Xingu Vivo.
23. These are the preconstruction, installation, and operation licenses, which must be sequentially granted for any proposed project according to Brazilian administrative procedures (Resolution 237/97 of the National Council for the Environment).
24. The IACHR never actually withdrew its finding against Brazil, although it was incorrectly reported to have done so in the nation's leading newspaper, *O Globo*.
25. This impact is particularly serious because fish is the main source of protein of those who reside in the Big Bend (RIMA Belo Monte). More than 16 million tons of fish died when the dam started filling up in November 2015, and indigenous peoples from the Juruna tribe, located near the site, were unable to continue dive-fishing for the ornamental fish they were accustomed to finding and then selling for use in aquariums. Fishing is the main livelihood of the tribe, and line fishing yields have also declined significantly as a result of the dam (Beeler 2016).
26. See Processo nº 0003072-96.2016.4.01.3903—Justiça Federal em Altamira (PA), and TRF1, Processo nº. 0053298-77.2016.4.01.0000.
27. This alliance was primarily composed of local municipal leaders and commercial interests.
28. For more, see the Movimento Gota d'Agua website at http://www.movimentogotadagua.com.br/.

29. The name Xingu +23 references the 23 years since the Encounter of the Xingu, which was in 1989. It was also meant to evoke ties between the timing of the event and that of the Rio +20 Earth Summit, which was taking place later that month.
30. A number of NGO-led meetings led to declarations against large dams and funding for them, beginning with the International Rivers Network's 1988 San Francisco declaration and involving subsequent declarations in 1994, 1997, 2002, and 2003, which were targeted at World Bank funding and establishing international moratoriums on large dam construction (Scudder 2012).
31. World Commission on Dams 2000.
32. The company's website itself noted in 2014: "As to relocation, Belo Monte is going to move hundreds of people involved in agriculture and around two thousand Altamira families who nowadays live under precarious conditions. Their homes, usually stilt houses, have water up to the floorboards during river flood seasons; and are surrounded by mud during the dry season. This environment is used both by children for playing and by inhabitants in general as a toilet, for there is no sanitation available. Everyone will be indemnified. Farmers will be transferred to agrovilas (organized farm settlements) and city residents will be taken to houses with urban infrastructure and sanitation, in places which will offer public facilities such as schools and leisure areas" (Norte Energia S.A. 2014).
33. This compares with a global average of only 13% renewables.
34. It is worth noting, however, that the New Development Bank's early lending portfolio was emphatically weighted toward renewable energy projects, especially solar and wind. The first New Development Bank loan to Brazil was a $300 million project for solar energy in 2017.
35. In the Brazilian BNDES context, investments are also substantial in the energy infrastructure sector and in smaller hydroelectric projects, though these are not included in the table for the sake of comparison.
36. Small-scale hydroelectric dams are included within the same strategy, but leaked documents from the Bank suggested that, largely for reasons of management efficiency and oversight, it is more efficient to take on big projects instead of smaller ones.
37. These include the National Electrical Energy Agency (ANEEL), the National Electrical System Operator (ONS), the recently created Energy Research Company (EPE), and large state electrical energy generators Eletrobras and Eletronorte.

Chapter 7

1. These include the Amazon Fund, established in 2008, which involves over $1 billion in foreign commitments aimed at reducing deforestation and thereby furthering global climate change emissions reduction goals. Also notable is funding for REDD+ programs, and Proambiente, a Brazilian payment-for-ecosystem-services program.
2. The origins of the term likely stem from the mid-1820s, when slaves were trafficked by boat into Brazil despite British prohibitions on doing so. Brazilian officials, who did not abolish slavery until 1888, doubtless considered the restrictions to be demagoguery,

imposed through the superior maritime control of the British. Rather than oppose the law directly, however, the Brazilian workaround simply involved hiding the trafficked slaves on their ships when British patrol boats were nearby and making other efforts to show that they were combating slavery.

3. Pará, G1. 2017. "Altamira lidera ranking de cidades mais violentas do Brasil, diz IPEA." *Globo.com*, June 5, 2017. http://g1.globo.com/pa/para/noticia/altamira-lidera-ranking-de-cidades-mais-violentas-do-brasil-diz-ipea.ghtml.

Methodological Appendix

1. These included interviews with individuals working at the Instituto SocioAmbiental, The Nature Conservancy, International Rivers Network, World Wildlife Fund, the Institute for Amazonian Environmental Research (IPAM), the Museu Emílio Goeldi, The National Institute for Amazonian Research, the Pará Society for Human Rights, the Pastoral Land Commission, Norte Energia, the Ministry of Mines and Energy, Ministry of Transportation, Ministry of Social Development, IBAMA, and FUNAI, among others.

References

"A Batalha de Belo Monte." 2013. December 16, 2013, *Tudo Sobre*. https://arte.folha.uol.com.br/especiais/2013/12/16/belo-monte/.

"Altamira lidera ranking de cidades mais violentas do Brasil, diz IPEA." 2017. *G1 Pará—Globo.com*, June 5, 2017. http://g1.globo.com/pa/para/noticia/altamira-lidera-ranking-de-cidades-mais-violentas-do-brasil-diz-ipea.ghtml.

"Asphalt and the Jungle." 2004. *The Economist*, July 22, 2004. https://www.economist.com/the-americas/2004/07/22/asphalt-and-the-jungle.

"The Belo Monte Dam Complex." 2014. Norte Energia S.A., (n.d.) http://norteenergiasa.com.br/site/ingles/belo-monte/.

"Brazil Takes Off." 2009. *The Economist*, November 12, 2009. https://www.economist.com/leaders/2009/11/12/brazil-takes-off.

"Colombia Apology for Devastation in Amazon Rubber Boom." 2012. *BBC News*, October 13, 2012. http://www.bbc.com/news/world-latin-america-19931443.

"Índia Repete a Ameaça que Fez a Diretor da Eletronorte em 1989." 2008. *Folha de São Paulo*, May 22, 2008, http://www1.folha.uol.com.br/fsp/brasil/fc2205200818.htm.

"No Pará, Morte de Peixes Preocupa Pescadores no Rio Xingu." 2016. *G1 Pará- Globo.com*, April 25, 2016. http://g1.globo.com/pa/para/noticia/2016/04/no-para-morte-de-peixes-preocupa-pescadores-no-rio-xingu.html.

. "Pará Concentra 40% Dos Crimes no Campo nos Dois Ultimos Anos." 2005. *Folha de São Paulo*, February 15, 2005.

"Para Moradores de Altamira, Belo Monte Trouxe Renda e Problemas." 2013. *Folha de São Paulo*, December 16, 2013, Opinão Publica. http://datafolha.folha.uol.com.br/opiniaopublica/2013/12/1386247-para-moradores-de-altamira-belo-monte-trouxe-renda-e-problemas.shtml.

"Peruvian Amazon Company: Compulsory Winding-Up." 1913. *The Mercury*, March 22, 1913. http://trove.nla.gov.au/ndp/del/article/10278671.

"The Rights and Wrongs of Belo Monte; Dams in the Amazon." 2013. *The Economist*, May 4 2013, 37–39.

Abers, Rebecca Neaera, and Margaret E. Keck. 2013. *Practical Authority: Agency and Institutional Change in Brazilian Water Politics*. New York: Oxford University Press.

ACTO. 2004. Brasília: Amazon Cooperation Treaty Organization (ACTO), Permanent Secretariat.http://www.itamaraty.gov.br/en/politica-externa/integracao-regional/6351-amazon-cooperation-treaty-organization-acto.

Adams, W.M. 2001. *Green Development*. 2nd ed. London: Routledge.

Agrawal, Arun. 2005. "Environmentality: Community, Intimate Government, and the Making of Environmental Subjects in Kumaon, India." *Current Anthropology* 46 (2):161–190.

Al-Saffar, Ali. 2014. Brazil Energy Outlook. Paris: International Energy Agency.

Aldrich, Stephen, Robert Walker, Cynthia Simmons, Marcellus Caldas, and Stephen Perz. 2012. "Contentious Land Change in the Amazon's Arc of Deforestation." *Annals of the Association of American Geographers* 102 (1):103–128.

Alencar, Ane. 2005. A Rodovia BR-163 e o Desafio da Sustentabilidade. In *MAPAS: Monitoramento Ativo da Participação da Sociedade*. Belém: INPA.

Allegretti, Marie H. 1990. "Extractive Reserves: An Alternative for Reconciling Development and Environmental Conservation in Amazonia." In *Alternatives to Deforestation: Steps Toward Sustainable Use of the Amazon Rain Forest*, edited by A.B. Anderson 252–264, New York: Columbia University Press.

Allegretti, Mary Helena. 1995. "The Amazon and Extracting Activities." In *Brazilian Perspectives on the Sustainable Development of the Amazon Region*, edited by M. Clüsener-Godt and Ignacy Sachs, 157–174. Paris: UNESCO.

Allen, Elizabeth. 2006. "Fire in Roraima, 1998—politics and human impact: What role for indigenous people in Brazilian Amazonia?" In *Human Impacts on Amazonia*, edited by Darrel Addison Posey and Michael J Balick, 51–84. New York: Columbia University Press.

Almeida, Alfredo Wagner Berno de. 1991. "O intransitivo de transição. O Estado, os conflitos agrários e a violência na Amazônia." In *Amazônia: A fronteira agrícola 20 anos depois*, edited by Philippe Léna and Adélia Engrácia de Oliveira, 259–290. Belém: Museu Paraense Emílio Goeldi.

Almeida, Anna Luiza Ozoria de. 1992. *The Colonization of the Amazon*. Austin: University of Texas Press.

Almeida, Mauro William Barbosa de. 1993. "The Rubber Tappers of the Upper Juruá River: The Making of a Forest Peasantry." PhD dissertation, Social Anthropology, Cambridge University.

Almeida, Claudio. 1999. *Grilagem: Relatório Final da CPI*. Belém, PA: Assembléia Legislativa do Pará.

Almeida, Thamyris F.T. 2015. "Araguaia: Maoist Uprising and Military Counterinsurgency in the Brazilian Amazon, 1967–1975." MA thesis, History, University of Massachusetts, Amherst (179).

Alonso, Angela, Valeriano Costa, and Débora Maciel. 2005. "The Formation of the Brazilian Environmental Movement." *IDS Working Paper #259*. Brighton: Institute for Development Studies.

Alston, Lee J., Gary D. Libecap, and Bernardo Mueller. 1999. *Titles, Conflict, and Land Use: The development of property rights and land reform on the Brazilian Amazon frontier*. Ann Arbor: University of Michigan Press.

Alves, Maria Helena Moreira. 1985. *State and Opposition in Military Brazil*. Austin: University of Texas Press.

Amado, Adriana Moreira, and Maria de Lourdes Rollemberg Mollo. 2015. "The 'Developmentalism' Debate in Brazil: Some Economic and Political Issues." *Review of Keynesian Economics* 3 (1):77–89.

Amann, Edmund, Werner Baer, Thomas Trebat, and Juan Villa Lora. 2016. "Infrastructure and Its Role in Brazil's Development Process." *The Quarterly Review of Economics and Finance* 62:66–73.

Anderson, Robin L. 1999. *Colonization as Exploitation in the Amazon Rain Forest, 1758–1911*. Gainsville: University of Florida.

Araujo, Claudio, Catherine Araujo Bonjean, Jean-Louis Combes, Pascale Combes Motel, and Eustaquio J. Reis. 2008. "Land reform and deforestation in the Brazilian Amazonia." Sociedade Brasileira de Economia, Administração e Sociologia Rural, Rio Branco: CERDI, July 20–23, 2008. https://ideas.repec.org/p/ags/sbrfsr/108618.html

Araújo, Elise, Paulo Barreto, Sara Baima, and Mayara Gomes. 2017. *Most Deforested Conservation Units in the Legal Amazon (2012–2015)*. Belém: Imazon.

Araújo, Roberto. 1991. "Campo religioso e trajetórias sociais na Transamazônica." In *Amazônia: A fronteira agrícola 20 anos depois*, edited by Philippe Léna and Adélia Engrácia de Oliveira, 125–143. Belém: Museu Paraense Emílio Goeldi.

Arima, Eugênia, Paulo Barreto, and Marky Brito. 2005. *Pecuária na Amazônia: Tendências e implicações para a conservação ambiental*. Belém: Imazon.

Arima, Eugênia, and Alberto Veríssimo. 2002. Brasil em Ação: Ameaças e Oportunidades Econômicas na Fronteira Amzônica. Belém: Imazon.

Arnaud, E., and A.R. Alves. 1974. "A Extinção dos Indios Kararaô (Kaiapó)—Baixo Xingu, Pará [The Extinction of the Kararao (Kaiapo) Indians—Lower Xingu, Para]." *Antropologia* 53:1–19.

Arrarás, Astrid, Luis Bitencourt, Clóvis Brigagão, Ralph H. Espach, Eduardo A. Gamarra, Thomas Guedes Da Costa, and Margaret E. Keck. 2002. Environment and Security in the Amazon Basin, edited by Joseph S. Tulchin and Heather A. Golding. Washington, DC: Woodrow Wilson Center Reports on the Americas.

Arruda, Hélio Palma de. 1977. *Os Problemas Fundiários na Estratégia do Desenvolvimento e da Segurança*. Brasilia: INCRA.

Arsenault, Chris. 2017. "Brazil, Home of the Amazon, Rolls Back Environmental Protection." *Reuters*, May 15, 2017. http://www.reuters.com/article/us-brazil-politics-environment-idUSKCN18B21P.

The Associated Press. 2005. "First Arrest Made in Nun's Slaying in the Amazon." *New York Times*, February 21, 2005. Americas. http://www.nytimes.com/2005/02/21/world/americas/firstarrest-made-in-nuns-slaying-in-amazon.html.

Azevedo, Reinaldo. 2011. "Belo Monte e as Magdas e os Magdos da TV Globo." *Veja*. November 24, 2011. https://veja.abril.com.br/blog/reinaldo/belo-monte-e-as-magdas-e-os-magdos-da-tv-globo-e-o-maior-festival-de-besteiras-jamais-ditas-num-video-e-olhem-que-a-concorrencia-e-grande/

Backstrand, Karin. 2006. "Democratizing Global Environmental Governance? Stakeholder Democracy after the World Summit on Sustainable Development." *European Journal of International Relations* 12 (4):467–498.

Bakker, Karen. 2010. "The Limits of 'Neoliberal Natures': Debating Green Neoliberalism." *Progress in Human Geography* 34 (6):715–735.

Baletti, Brenda. 2012. "Ordenamento Territorial: Neo-developmentalism and the Struggle for Territory in the Lower Brazilian Amazon." *Journal of Peasant Studies* 39 (2):573–598.

Baletti, Brenda. 2014. "Saving the Amazon? Sustainable Soy and the New Extractivism." *Environment and Planning A* 46 (1):5–25.

Balick, Michael J. 2006. "Thoughts on the Future of Amazonia: The Region, Residents, Researchers, and Realities." In *Human Impacts on Amazonia*, edited by Darrel Addison Posey and Michael J Balick, 1–5. New York: Columbia University Press.

Ban, Cornel. 2012. "Brazil's Liberal Neo-Developmentalism: New Paradigm or Edited Orthodoxy?" *Review of International Political Economy* 20 (2):298–331.

Barbanti, Olympio. 2013. "From Peasants to 'Project Beneficiaries': The Case of the Brazilian Amazon PPG7 Demonstration Projects." *Agrarian South: Journal of Political Economy* 2 (1):71–92.

Barber, Christopher, Mark A. Cochrane, Carlos M. Souza Jr., and William F. Laurance. 2014. "Roads, Deforestation, and the Mitigating Effect of Protected Areas in the Amazon." *Biological Conservation* 147:203–209.

Barbosa, Luis C. 2000. *The Brazilian Amazon Rainforest: Global Ecopolitics, Development, and Democracy*. Lanham: University Press of America.

Bárham, Bradford L., and Oliver T. Coomes. 1994. "Reinterpreting the Amazon Rubber Boom: Investment, the State, and Dutch Disease." *Latin American Research Review* 29 (2):73–109.

Barrientos, Armando, and Edmund Amman. 2015. "Is There a Brazilian Model of Development?" *Policy In Focus*, 12 (3), International Policy Centre for Inclusive Growth: UNDP.

Barros-Platiau, Ana Flávia. 2010. "When Emergent Countries Reform Global Governance of Climate Change: Brazil Under Lula." *Revista Brasileira de Politíca Internacional* 53 (special edition):73–90.

Beck, Ulrich, Anthony Giddens, and S. Lash. 1994. *Reflexive Modernisation*. Cambridge: Polity.

Becker, Bertha. 1999. "Os Eixos de Integração e Desenvolvimento e a Amazônia." *Território* 6:29–42.

Becker, Bertha. 2005. "Geopolítica da Amazônia." *Estududos Avançados* 19 (53):71–86.

Becker, Bertha, and Philippe Léna. 2002. "Pequenos Empreendimentos Alternativos na Amazônia." *Proposição de Políticas para Promoção de Sistemas Produtivos Locais de Micro Pequenas e Medias Empresas* September 2002, Rede de Sistemas Produtivos e Inovativos Locais, UFRJ. http://www.redesist.ie.ufrj.br

Beeler, Carolyn. 2016. "Brazil's Huge Dam is Built, But These Women Won't Stop Fighting." *PRI's The World*, February 26, 2016. https://www.pri.org/stories/2016-02-25/women-lead-fight-protect-amazonia-impacts-huge-dam

Belo Sun Mining Corporation. 2016. Presentation to Investors. Belo Sun Mining Corp. http://www.belosun.com/investor_center/presentations/

Benevides, Maria Victoria de Mesquita. 1976. *O governo Kubitschek: desenvolvimento economico e estabilidade politica, 1956–1961*. Rio de Janeiro: Paz e Terra.

Berchin, Issa Ibrahim, Jéssica Garcia, Mauri Luiz Heerdt, et al. 2015. "Energy Production and Sustainability: A Study of Belo Monte Hydroelectric Power Plant." *Natural Resources Forum* 39 (3–4):224–237.

Bermann, Célio, and Osvaldo Stella Martins. 2000. "Sustentabilidade energética no Brasil: limites e possibilidades para uma estratégia energética sustentável e democrática."

Bernstein, Steven. 2000. "Ideas, Social Structure and the Compromise of Liberal Environmentalism." *European Journal of International Relations* 6 (4):464–512.

Bernstein, Steven. 2002. "Liberal Environmentalism and Global Environmental Governance." *Global Environmental Politics* 2(3):1–16.

Bevins, Vincente. 2012. Brazil Workers Exploited as Modern-day Amazon Slaves. *Los Angeles Times*, June 7, 2012. https://www.latimes.com/world/la-xpm-2012-jun-07-la-fg-brazil-slave-labor-20120607-story.html.

Bingham, Alexa. 2010. "Discourse of the Dammed: A Study of the Impacts of Sustainable Development Discourse on Indigenous Peoples in the Brazilian Amazon in the Context of the Proposed Belo Monte Hydroelectric Dam." *POLIS Journal (University of Leeds)* 4 (1):1–47.

Binswanger, Hans P. 1991. "Brazilian Policies that Encourage Deforestation in the Amazon." *World Development* 19 (7):821–829.

Blakie, Piers. 2008. "Epilogue: Towards a Future for Political Ecology that Works." *Geoforum* 39:765–772.

Bolaños, Omeira. 2014. "Redefining Identities, Redefining Landscapes: Indigenous Identity and Land Rights Struggles in the Brazilian Amazon." In *Amazonian Geographies: Emerging Identities and Landscapes*, edited by Jacqueline M. Vadjunec and Marianne Schmink, 45–72. New York: Routledge.

Borges, André. 2017. "Governo do Pará ignora Funai e libera mina de ouro ao lado de Belo Monte." *Estadão*, February 2, 2017. http://economia.estadao.com.br/noticias/geral,governo-do-para-ignora-funai-e-libera-mina-de-ouro-ao-lado-de-belo-monte,70001651266.

Bowman, Isaiah. 1913. "Geographical Aspects of the New Madeira-Mamore Railroad." *Bulletin of the American Geographical Society* 45 (1):275–281.

Boxer, C.R. 1962. *The Golden Age of Brazil*. Berkeley: University of California Press.

Braga de Souza, Oswaldo. 2016. ISA entrega à relatora da ONU dados do aumento de invasões e desmatamento na Terra do Meio (PA). *Notícias Socioambientais* Programa Xingu. https://www.socioambiental.org/pt-br/noticias-socioambientais/isa-entrega-a-relatora-da-onu-dados-do-aumento-de-invasoes-e-desmatamento-na-terra-do-meio-pa.

Braga de Souza, Oswaldo. 2017. Base parlamentar de Temer abre florestas ao desmatamento e grilagem. *Notícias Socioambientais* Instituto Socioambiental, accessed May 30, 2019. https://www.socioambiental.org/pt-br/noticias-socioambientais/base-parlamentar-de-temer-abre-florestas-ao-desmatamento-e-grilagem

Brainard, Lael and Leonardo Martinez-Diaz, eds. 2009. *Brazil as an Economic Superpower? Understanding Brazil's Changing Role in the Global Economy*. Columbia: Brookings Institute.

Brandão, Ignácio de Loyola. 1981. *Não Verás País Nenhum: Memorial Descritivo*. Rio de Janeiro: Codecri.

Branford, Sue. 2016. BNDES Speaks Out: Giant Brazilian bank offers rare in-depth interview, *Mongabay*, April 6, 2016. https://news.mongabay.com/2016/04/bndes-speaks-out-giant-brazilian-bank-offers-rare-in-depth-interview/

Branford, Sue, and Oriel Glock. 1992. *The Last Frontier: Fighting over Land in the Amazon*. London: Zed Books.

Branford, Sue, and Mauricio Torres. 2017. "Getting There: The rush to turn the Amazon into a soy transport corridor." *Mongabay*, February 15, 2017. https://news.mongabay.com/2017/02/getting-there-the-rush-to-turn-the-amazon-into-a-soy-transport-corridor/.

Bratman, Eve. 2011. "Villains, Victims, and Conservationists? Representational Frameworks and Sustainable Development on the Transamazon Highway." *Human Ecology* 39 (4):441–453.

Bratman, Eve Z. 2014. "Contradictions of Green Development: Human Rights and Environmental Norms in Light of Belo Monte Dam Activism." *Journal of Latin American Studies* 46 (02):261–289.

Bratman, Eve. 2015. "Passive revolution in the green economy: activism and the Belo Monte dam." *International Environmental Agreements: Politics, Law and Economics* 15 (1):1–17.

Bratman, Eve, and Cristiane Bená Dias. 2018. "Development Blind Spots in Environmental Impact Assessment: Tensions between Policy, Law and Practice in Brazil's Xingu River Basin." *Environmental Impact Assessment Review* 70:1–10.

Brazil, Government of. 2011. Response from the State of Brazil, Indigenous Communities of the Xingu River Basin, Pará v. Brazil, Inter-American Commission on Human

Rights (IACHR), PM 382/10, July 29, 2011. https://www.oas.org/en/iachr/indigenous/protection/precautionary.asp

Bresser-Pereira, Luiz Carlos. 2011. "An Account of New Developmentalism and the Structuralist Macroeconomics." *Revista de Economia Política* 31 (3):493–502.

Bresser-Pereira, Luiz Carlos 2009. *Developing Brazil: Overcoming the Failure of the Washington Consensus*. Boulder: Lynne Rienner.

Bringel, Fabiano Oliveira. 2014. "Territorialização Camponesa e Fronteira Agrária—O Caso do Projeto de Desenvolvimento Sustentável (PDS) Esperança em Anapu—Pará—Brasil." *Boletim Gaúcho de Geografia* 41 (2):384–403.

British Library. 2017. "Thomas More's Utopia (1516)." In *Learning: English Timeline*: British Library.

Brosius, J. Peter. 1999. "Analysis and Interventions: Anthropological Engagements with Environmentalism." *Current Anthropology* 40 (3):277–309.

Browder, John O., and Brian Godfrey. 1993. *Rainforest Cities: Urbanization, Development, and Globalization in the Brazilian Amazon*. New York: Columbia University Press.

Brown, J. Christopher, and Mark Purcell. 2005. "There's Nothing Inherent About Scale: Political Ecology, the Local Trap, and the Politics of Development in the Brazilian Amazon." *Geoforum* 36 (5):607–624.

Brum, Eliane. 2014. "Belo Monte: A anatomía de etnocídio." *El País*, December 1, 2014, Opinion. http://brasil.elpais.com/brasil/2014/12/01/opinion/1417437633_930086.html.

Brundtland, Gro Harlem. 1987. "Our Common Future: Report of the World Commission on Environment and Development." Report of the World Commission on Environment and Development. https://sustainabledevelopment.un.org/content/documents/5987our-common-future.pdf.

Bruner, A.G., R.E. Gullison, R.E. Rice, and G.A. da Fonseca. 2001. "Effectiveness of Parks in Protecting Tropical Biodiversity." *Science* 291 (5501):125–128.

Bulkeley, Harriet. 2005. "Reconfiguring Environmental Governance: Towards a Politics of Scales and Networks." *Political Geography* 24 (8):875–902.

Bulkeley, Harriet, and Michele M. Betsill. 2003. *Cities and Climate Change: Urban Sustainability and Global Environmental Governance*. New York: Routledge.

Bunker, Stephen G. 1985. *Underdeveloping the Amazon: Extraction, Unequal Exchange, and the Failure of the Modern State*. Chicago: University of Chicago Press.

Bunker, Stephen G., and Paul S. Ciccantell. 2005. "From Amsterdam to Amazonia: How Space and Technology Matter in the Formation of the Capitalist State." In *Nature, Raw Materials and Political Economy*, edited by P.D. Smite G. Seidman, 253–285. Oxford: JAI/Elsevier Press.

Burns, Bradford E. 1993. *A History of Brazil*. 3rd ed. New York: Columbia University Press.

Busch, Jonah, and Kalifi Ferretti-Gallon. 2017. "What Drives Deforestation and What Stops It? A Meta-Analysis." *Review of Environmental Economics and Policy* 11 (1):3–23.

Butler, Rhett. 2014. "Brazil Rainforests Country Profile." *Mongabay.com*. http://rainforests.mongabay.com/20brazil.htm.

Butler, Rhett. 2017. "Calculating Deforestation Figures for the Brazilian Amazon." Mongabay.com, January 26, 2017. http://rainforests.mongabay.com/amazon/deforestation_calculations.html.

Buttel, Frederick H. 2000. "Ecological Modernization as Social Theory." *Geoforum* 31 (1):57–65.

Büscher, Bram, and Wolfram Dressler. 2007. "Linking Neoprotectionism and Environmental Governance: On the Rapidly Increasing Tensions between Actors in the Environment-Development Nexus." *Conservation and Society* 5 (4):586–611.

Campbell, Jeremy M. 2012a. "Between the Material and the Figural Road: The Incompleteness of Colonial Geographies in Amazonia." *Mobilities* 7 (4):481–500.

Campbell, Jeremy M. 2012b. "Brazil's Deferred Highway: Mobility, Development, and Anticipating the State in Amazonia." *Boletín de Antropología* 27 (44):102–126.

Campbell, Jeremy M. 2015. *Conjuring Property: Speculation and Environmental Futures in the Brazilian Amazon*. Seattle: University of Washington Press.

Campbell, Ullisses. 2006. "Pará Sofre a Violência no Campo." *Correio Braziliense*, November 5, 2006. http://www.amazonia.org.br/noticias/noticia.cfm?id=208352.

Campos, Luiz Otavio Oliveira. 1999. Pronunciamento de Luiz Otavio. Edited by PPB—Partido Progressista Brasileiro/PA. Brasilia: Senado Federal.

Campos, Marina T., and Daniel Nepstad. 2006b. "Smallholders, the Amazon's New Conservationists." *Conservation Biology* 20 (5):1553–1556.

Cardoso, Fernando H. 1979. "On the Characterization of Authoritarian Regimes in Latin America." In *The New Authoritarianism in Latin America*, edited by David Collier, 33–57. Princeton: Princeton University Press.

Cardoso, Fernando H., and Geraldo Müller. 2008 [1977]. *Amazônia: Expansão do Capitalismo*. São Paulo: Editora Brasiliense.

Carneiro da Cunha, Manuela Mauro W.B. Almeida. 2004. "Traditional Populations and Environmental Conservation." In *Biodiversity in the Brazilian Amazon*, edited by Adalberto Verissimo et al., 182–191. São Paulo: Instituto Socioambiental.

Carneiro da Cunha, Manuela, and Mauro W.B Almeida. 2000. "Indigenous People, Traditional People, and Conservation in the Amazon." *Daedlus* 129 (2):315–338.

Carrier, J.G., and D. Miller. 1998. *Virtualism: A New Political Economy*. Oxford: Berg.

Carter, Miguel. 2010. "The Landless Rural Workers Movement and Democracy in Brazil." *Latin American Research Review* 45 (S):186–217.

Carvalho, David Ferreira. 2002. "Industrialização Tardia e Grandes Projetos." In *Amazônia e a Crise de Modernização*, edited by Maria Angela D'Incao Isolda Maciel da Silveira, 427–446. Belém: Museu Paraense Emílio Goeldi.

Carvalho, G.O. 2006. "Environmental Resistance and the Politics of Energy Development in the Brazilian Amazon." *The Journal of Environment & Development* 15 (3):245–268.

Castro, Edna. 2002. "Processos de Trabalho e Relações de Poder no Carajás." In *Amazônia e a Crise de Modernização*, edited by Maria Angela D'Incao and Isolda Maciel de Silveira, 457–472. Belém: Museu Paraense Emílio Goeldi.

Castro, Edna. 2012. "Expansão da Fronteira, Megaprojetos de Infraestrutura e Integração Sul-Americana." *Caderno CRH* 25 (64):45–61.

Castro, João Augusto de Araujo. 2004. "Environment and Development: The Case of the Developing Countries." In *Green Planet Blues: Environmental Politics from Stockholm to Rio*, edited by Ken Conca and Geoffrey Dabelko, 29–36. Boulder: Westview Press.

Castro, João Augusto de Araujo. 2015 (1992). "Environment and Development: The Case of the Developing Countries." In *Green Planet Blues*, edited by Ken Conca and Geoffrey Dabaelko, 30–37. Boulder: Westview Press.

Chernela, Janet. 2005. "The Politics of Mediation: Local-Global Interactions in the Central Amazon of Brazil." *American Anthropologist* 107 (4):620–631.

Christoff, Peter. 1996. "Ecological Modernization: Ecological Modernities." *Environmental Politics* 5 (3):476–500.

Cicogna, Marcelo Augusto. 2004. "Sistema de suporte a decisão para o planejamento e a programação da operação de sistemas de energia elétrica." PhD, Engenharia Elétrica (Electrical Engineering), UNICAMP.

Clark, Dana, Jonathan Fox, and Kay Treakle, eds. 2003. *Demanding Accountability: Civil-Society Claims and the World Bank Inspection Panel*. Lanham and Oxford: Rowman & Littlefield.

Cleary, David. 1991. "The Greening of the Amazon." In *Environment and Development in Latin America: The Politics of Sustainablilty*, edited by David Goodman and Michael Redclift, 116–140. Manchester: Manchester University Press.

Cleary, David. 1993. "After the Frontier: Problems with the Political Economy in the Modern Brazilian Amazon." *Journal of Latin American Studies* 25 (2):331–349.

Clement, Charles R. 2006. "Demand for Two Classes of Traditional Agroecological Knowledge in Modern Amazonia." In *Human Impacts on Amazonia: The Role of Traditional Ecological Knowledge*, edited by Darrell Addison Posey and Michael J. Balick, 33–50. New York: Columbia University Press.

Clüsener-Godt, M., and Ignacy Sachs. 1995. "Introduction." In *Brazilian Perspectives On Sustainable Development of the Amazon Region*, edited by M. Clüsener-Godt, M., and Ignacy Sachs, 1–8. Paris and New York: UNESCO and the Parthenon Publishing Group.

CNN. 2014. "Manaus World Cup Stadium Suffers Third Death." February 7, 2014. https://edition.cnn.com/2014/02/07/sport/football/football-manaus-stadium-world-cup-death/index.html.

Collier, David. 1979. "Overview of the Bureaucratic-Authoritarian Model." In *The New Authoritarianism in Latin America*, edited by David Collier, 19–32. Princeton: Princeton University Press.

Conca, Ken. 2006. *Governing Water: Contentious Transnational Politics and Global Institution Building*. Boston: MIT Press.

Conectas. 2011. Belo Monte Case Brought to UN Human Rights Council. *Conectas* June 3, 2011. https://www.conectas.org/en/news/un-human-rights-council-concludes-its-17th-session

Conklin, Beth A., and Laura R. Graham. 1995. "The Shifting Middle Ground: Amazonian Indians and Eco-Politics." *American Anthropologist* 97 (4):695–710.

Cook, Sarah, and Kiah Smith. 2012. "Introduction: Green Economy and Sustainable Development: Bringing Back the 'Social'." *Development* 55 (1):5–9.

CPI (Comissão Parlamentar de Inquérito). 2001. Ocupação de Terras públicas na Região Amazônica: Relatório da Comissão Parlamentar de Inquérito Destinada a Investigar a Ocupação de Terras Públicas na Região Amazônica. Brasília: Comissão Parlamentar de Inquérito, Câmara dos Deputados.

Cornwall, Andrea, and Deborah Eade, eds. 2010. *Deconstructing Development Discourse: Buzzwords and Fuzzwords*. Warwickshire: Oxfam/Practical Action Publishing, Ltd.

Corrêa, Roberto Lobato. 1987. "A Periodização da Rede Urbana da Amazônia." *Revista Brasileira de Geografia* 49 (3):39–68.

Costa, Flávio. 2011. "A Violência que Veio com a Usina." *Isto É*, December 16, 2011.

Couto, Marlen. 2016. "Conflito agrário pode levar Força Nacional ao Pará." *O Globo*, July 30, 2016. http://oglobo.globo.com/brasil/conflito-agrario-pode-levar-forca-nacional-ao-para-19815560#ixzz4LTPAlO1G.

CPT. 2015. Conflitos no Campo 2015. Goiânia: Comissão Pastoral da Terra.

Cromberg, Marina. 2014. "Local Participation in REDD+: Lessons from the Eastern Brazilian Amazon." *Forests* 5 (4):579–598.

Cronkleton, Peter et al. 2008. *Environmental Governance and the Emergence of Forest-Based Social Movements*. Bogor: Center for International Forestry Research (CIFOR).

Cronon, William. 1995. "The Trouble with Wilderness, or, Getting Back to the Wrong Nature." In *Uncommon Ground: Rethinking the Human Place in Nature*, edited by William Cronon, 69–90. New York: W.W Norton.

Cruickshank, Emlyn W, Kirsty Schneeberger, and Nadine Smith, eds. 2012. *A pocket guide to sustainable development governance, second edition*, edited by Commonwealth Secretariat Stakeholder Forum. 2nd ed. London: Commonwealth Secretariat.

Cunha, Euclides da. 2000. *Um Paraíso Perdido. Ensaios Amazônicos*. Brasília: Senado Federal.

Cunningham, Nick. 2014. "Brazil's Petrobras Ramps Up Production of Pre-Salt Oil." *Oilprice.com*, August 11, 2014. http://oilprice.com/Energy/Crude-Oil/Brazils-Petrobras-Ramps-Up-Production-of-Pre-Salt-Oil.html.

da Costa Ferreira, Leila, and Sergio B. F. Tavolaro. 2008. "Environmental Concerns in Contemporary Brazil: An Insight into Some Theoretical and Societal Backgrounds (1970s–1990s)." *International Journal of Politics, Culture, and Society* 19 (3-4):161–177.

da Fonseca, Patricia Galindo, and Antoine Bourgoignie. 2011. "The Belo Monte Dam Case." *Environmental Policy and Law* 41 (2):104–107.

Da Matta, Roberto. 1987. "The Quest for Citizenship in a Relational Universe." In *State and Society in Brazil*, edited by J. D. Wirth, E. O. Nunes and T. E. Bogenschild, 318–319. Boulder: Westview.

da Silva, Luiz Inácio. 2010. Speech by Pres. Lula at a rally for the Belo Monte Dam. Altamira: International Rivers Network.

Davidov, Veronica. 2013. "Amazonia as Pharmacopia." *Critique of Anthropology* 33 (3):243–262.

Davidson, E.A., A.C. de Araujo, P. Artaxo, J.K. Balch, I.F. Brown, C. Bustamante MM, et al. 2012. "The Amazon Basin in Transition." *Nature* 481 (7381):321–328. 17.

Davis, Wade. 1996. *One River: Explorations and Discoveries in the Amazon Rainforest*. New York: Simon & Schuster.

de Barros, João. 2005. "O Maior Grileiro do Mundo." *Caros Amigos* 9 (102):26–33.

de Lima, Ismar Borges, and Leszek Buszynski. 2011. "Local Environmental Governance, Public Policies and Deforestation in Amazonia." *Management of Environmental Quality* 22 (3):292–316.

de Magalhães Lima, Deborah. 1999. "A Construção Histórica do Termo Caboclo: Sobre Estruturas e Representações Sociais no Meio Rural Amazônico." *Novos Cadernos NAEA* 2 (2):5–32.

de Oliveira, Francisco. 2002. "A Reconquista da Amazônia." In *Amazônia e a Crise de Modernização*, edited by Maria Angela D'Incao and Isolda Maciel da Silveira, 85–95. Belém: Museu Paraense Emílio Goeldi.

De Onis, Juan. 1992. *The Green Cathedral: Sustainable Development in Amazonia*. New York: Oxford University Press.

de Sousa Júnior, Wilson Cabral, and John Reid. 2010. "Uncertainties in Amazon Hydropower Development: Risk Scenarios and Environmental Issues Around the Belo Monte Dam." *Water Alternatives* 3 (2):249–268.

de Sousa Júnior, Wilson Cabral, John Reid, and Neidja Cristine Silvestre Leitão. 2006. *Custos e Benefícios do Complexo Hidrelétrico Belo Monte: Uma abordagem econômico ambiental*. Arcata: Conservation Strategy Fund.

de Souza Martins, José. 1975. *Capitalismo e Tradicionalismo: Estudos sobre as Contradições da Sociedade Agrária no Brasil*. São Paulo: Livraria Pioneira Editora.

Dean, Warren. 1987. *Brazil and the Struggle for Rubber: A Study in Environmental History*. Cambridge: Cambridge University Press.

Dear, John. 2007. "Sr. Dorothy Stang, Martyr of the Amazon." *National Catholic Reporter*, October 2, 2007, On the Road to Peace. https://www.ncronline.org/blogs/road-peace/sr-dorothy-stang-martyr-amazon.

Delmas, Magali A., and Oran Young, eds. 2009. *Governance For The Environment: New Perspectives*. Cambridge: Oxford University Press.

Dingwerth, Klaus. 2005. "The Democratic Legitimacy of Public–Private Rule Making: What Can We Learn from the World Commission on Dams?" *Global Governance* 11 (1):65–83.

Diversi, Marcelo. 2014. "Damming the Amazon: The Postcolonial March of the Wicked West." *Cultural Studies ↔ Critical Methodologies* 14 (3):242–246.

Dore, Elizabeth. 1996. "Capitalism and Ecological Crisis: Legacy of the 1980s." In *Green Guerrillas: Enviromental Conflicts and Initiatives in Latin America and the Caribbean*, edited by Helen Collinson, 8–19. London: Latin American Bureau.

Dornelas, Pe. Nelito Nonato. 2006. "A Identidade das CEBs." *Vida Pastoral*, 47 (248):3–5.

dos Santos, Eduardo. 2017. "Hydropower Can Work for Everyone's Good." *The Guardian*, May 31, 2017, Letters. https://www.theguardian.com/theguardian/2017/may/31/hydropower-can-work-for-everyones-good.

Doty, Roxanne Lynn. 1996. *Imperial Encounters: The Politics of Representation in North–South Relations*. Minneapolis: University of Minnesota Press.

Dreifuss, René Armand. 1981. *1964, A Conquista do Estado: Ação política, poder e golpe de classe*. Petrópolis: Vozes.

Duffy, Gary. 2007. "Brazil announces new oil reserves." *BBC*, November 9, 2007. http://news.bbc.co.uk/2/hi/americas/7086264.stm.

ECOPLAN Engenharia Ltda. 2002. Relatório de Impacto Ambiental: Pavimentação BR163-BR230 (Environmental Impact Study: Paving BR-163-BR-230). Porto Alegre: Departamento Nacional de Infra-Estrutura de Transportes (DNIT). http://www.dnit.gov.br/download/meio-ambiente/acoes-e-atividades/estudos-ambientais/br-230-163-pa-.pdf

Eicher, Carl K., and John M. Staatz, eds. 1990. *Agricultural Development in the Third World*. Baltimore: Johns Hopkins University Press.

Eletronorte. 2002. "Complexo Hidrelétrico de Belo Monte–Estudos de Viabilidade-Relatório Final." Volumes 1 and 2. Brasília: EPE/MME.

Elizondo, Gabriel. 2009. "Kaipaó Protest in Brazil Against Dams." *Al Jazeera* October 29, 2009. http://blogs.aljazeera.com/blog/americas/kaipa%C3%B3-protest-brazil-against-dams.

Elizondo, Gabriel. 2012. Dam it: Brazil's Belo Monte Stirs Controversy. *Al Jazeera*, January 20, 2012. https://www.aljazeera.com/indepth/features/2012/01/201212015366764400.html

Escada, Maria Isabel Sobral et al. 2005. "Processos de Ocupação nas Novas Fronteiras da Amazônia: O Intervfluvio do Xingu-Iriri." *Dossiê Amazônia Brasileira II, Estudos Avançados* 19 (54):9–23.

Escobar, Arturo. 1995. *Encountering Development: The making and unmaking of the Third World*. Princeton: Princeton University Press.

Escobar, Arturo. 2010. "Latin America at a Crossroads." *Cultural Studies* 24 (1):1–65.

Espach, Ralph H. 2002. "The Brazilian Amazon in Strategic Perspective." In *Woodrow Wilson Center Reports on the Americas*, edited by Joseph S. Tulchin and Heather A. Golding, 1–30. Washington, DC: Woodrow Wilson Center for International Scholars.

Esterci, Neide. 2003. "A Luta Pela Terra e a Função Ambiental da Propriedade." In *Reforma Agrária e Meio Ambiente*, edited by Neide Esterci and Raul Silva Telles do Valle, 9–18. São Paulo: Instituto Socioambiental.

Esteva, Gustavo. 1992. "Development." In *The Development Dictionary*, edited by Ignacy Sachs, 6–25. London: Zed Books.

Evans, Peter. 1979. *Dependent Development: The Alliance of Multinational, State, and Local Capital in Brazil*. Princeton: Princeton University Press.

Evans, Peter B. 2002. "Introduction: Looking for Agents of Urban Liveability in a Globalized Political Economy." In *Liveable Cities? Urban Struggles for Livelihood and Sustainability*, edited by Peter B. Evans, 1–30. Berkeley: University of California Press.

Experts Panel. 2009. Análise Crítica do Estudo de Impacto Ambiental do Aproveitamento Hidrelétrico de Belo Monte, edited by Sônia Maria Simões Barbosa Magalhães Santos and Francisco del Moral Hernandez. Belém.

Fearnside, Philip M. 1984. "Brazil's Amazon Settlement Schemes: Conflicting Objectives and Human Carrying Capacity." *Habitat International* 8 (1):45–61.

Fearnside, Philip M. 2002. "Avança Brasil: Environmental and Social Consequences of Brazil's Planned Infrastructure in Amazonia." *Environmental Management* 30 (6):735–747.

Fearnside, P.M. 2005. "Dams in the Amazon: Belo Monte and Brazil's Hydroelectric Development of the Xingu River Basin." *Environmental Management* 38 (1):16–27.

Fearnside, Philip M. 2007a. "Brazil's Cuiabá- Santarém (BR-163) Highway: The Environmental Cost of Paving a Soybean Corridor Through the Amazon." *Environmental Management* 39 (5):601–614.

Fearnside, Philip M. 2007b. "Deforestation in Amazonia." In *Encyclopedia of the Earth*, edited by Mryka Hall-Beyer. http://www.eoearth.org/article/Deforestation_in_Amazonia

Fearnside, Philip M. 2008. "The Roles and Movements of Actors in the Deforestation of Brazilian Amazonia." *Ecology and Society* 13 (1):23–45.

Fearnside, Philip M. 2012a. Belo Monte Dam: A spearhead for Brazil's dam building attack on Amazonia? Canberra: Global Water Forum.

Fearnside, Philip M. 2012b. "Brazil's Amazon Forest in Mitigating Global Warming: Unresolved Controversies." *Climate Policy* 12 (1):70–81.

Fearnside, Philip M. 2013. "Carbon Credit for Hydroelectric Dams as a Source of Greenhouse-gas Emissions: The Example of Brazil's Teles Pires Dam." *Mitigation and Adaptation Strategies for Global Change* 18 (5):691–699.

Fearnside, Philip M. 2016a. "Environmental Policy in Brazilian Amazonia: Lessons from Recent History." *Novos Cadernos NAEA* 19 (1):27–46.

Fearnside, Philip M. 2016b. "Greenhouse Gas Emissions from Brazil's Amazonian Hydroelectric Dams." *Environmental Research Letters* 11 (1):011002.

Feitosa, Orange Matos, and Alexandre Macchione Saes. 2013. "The Rubber Defense Plan: Between 'Developmentalism' and Policy Neglect in the Northern Brazil, 1900-1915." *América Latina en la historia económica* 20 (3):138–168.

Ferguson, James. 1994. *The Anti-politics Machine: "Development," Depoliticization, and Bureaucratic Power in Lesotho*. Minneapolis: University of Minnesota Press.

Ferguson, James. 1999. *Expectations of Modernity: Myths and Meanings of Urban Life on the Zambian Copperbelt*. Berkeley: University of California Press.

Fernandes, Florestan. 1975. *A revolução burguesa no Brasil: Ensaio de interpretação sociológica*. Rio de Janeiro: Zahar.

Ferreira, J., L.E.O.C. Aragão, J. Barlow, P. Barreto, E. Berenguer, M. Bustamante, et al. 2014. "Brazil's Environmental Leadership at Risk." *Science* 346 (6210):706–707.

Fiechter, Georges-André. 1975. *Brazil Since 1964: Modernisation under a Military Régime*. Translated by Alan Braley. New York: Halsted Press, John Wiley.

Finer, Matt, and Clinton N. Jenkins. 2012. "Proliferation of Hydroelectric Dams in the Andean Amazon and Implications for Andes-Amazon Connectivity." *PLOS ONE* 7 (4):e35126.

Fisher, William. 1996. "Native Amazonians and the Making of the Amazonian Wilderness: From Discourse of Riches to Sloth and Underdevelopment." In *Creating the Countryside: The Politics of Rural and Environmental Discourse*, edited by E. Melanie Dupuis and Peter Vandergeest, 166–203. Philadelphia: Temple University Press.

Flanders, Stephanie. 1997. "Truce Called in Battle of the Dams." *Financial Times*. April 14, 1997.

Flaskerud, George. 2003. Brazil's Soybean Production and Impact. Fargo: North Dakota State University Extension Service.

Fonseca, Antônio, Marcelo Justino, Carlos Souza Jr., and Adalberto Veríssimo. 2015. *Deforestation Report for the Brazilian Amazon*. Belém: Imazon.

Font, Mauricio A. 2003. *Transforming Brazil: A Reform Era in Perspective*. New York: Rowman & Littlefield.

Forsyth, Tim. 2008. "Political Ecology and the Epistemology of Social Justice." *Geoforum* 39:756–764.

Foweraker, Joe. 1981. *The Struggle for Land: A Political Economy of the Pioneer Frontier in Brazil from 1930 to the Present Day*. Cambridge: Cambridge University Press.

Franco, Roberto Messias. 1995. "Development and Management Plans for the Amazon Region: Lessons from the past, proposals for the future." In *Brazilian Perspectives on Sustainable Development of the Amazon Region*, edited by M. Clusener-Godt and Ignacy Sachs, 23–51. Paris: UNESCO.

Freire, Paulo. 1970. *Pedagogy of the Oppressed*. 30th Anniversary Edition ed. New York: Continuum.

Friedman-Rudovsky, Jean. 2012. "In Bolivia, A Battle Over A Highway and a Way of Life." *Environment 360*, August 27, 2012,. http://e360.yale.edu/feature/in_bolivia_a_battle_over_a_highway_and_a_way_of_life/2566/.

Fujikura, Ryo, and Mikiyasu Nakayama. 2009. "Lessons Learned from the World Commission on Dams." *International Environmental Agreements: Politics, Law and Economics* 9 (2):173–190.

FUNAI. 2009. Parecer Técnico edited by FUNAI: Government of Brazil.

Furley, Peter A. 1994. *The Forest Frontier: settlement and change in Brazilian Roraima*. New York: Routledge.

Furtado, Celso. 1962. *A Pré-revolução Brasileira*. Rio de Janeiro: Fundo de Cultura.

Galvao, Andea. 2014. "The Brazilian Labor Movement under PT Governments." *Latin American Perspectives* 41 (5):184–199.

Garcia-Navarro, Lourdes. 2015. "Brazil's World Cup Legacy Includes $550M Stadium-Turned-Parking Lot." May 11, 2015. *All Things Considered* NPR. https://www.

npr.org/sections/parallels/2015/05/11/405955547/brazils-world-cup-legacy-includes-550m-stadium-turned-parking-lot.

Garfield, Seth. 2001. *Indigenous Struggle at the Heart of Brazil: State Policy, Frontier Expansion, and the Xavante Indians, 1937-1988*. Durham: Duke University Press.

Garfield, Seth. 2013. *In Search of the Amazon: Brazil, the United States, and the Nature of a Region, American Encounters/Global Interactions*. Durham: Duke University Press.

Gauld, Charles Anderson. 1964. *The Last Titan: Percival Farquhar, American Entrepreneur in Latin America*. Palo Alto: Institute of Hispanic American and Luso-Brazilian Studies, Stanford University.

Geromel, Ricardo. 2013. "Meet Blairo Maggi: From Soybean King to Politician to One of the World's Most Powerful People to Tree Hugger." *Forbes*, November 8, 2013. https://www.forbes.com/sites/ricardogeromel/2013/11/08/meet-blairo-maggi-from-soybean-king-to-politician-to-one-of-the-worlds-most-powerful-people-to-tree-hugger/#4a70c2f63674

Gheerbrant, Alain. 1953. *The Impossible Adventure; Journey to the Far Amazon*. Translated by Edward Fitzgerald. London: Gollancz. Original edition, L'expédition Orénoque Amazone, 1948–1950.

Ghosh, Amitav. 2016. *The Great Derangement*. Chicago: University of Chicago Press.

Giaimo, Michael. 1988. "Deforestation in Brazil: Domestic Political Imperative—Global Ecological Disaster." *Environmental Law* 18:537–570.

Gibson-Graham, J.K. 1996. *The End of Capitalism (as we knew it): A Feminist Critique of Political Economy*. Oxford and Cambridge: Blackwell Publishers.

Gibson-Graham, J.K. 2006. *A Postcapitalist Politics*. Minneapolis: University of Minnesota Press.

Giddens, Anthony. 1990. *The Consequences of Modernity*. Palo Alto: Stanford University Press.

Global, Justiça. 2014. Situação do Direito de Acesso a Justiça e a Suspensão de Decisões Judiciais (ação de suspensão de segurança no Brasil) (The Situation of the Right of Access to Justice and the Suspension of Judicial Decisions). edited by 150th Ordinary Session of the Inter-American Commission on Human Rights (March 2014). Washington, DC: Inter-American Commission on Human Rights.

Godar, Javier, Toby A. Gardnera, E. Jorge Tizadob, and Pablo Pacheco. 2014. "Actor-Specific Contributions to the Deforestation Slowdown in the Brazilian Amazon." *Proceedings of the National Academy of Sciences* 111 (43):15591–15596.

Godar, Javier, Emilio Jorge Tizado, and Benno Pokorny. 2012. "Who is Responsible for Deforestation in the Amazon? A Spatially Explicit Analysis Along the Transamazon Highway in Brazil." *Forest Ecology and Management* 267 (0):58–73.

Godar, Javier, Emilio Jorge Tizado, Benno Pokorny, and James Johnson. 2012. "Typology and Characterization of Amazon Colonists: A Case Study Along the Transamazon Highway." *Human Ecology* 40 (2):251–267.

Goldman, Michael. 2005. *Imperial Nature: The World Bank and Struggles for Social Justice in the Age of Globalization, Yale Agrarian Studies Series*. New Haven: Yale University Press.

Goodland, Robert, and Howard S. Irwin. 1975. *Amazon Jungle: Green Hell to Red Desert?: An Ecological Discussion of the Environmental Impact of the Highway Construction Program in the Amazon Basin*. Amsterdam: Elsevier Scientific Publishers.

Graeber, David. 2012. "On Social Currencies and Human Economies: Some Notes on the Violence of Equivalence." *Social Anthropology* 20 (4):411–428.

Graeff, Bibiana. 2012. "Should we Adopt a Specific Regulation to Protect People that are Displaced by Hydroelectric Projects? Reflections Based on Brazilian Law and the "Belo Monte Case"." *Florida A & M Law Review* 7 (2):261–288.

Gramsci, Antonio. 1971. *Selections From The Prison Notebooks Of Antonio Gramsci*. Translated by Quintin Hoare and Geoffrey Nowell Smith. New York: International Publishers.

Grandin, Greg. 2009. *Fordlândia: The Rise and Fall of Henry Ford's Forgotten Jungle City*. New York: Metropolitan Books.

Greenpeace. 2003. State of Conflict: An Investigation into the Landgrabbers, Loggers and Lawless Frontiers in Pará State, Amazon. Greenpeace: Netherlands. https://www.greenpeace.org/usa/wp-content/uploads/legacy/Global/usa/report/2007/8/state-of-conflict.pdf.

Greenpeace. 2006. "Eating Up the Amazon." April 21, 2006. Greenpeace: Netherlands. https://www.greenpeace.org/usa/wp-content/uploads/legacy/Global/usa/report/2010/2/eating-up-the-amazon.pdf.

Grindle, Merilee S. 2011. "Good Enough Governance Revisited." *Development Policy Review* 29:s199–s221.

Group, World Bank. 2011. Energizing Sustainable Development: Energy Sector Strategy of the World Bank Group. edited by Committee on Development Effectiveness. Washington, DC: World Bank.

Grupo de Trabalho Interministerial. 2005. Plano de Ação para Prevenção e Controle sobre Desmatamento na Amazônia. Brasilia, DF: Ministerio do Meio Ambiente.

Gudynas, Eduardo. 2011. "Buen Vivir: Today's Tomorrow." *Development* 54 (4):441–447.

Gudynas, Eduardo. 2016. "Beyond Varieties of Development: Disputes and Alternatives." *Third World Quarterly* 37 (4):721–732.

Haidar, D., and V. Gorczeski. 2016. "Delação da Andrade Gutierrez mostra um belo monte de propinas." *Época*, April 8, 2016. http://epoca.globo.com/tempo/noticia/2016/04/delacao-da-andrade-gutierrez-mostra-um-belo-monte-de-propinas.html.

Haidar, Daniel. 2012. "Manifestantes depredam escritório de hidrelétrica de Belo Monte." *O Globo*, June 16, 2012, Rio +20. http://oglobo.globo.com/economia/rio20/manifestantes-depredam-escritorio-de-hidreletrica-de-belo-monte-5230223#ixzz3GQrJhD2k.

Hajer, Maarten A. 1993. "Discourse Coalitions and the Institutionalization of Practice: The Case of Acid Rain in Britain." In *The Argumentative Turn in Policy Analysis and Planning*, edited by Frank Fisher and John Forester, 43–76. Durham: Duke University Press.

Hajer, Maarten A. 1995. *The Politics of Environmental Discourse: Ecological Modernization and the Policy Process*. Oxford: Oxford University Press.

Hall, A. 2008. "Better RED than Dead: Paying the People for Environmental Services in Amazonia." *Philosophical Transcripts of the Royal Society of London, B: Biological Sciences* 363 (1498):1925–1932.

Hall, A., and S. Branford. 2012. "Development, Dams and Dilma: the Saga of Belo Monte." *Critical Sociology* 38 (6):851–862.

Hall, Anthony, ed. 2000. *Amazonia At The Crossroads: The Challenge Of Sustainable Development*. London: Institute of Latin American Studies.

Hall, Anthony L. 1989. *Developing Amazonia: Deforestation and Social Conflict in Brazil's Carajás Programme*. Manchester: Manchester University Press.

Hall, Anthony L. 1996. "Did Chico Mendes Die In Vain? Rubber Tappers and Lessons of the 1990s." In *Green Guerrillas: Environmental Conflicts and Initiatives in Latin America and the Caribbean*, edited by Helen Collinson, 93–102. London: Latin American Bureau.

Hall, Stuart. 1996. "On Postmodernism and Articulation: An Interview with Stuart Hall." In *Stuart Hall: Critical Dialogues in Cultural Studies*, edited by David Morley and Kuan-Hsing Chen, 45–60. London: Routledge.

Hamelin, Francisco. 1991. "O Fracasso Anunciado." In *Amazônia: A Fronteira Agrícola 20 Anos Depois*, edited by Philippe Léna and Adélia Engrácia de Oliveira, 161–176. Belém: Museu Paraense Enílio Goeldi.

Hardenburg, Walter Earnest. 1912. *The Putumayo, The Devil's Paradise: Travels in the Peruvian Amazon Region and an Account of the Atrocities Committed upon the Indians Therein*. London: T. Fisher Unwin.

Harlow, John, Aaron Golub, and Braden Allenby. 2013. "A Review of Utopian Themes in Sustainable Development Discourse." *Sustainable Development* 21 (4):270–280.

Harris, Mark. 2006. "Peasant Riverine Economies and Their Impact in the Lower Amazon." In *Human Impacts on Amazonia*, edited by Darrel Addison Balick Posey, Michael J, 222–237. New York: Columbia University.

Harvey, David. 1996. *Justice, Nature, and the Geography of Difference*. Oxford: Blackwell.

Hecht, Susanna. 2005. "Soybeans, Development and Conservation on the Amazon Frontier." *Development and Change* 36 (2):375–404.

Hecht, Susanna. 2007. "Factories, Forests, Fields and Family: Gender and Neoliberalism in Extractive Reserves." *Journal of Agrarian Change* 7 (3):316–347.

Hecht, Susanna. 2011a. "The New Amazonian Geographies: Insurgent Citizenship, 'Amazon Nation' and the Politics of Environmentalism." *Journal of Cultural Geography* 28 (1):203–223.

Hecht, Susanna. 2011b. "From Eco-Catastrophe to Zero Deforestation? Interdisciplinarities, Politics, Environmentalisms and Reduced Clearing in Amazonia." *Environmental Conservation* 39 (01):4–19.

Hecht, Susanna B. 2013. *Scramble for the Amazon and the "Lost Paradise" of Euclides da Cunha*. Chicago: University of Chicago Press.

Hecht, Susanna B. 2014. "Forests Lost and Found in Tropical Latin America: The Woodland 'Green Revolution'." *The Journal of Peasant Studies* 41 (5):877–909.

Hecht, Susanna, and Alexander Cockburn. 1990. *The Fate of the Forest: Developers, Destroyers, and Defenders of the Amazon*. New York: Harper & Row Publishers.

Hecht, Susanna, K.D. Morrison, and C. Padoch. 2014. *The Social Lives of Forests: Past, Present, and Future of Woodland Resurgence*. Chicago: University of Chicago Press.

Hecht, Susanna, Richard Norgaard, and Georgio Possio. 1988. "The Economics of Cattle Ranching in Eastern Amazonia." *Interciência* 13 (5):233–240.

Heckenberger, Michael, J. Christian Russell, Carlos Fausto, Joshua R. Toney, Morgan J. Schmidt, Edithe Pereira, et al. 2008. "Pre-Columbian Urbanism, Anthropogenic Landscapes, and the Future of the Amazon." *Science* 321:1214–1217.

Hedrén, Johan, and Björn-Ola Linnér. 2009a. "Utopian Thought and Sustainable Development." *Futures* 41 (4):197–200.

Hedrén, Johan, and Björn-Ola Linnér. 2009b. "Utopian Thought and the Politics of Sustainable Development." *Futures* 41 (4):210–219.

Hemming, John 2006. "Romance and Reality: The First European Vision of Brazilian Indians." In *Human Impacts on Amazonia*, edited by Darrell Addison Posey and Michael J. Balick, 5–16. New York: Columbia University Press.

Hempel, Lamont C. 1995. *Environmental Governance: the global challenge*. Washington DC: Island Press.

Hepple, Leslie W. 1992. "Metaphor, Geopolitical Discourse, and the Military in South America." In *Writing Worlds: Discourse, Text and Metaphor in the Representation of Landscape*, edited by Trevor J. Barnes and James S. Dunken, 136–154. New York: Routledge.

Hernandez, Francisco Del Moral. 2012. "Hydropower in the Amazon: Renewability and Non-Renewability of Energy Policy. What is Desired the Search for Renewable Energy Conversion Why not Renew the Energy Policy as Well?" *Boletin do Museu Paraense Emílio Goeldi. Ciências Humanas*. 7 (3):791–811.

Hetherington, Kregg, and Jeremy M. Campbell. 2014. "Nature, Infrastructure, and the State: Rethinking Development in Latin America." *The Journal of Latin American and Caribbean Anthropology* 19 (2):191–194.

Higbee, Edward C. 1951. "Of Man and the Amazon." *Geographical Review* 41 (3):401–420.

Hobson, Kersty. 2013. "On the Making of the Environmental Citizen." *Environmental Politics* 22 (1):56–72.

Hochstetler, Kathryn. 2002. "After the Boomerang: Environmental Movements and Politics in the La Plata River Basin." *Global Environmental Politics* 2 (4):35–57.

Hochstetler, Kathryn. 2011. "The Politics of Environmental Licensing: Energy Projects of the Past and Future in Brazil." *Studies in Comparative International Development (SCID)* 46 (4):349–371.

Hochstetler, Kathryn, and Margaret E. Keck. 2007. *Greening Brazil*. Durham: Duke University Press.

Hochstetler, Kathryn, and Margaret E. Keck. 2008. "Creative Approaches to Preserving Biodiversity in Brazil and the Amazon." In *Saving Biological Diversity*, edited by Robert A. Askins, Glenn Dryer, Gerald Visgilio and Diana Whitelaw, 177–186. New York: Springer.

Hochstetler, Kathryn, and Alfred P. Montero. 2013. "The Renewed Developmental State: The National Development Bank and the Brazil Model." *Journal of Development Studies* 49 (11):1484–1499.

Hochstettler, Kathryn, and Margaret Keck. 2007. *Greening Brazil: Environmental Activism in State and Society*. Durham: Duke University Press.

Hoelle, Jeffrey. 2015. *Rainforest Cowboys: The rise of ranching and cattle culture in Western Amazonia*. Austin: University of Texas Press.

Human Rights Watch. 2014. *World Report 2014: Events of 2013*. United States: Human Rights Watch.

Human Rights Watch. 2017. Brazil: Events of 2016. New York: Human Rights Watch.

Hurrell, Andrew. 1992. "Brazil and the International Politics of Amazonian Deforestation." In *The International Politics of the Environment*, edited by Andrew Hurrell and Barbara Kingsbury, 398–429. Oxford: Clarendon.

Ianni, Octavio. 1979. *Colonização e Contra-Reforma Agrária na Amazônia, Coleção Sociologia brasileira*. Petrópolis: Vozes.

Ianni, Octávio. 1975. *O Colapso do Populismo no Brasil*. Rio de Janeiro: Civilização Brasiliera.

IBAMA. 2010. Análise técnica das complementações solicitadas no Parecer nº 114/2009, referente ao Aproveitamento Hidrelétrico Belo Monte. Brasília: Government of Brazil. https://ox.socioambiental.org/sites/default/files/ficha-tecnica//node/202/edit/2019-02/RELAT%C3%93RIO_PROCESSO_LICENCIAMENTO_LI.pdf.

IBGE (Conselho Nacional de Geografia). 1942. *Goiânia, coletânea especialmente editada.* Rio de Janeiro: Serviço gráfico do Instituto Brasileiro de Geografia e Estatística.

INCRA. 1973. "Propõe-se a Rever Política Para Amazônia." *Journal do Brasil*, February 20, 1973.

INPE (Instituto Nacional de Pesquisas Espaciais). 2012. Desmatamento por Município. São Paulo: PRODES/DPI. http://www.dpi.inpe.br/prodesdigital/municipios.html

Instituto SocioAmbiental. 2007. "Basta de Promessas! Sociedade civil exige implantação imediata do Plano BR-163 Sustentável." *Notícias Socioambientais*, June 15, 2007. https://site-antigo.socioambiental.org/nsa/detalhe?id=2483.

International Energy Agency. 2013. *World Energy Outlook*. OECD/IEA. Paris: International Energy Agency.

International Rivers. 2012. Belo Monte Massive Dam Project Strikes at the Heart of the Amazon. Fact Sheet, May, 2012. https://www.internationalrivers.org/sites/default/files/attached-files/Belo_Monte_FactSheet_May2012.pdf.

IPAM. 2006. *A Grilagem de Terras Públicas na Amazônia Brasileira*. Vol. 8, Série Estudos. Brasília: MMA.

IRENA. 2015. Renewable Energy Policy Brief: Brazil. Abu Dhabi: International Renewable Energy Agency.

ISA. 2008. Criacao da Resex do Médio Xingu marca Dia Mundial do Meio Ambiente. June 5, 2008. *Instituto SocioAmbiental*. https://nuestrosparques.info/en/noticia/56971.

IUCN. 1980. *World Conservation Strategy: Living resource conservation for sustainable development*. Geneva: IUCN. https://portals.iucn.org/library/efiles/documents/wcs-004.pdf.

Ivanova, Maria. 2003. "Partnerships, International Organizations, and Global Environmental Governance." In *Progress or Peril? Partnerships and Networks in Global Environmental Governance: The Post-Johannesburg Agenda*, edited by J.M. Witte, C. Streck and T. Brenner, 9–36. Washington, DC: Global Policy Institute.

Jackson, Joe. 2008. *The Thief at the End of the World: Rubber, Power, and the Seeds of Empire*. New York: Penguin Group.

Jaichand, Vinodh, and Alexandre Andrade Sampaio. 2013. "Dam and Be Damned: The Adverse Impacts of Belo Monte on Indigenous Peoples in Brazil." *Human Rights Quarterly* 35 (2):408–447.

Jampolsky, Jacquelyn Amour. 2012. "Activism is the New Black! Demonstrating the Benefits of International Celebrity Activism Through James Cameron's Campaign Against the Belo Monte Dam." *Colorado Journal of International Environmental Law and Policy* 23 (1):227–256.

Jordan, Andrew, Rüdiger K.W. Wurzel, and Anthony Zito. 2005. "The Rise of 'New' Policy Instruments in Comparative Perspective: Has Governance Eclipsed Government?" *Political Studies* 53 (3):477–496.

Jr., Saturnino M. Borras. 2003. "Questioning Market-Led Agrarian Reform: Experiences from Brazil, Colombia and South Africa." *Journal of Agrarian Change* 3 (3):367–394.

Junior, Policarpo. 1999. "O Maior Latifundiário do Mundo." *Veja*, January 13, 1999.

Kanai, J.M., and R. da Silva Oliveira. 2014. "Paving (through) Amazonia: Neoliberal Urbanism and the Reperipheralization of Roraima." *Environment and Planning A* 46 (1):62–77.

Kanai, J. Miguel. 2016. "The Pervasiveness of Neoliberal Territorial Design: Cross-Border Infrastructure Planning in South America Since the Introduction of IIRSA." *Geoforum* 69:160–170.

Kauffman, Craig M. 2017. *Grassroots Global Governance: Local Watershed Management Experiments and the Evolution of Sustainable Development*. New York: Oxford University Press.

Kauffman, Craig M., and Pamela L. Martin. 2017. "Can Rights of Nature Make Development More Sustainable? Why Some Ecuadorian Lawsuits Succeed and Others Fail." *World Development* 92:130–142.

Keck, Margaret. 1995. "Social Equity and Environmental Politics in Brazil: Lessons from the Rubber Tappers of Acre." *Comparative Politics* 27 (4):409–424.

Keck, Margaret E. 1998. "Planafloro in Rondônia: The Limits of Leverage." In *The Struggle for Accountability: The World Bank, NGOs, and Grassroots Movements*, edited by Jonathan Fox and L. David Brown, 181–218. Cambridge: MIT Press.

Keck, Margaret, and Kathryn Sikkink. 1998. *Activists Beyond Borders*. Ithaca: Cornell University Press.

Kemp, René, Saeed Parto, and Robert Gibson. 2005. "Governance for Sustainable Development: Moving from Theory to Practice." *International Journal for Sustainable Development* 8 (1/2):12–29.

Khagram, Sanjeev. 2004. *Dams and Development: Transnational Struggles for Water and Power*. Ithaca, NY: Cornell University Press.

Killeen, Timothy. 2007. A Perfect Storm in the Amazon Wilderness: Development and Conservation in the Context of the Initiative for the Integration of the Regional Infrastructure of South America (IIRSA). Arlington: Conservation International. https://www.conservation.org/publications/Documents/Migrated%20Files/AABS.7_Perfect_Storm_English.low.res.pdf

Kimmerling, Judith. 2013. "Oil, Contact, and Conservation in the Amazon: Indigenous Huaorani, Chevron, and Yasuni." *Colorado Journal of International Environmental Law and Policy* 24 (1):43–115.

Kington, Tom. 2008. "Pavarotti Mimed at Final Performance." *The Guardian*, April 6, 2008, Classical music. http://www.theguardian.com/music/2008/apr/07/classicalmusicandopera.italy.

Kooiman, Jan. 1993. "Findings, Speculations and Recommendations." In *Modern Governance: New Government-Society Interactions*, edited by Jan Kooiman, 249–262. London: Sage.

La Freniere, Gilbert F. 1990. "Rousseau and the European Roots of Environmentalism." *Environmental History Review* 14 (4):41–72.

La Rovere, Emilio L., and F.E. Mendes. 2000. Tucuruí Hydropower Complex Brazil. In *A WCD case study prepared as an input to the World Commission on Dams*. Cape Town.

Langfur, Hal. 2014. Recovering Brazil's Indigenous Pasts." In *Native Brazil: Beyond the Convert and the Cannibal, 1500–1900*, edited by Hal Langfur, 1–28 Albuquerque: University of New Mexico Press.

Latour, Bruno. 1996. *Aramis, or the Love of Technology*. Translated by Catherine Porter. Cambridge: Harvard University Press.

Latour, Bruno. 1998. "To modernise or ecologise? That is the question." In *Remaking Reality: Nature at the Millennium*, edited by B. Braun and N. Castree, 221–242. London: Routledge.

Latour, Bruno. 2003. "Is Re-modernization Occurring—And if so, How to Prove it? A Commentary on Ulrich Beck." *Theory, Culture and Society* 20 (2):35–48.

Laurance, William F., A.K.M. Albernaz, P.M. Fearnside, H.L. Vasconcelos, and L.V. Ferreira. 2004. "Deforestation in Amazonia." *Science* 304 (5674):1109–1111.

le Breton, Binka. 2007. *The Greatest Gift: The Courageous Life and Martyrdom of Sister Dorothy Stang*. New York: Doubleday.

Le Tourneau, François-Michel, Guillaume Marchand, Anna Greissing, Stéphanie Nasuti, Martine Droulers, Marcel Bursztyn, et al. 2013. "Assessing the Impacts of Sustainable Development Projects in the Amazon: the DURAMAZ Experiment." *Sustainability Science* 8 (2):199–212.

Leahy, Joe. 2015. "BNDES: Leader of First Resort for Brazil's Tycoons." *Financial Times*, January 11, 2015. https://www.ft.com/content/c510368e-968e-11e4-922f-00144feabdc0.

Lefebvre, Henri. 1991 (1974). *The Production of Space*. Translated by Donald Nicholson-Smith. Oxford: Basil Blackwell.

Leslie, Jacques. 2005. *Deep Water: The epic struggle over dams, displaced people, and the environment*. New York: Picador.

Levins, R., and R. Lewontin. 1985. *The Dialectical Biologist*. Cambridge: Harvard University Press.

Lewis, Colin M. 1983. "The Financing of Railway Development in Latin America, 1850–1914." *Ibero-amerikanisches Archive* 9 (3/4):255–278.

Lewis, David. 2005. "Anthropology and Development: The Uneasy Relationship." In *Originally in A Handbook of Economic Anthropology*, 472–486. London: LSE Online.

Lewis, W. Arthur. 1954. "Economic Development with Unlimited Supplies of Labour." *Manchester School of Economics and Social Studies* 22 (2):139–191.

Li, Tania Murray. 1999. "Compromising Power: Development, Culture and Rule in Indonesia." *Cultural Anthropology* 14 (3):295–322.

Li, Tania Murray. 2000. "Articulating Indigenous Identity in Indonesia: Resource Politics and the Tribal Slot." *Comparative Studies in Society and History* 42 (1):149–179.

Li, Tania Murray. 2007. *The Will to Improve: Governmentality, Development, and the Practice of Politics*. Durham: Duke University Press.

Lilley, Sasha. 2004. "Paving the Amazon with Soy." *Corp Watch*, December 16, 2004. https://corpwatch.org/article/paving-amazon-soy.

Lisansky, Judith. 1990. *Migrants to Amazonia: spontaneous colonization in the Brazilian frontier*. Boulder: Westview Press.

Lohman, Larry. 1993. "Green Orientalism." *The Ecologist* 23 (6):202–204.

Loyola, Rafael. 2014. "Brazil Cannot Risk its Environmental Leadership." *Diversity and Distributions* 20 (12):1365–1367.

Luke, Timothy W. 1997. *Ecocritique: Contesting the Politics of Nature, Economy, and Culture*. Minneapolis: University of Minnesota Press.

Luomi, Mari. 2014. *Sustainable Energy in Brazil: Reversing Past Achievements or Realizing Future Potential*. Oxford: Oxford Institute for Energy Studies.

Lélé, Sharachandra M. 1991. "Sustainable Development: A Critical Review." *World Development* 19 (6):609–621.

Léna, Philippe, and Adélia Engrácia de Oliveira. 1991. *Amazônia: a fronteira agrícola 20 anos depois*: Governo do Brasil, SCT/CNPq, Museu Paraense Emílio Goeldi.

López, Ramón, and I. Galinato Gregmar. 2005. "Trade Policies, Economic Growth, and the Direct Causes of Deforestation." *Land Economics* 81 (2):145–169.

Magalhães, Sonia Barbosa. 2002. "As Grandes Hidreléticas e as Populaçoes Camponesas." In *Amazônia e a Crise de Modernização*, edited by Maria Angela D'Incao and Isolda Maciel de Silveira, 447–456. Belém: Museu Paraense Emílio Goeldi.

Magiera, Leone. 2008. *Pavarotti Up Close*. New York: Ricordi.

Mahar, Dennis J. 1978. *Desenvolvimento econômico da Amazônia: uma análise das políticas governamentais*. Rio de Janeiro: IPEA/INPES.

Mann, Charles C. 2006. *1491: New Revelations of the Americas Before Columbus*. New York: Vintage.

Martino, Diego. 2007. "Deforestation in the Amazon: Pressures and Outlook." *Third World Resurgence* 200 (April 2007):2–5.

Martins, José Souza. 1980. "Fighting for the Land: Indians and Posseiros in Legal Amazonia." In *Land, People and Planning in Contemporary Amazonia*, edited by Françoise Barbira-Scazzocchio, 95–104. Cambridge: Cambridge University Centre of Latin American Studies.

Marx, Karl. 2004 (1818-1883). *The Eighteenth Brumaire of Louis Bonaparte*. Translated by Daniel de Leon. Montana: Kessinger Publishers.

Mathews, Andrew S. 2011. *Instituting Nature: Authority, Expertise, and Power in Mexican Forests*. Cambridge: MIT Press.

Maybury-Lewis, Biorn. 1994. *The Politics of the Possible: The Brazilian Rural Workers' Trade Union Movement, 1964-1985*. Philadelphia: Temple University Press.

McCarthy, James, and Scott Prudham. 2004. "Neoliberal Nature and the Nature of Neoliberalism." *Geoforum* 35 (3):275–283.

McElhinny, Vince. 2011. The World Bank & Development Policy Lending: Lessons for Revising OP 8.60. *Bank Information Center Evaluation Policy Report*. Washington, DC: Bank Information Center.

McGrath, David. 1999. "Parceiros no Crime: O Regatão e a Resistência Cabocla na Amazônia Tradicional." *Novos Cadernos Núcleo Avançado de Estudos Amazônicos* 2 (2):57–72.

McGrath, David G. 1989. "The Paraense Traders: Small-scale, long-distance trade in the Brazilian Amazon." PhD dissertation, Geography; Latin American History, University of Wisconsin-Madison.

Meggers, Betty. 1971. *Amazonia: Man and Culture in a Counterfeit Paradise*. Wheeling: Harlan Davidson.

Melo, Licio. 2017. "Belo Sun Investirá US $5 milhões no Pará em 2017." *BVMI*. São Paulo.

Mendes, Carlos. 2006. "Justiça Indisponibiliza 1,1 Milhão de Hectares do Grupo CR Almeida." *Agência Estado*, April 7, 2006.

Mendes, Chico. 1989. *Fight for the Forest: Chico Mendes in his Own Words*. London: Latin America Bureau.

Mendes, Josilene Ferreira, and Noemi S. Miyasaka Porro. 2015. "Social Conflicts in Times of Environmentalism: Living Law Rights to Land in Settlements with a Conservationist Focus." *Ambiente & Sociedade* 18 (2):93–110.

Mendonça, José Maria. 2011. "Belo Monte: fonte de energia limpa." FIEPA (Federação das Industrias do Pará), March 28, 2011. http://www.fiepa.org.br/component/content/article/60-artigos/184-belo-monte-fonte-de-energia-limpa.html?lang=pt.

Milanez, Bruno, and Ton Buhrs. 2008. "Ecological Modernisation Beyond Western Europe: The Case of Brazil." *Environmental Politics* 17 (5):784–803.

Ministério de Meio Ambiente (MMA). 2006. Governo lança pacote para promover o desenvolvimento sustentável na Amazônia, edited by Marluzza Matos and Daniela Mendes, June 4, 2006. Brasília: Government of Brazil.

Ministério de Minas e Energia. 2011. *Projeto da Usina de Belo Monte—Perguntas mais Frequentes*. Brasília: Governo do Brasil.

Miotto, Karina. 2011. Obras provocam redução de unidades de conservação. *O Eco Amazonia*. June 8, 2011. https://uc.socioambiental.org/pt-br/noticia/102849

Mitchell, Sean T. 2010. "Paranoid Styles of Nationalism after the Cold War: Notes from an Invasion of the Amazon." In *Anthropology and Global Counterinsurgency*, edited by John D. Kelly, Beatrice Jauregui, Sean T. Mitchell and Jeremy Walton, 89–104. Chicago: University of Chicago Press.

Ministério de Meio Ambiente (MMA). 2011. UHE Belo Monte Perguntas e Respostas. MMA/Secretaria de Comunicação Social /PR. Brasília: Government of Brazil.

Ministério dos Direitos Humanos. 2017. Relatório parcial CNDH—Belo Monte/ Belo Sun. October 2, 2017. Brasilia: Government of Brazil. https://www.mdh.gov.br/informacao-ao-cidadao/participacao-social/conselho-nacional-de-direitos-humanos-cndh/Relatorioparcial_BeloMonteBeloSun_Aprovado_final.pdf/view.

Ministério dos Transportes. 2017. "Pavimentação da BR-163 é prioridade, diz ministro." *Portal Brasil*, May 16, 2017. http://www.brasil.gov.br/infraestrutura/2017/05/paviementacao-da-br-163-e-prioridade-diz-ministro.

Mol, Arthur P.J. 2010. "Ecological Modernization as a Social Theory of Environmental Reform." In *The International Handbook of Environmental Sociology*, edited by Michael Redclift and Graham Woodgate, 63–76. Cheltenham: Edward Elgar.

Momsen, Richard P. 1968. *Brazil: A Giant Stirs*. New York: D. Van Nostrand.

Monteiro, Marko S. A., Sonia Regina da Cal Seixas, and Simone Aparecida Vieira. 2014. "The Politics of Amazonian Deforestation: Environmental Policy and Climate Change Knowledge." *Wiley Interdisciplinary Reviews: Climate Change* 5 (5):689–701.

Moore Jr., Barrington 1978. *Injustice: The Social Bases of Obedience and Revolt*. White Plains: M.E. Sharpe.

Moore, Molly. 2008. "EDF's Schwartzman Remembers Chico Mendes." *EDF Talks Global Climate*. http://blogs.edf.org/climatetalks/2008/12/24/edfs-schwartzman-remembers-chico-mendes/?_ga=1.223738139.1836927054.1470337109.

Morais, Lecio, and Alfredo Saad-Filho. 2012. "Neo-Developmentalism and the Challenges of Economic Policy-Making under Dilma Rousseff." *Critical Sociology* 38 (6):789–798.

Moran, Emilio F. 1974. "The Adaptive System of the Amazonian Coboclo." In *Man in the Amazon*, edited by Charles Wagley, 136–159. Gainesville: University of Florida Press.

Moran, Emilio F. 1981. *Developing the Amazon*. Bloomington: University of Indiana Press.

Moran, Emilio F. 1993. *Through Amazonian Eyes: The Human Ecology of Amazonian Populations*. Iowa City: University of Iowa Press.

Moran, Emilio F., and Elinor Ostrom, eds. 2005. *Seeing the Forest and the Trees: Human–Environment Interactions in Forest Ecosystems*. Boston: MIT Press.

Morton, D.C., R.S. DeFries, Y.E. Shimabukuro, L.O. Anderson, E. Arai, F. del Bon Espirito-Santo, et al. 2006. "Cropland Expansion Changes Deforestation Dynamics in the Southern Brazilian Amazon." *Proceedings of the National Academy of Sciences U S A* 103 (39):14637–14641.

Morton, Ella. 2014. Teatro Amazonas: The Dramatic Story of an Unlikely Opera House. *Slate*. January 14, 2014. http://www.slate.com/blogs/atlas_obscura/2014/01/14/teatro_amazonas_the_unlikely_opera_house_in_manaus_brazil.html.

Mosse, David. 2004. "Is Good Policy Unimplementable? Reflections on the Ethnography of Aid Policy and Practice." *Development and Change* 35 (4):639–671.

Mosse, David. 2005a. *Cultivating Development: An Ethnography of Aid Policy and Practice*. London: Pluto Press.

Mosse, David. 2005b. "Is Good Policy Unimplementable? Reflections on the Ethnography of Aid Policy and Practice." *Development and Change* 35 (4):639–671.

Movimento Xingu Vivo Para Sempre. 2013. "Funcionário de Belo Monte é flagrado espionando Xingu Vivo para informar ABIN." Xingu Vivo Para Sempre, February 25, 2013. http://www.xinguvivo.org.br/2013/02/25/funcionario-de-belo-monte-e-flagrado-espionando-reuniao-do-xingu-vivo-para-informar-bin/.

Moya, Carlos Alberto de Figueira, Hélio Costa de Barros Franco, and Paulo Fernando Vieira Souto Rezende. 2007. "AHE Belo Monte—Evolução dos Estudos." Comitê Brasileiro de Barragens—27th National Seminar on Large Dams, Belém, Pará, June 3–7, 2007.

Muchagata, Marcia, et al. 2003. "A Participação da Sociedade Civil na Elaboração e Implementação de Políticas Agrárias e Ambientais na Amazônia Oriental nos Anos 90." In *Reforma Agrária e Meio Ambiente*, edited by Neide Esterci and Raul Silva Telles do Valle, 89–106. São Paulo: Instituto Socioambiental.

Murphy, Roseanne. 2007. *Martyr of the Amazon: The Life of Sister Dorothy Stang*. Maryknoll: Orbis Books.

Neeleman, Gary, and Rose Neelman. 2013. *Tracks in the Amazon: The Day-to-Day Life of the Worker on the Madeira-Mamoré Railroad*. Glen Canyon: University of Utah Press.

Nelsen, Aaron. 2012. "Dam Project Threatens a Way of Life in Peru." *New York Times*, May 15, 2012. http://www.nytimes.com/2012/05/16/world/americas/dam-project-would-displace-villages-in-jungle-valley-of-peru.html?_r=0.

Nepstad, D., S. Schwartzman, B. Bamberger, M. Santilli, D. Ray, P. Schlesinger, et al. 2006. "Inhibition of Amazon Deforestation and Fire by Parks and Indigenous Lands." *Conservation Biology* 20 (1):65–73.

Nepstad, Daniel, C. Azevedo-Ramos, E. Lima, D. McGrath, C. Perreira, and F. Merry. 2004. "Managing the Amazon Timber Industry." *Conservation Biology* 18 (2):575–577.

Nepstad, Daniel, J.P. Capobianco, A.C. Barros, G. Carvalho, P. Moutinho, U. Lopes, et al. 2000. *Avança Brasil: Os custos ambientais para a Amazônia*. Belém: Cenários futuros para a Amazônia.

Nepstad, Daniel, David McGrath, Ane Alencar, A.C. Barros, Georgia Carvalho, M. Santilli, and M. del C. Vera Diaz. 2002. "Frontier Governance in Amazonia." *Science* 295:629–631.

Nepstad, Daniel, David McGrath, Claudia Stickler, Ane Alencar, Andrea Azevedo, Briana Swette, et al. 2014. "Slowing Amazon Deforestation Through Public Policy and Interventions in Beef and Soy Supply Chains." *Science* 344 (6188):1118–1123.

Nepstad, Daniel, C.M Stickler, B. Soares-Filho, and F. Merry. 2008. "Interactions Among Amazon Land Use, Forests and Climate: Prospects for a Near-term Forest Tipping Point." *Philosophical Transactions of the Royal Society of London Series B, Biological Sciences* 363 (1498):1737.

Neto, Wenceslau Gonçalves. 1997. *Estado e Agricultura no Brasil: Política agrícola e modernização econômica Brasileira 1960–1980*. São Paulo: Editora HUCITEC.

Neves, João Augusto de Castro. 2012. "Brazil Wants Some Security Council Love, but it Won't Get it, Yet." *Foreign Policy*, April 3, 2012.

Nixon, Rob. 2011. *Slow Violence and the Environmentalism of the Poor*. Cambridge: Harvard University Press.

Norte, Programa Calha. 2016. "Programa Calha Norte." Ministério da Defesa. http://www.defesa.gov.br/programas-sociais/programa-calha-norte.

North, Liisa L., and Ricardo Grinspun. 2016. "Neo-Extractivism and the New Latin American Developmentalism: The Missing Piece of Rural Transformation." *Third World Quarterly* 37 (8):1483–1504.

Novitski, Joseph. 1972. "Brazil Shunning Pollution Curbs." *New York Times*. February 13, 1972, 11. https://www.nytimes.com/1972/02/13/archives/brazil-shunning-pollution-curbs-seeks-to-bring-industries-from.html

Nugent, Stephen. 1981. "Amazonia: Ecosystem and Social System." *Man* 16 (1):62–74.

Nugent, Stephen. 1993. *Amazonian Caboclo Society: An Essay on Invisibility and Peasant Economy*. Oxford: Berg.

Nugent, Stephen. 2002. "Whither O Campesinato? Historical Peasantries of Brazilian Amazonia." *The Journal of Peasant Studies* 29 (3-4):162–189.

Nugent, Stephen. 2006. "Euphamism in the Forest: Ahistoricism and the Valorization of Indigenous Knowledge." In *Human Impacts on Amazonia*, edited by Michael J. Balik and Darrell Posey, 273–285. New York: Columbia University Press.

O'Donnell, Guillermo. 1973. *Modernization and Bureaucratic-Authoritarianism, Studies in South American Politics*. Berkeley: University of California.

O'Donnell, Guillermo. 1978. "Reflections on the Patterns of Change in the Bureaucratic-Authoritarian State." *Latin American Research Review* 13 (1):3–38.

Olsson, Lennart, Jean-Charles Hourcade, and Jonathan Köhler. 2014. "Sustainable Development in a Globalized World." *The Journal of Environment & Development* 23 (1):3–14.

Orr, David. 2010. *Hope is an Imperative: The Essential David Orr*. Washington, DC: Island Press.

Ostrom, Elinor. 1999. "Design Principles in Long-Enduring Irrigation Institutions." In *Polycentric Governance and Development*, edited by Michael McGinnis, 74–86. Ann Arbor: University of Michigan Press.

Ostrom, Vincent. 1980. "Artisanship and Artifact." *Public Administration Review* 40:309–317.

Pacheco, Pablo. 2009a. "Agrarian Change, Cattle Ranching and Deforestation: Assessing their Linkages in Southern Pará." *Environment and History* 15 (4):493–520.

Pacheco, Pablo. 2009b. "Smallholder Livelihoods, Wealth and Deforestation in the Eastern Amazon." *Human Ecology* 37 (1):27–41.

Padoch, Christine, Eduardo Brondizio, Sandra Costa, Miguel Pinedo-Vasquez, Robin R. Sears, and Andrea Siqueira. 2008. "Urban Forest and Rural Cities: Multi-sited Households, Consumption Patterns, and Forest Resources in Amazonia." *Ecology and Society* 13 (2):2–18.

Palacios, José Agustin 1869. "Exploration of the Rivers and Lakes of the Department of the Beni, Bolívia, from 1844 to 1847, and his Notes Relative to the Department of Mojós." In *Explorations Made in the Valley of the River Madeira, from 1749 to 1868*, edited by George Earl Church, 77–121. London: National Bolivian Navigation Company.

Panja, Tariq. 2013. "Brazil World Cup Stadium Could Be Used for Prisoners, Judge Says." *Bloomberg Business*, September 24, 2013. https://www.bloomberg.com/news/articles/2013-09-24/brazil-world-cup-stadium-could-be-used-for-prisoners-judge-says.

Paraguassu, Lisandra, and Pedro Fonesca. 2017. "PF investiga fraude em aporte bilionário do BNDES na JBS." *Reuters Brasil*, May 12, 2017. http://br.reuters.com/article/topNews/idBRKBN1881LI-OBRTP.

Patterson, Brittany. 2017. "Funding Gutted for Brazil's Environment Agencies." *Climate Wire*, April 7, 2017, E&E news. https://www.eenews.net/climatewire/2017/04/07/stories/1060052762.

Pearce, David, Anil Markandya, and Edward Barbier. 1989. *Blueprint 1: For a Green Economy*. New York: Earthscan.

Peet, Richard, and Michael Watts. 1996. *Liberation Ecologies: Environment, Development, Social Movements*. New York: Routledge.

Pepper, David. 1998. "Sustainable Development and Ecological Modernization: A Radical Homocentric Perspective." *Sustainable Development* 6:1–7.

Perfecto, Ivette, John H. Vandermeer, and Angus Lindsay Wright. 2009. *Nature's Matrix: Linking Agriculture, Conservation and Food Sovereignty, Nature*. London: Earthscan.

Perney, Linda. 1996. "The Rubber Tappers Under Fire Again." In *Fighting for the Soul of Brazil*, edited by Kevin Danaher and Michael Schellenburger, 109–112. New York: Monthly Review Press.

Pfaff, Alexander, Juan Robalino, Diego Herrera, and Catalina Sandoval. 2015. "Protected Areas' Impacts on Brazilian Amazon Deforestation: Examining Conservation—Development Interactions to Inform Planning." *PLOS ONE* 10 (7):e0129460.

Pfaff, Alexander S. P. 1999. "What Drives Deforestation in the Brazilian Amazon?: Evidence from Satellite and Socioeconomic Data." *Journal of Environmental Economics and Management* 37 (1):26–43.

Picoli, Fiorelo. 2006. *O Capital e a Devastação Amazônica: Uma Abordagem do Pensamento Hegemônico e do Alargamento da Fronteira*. São Paulo: Editora Expressão Popular.

Pinto, Lúcio Flávio. 2002. "A Amazônia Entre Estruturas Disfavoráveis." In *Amazônia e a Crise de Modernizaçâo*, edited by Maria Angela D'Incao and Isolda Maciel de Silveira, 111–117. Belém: Museu Paraense Emílio Goeldi.

Pinto, Lúcio Flávio. 2012. "De Tucuruí a Belo Monte: a História Avança Mesmo?" *Boletim do Museu Paraense Emílio Goeldi. Ciências Humanas* 7 (3):777–782.

Pokorny, Benno. 2013. *Smallholders, Forest Management and Rural Development in the Amazon, The Earthscan Forest Library*. New York: Earthscan.

Poletto, Ivo. 1985. "A CPT, a igreja e o camponeses." In *Conquistar a terra, reconstruir a vida: Comissão Pastoral da Terra—dez aos de caminhada*, edited by Pedro Casaldáliga, 29–66. Goiânia: Editora Vozes Ltda.

Pontes, Felipe. 2016. "Onze anos após assassinato de Dorothy Stang, mortes em Anapu disparam." *Agência Brasil*, April 15, 2016, Direitos Humanos. http://agenciabrasil.ebc.com.br/direitos-humanos/noticia/2016-04/onze-anos-apos-assassinato-de-dorothy-stang-mortes-em-anapu.

Porter, Doug J. 1995. "Scenes from Childhood: The Homesickness of Development Discourse." In *Power of Development*, edited by Jonathan Crush, 63–86. London and New York: Routledge.

Posey, Darrell Addison, and Michael J. Balick. 2006. *Human Impacts on Amazonia: The Role of Traditional Ecological Knowledge*. New York: Columbia University Press.

Powell-Cotton, P. H. G. 1907. "Notes on a Journey Through the Great Ituri Forest." *Journal of the African Society* 7 (25):1–12.

Prado, Rosane. 1995. "Small Town Brazil: Heaven and Hell of Personalism." In *The Brazilian Puzzle: Culture on the Borderlands of the Western World*, edited by David J. Hess and Roberto da Matta, 59–82. New York: Columbia University Press.

Princen, Thomas P. 2010. "Speaking of Sustainability: The Potential of Metaphor." *Sustainability: Science, Practice, & Policy* 6 (2):60–65.

Rabben, Linda. 1998. *Unnatural Selection: The Yanomami, the Kayapó, and the Onslaught of Civilization*. Seattle: University of Washington Press.

Randell, Heather. 2016. "Structure and Agency in Development-Induced Forced Migration: The Case of Brazil's Belo Monte Dam." *Population and Environment* 37 (3):265–287.

Rangel, Alberto. 2008 [1908]. *Inferno Verde: Cenas e Cenários do Amazonas*. 6th ed. Manaus: Valer.

Rapoza, Kenneth. 2014. "Was Brazil's Belo Monte Dam A Bad Idea?" *Forbes*, March 7, 2014. https://www.forbes.com/sites/kenrapoza/2014/03/07/was-brazils-belo-monte-dam-a-bad-idea/#63001c692a4e.

Redclift, Michael. 1989. *Sustainable Development: Exploring the Contradictions*. London: Routledge.

Redford, Kent H., and Christine Padoch, eds. 1992. *Conservation of Neotropical Forests: Working from Traditional Resource Use*. New York: Columbia University Press.

Reel, Monte. 2014. "Traveling From Ocean to Ocean Across South America." *The New York Times Magazine*, February 19, 2014.

Repórter Brasil. 2011. BNDES and its Environmental Policy. February, 2011. Brasilia: NGO Repórter Brasil. https://reporterbrasil.org.br/documentos/BNDES_English.pdf.

Revkin, Andrew. 1990. *The Burning Season: the Murder of Chico Mendes and the Fight for the Amazon Rain Forest*. Washington, DC: Island Press.

Ricardo Bonalume, Neto. 2003. "GM Confusion in Brazil." *Nature Biotechnology* 21 (11):1257–1258.

Ricardo, Fany, and Alicia Rolla. 2006. *Mineraçao em Unidades de Conservação na Amazônia Brasileira*. São Paulo: Instituto Socioambiental.

Rich, Bruce. 1995. *Mortgaging the Earth: The World Bank, Environmental Impoverishment, and the Crisis of Development*. Boston: Beacon Press.

Rippy, J Fred. 2000. *British Investments in Latin America, 1822–1949: A Case Study in the Operations of Private Enterprise in Retarded Regions*. Vol. 1: Psychology Press.

Robbins, Paul. 2004. *Political Ecology: A Critical Introduction*. Malden: Blackwell.

Robbins, Paul, and Kristina Monroe Bishop. 2008. "There and Back Again: Epiphany, Disillusionment, and Rediscovery in Political Ecology." *Geoforum* 39 (2):747–755.

Robinson, John. 2004. "Squaring the Circle? Some Thoughts on the Idea of Sustainable Development." *Ecological Economics* 48 (4):369–384.

Rocha, Diogo. 2015a. Um Ano Após Primeiro Jogo da Copa, Manaus Ainda Aguarda Melhorias Prometidas. *D24am*, October 19, 2015.

Rocha, Djogo. 2015b. "Deforestation, inter-ethnic conflicts and violence in Gleba Nova Olinda, Pará, Brazil." *EJOLT Factsheet*, #024, February 10, 2015. Liabilities Environmental Justice Organizations, and Trade (EJOLT). http://www.ejolt.org/wordpress/wp-content/uploads/2015/07/FS-24.pdf.

Rodrigues, Gomercindo. 2007. *Walking the Forest with Chico Mendes: Struggle for Justice in the Amazon*. Translated by Linda Rabben. Austin: University of Texas Press.

Rodrigues, Maria Guadeloupe Moog. 2004. *Global Environmentalism and Local Politics: Transnational Advocacy Networks in Brazil, Ecuador, and India*. Albany: SUNY Press.

Rohter, Larry. 2002. "José Lutzenberger, Brazilian Environmentalist, Dies at 75." *New York Times*, May 17, 2002.

Rohter, Larry. 2005. "Brazil Promises Crackdown After Nun's Shooting Death." *New York Times*, February 14, 2005. http://www.nytimes.com/2005/02/14/world/americas/brazil-promises-crackdown-after-nuns-shooting-death.html.

Roosevelt, Anna Curtenius. 1991. *Moundbuilders of the Amazon: Geophysical Archaeology on Marajo Island, Brazil*. Waltham: Academic Press.

Roosevelt, Theodore. 1914. *Through the Brazilian Wilderness, October 4, 1913 - May 19, 1914*. Morristown: Digital Antiquaria.

Rorty, Richard. 1979. *Philosophy and the Mirror of Nature*. Princeton: Princeton University Press.

Rose, Nikolas. 1999. *Power of Freedom: Reframing Political Thought*. Cambridge: Cambridge University Press.

Rousseff, Dilma. 2011. "Dilma Rousseff Inauguration Speech: Brazil's First Female President Addresses Congress In Brasilia." *Ministry of Foreign Affairs, Government of Brazil*. January 1, 2011. http://www.itamaraty.gov.br/en/speeches-articles-and-interviews/president-of-the-federative-republic-of-brazil-speeches/4661-address-of-dilma-vana-rousseff-president-of-the-republic-inaugural-speech-to-congress-english-version.,

Rudel, Thomas. 2013. *Defensive Environmentalists and the Dynamics of Global Reform*. London: Cambridge University Press.

Sabatini, Christopher. 2016. "Bridges to Nowhere: Corruption in the BRICS." *Foreign Affairs*. July 18, 2016 (10):42–47.

Sachs, Ignacy. 1995. "What Future for Amazonia?" In *Fighting for the Soul of Brazil*, edited by Kevin Danaher and Michael Schellenburger, 103–108. New York: Monthly Review Press.

Sachs, Jeffrey. 2015. *The Age of Sustainable Development*. New York: Columbia University Press.

Sachs, Wolfgang. 1993. "Global Ecology and the Shadow of Development." In *Global Ecology: A New Arena of Political Conflict*, edited by Wolfgang Sachs, 3–21. London: Zed Books.

Salazar, Katya. 2012. "Reflections on Strengthening the Inter-American Human Rights System." *Aportes DPLf (Magazine of the Due Process of Law Foundation)* 16 (5):1.

Santilli, J. 2005. *Socioambientalismo e Novos Direitos: Proteção jurídica à diversidade biológica e cultural*. Goiânia: CPT/Justiça Global/Terra de Direitos.

Santos, Roberto Araújo de Oliveira. 1980. *História Econômica da Amazônia: 1800–1920*. São Paulo: T.A. Queiroz.

Sartre, Xavier Arnauld de, and Romain Taravella. 2009. "National Sovereignty vs. Sustainable Development: Lessons from the Narrative on the Internationalization of the Brazilian Amazon." *Political Geography* 28:406–415.

Sauer, Sergio. 2005. *Violação dos direitos humanos na Amazônia: conflito e violência na fronteira paraense*. Goiânia: CPT.

Sauer, Sergio. 2009. "Market-led 'Agrarian Reform' in Brazil: A Dream has Become a Debt Burden." *Progress in Development Studies* 9 (2):127–140.

Sawakuchi, A.O., G.A. Hartmann, H.O. Sawakuchi, F.N. Pupim, D.J. Bertassoli, M. Parra, Jet al. 2015. "The Volta Grande do Xingu: Reconstruction of Past Environments and Forecasting of Future Scenarios of a Unique Amazonian Fluvial Landscape." *Scientific Drilling* 20:21–32.

Sawyer, Donald R. 1984. "Frontier Expansions and Retraction in Brazil." In *Frontier Expansion in Amazonia*, edited by Marianne Schmink and Charles Wood, 180–203. Gainesville: University Presses of Florida.

Sawyer, Donald R. 1990. "Possibilidades e limites de formas alternativas de exploração econômica da Amazônia brasileira." *Nova Economia (UFMG)*, Belo Horizonte, 1 (1):91–108.

Schmink, Marianne, and Charles Wood, eds. 1984. *Frontier Expansion in Amazonia*. Gainesville: University Presses of Florida.

Schmink, Marianne, and Charles Wood. 1992. *Contested Frontiers in Amazonia*. New York: Columbia University Press.

Schneider, Cecile, E. Coudel, F. Cammelli, and P. Sablayrolles. 2015. "Small-Scale Farmers' Needs to End Deforestation: Insights for REDD+ in São Felix do Xingu (Pará, Brazil)." *International Forestry Review* 17 (S1):124–142.

Scholz, Imme. 2006. "Negotiating Solutions for Local Sustainable Development and Preventing Deforestation in the Brazilian Amazon." In *Partnerships in Sustainable Forest Resource Management: Learning from Latin America*, Leiden: Brill-CEDLA Latin America Studies, edited by Mirjam Ros-Tonen, 94 (39/40): 279–300.

Schwartzman, Stephan, André Villas Boas, Katia Yukari Ono, Marisa Gesteira Fonseca, Juan Doblas, Barbara Zimmerman, et al. 2013. "The Natural and Social History of the Indigenous Lands and Protected Areas Corridor of the Xingu River Basin." *Philosophical Transactions of the Royal Society B: Biological Sciences* 368 (1619):20120164.

Schweickardt, Kátia. 2003. "Reforma Agrária e Política Ambiental na Amazônia—encontros e desencontros." *Somanlu* 3 (2):111–124.

Scott, James C. 1985. *Weapons of the Weak: Everyday Forms of Peasant Resistance*. New Haven: Yale University Press.

Scott, James C. 1990. *Domination and the Arts of Resistance*. New Haven: Yale University Press.

Scott, James C. 1998. *Seeing Like a State: How Certain Schemes to Improve the Human Condition Have Failed*. New Haven: Yale University Press.

Scott, Joan Wallach, Cora Kaplan, and Debra Keates. 1997. *Transitions, Environments, Translations: Feminisms in International Politics*. New York: Routledge.

Scudder, T. 2012. *The Future of Large Dams: Dealing with Social, Environmental, Institutional and Political Costs*. New York: Earthscan.

SDDH. 2016. Universal Periodic Review: Brazil: The UHE Belo Monte Dam Project. Belém, Pará: Movimento Xingu Vivo Para Sempre, Painel de Especialistas, Sociedade Paraense de Defesa dos Direitos Humanos, Justiça Global, Asociación Interamericana para la Defensa del Ambiente.

Serbin, Kenneth P. 2000. *Secret Dialogues: Church-State Relations, Torture, and Social Justice in Authoritarian Brazil*. Pittsburgh: University of Pittsburgh Press.

Serrill, M.S. 1997. "Ghosts of the Forest." *Time* 150 (17A Special Issue):50–55.

Sevá Filho, A. Oswaldo, ed. 2005. *Tenotã Mõ: Alertas sobre as conseqüências dos projetos hidrelétricos no rio Xingu*. Brasilia: International Rivers Network (IRN).

Sezgin, Zeynep. 2013. "Ecological Modernization at the Intersection of Environment and Energy." *International Journal of Energy Economics and Policy* 3 (Special Issue):93–101.

Sherwood, Louise. 2010. "Brazil's Devil's Railway gets new lease of life." *BBC News*, November 27, 2010. http://www.bbc.co.uk/news/world-latin-america-11578463.

Shohat, Ella, and Robert Stam. 2013. *Flagging Patriotism: Crises of Narcissism and Anti-Americanism*. New York: Routledge.

Sikkink, Kathryn. 1991. *Ideas and Institutions: Developmentalism in Brazil and Argentina*. Ithaca: Cornell University Press.

Simmons, Cynthia S., Robert T. Walker, Eugenio Y. Arima, Stephen P. Aldrich, and Marcellus M. Caldas. 2007. "The Amazon Land War in the South of Pará." *Annals of the Association of American Geographers* 97 (3):567–593.

Siscú, João, Luiz Fernando de Paulo, and Renalt Michel. 2007. "Por que Novo-Desenvolvimentismo?" *Revista de Economia Política* 27 (4):507–524.

Slater, Candace. 2002. *Entangled Edens: Visions of the Amazon*. Berkeley: University of California Press.

Slater, Candace. 2015. "Visions of the Amazon: What Has Shifted, What Persists, and Why This Matters." *Latin American Research Review* 50 (3):3–23.

Smith, Neil. 1996. "The Production of Nature." In *FutureNatural: Nature, Science, Culture*, edited by George Robertson, Melinda Mash, Lisa Tickner, Jon Bird, Barry Curtus and Tim Putnam, 35–54. London: Routledge.

Smith, Nigel J. H. 1978. "Agricultural Productivity along Brazil's Transamazon Highway." *Agro-Ecosystems* 4:415–432.

Smith, Nigel J. H. 1981. "Colonization Lessons from a Tropical Forest." *Science* 214 (4522):755–761.

Smith, Nigel J. H. 1982. *Rainforest Corridors: The Transamazon Colonization Scheme*. Berkeley: University of California Press.

Smucker, Jonathan Matthew. 2017. *Hegemony How-To: A Roadmap for Radicals*. Chico: AK Press.

Snow, David A., and Danny Trom. 2002. "The Case Study and the Study of Social Movements." In *Methods of Social Movement Research*, edited by Bert Klandermans and Suzanne Staggenborg. Minneapolis: University Minnesota Press.

Sotero, Paulo. 2012. "El Desafío Brasileño: Cómo Gestionar las Relaciones Regionales Asimétricas más Allá de la OEA." *Revista CIDOB d'afers internacionals* 97-98:101–116.

Souza, Ana Paula. 2006. *O Desenvolvimento socioambiental na Transamazônica: a trajetória de um discurso a muitas vozes*. Masters Thesis, Centro Agropecuário Programa de Pós-Graduação em Agriculturas Amazônicas, Universidade Federal do Pará, Belém.

Stepan, Alfred. 1971. *The Military in Politics: Changing Patterns in Brazil*. Princeton: Princeton University Press.

Stepan, Nancy Leys. 2006. "Constructing Tropical Nature." In *Human Impacts on Amazonia*, edited by Michael J. Balik Darrell Posey, 17–32. New York: Columbia University Press.

Strassburg, Bernardo B.N., Agnieszka E. Latawiec, Luis G. Barioni, Carlos A. Nobre, Vanderley P. da Silva, Judson F. Valentim, et al. 2014. "When Enough Should be Enough: Improving the Use of Current Agricultural Lands Could Meet Production Demands and Spare Natural Habitats in Brazil." *Global Environmental Change* 28:84–97.

Streck, C. 2001. "The Global Environment Facility—a Role Model for International Governance?" *Global Environmental Politics* 1 (2):71–94.

Strochlic, Nina. 2015. Henry Ford's Lost City in the Amazon. *The Daily Beast*, May 24, 2015 https://www.thedailybeast.com/henry-fords-lost-city-in-the-amazon.

Strong, Maurice F. 1992. "Opening Statement to the Rio Summit." United Nations Conference on Environment and Development, Rio de Janeiro, Brazil, June 3.

Sutter, Christoph, and Juan Carlos Parreño. 2007. "Does the Current Clean Development Mechanism (CDM) Deliver its Sustainable Development Claim? An Analysis of Officially Registered CDM projects." *Climactic Change* 84:75–90.

Swyngedouw, Erik. 2006. "Circulations and Metabolisms: (Hybrid) Natures and (Cyborg) Cities." *Science as Culture* 15 (2):105–121.

Swyngedouw, Erik. 2015. *Liquid Power: Water and Contested Modernities in Spain, 1898–2010*. Boston: MIT Press.

Taussig, Michael. 1980. *The Devil and Commodity Fetishism in Latin America*. Chapel Hill: University of North Carolina Press.

Taussig, Michael. 1987. *Shamanism, Colonialism and the Wildman*. Chicago: University of Chicago Press.

Tavares, Paulo. 2013. "The Geological Imperative: On the Political Ecology of the Amazonia's Deep History." In *Architecture in the Anthropocene: Encounters Among Design, Deep Time, Science and Philosophy*, edited by Etienne Turpin. Ann Arbor: Michigan Publishing, Open Humanities Press.

Teixeira, Marcelo 2017. "Protests on Brazil Road Impact Flow of Grains to Northern Ports." *Reuters*. July 11, 2017. https://www.reuters.com/article/us-brazil-grains-protests/protests-on-brazil-road-impact-flow-of-grains-to-northern-ports-idUSKBN19W2PQ.

Terborgh, John. 1999. *Requiem for Nature*. Washington, DC: Island Press/ Shearwater Books.

Thadeu, Raul. 2007. "Cartórios de Altamira Lideram Fraude." *O Liberal*, December 2, 2007.

Timo, Pétalla Brandão. 2013. "Development at the Cost of Violations: The Impact of Mega-Projects on Human Rights in Brazil." *Sur International Journal on Human Rights* 10 (18):136–157.

Toni, Fabiano. 2006. "Institutional Choices on the Brazilian Agricultural Frontier: Strengthening Civil Society or Outsourcing Centralized Natural Resource Management?" Survival of the Commons: Mounting Challenges and New Realities, 11th Conference of the International Association for the Study of Common Property, Bali, Indonesia, June 19–23, 2006.

Toni, Fabiano, Anna Paula Santos Souza, and Noemi Myasaka Porro. 2006. "Governança Ambiental e Desenvolvimento Territorial Rural na Fronteira Agrícola: o Papel das Redes de Movimentos Sociais na Região da Transamazônica." Seminario Territórios Rurales em Movimiento, Santiago, Chile, April 23–26, 2006.

Torres, Mauricio, Juan Doblas, and Daniela Fernandes Alarcon. 2017. *"Dono é Quem Desmata": Conexões entre grilagem e desmatamento no sudoeste paraense*. São Paulo: Instituto Agronômico da Amazônia.

Tsing, Anna L. 2005. *Friction: An Ethnography of Global Connection*. Princeton: Princeton University Press.

Tsing, Anna Lowenhaupt. 1997. "Transitions as Translations." In *Transitions, Environments, Translations*, edited by Joan W. Scott, 253–272. New York: Routledge.

Tully, John A. . 2011. *The Devil's Milk: A Social History of Rubber*. New York: Monthly Review Press.

Turner, Frederick J. 1894. *The Significance of the Frontier in American History*. Madison: Silver Buckle Press.

UK Foreign & Commonwealth Office and Sir Mark Lyall Grant. 2014. Speech. "Security Council Reform: The UK supports new permanent seats for Brazil, Germany, India and

Japan, alongside permanent African representation." November 12, 2014. New York. https://www.gov.uk/government/speeches/security-council-reform-the-uk-supports-new-permanent-seats-for-brazil-germany-india-and-japan-alongside-permanent-african-representation

UN Working Group on Business and Human Rights. 2015. Statement at the end of visit to Brazil by the United Nations Working Group on Business and Human Rights. Brasilia: United Nations High Commission on Human Rights.

UNDP. n.d. "Green Economy." https://sustainabledevelopment.un.org/index.php?menu=1446.

US Energy Information Administration. 2015. Brazil: International Energy and Data Analysis. Washington, DC: US Energy Information Administration (US EIA).

Uphoff, Norman Thomas. 1986. *Local Institutional Development: An Analytical Sourcebook with Cases*. West Hartford: Kumarian Press.

Valente, Ana Lucia. 2008. "What Kind of Agrarian Reform, After All?": Revisiting an Unfinished Debate in Brazil." *Estudos Sociedade e Agricultura* 4:86–120.

van Dijck, Pitou. 2008. "Troublesome Construction: The Rationale and Risks of IIRSA." *Revista Europea de Estudios Latinoamericanos y del Caribe/European Review of Latin American and Caribbean Studies* (85):101–120.

Vanden, Harry E. 2012. "The Landless Rural Workers' Movement and their waning influence on Brazil's Workers' Party government." In *Social Movements and Leftist Governments in Latin America: Confrontation or Co-operation?*, edited by Carl Prevost, Carlos Oliva Campos and Harry E. Vanden, 34–48. London: Zed.

Veiga, J.B., J.F. Tourrand, R. Poccard-Chapuis, and M.G. Piketty. 2003. "Cattle Ranching in the Amazon Rainforest." XII World Forestry Congress, Quebec, Canada, (0568-B1). http://www.fao.org/3/XII/0568-B1.htm.

Vera-Diaz, Maria del Carmen, Robert K. Kaufmann, and Daniel Nepstad. 2009. "The Environmental Impacts of Soybean Expansion and Infrastructure Development in Brazil's Amazon Basin." *Global Development and Environment Institute* Working Paper (09-05):25.

Vespucci, Amerigo. 1504. "Amerigo Vespucci to Piero Soderini, Lisbon." In *Letters from a New World: Amerigo Vespucci's Discovery of America*, September 4, 1504, edited by Luciano Formisano. New York: Marsilio.

Vieira, Marco A. 2013. "Brazilian Foreign Policy in the Context of Global Climate Norms." *Foreign Policy Analysis* 9 (4):369–386.

Wagley, Charles. 1967. "The Folk Culture of the Brazilian Amazon." In *Acculturation in the Americas*, edited by S. Tax, 224–230. New York: Cooper Square Publishers.

Wagley, Charles. 1974. *Man in the Amazon*. Gainsville: University of Florida Press.

Walker, R.S., and M.J. Hamilton. 2014. "Amazonian Societies on the Brink of Extinction." *American Journal of Human Biology* 26 (4):570–572.

Walker, Robert, and Eugenio Arima. 2011. "Smallholder Timber Sales Along the Transamazon Highway: A Comment." *Ecological Economics* 70 (9):1565–1567.

Walker, Robert et al. 2000. "Deforestation and Cattle Ranching in the Brazilian Amazon: External Capital and Household Process." *World Development* 28 (4):683–699.

Walker, Robert S., and Kim R. Hill. 2015. "Protecting Isolated Tribes." *Science* 348 (6239):1061.

Walker, Robert, Cynthia Simmons, Stephen Aldrich, Stephen Perz, Eugenio Arima, and Marcellus Caldas. 2011. "The Amazonian Theater of Cruelty." *Annals of the Association of American Geographers* 101 (5):1156–1170.

Wapner, Paul K. 1996. *Environmental Activism in Civic World Politics, International Environmental Policy & Theory*. Albany: State University of New York Press.

Wapner, Paul K. 2003. "World Summit on Sustainable Development: Toward a Post-Jo'burg Environmentalism." *Global Environmental Politics* 3 (1):1–10.

Wapner, Paul K. 2008. "The Importance of Critical Environmental Studies in the New Environmentalism." *Global Environmental Politics* 8 (1):6–13.

Wapner, Paul K. 2011. "The Politics of Planetary Bandwagoning." *Global Environmental Politics* 11 (3):137–144.

Watts, Jonathan. 2014. "Belo Monte, Brazil: The Tribes Living in the Shadow of a Megadam." *The Guardian*, December 16, 2014. https://www.theguardian.com/environment/2014/dec/16/belo-monte-brazil-tribes-living-in-shadow-megadam.

WCD (World Commission on Dams). 2000. *Dams and Development: A New Framework for Decision-Making*. London: Earthscan.

Weinstein, Barbara. 1983. *The Amazon Rubber Boom, 1850–1920*. Stanford: Stanford University Press.

Weisbrot, Mark, Jake Johnston, and Stephan Lefebvre. 2014. The Brazilian Economy in Transition: Macroeconomic Policy, Labor and Inequality. Washington, DC: Center for Economic and Policy Research.

West, Paige. 2006. *Conservation Is Our Government Now: The Politics of Ecology in Papua New Guinea, New Ecologies for the Twenty-First Century*. Durham: Duke University Press.

West, Paige, James Igoe, and Dan Brockington. 2006. "Parks and Peoples: The Social Impact of Protected Areas." *Annual Review of Anthropology* 35 (1):251–277.

Whitehead, Neil L. 1993. "Ethnic Transformation and Historical Discontinuity in Native Amazonia and Guayana, 1500–1900." *L'Homme* 33 (126–128):285–305.

Williams, Colin C., and Andrew C. Millington. 2004. "The Diverse and Contested Meanings of Sustainable Development." *The Geographic Journal* 7 (2):99–104.

Wolford, Wendy. 2005. "Agrarian Moral Economies and Neoliberalism in Brazil: Competing Worldviews and the State in the Struggle for Land." *Environment and Planning A* 37 (2):241–261.

World Bank. 2012. How to decrease freight logistics costs in Brazil. *Transport Papers*. April 1, 2012, 39 (46885). Washington, DC: World Bank. http://documents.worldbank.org/curated/en/348951468230950149/Brazil-How-to-decrease-freight-logistics-costs-in-Brazil.

WRI Brazil. 2017. "Open Letter: Reducing forest protection threatens Brazil's international commitments." May 25, 2017. São Paulo: WRI Brazil. https://wribrasil.org.br/en/news/open-letter-reducing-forest-protection-threatens-brazils-international-commitments

Xinkrin Xingu. 2012. O que exigimos (What we demand). *Ocupação de Belo Monte—Índios do Xingu*. June 25, 2012. http://xingubacajairiri.blogspot.com.br/2012/06/o-que-exigimos.html.

York, Richard, Eugene Rosa, and Thomas Deitz. 2010. "Ecological Modernization Theory: Theoretical and Empirical Challenges." In *The Handbook of Environmental Sociology (2nd Ed.)*, edited by Michael Redclift and Graham Woodgate, 77–90. Cheltenham: Edward Elgar.

Zainulbhai, Hani. 2015. "Brazil's Corruption Scandal, Economy Drive Rousseff's Ratings to Record Low." *Pew Research Center FactTank*, August 17, 2015. https://www.pewresearch.org/fact-tank/2015/08/17/brazils-corruption-scandal-economy-drive-rousseffs-ratings-to-record-low/.

Zarin, Daniel, Janaki R. R. Alavalapati, Frances E. Putz, and Marianne Schmink, eds. 2004. *Working Forests in the Neotropics: Conservation Through Sustainable Management? (Biology and Resource Management Series*. New York: Columbia University Press.

Zarin, Hilary L. 2010. "Making Place and Identity in the Interstices: Ribeirinho Landscapes in the Terra do Meio ("Land of the Middle"), Para, Brazil." 3446960 PhD dissertation, University of Florida.

Zelli, Fariborz, Aarti Gupta, and Harro van Asselt. 2013. "Institutional Interactions at the Crossroads of Trade and Environment: The Dominance of Liberal Environmentalism?" *Global Governance* 19 (1):105–118.

Zhouri, Andréa. 2010. "Adverse Forces' in the Brazilian Amazon: Developmentalism Versus Environmentalism and Indigenous Rights." *The Journal of Environment and Development* 19 (3):252–273.

Zibechi, Raúl. 2014. *The New Brazil: Regional Imperialism and the New Democracy*. Translated by Ramor Ryan. Chico: AK Press.

Zimmerer, Karl S., and Thomas J. Bassett. 2003. *Political Ecology: An Integrative Approach To Geography And Environment-Development Studies*. New York: Guilford Press.

Index

Note: Tables and figures are indicated by *t* and *f* following the page number

For the benefit of digital users, indexed terms that span two pages (e.g., 52–53) may, on occasion, appear on only one of those pages.

Printed in the USA/Agawam, MA
November 10, 2020

763870.003